The Law for Comic
Book Creators

The Law for Comic Book Creators

Essential Concepts and Applications

JOE SERGI

McFarland & Company, Inc., Publishers
Jefferson, North Carolina

Library of Congress Cataloguing-in-Publication Data

Sergi, Joe, 1970– , author.
The law for comic book creators : essential
concepts and applications / Joe Sergi.
p.   cm.
Includes bibliographical references and index.

ISBN 978-0-7864-7360-1 (softcover : acid free paper) ∞
ISBN 978-1-4766-1733-6 (ebook)

1. Law—Anecdotes.   2. Graphic novels—History and
criticism.   3. Comic books, strips, etc.—United States—
History and criticism.   4. Law and literature.   I. Title.

K183.S47 2015   346.7304'8—dc23   2014038674

British Library cataloguing data are available

Cover graphics © iStock/Thinkstock

Printed in the United States of America

*McFarland & Company, Inc., Publishers
Box 611, Jefferson, North Carolina 28640
www.mcfarlandpub.com*

To the writers, artists, and companies in this book
who are dedicated to storytelling
and not afraid to fight for what they believe in.
And the lawyers that represented them.

Acknowledgments

Acknowledgments are hard. Invariably, the author misses someone. To that someone, I apologize. Obviously, I have to thank my family. My wife and daughter have no idea how much they did to make this book a reality. From a quiet bit of encouragement to knowing when to leave me alone to finish a thought before it faded into obscurity. I also have to thank my parents. Without them buying me my first comics for sending me to law school, this book could never have become a reality.

Next, there is the practical help. This book would still be an idea if not for my good friend Rob Anderson, who not only introduced me to McFarland and is a talented comic book creator, but, as a lawyer himself, was invaluable in discussing the cases during our regular lunches. In addition, Andy Schmidt and his Comics Experience work group provided an excellent conduit to discuss what issues were relevant to today's creator. My nephew Dan Sherrier, a talented novelist in his own right, helped make sure I was making sense. Thanks to my current and former co-workers in my unnamed government agency, especially Adair, Beatrice, Chad, David, Jennifer, Jeremy, Karen, Kari, Kaycee, and Virginia, who had to listen to more obscure comic book law facts than any human should endure and were always there to discuss legal and trial theories. Thanks also goes out to the folks at the CBLDF, especially Charles Brownstein and Betsy Gomez, for the great work they do they and for helping me hone my research skills through my work with their site. I would also like to thank the numerous court clerks, research librarians, and legal scholars that patiently create, maintain, and provide access to sometimes decades-old case dockets and filings.

Table of Contents

Preface

Since the creation of the comic book, there has been legal conflict and confusion. The first comic strip, *Hogan's Alley*, resulted in the first lawsuit over licensing. Superman, the first comic book superhero, spawned a seemingly never ending battle over who owned the character. In the forties and fifties, the comic industry came under fire for contributing to the delinquency of minors, which resulted in the passage of several criminal anti-comic laws and the creation of the self-regulating body known as the Comics Code Authority. It can all be very confusing to the lay person. This is especially true when you consider concepts such as public domain, unincorporated entities, and moral rights. As a result, comic creators are frequently concerned about whether they are protecting themselves. They have many questions and no single place to find the answers. *The Law for Comic Book Creators* strives to provide those answers.

The Law for Comic Book Creators examines the legal history of comics and presents the information in a way that is understandable to the layperson. It is not a "how to" book, a legal reference book, or a case book. It does not seek to provide legal advice. Instead, *The Law for Comic Book Creators* presents the legal background in easy to understand language and explores the stories behind the cases. And just as every lawsuit has a story, every case has lessons to be learned. As the book explores these lessons, the reader will learn the importance of contracts, the precautions necessary when working with public domain characters, and the effect of censorship. This book seeks to entertain as it instructs.

The book you hold in front of you was not an easy one to write. Immeasurable amounts of research went into creating it. But, it was a labor of love. To understand this, perhaps you should understand something about me and why I wrote this book.

I have two passions, both of which were inspired by fictional characters.

The first is litigation. I have been told that as a child, I was read a copy of *To Kill a Mockingbird*. In the scene when Atticus Finch loses the trial and walks past the galley, the townspeople respectfully stand up and when Scout asks why, the Reverend Sykes replies, "Miss Jean Louise, stand up. Your father's passin'." I must have been influenced by this since it fueled me through law school and an LL.M. (Master of Laws) in taxation. For nearly two decades, I have worked as a trial attorney and I am honored to represent the federal government as a senior litigation counsel.

The second is comics, especially superheroes. I remember the day I fell in love with superheroes. I sat in a red velvet seat in the Woodbridge Center Cinema next to my mother.

On the screen a larger than life Lois Lane clutched onto the seat belt of a crashed helicopter as it dangled what seemed hundreds of stories above the street of the Metropolis. Slowly her grip slipped. I leaned forward, not even realizing I was holding my breath. As she slipped closer to doom, mild mannered Clark Kent rushed through a revolving door where he changed into a familiar red and blue costume. All the while, a slow march played, "dun dun dun dun." Then Lois fell. The music picked up the pace. All seemed lost. And then, Superman caught Lois Lane as his anthem played. With a smile, Superman announced, "Don't worry, Miss, I've got you." She shrieked back, "You've got me? Who's got you?" The precipitously angled helicopter chose this moment to give way. I gasped again. But neither Superman nor that anthem could be beaten; he merely held Lois in one hand and caught the copter in his other. He gently flew them both to the roof and then, after making sure Lois and the pilot were okay, politely smiled and said, "I hope this experience hasn't put you off flying, Miss Lane. Statistically speaking, it's still the safest way to travel." With that he took off into the night sky. Afterwards, my mother took me into the nearby Toys "R" Us, where she bought me Superman comics, a poster, a cape, and a Superman action figure (a year earlier, she had bought me my first comic, a *Star Wars* comic, so this is all her fault on multiple levels). I never gave up on comics or on superheroes—not in high school, not in college, not in law school, and not during the god-awful nineties. Now, I create my own comics and novels and hope to someday write the mainstream superheroes I grew up with.

The Law for Comic Book Creators is the perfect blend of my two passions and a dream project. As a creator, I attend a lot of shows and make a lot of appearances at comic cons, book festivals and on podcasts. It is also no secret that I am a lawyer. I have also found that everyone is looking for free legal advice. As a result of these three things, I am frequently asked questions about legal topics related to comics. These questions range from contract law to whether the fictional Superhero Registration Act is constitutional. A lot of questions come from creators, who are inspired by more than simple curiosity because, in some cases, this is their livelihood. As a practicing lawyer for the federal government, I cannot advise anyone or offer legal advice. Over the years, I have learned that sometimes giving an historical overview to their issue and explaining what things mean will allow people to draw their own conclusions and find the solution. Sadly, I have discovered there is a lot of misinformation being dispersed. For example, it's surprising just how many creators believe the urban legend that copyright can be established when someone mails their material to themselves and keeps the date stamped sealed envelope.

As a result of these questions and the general misinformation in the industry, I asked numerous comic creators (both big name and newcomers) whether they would be interested in a book on the legal cases and concepts relevant to creators. The response was overwhelming not only that such a book should exist, but that I was the one that had to write it because of my unique perspective developed through my litigation background and my comic book experiences as both a creator and a fan. I followed up with these creators to determine what topics they would like to see included in the book. As a result of these conversations, I generated a list of subjects and the basic concept for this book was born. You hold in your hand the final product of that concept.

I hope that you enjoy it.

Introduction

So, who is the target audience for this book? Ideally, anyone who is interested in the history of comics should enjoy it. However, the book is especially designed with the comic creator in mind. Of course, this book does not offer legal advice. It must not be treated as anything but a historical retrospective full of cautionary tales. Hopefully, folks can learn a few things from the plights of Siegel and Kirby when dealing with contracts. People can understand the censorship that nearly shut down the industry in the fifties and be better informed on how to prevent it in the present. Creators and fans can understand complex concepts like work for hire, public domain, and fair use. Most of all, everyone can honor these great creators and the sacrifices that have been made, in and out of the courtrooms, for their art.

In short, this book is written for the professional, suitable for the fan, and dedicated to the creators.

There are two types of chapters in this book.

First, there are chapters that provide background on a particular area of law. These chapters cover litigation, intellectual property, copyright, trademark, contracts, the public domain, business structure and censorship. This material is meant to provide a background to these areas of law. Once again, these chapters are not presented as legal advice, but they offer enough information to foster an understanding of how each area of law functions, which will be helpful when seeking advice from professionals and when reading the various case studies in this book.

Second, there are chapters that present the backgrounds of the cases. A good litigator knows that every case has a story. These chapters tell those stories. Not only do these stories shed light on and apply the legal principles discussed in the law chapters, but they also provide a unique historical view into the world of comics and the origin of some of its most beloved creations. These chapters are based entirely on the public records of the cases: the filings, the testimony, the exhibits, and the opinions.

There are also a few things that anyone reading this book should understand. The first thing is the inherent conflict that exists in the world of comics. On one side, the comic medium is art. Talented creators shatter preconceptions and utilize novel storytelling to challenge conventions and convey their message through a mixture of art, text, color, and lettering. On the other side, the comic industry is a multi-billion dollar business where multinational corporations race to produce salable goods to a target market at the cheapest price. These two sides are often at odds with each other, constantly pushing and pulling the laws of intellectual property, contracts, and censorship in an effort to reach the proper result.

The second thing may be the hardest for comic book readers and creators to accept. While there are winners and losers,[1] there are no good guys or bad guys in this book. There are no heroes or villains. Instead, there are two litigants who so believe in their position that they are willing to go to court. And there are issues that are such close calls that it takes several levels of court review, and often several reversals and remands, before a final decision can be reached.

It would be very easy to come into these stories blaming the evil company or the greedy creator, when in fact both sides are just looking to do what they believe is correct under the law. In fact, even Doctor Fredric Wertham, who is uniformly blamed for the downfall of comics in the fifties, still acted with the noblest intentions—protecting children. In any other story, he might be the hero of the tale. Some people believe he is a villain. In this book, he is merely a participant.

The third point ties closely to the second. Readers must remember that real people are involved in these cases. They may be famous artists and writers, but they are also human beings. No one likes to go to court except trial lawyers. No one likes to testify, including trial lawyers. Many of the people involved in these cases did just that. And when the cases were over, many of them had to go back to work with the people they had just sued. For the most part, these litigants were professional, civil, and respectful of their adversaries. The readers of this book should strive to be the same.

Finally, I should add a word about sources. The stories in this book come entirely from the public records in the cases. All quotes are from the judicial opinions, the deposition or trial testimony, or, in a few minor cases, the exhibits used in the case. Care was taken to eliminate personal information, such as home addresses, as well as other personal identifiers unless relevant to the outcome of the case. In addition, negative comments either by or about the litigants, or their lawyers, have been omitted unless directly relevant to the outcome of the case.

With those caveats in mind, it is time to forge ahead into the world of *The Law for Comic Book Creators*.

CHAPTER 1

Litigation in Brief

Tens of millions of civil lawsuits are filed in the state and federal courts each year. And, with few exceptions, they all follow the same procedure. The purpose of this chapter is to explain this process in very general layman terms. Given the oversaturation of legal dramas, dramadies, and procedural shows, the process should be very familiar to most readers. Needless to say, cases usually take a lot longer than an hour (or forty-two minutes with commercials) to resolve.

When going to court, an individual can be represented by an attorney or represent themselves (called *pro se*). A corporation, however, must always be represented by a lawyer. A court case begins when one side (called a plaintiff) files something called a Complaint and gives it to the other side (the defendant).

A Complaint is basically a bare bones listing of everything that the defendant did wrong and includes what the plaintiff wants. This is usually money, but sometimes for something else like stopping someone from doing something (injunction), forcing someone to do something (specific performance) or just a statement as to the truth (a declaratory judgment).

Once a defendant receives the Complaint (through service of process), they can do a few things. First, they can ignore it and risk a finding of default. More likely, a defendant will respond. A defendant can simply file an Answer, which is a written response to all of the allegations in the Complaint. Sometimes, a defendant files a counterclaim and sues the plaintiff back. Sometimes, a defendant can cross claim, which means that they bring a necessary third party into the suit. Or they can file a motion to dismiss the case for a variety of reasons such as procedural (e.g., the Complaint was not delivered correctly) or jurisdictional (the court isn't allowed to hear the type of case [subject matter jurisdiction] or the court cannot enforce its ruling upon the parties involved [personal jurisdiction]) or substantive (e.g., if the complaint doesn't state a claim upon which relief can be granted, which is a fancy way to say that even if everything plaintiff says is true, they can't win).

If the case survives and proceeds after the initial pleadings and motions, discovery commences. Discovery is that phase of litigation where both sides find out or discover what kind of case and evidence the other side has. Discovery can be conducted through written questions (interrogatories), requests for documents obtained from both sides and third parties (requests for production), true/false question that must be answered truthfully (requests for admissions), and interviews of witnesses taken under oath (depositions). Sometimes, one or both sides will hire specialists (known as experts) who must provide detailed expert reports showing not only their qualifications, but the specific facts and methodology they used in rendering their opinion. Those experts also must subject themselves to a deposition.

At the end of discovery (sometimes before), one or both sides may move for something called summary judgment. Basically, a Motion for Summary Judgment asks the court to rule that one side wins as a matter of law when the material facts are not in dispute. For example, in a contract case, if both sides don't dispute that the goods were delivered to a different address than the one specified in the contract, the court may take that fact as true and then determine, under the law, whether the delivery was valid under the contract. If there are facts in dispute, then the case goes to trial where either the judge or a jury will determine what facts are true based on the admissible evidence put in by the parties.[1]

Although the process can be streamlined,[2] the procedure for trial follows the same basic pattern. First, both sides make opening statements where they present what facts they will show in the trial. The plaintiff usually goes first because they are the ones who have to prove they win (this is called the burden of proof) whereas the defendant just has to show that plaintiff hasn't met its burden. Next, both sides (plaintiff and then defendant and then sometimes plaintiff again) present evidence to prove his or her case is true through the testimony of witnesses and the use of documents (referred to as exhibits). But not everything comes in. While far too complicated to discuss fully here, the rules of evidence are designed so that only reliable and relevant information gets seen by the fact finder. For example, junk science and uncorroborated one-sided statements are kept out. Sadly, this means that sometimes the whole story that is "known" to the public does not appear in the courtroom. Every litigator knows that there is a difference between knowing one is correct and proving one is correct in a court of law. It's not a perfect system, but the truth usually comes out. After all the evidence comes in, the judge applies the law to the facts and renders a decision.

An example may be helpful. Suppose Peter is driving a spider mobile through an intersection where he collides with a clown car driven by Joe Kerr. Joe sues Peter by serving him a Complaint that says Peter ran a red light and hit him. Peter counterclaims and says that Joe ran the red light. During discovery the parties find out that Kal witnessed the whole thing with his X-ray vision and told his friend Bruce that Joe ran the red light. On the day of trial, Kal is in the parallel prison dimension, so Bruce takes the stand and tells the judge what Kal told him. Peter also puts up Stephen, a doctor of all that is strange, as an expert to opine on Joe's bad aura, which convinces Stephen that Joe is lying. Unfortunately, neither of these things can be considered by the fact finder. Bruce cannot say what Kal said, because Joe has no way to cross examine Kal to make sure of what he saw (for example, there could have been a lot of lead in the way). Stephen's testimony would equally be thrown out because aura analysis is not an accepted way of telling whether someone is being truthful. Instead, the court would have to listen to the testimony of Joe and Peter and decide whose story is more credible. If the court finds it is Joe then he will win, even though everyone knows Kal would never lie about what he saw.

After the trial court issues its decision, the losing party has a few options. They can file a Motion for Reconsideration, which basically asks the trial court to see if it was wrong when it made its decision. As one can guess, this doesn't happen very often. The next step is that the losing side can file an appeal and ask the next highest court to review the lower court's ruling. Unlike the trial level, there is no additional discovery or a new trial. Instead, both sides submit papers and get a short oral argument before a panel of judges on the appellate court. This appellate court then reviews the record to determine whether the lower court got the facts or the law wrong. If it finds that it did, the appellate court can reverse the lower court's decision (thus making the loser the winner) or remand the decision (which means it sends it back to the lower court to do something, like look for additional facts). A few comments are needed here. First, the lower court is granted great deference for the facts and a judge's findings have to be clearly erroneous before a case is reversed and a jury's findings are usually beyond reproach (although one can argue they were asked the wrong questions). Second, it should be added that very few cases are actually reversed.[3]

Once the appellate court issues its ruling, the losing party has the right to ask for the panel to reconsider the decision (called a petition for rehearing) or for the case to be heard by every judge on the appellate court (an en banc hearing). There is no guarantee that either of things will happen and they usually don't. In state courts, there is another level of appeal before the United States Supreme Court. These are the highest level of state court review and the process works the same as the intermediary level except that the whole court hears the case the first time.

If after all of this, the losing side still wants to continue, they can ask the Supreme Court of the United States to hear the case by filing a Petition for a Writ of Certiorari. The Supreme Court takes very few cases each year and requires either a constitutional right to be at issue (such as the freedom of speech) or requires that several courts of appeals throughout the country have ruled differently (called a circuit split). Once the Supreme Court rules, the case is over. The winner wins and the loser loses.

Once again, it should be stressed that this is a general background discussion and there are several specific complex exceptions that have been ignored (such as jurisdiction and criminal procedure). It is hoped that this general background will provide more context to the stories that follow.

CHAPTER 2

Intellectual Property and
State Law in Brief

The subject of intellectual property touches nearly every aspect of commerce and society. In an early Supreme Court case, Justice Story referred to intellectual property as the metaphysics of the law. And, as the world moves into the digital age, it is more important than ever for people to have a basic understanding of these rights. This is especially true in the comic book industry, where fantastic ideas, colorful characters, and amazing adventures spring from the imagination of creators. Intellectual property law provides a method to both incentivize and protect this imaginative thinking. However, it may also result in a trap for the unwary creator.

Of course, given the current increase of technology and the fast pace at which innovation occurs, the intellectual property law is constantly being changed by Congress, the courts, and the international community. And for that reason, among others, this chapter should be not viewed as a how to or legal advice; however, hopefully this chapter will help provide a roadmap to understand the complex legal terrain or at the very least, provide a basic background to better enjoy the stories that follow.

At its essence, intellectual property law gives protection to the creations of the mind. There are several legal subject matters that fall under the rubric of intellectual property law. There are the three main areas of federal protection that are included as part of intellectual property. These are: copyright (discussed in chapter 3); trademarks (discussed in chapter 8), and patents[1] (beyond the scope of this book). In addition, there are several areas of intellectual property that do not fit directly in the three areas and that are discussed in this chapter. These include the concepts of trade secrets, unfair competition law, and the right of publicity. A single comic may embody several intellectual property rights; from the writing of a script, to the drawing of the art, to the name of the characters, to the process by which the book is created, each step of the comic book creation process is covered. Of course, the one thing intellectual property does not cover is the tangible form of the final comic that embodied the intangible ideas of the creator. Put another way, while comic fans can buy and own the physical copy of the comic book, they do not own the underlying intellectual property that made the book a reality.

Unfair Competition

Unfair competition is a common law principle that refers to a number of judge-made causes of action that protect against commercial abuse of intellectual property. These are very flexible protections that can be adapted by the courts to account for changing economic conditions and the marketplace. Two of these doctrines are of interest to the comic book creator: (1) misappropriation and (2) passing off.

The common law created doctrine of misappropriation is an equitable remedy that protects the owner of intellectual property when a need for protection is apparent, but the law of trademark, patent, or copyright fail to protect the work. Usually, the doctrine is applied in situations where there is a substantial investment by one party to create an intangible right and then another party misappropriates the right for personal gain while injuring the first party and preventing the first party from continuing to create the work.

For example, assume the East Coast based DP Newswire embeds journalists to cover a civil war in the country of Kahndaq. Each morning, the reporters wire the news to the states where it is placed into the DP Newswire's syndicated *Daily Planet* newspapers. Each day, however, DP Newswire's biggest competitor, the West Coast based Coast City Newstime, buys the earliest edition of the East Coast edition of the *Planet* and has its reporters completely rewrite the stories based on the facts gathered by the DP Newswire and distribute them to their *Coast City Reporter* papers. As a result, the West Coast edition of the *Daily Planet* and the *Coast City Reporter* would come out at the same time. As described later in chapter 3, copyright does not apply to the underlying facts, only to the expression of the idea. As a result, because the *Coast City* reporters completely rewrote the stories, they would not be subject to a copyright infringement claim. In addition, there is no case to make against the Coast City Newswire under patent or trademark. However, DP Newswire could sue for misappropriation and unfair competition. This is precisely what the Supreme Court determined in *International News Service v. The Associated Press* when it heard a case with nearly identical facts. The Court found that there is a quasi-property right in the news as it is "stock in trade to be gathered at the cost of enterprise, organization, skill, labor and money, and to be distributed and sold to those who will pay money for it." The court further held that the West Coast news agency was a free rider "endeavoring to reap where it ha[d] not sown."

There are four elements necessary to prove misappropriation in court. First, the infringed party must prove that it made a substantial investment to collect or gather information with the expectation of commercial profits. Second, the infringed party must show the infringer has appropriated the information for commercial use with little or no effort. Third, the infringed party must show it suffered economic harm. Fourth, the infringed party must show that it is fairly and equitably entitled to relief (i.e., that they have clean hands). Of course, courts are reluctant to apply this doctrine as anything other than a last resort. This is because there are other adequate remedies under the traditional statutory intellectual property law that could be usurped by this doctrine.

Another common law judicial doctrine that protects intellectual property is the law of passing off. The law of passing off involves a situation where a person makes a false representation that tends to make consumers believe that his goods come, or are related to, a second (usually more recognized or respected) party and the false misrepresentation harms the second party. This misrepresentation can be direct or indirect. For example, assume that Otis makes horrible tasting candy. However, in his store, he puts out samples of the higher quality Teschmacher Chews and represents that they are his. Otis is violating the doctrine of passing off. Similarly, Otis can violate this rule by simply stating that his candy has some type of connection to those created by Teschmacher in an effort to get people to buy his goods. When people think they are buying Teschmacher Chews, but in fact are getting Otis candy, then those purchases are not buying candy from Teschmacher directly and damaging her. Indirectly, Teschmacher's reputation is being hurt by being associated with the subpar Otis Candies. This would most likely make Otis liable to Teschmacher for the damages he caused by passing off his product as hers.

The false representation is considered to be to the detriment of the competitor if the infringed party can prove several elements. First, they must show the misrepresentation is material and likely to affect the purchases of potential customers. Second, there has to be a reasonable basis that that the misrepresentation has caused economic value to move from the infringed to the infringer or has harmed their goodwill.

Consumers cannot sue for passing off; it only applies in lawsuits between competitors. The policy behind the doctrine is that businesses should be able to build consumer goodwill by creating quality products and consumers should not be confused when selecting among goods and service providers. In fact, the law of passing off was the foundation for the passage of the Lanham Trademark Act in 1946. Over the past years, the doctrine of passing off has fallen into disuse as state and federal trademark law has become more and more prevalent.

The Right of Publicity

Most people understand the power of celebrity. And many comic creators would like to harness that power in their books.[2] As a result, it is necessary to take a moment and address the right to publicity. If someone uses the name, photograph, or likeness of a celebrity without permission, the celebrity may have a right to enjoin (stop) the infringer from doing so under the right of publicity. Simply put, the right of publicity protects against the unauthorized commercial use of a person's attributes (e.g., name, voice, appearance, likeness, personality, signature, and even acting roles) in a way that causes commercial damage to the person whose likeness is used.

In order to prove a case for infringement of the right of publicity, courts will require the celebrity to prove four elements. (1) The infringer must use the celebrity's identity.[3] (2) The use of the celebrity's identity is used to the infringer's benefit. (3) Lack of consent by the celebrity. And (4) Injury to the celebrity because of the use. This injury could take several forms. For example, if the infringer's goods are of an offensive nature or of low quality, the celebrity's image may suffer by being associated with the product. In addition, including a celebrity's image without their permission may limit future chances for that celebrity to received authorized endorsement opportunities for the same type of products. Given the difficulties in quantifying these damages, most courts will award an injunction and simply stop the infringement.

Three cases describe this right as it relates to comics: *Molony v. Boy Publishers*; *Tony Twist v. McFarlane*; and *Winter Brothers v. DC Comics*. Each will be discussed in turn.

Molony v. Boy Comics Publishers, Inc.

The first case involves a seventeen-year-old serviceman named Donald P. Molony. On July 28, 1945, Molony was standing in front of the Empire State Building when a plane crashed into the 79th floor of the building. Heedless of his own safety, Molony rushed into the building and rescued several injured people, procured medical equipment, and administered first aid to the victims. His heroism earned him the Medal of Valor from the American Legion. It also earned him a place as the star in the pages of *Boy Comics*, who recounted the plane crash and Molony's actions in a five page story entitled "The True Story of the Empire State Building, Real Hero."

After the story was published, Molony sued Boys Comics Publishers in the Supreme Court of New York on the grounds that the company had violated his right to privacy. Under New York law, a company was prohibited from using of the name, portrait, or picture of a living person, without his consent, for advertising purposes, or for the purposes of trade. Initially, the trial court ruled in Molony's favor. However, the appeals court reversed and found that Boy Comics Publishers had not violated Molony's right because it had not fictionalized the account for the purposes of comics. Initially, the court acknowledged that the fact that the story appeared in a comic was irrelevant in the determination of whether the story was fictional. Next, the court determined that whether Molony's reputation had been enhanced or degraded had nothing to do with the verisimilitude of the story. As a result, the court found that because the book was based on the actual events, as reported in the newspaper, Boy Comics Publishing did not invade Molony's right of privacy.

Tony Twist v. Todd McFarlane

Todd McFarlane named one of the villains in his *Spawn* book after Anthony Twist, a former professional hockey player in the National Hockey League. The character, who was named "Anthony 'Tony Twist' Twistelli," bore no physical resemblance to the hockey player. Twist filed for an injunction and sought damages for misappropriation of his name. The jury ruled for Twist and awarded him $24.5 million in damages. However, the trial court granted McFarlane's motion for judgment notwithstanding the verdict (his request to have the judge replace the jury's ruling with his own) and awarded nothing. The Missouri Court of Appeals affirmed the trial court's ruling, reasoning that because Twistelli was not a depiction of Twist and because McFarlane never used Twist's identity to propose a commercial transaction, the First Amendment absolutely barred Twist's claims. Twist appealed to the Missouri Supreme Court, which reversed. In reaching its decision, the court concluded that

Twist was really making a right of publicity claim. As a result, the Supreme Court of Missouri applied the predominant purpose test under the law of the right of publicity, to find that the predominant purpose of McFarlane was to obtain a commercial advantage by attracting consumer attention to the product and found in favor of the former hockey player.[4] The Missouri Supreme Court ordered a new trial. In July 2004, a jury awarded Twist $15 million. This judgment was affirmed by the Missouri Court of Appeals in June 2006. In 2007, Twist and McFarlane settled the lawsuit out of court.

Winter Brothers v. DC Comics

In 1995, DC Comics included, as part of a *Jonah Hex* mini-series, two characters called Johnny and Edgar Autumn, the "Autumn Brothers." The Autumn Brothers were created by Joe Lansdale and Tim Truman as a work of fiction and parody. On March 6, 1996, the Winter brothers filed suit in California state court alleging defamation and invasion of privacy and alleged that the comic falsely portrayed them as "vile, depraved, stupid, cowardly, subhuman individuals who engage in wanton acts of violence, murder and bestiality for pleasure and who should be killed."

DC Comics won the case on summary judgment on First Amendment grounds. The Court of Appeals initially affirmed the judgment, but later remanded part of the case for trial on whether the First Amendment protected against the misappropriation of likeness. Prior to trial, the California State Supreme Court granted DC Comic's petition for review. On appeal, the California Supreme Court ruled in DC Comics favor stating, "Although the fictional characters Johnny and Edgar Autumn are less-than-subtle evocations of Johnny and Edgar Winter, the books do not depict plaintiffs literally.... Instead, plaintiffs are merely part of the raw materials from which the comic books were synthesized. To the extent the drawings of the Autumn brothers resemble plaintiffs at all, they are distorted for purposes of lampoon, parody or caricature.... The characters and their portrayals do not greatly threaten plaintiffs' right of publicity."[5]

Protection of Submitted Ideas

Although many people believe that ideas are not covered by intellectual property, there is a narrow doctrine that protects submitted ideas. There are two prerequisite requirements for someone to prevail when someone has inappropriately taken their idea. First, the idea must be novel. This means that the idea must be original, not common knowledge, and of a creative or inventive nature. Second, courts will require that idea be reduced to tangible form, like a writing. In other words, the ideal must be sufficiently detailed and not a stream of consciousness brainstorm.

If an idea holder meets the basic threshold of novelty and concreteness, a court is free to choose from several theories to award damages. These include express contract, implied contracts, and breach of a confidential relationship. As one can see, in order for a court to award damages for a violation of the protection of submitted ideas requires a pre-existing relationship between the idea maker and the infringer.

Hopefully, this chapter helps provide a basic understanding of intellectual property as the backdrop for what will come.

CHAPTER 3

Copyright
An Overview

Perhaps the first question many comic creators may ask when confronted with the highly technical subject matter of copyright is whether it should exist at all. After all, William Shakespeare, Ludwig van Beethoven, and Leonardo da Vinci did not need to rely on the benefit of copyright law to protect themselves or their works. So, given this, why is it that creators and artists today need to worry about complex statutory and common law definitions and rules to protect their creations? The answer is a practical one. Before the advent of copyright law, copying was simply too impracticable to be a problem. Mozart did not have to worry that Antonio Salieri would record his symphonies or photocopy his sheet music. However, in the modern age, copying has become so easy that more protection is necessary. In this way, copyright law can be viewed as the legal response to the advent of more efficient technology. The more advanced the technological ability to copy, the more complex copyright law must be to combat it.[1] In short, the importance of copyright law has gained more prominence as technology advances.

The Origin of Copyright Law

Traditionally, there are considered to be two alternative justifications for the use of copyright. The first is based on the concept of moral entitlement. This is sometimes referred to as the continental theory since it arose in continental Europe. Under this theory, artistic creations are considered an extension of the creator and therefore they are protected against copying and other actions that may harm the creations and, in direct response, the creator. And while the United States incorporates moral entitlement into its copyright structure, it is given far less weight than in Europe. Instead, the United States copyright system utilizes a second theory, which is based on economics. This theory is premised on a belief that without an economic incentive there would be no creativity. In other words, authors and artists would not create a work unless it were protected. Basically, in order to keep comic artists at their drawing boards, copyright law needs to exist to help capture economic value for their work; otherwise they would never bother to draw.[2]

On the flip side, although the copyright system exists to protect the creator as a moral right and to provide an economic incentive, there are also some concerns that needed to be addressed to limit the otherwise unfettered ownership rights. The first concerns the ability of later creators to build on the work of their predecessors. In part, this is based on theory that all art is derivative. Without this limitation on protection, only the originator of a work would have an incentive because she would have unlimited rights. However, she would be the only one with this incentive as all late-comers would simply be out of luck infringers. The second concern limiting copyright protection is based on the First Amendment, which permits citizens to freely express their views, opinions, and ideas. If the copyright law were too limiting, it would affect these rights.[3]

These countervailing considerations, when balanced with the moral and economic justifications, result in a copyright law that is complex, encompassing, but also flexible by necessity. Rights are provided, but these rights are not absolute as there are both temporal and use exceptions to its applicability. The remainder of this chapter focuses on these rules, which provide a background for many of the cases that follow. Given that copyright law changes so often, and at the risk of repetition, this chapter should not viewed as an analysis of the current state of the law or legal advice in any way.

The Source of United States Copyright Law

Many people don't realize that copyright law, along with patent law, comes from the founding fathers. In fact, copyright protection was included in the original draft of the United States Constitution. During a very hot summer in 1787, the Constitutional Convention met in Philadelphia to discuss the rights and duties of the United States Congress. On August 18, the Committee discussed three proposals made related to intellectual property rights. The first proposal was advanced by Charles Pinckney, who wanted to secure authors with exclusive rights for a limited time. The other two proposals were offered by James Madison, a strong proponent of creator rights.[4] Madison suggested language that would permit Congress to secure to literary authors their copyrights for a limited time, or, in the alternative, to encourage, by proper premiums and provisions, the advancement of useful knowledge and discoveries. On September 5, 1787, these proposals were incorporated into the following clause: "The Congress shall have power to ... promote the progress of science and useful arts, by securing for limited times to authors and inventors the exclusive right to their respective writings and discoveries."

On September 17, 1787, the members of the Convention unanimously voted to include the clause in the Constitution. Interestingly, while many other topics were hotly discussed, there was no debate on the inclusion or wording of the copyright language. This provision embodies the economic incentive theory and balances the offsetting concerns as the clause refers to both promoting the progress of science and useful arts and a reference to limitations.

Under the powers granted by the Constitution, Congress enacted several Copyright Acts. Congress enacted the first federal copyright law on May 1790, which granted authors the exclusive right to publish and vend maps, charts and books for a term of 14 years.[5] The

Copyright Act of 1831 extended the term to 28 years and allowed for 14-year renewal of protection.

As comics did not appear in America until 1933, for the purpose of this chapter, and book, there are only two relevant copyright laws that will be discussed. In fact, these are the only two Acts that would apply to works today. The first is the Copyright Act of 1976, which is the current copyright law in the United States. However, since Copyright Acts are generally not retroactively applied, works created prior to the enactment of the 1976 Act will be governed, for the most part, by the previous Act.[6] As a result, the second important Act covered in detail is the Copyright Act of 1909, which governs protected work created prior to 1978.

Protected Subject Matter Covered by Copyright

Under the current law, copyright will only apply to original works that are fixed in a tangible medium of expression. As this book is about comic books and their creators, the discussion will be limited to that medium.

There are two general requirements before copyright can attach. The first general requirement is that the work becomes fixed. This is fairly self-explanatory. Basically, to be considered "fixed" it must be permanently or stably embodied in physical form. For example, an improve comedy troop cannot copyright its show unless it is written down. Comics meet this requirement fairly easily. The script becomes permanent when it is written, the art becomes permanent when it is drawn, and the final comic becomes permanent when it is produced. As explained more fully below, under current law, copyright protection attaches the moment the work becomes fixed. Unlike other areas of intellectual property (e.g. patent, trademark), there is no need to take any other affirmative steps to protect a creator's work. And while there are certain affirmative steps that a creator can take to strengthen its protection, it is important to point out that the protection arises the second the script, the drawing, or the comic is finished.

The second general requirement for copyright protection is the need for originality. Once again, common sense applies to the definition and there are two subparts to this test. First, for a work to be considered "original" it must not have been copied. This means that the work must be made through independent intellectual or artistic effort. As an example, if someone were to copy *Romeo and Juliet* word for word, the copier could not get copyright protection as the work is not original. On the other hand, if the creator were to copy part of *Romeo and Juliet* and add a non-trivial amount of new material, such as having the couple receive romance advice from a wacky alien who magically appears, this would be considered an original work and be protected to the extent of the new material. In this example, other creators could still utilize *Romeo and Juliet* in their new work, but the portion of the work involving the alien would be protected by copyright. The second subpart for the originality test is that the work must be minimally creative. Now, there is no requirement of artistic merit and this does not mean that the work is sophisticated or even has to be good. However, a creator needs to display some minimal level of creativity. For example, a drawing of a square is not protected, but a poorly drawn square that looks like it is supposed to be a cow would be covered.

At this point, it is important to point out a major limitation on the scope of copyright. As copyright protection extends only to the expressions that are fixed in a tangible medium, it does not extend to the underlying ideas in the work.[7] For example, copyright will not protect the idea of a boy who dresses as a creature of the night and dedicates his life to fighting crime after his parents are murdered in front of him. Instead, the copyright law would protect the expression of the idea and would protect the exact wording and art that the creator uses to describe the hero's origin and adventures. In short, ideas are not protected by copyright and expression is protected by copyright.[8] Of course, there is a point at which the details of the new story so closely resemble the original story that the copier has become an infringer of the expression. The issue of determining which parts of a work is protected expression and which parts are unprotected ideas is at the focal point of most infringement litigation and will be discussed more thoroughly below.

In addition to the general requirements in the copyright law, the United States copyright law specifically provides for copyright protection for eight specific non-exclusive categories. Comics fall under the protection of literary and artistic works.[9] As described above, this protection extends to the pictorial or written expression contained in the work. Thus a drawing, picture, depiction, or written description of a character can be registered for copyright. However, not everything is covered. For example, copyright protection does not arise for the title, the general theme, the general idea or name for characters depicted, or their intangible attributes.[10]

The category of literary works is defined as anything in words or symbols and includes both fiction and nonfiction works. It should be noted that although nonfiction is covered by copyright, the historical research or factual discoveries are not protected by copyright. For example, assume someone creates a comic that utilizes the creator's extensive research into the history of Jack the Ripper and the Freemasons and, in the course of this research, it is discovered that there is a connection between the two. The creator puts that connection in his book, which is protected by copyright. If another creator were to come along and write a story based on this connection, that would not violate copyright because the courts treat facts just like ideas—they are not covered by copyright. Put another way, one does not create facts, one discovers them. Therefore, the underlying facts are not covered by copyright.

Comics can also be considered protected as a pictorial graphic work. The main limitation here is that copyright protection is not provided for works if they serve a utilitarian purpose. Usually, there isn't really a debate as to whether the work is a useful article under the statute. However, as explained in chapter 6, a recent case involving the copyrightability and trademarkability of real-life Batmobiles addressed this specific issue.[11]

The final category of copyright in which comics could be considered is not in the specific list of eight specific categories. That category is for compilations. A compilation is a collection of either data or, as is more relevant here, pre-existing works. If the compilation consists of previous work that is covered by copyright, the compilation-author needs permission from the copyright owner of each individual work before it can be included in the compilation. Assuming there is no copyright problem in the underlying work, once the material is put together, the person who compiled the work is entitled to a separate copyright for the compilation.[12] Of course, the original owners of the copyrights in the included stories would each retain their original copyright unless it is assigned.

Copyright Protection for Fictional Characters

In the area of fiction, there has been quite a bit of litigation concerning whether or not there should be protection for fictional characters. In fact, several of the cases in this book deal with this very notion. In the comic's world, it is much easier to get character protection than in the prose world. Unfortunately, there really hasn't been uniformity in court decisions in establishing this protection. Generally, courts have applied two tests: (1) whether the character is capable of copyright and not a vague, undeveloped character and therefore not capable of copyright (the distinct delineation test); and (2) whether the characters are not the story but rather merely a vehicle for the story being told, which is referred to as the story being told test. The Supreme Court created the distinct delineation test in a case involving two screenplays (a play and a movie) about comedies involving interfaith marriage. The court determined the characters in the two works were "stock" and lacked distinct features and characteristics, and therefore the movie did not infringe the play. As described in chapter 4, the same test was applied to Superman in two early cases (involving Wonderman and Shazam) where the courts held that the pictorial representations and verbal descriptions of Superman weren't a mere delineation of a stock hero (like Hercules) but embodied original expression and were therefore protected by copyright and could be infringed. Despite this, in a third case involving Superman (and the television show *The Greatest American Hero*), the court determined that the "overall perception" of the main character in the television show was substantially different and would not be considered an infringement of Superman even though the character shared "some of the superhuman traits popularized by the Superman character and now widely shared within the superhero genre."

In the leading case under the story being told test, a court found that Dashiell Hammett's *Maltese Falcon* characters (including Sam Spade) were not the story but rather merely a vehicle for the story being told. The court stated, "[I]f the character is only the chessman in the game of telling the story he is not within the area of the protection afforded by the copyright." It was later determined, in *Disney v. Air Pirates*, that the story being told wouldn't apply to characters that are graphically represented. The same result happened in the *Spawn* case, discussed in chapter 7, which also has language to imply the test no longer applies to prose.[13]

The short answer is that determining copyright protection for comic book characters is much easier as they are visually unique. Instead, most of the cases have arisen with the use of literary characters. This is because many are merely generic stock characters. Examples would include: the hardnosed detective; the mischievous child; the sex starved teenager; and the suave spy. Because these characters are nothing more than stock ideas, courts generally are reluctant to allow copyright protection for them. On the other hand, if a character is created with such specificity and uniqueness, or given a unique look or manner of dress, courts may consider the character to be expressive and eligible for protection.[14]

Derivative Works

Given the continuing storylines, the fact that comics come out monthly, and that some characters have been around for over 75 years, the concept of derivative works is a very important one for the comic creator. This is especially true given the reinvention and retconning (retroactively changing history to fit a current storyline) that goes on in an effort to reinvigorate the industry every few years. A derivative work is a new work that is based on an earlier work, a transformation of the earlier work into something new. A common explanation is when a comic or novel is transformed into a screenplay. However, as can be seen in the *Spawn* case in chapter 7, the concept equally applies to later variations of spin-off characters or, as can be seen in the Superman litigation discussed in chapter 15, even later versions of the same character.

A derivative work is entitled to its own, separate copyright. However, the creator of the derivative work must obtain permission of the copyright owner of the underlying work if it is subject to copyright protection. If a creator fails to obtain this permission it is considered an infringement of the earlier work and will not itself be eligible for copyright. As can be seen in the *Spawn* case, there must be a "non-trivial" difference between the underlying work and the derivative work in order for it to be eligible for copyright protection.

The Owner of a Copyright

Until this point, the discussion has focused on the work. Next, it is important to note, under copyright law, who can be considered the owner of a work.

The first important thing to remember is that the ownership in the physical work is different from the ownership of the copyright. For example, if someone were to get a sketch done at a comic convention, the purchaser would own the physical copy of that sketch, but the artist would still retain the copyright in that sketch. More importantly, if a writer were to hire an artist without a contract to draw a comic, the artist would continue to own the copyright in those drawings. As a result, the owner of the copyrighted work and the owner of the physical object that embodies the work can be, and often are, two different people.

With that caveat in mind, the general rule is that the creator of the work is the owner of the copyright in that work. However, in the collaborative world of comics, this general rule may get confusing. Many people come together to make comics: a writer, an artist (who may be further broken down into an inker and a penciler), a letterer, and a toner or colorist.[15] Add to this the multiplicity of other people working on mainstream comics, which employ numerous editors and assistant editors to oversee the work on well-established licensed characters and the layout of the book, and the matter of ownership becomes quite complex.

The first issue that arises is the concept of joint ownership. The question is whether the parties intend to produce "joint work." To make that determination, courts examine a two part test: (1) each party must contribute copyrightable expression to the final product; and (2) the parties must each have the requisite intent to make a joint work at the time. So, for example, when a writer hands his script to an artist and that artist creates the comic book layout and underlying art to produce a final comic, the pair will be considered joint owners of the work. On the flip side, if someone were to contribute merely the idea for a story and another creator were to write the script and draw the story, then that would not be considered a joint work and only the creator would hold the copyright while the idea generator would not be considered a joint owner.[16]

Of course, as one can imagine, the second requirement, which involves the intent of the parties to create a joint work, may be troublesome to prove. Years later, when a property becomes valuable, there may a question as to what the intention of the original collaborators was when they first created a work. As a result, courts tend to look at circumstantial evidence to meet this prong. Specifically, courts give great weight to the way the work is credited. For example, if on the title page, the creation of a character is credited to two individuals, courts view this as very good evidence that there was an intention to create a joint work. This can be seen in several stories in the book, most notably, in the *Ghost Rider* case, and in the *Spawn* case. However, there also could be circumstances in which each creator has a separate copyright in the work. For example, assume a writer drafts a script to their idea for Muddy Walter, a hero with feet of clay. As soon as the script is complete, copyright attaches. The writer then shops around the script and the Untimely Company likes the concept and buys a nonexclusive right to produce a comic based on the script. The writer's involvement ceases and Untimely uses one of their in-house artists to draw the script. The result will not be considered a joint work. Instead, it is a derivative work. If, a year later, the writer sells the same script to Distinguished Competition Comics and they use their in-house artist, who draws the book completely differently, Untimely will not be able to claim infringement. However, if the Distinguished Competition artist uses the Untimely characters as models, then Untimely would have an infringement claim.

So assuming joint ownership, each creator owns an undivided share in a joint work. This means that each creator can exploit the joint work without getting permission of co-authors. However, there is a duty to account and share the royalties to their co-authors for any profits earned from the exploited work. Similarly, each joint owner can make derivative works based on the original work without permission of co-authors. More importantly, this derivative work would not be considered itself to be a joint work and is separately copyrightable by the new creator.

An example may be helpful. Assume Steven and George write a book together about an adventurous archeologist named Henry. They are joint creators. After the book is a success, George decides to write a sequel that involves adventurers of a Young Henry and his dog, Indiana. George can do this, but he is required to split the profits with Steven. However, Steven has no ownership over the dog as that is a new element in the derivative work. So, if Steven wanted to create a book where Indiana faces off against a killer shark, he would need George's permission. Similarly, if George were write a story without Henry in which

Indiana meets Han, changes his name to Chewie, and has space adventures, George would not owe any money to Steven as he is the sole owner of the derivative elements.

Work for Hire

Work for hire is a very important issue in the comics industry. From its early beginnings, it was common for companies to hire people to perform creative work. The job of these writers and artists is to create copyrighted work for other people. Thus, the issue arises as to who owns the copyright: the creator of these works or the person that hired the creator? The Copyright Act of 1976 provides that when the work is work made for hire, the hiring party, rather than the actual author, is the owner of the copyright. Of course, this begs the question of when someone would be considered to be performing a work for hire. Under the current copyright law, the test is fairly simple.

The first step in this analysis is to determine whether the person creating the work is acting as an employee of the company and the work is performed within the scope of his or her job duties. If so, the work will be considered a work for hire. In order to determine whether someone is working as an employee, courts have looked at several factors that have been created as part of the law of agency. For example, the Supreme Court in *Community for Creative Non-Violence v. Reid* stated that the following factors would be considered important to the analysis:

> In determining whether a hired party is an employee under the general common law of agency, we consider the hiring party's right to control the manner and means by which the product is accomplished. Among the other factors relevant to this inquiry are the skill required; the source of the instrumentalities and tools; the location of the work; the duration of the relationship between the parties; whether the hiring party has the right to assign additional projects to the hired party; the extent of the hired party's discretion over when and how long to work; the method of payment; the hired party's role in hiring and paying assistants; whether the hiring party is in business; the provision of employee benefits; and the tax treatment of the hired party. No one of these factors is determinative.

Probably the easiest example of a comic creator being treated as an employee would be the story of Stan Lee. Throughout his career, Stan Lee has been an employee of Marvel Comics. In fact at times in the '50s, he was arguably the sole employee of Marvel Comics.[17]

However, even if the creator of the work is not considered an employee, the inquiry does not end there. This is because the work may still be considered a work for hire under a second alternative test set up under the copyright statute. There are two prongs that must be met in order for a non-employee to create a work made for hire. First, the work created must fall within a list of nine specific categories of work listed in the statute. Comics fall into this list as contribution to collective works.[18]

If the work falls within the nine types of work, like comics, the next step is to determine whether there is a written agreement between the parties specifically establishing work for hire status. If there is an agreement establishing that the work was done for hire than the work will be considered a work for hire. Without any writing, it is not a work for hire. For example, if there is only an oral agreement, the relationship will not be considered a work for hire relationship.

Of course, the work for hire definition was very different under the previous rules, as can be seen in the *Kirby* case in chapter 14. Simply put, it was much easier for a company to establish work for hire under the 1909 Act applying what was known as the instance and expense test. Under the test, courts examine who asked for the work to be done, and who was in charge of supervising. It is important to note that there doesn't actually need to be supervision, just the right to direct and supervise the manner in which the writer performs his work.

The Traditional Rights of a Copyright Holder

Under current copyright law, copyright owners have several rights. As originally enacted, the 1976 copyright gave copyright owners five exclusive rights. They were: (1) the right to reproduce the work into copies and phonorecords; (2) the right to create derivative works of the original work; (3) the right to distribute copies and phonorecords of the work to the public by sale, lease, or rental; (4) the right to perform the work publicly (if the work is a literary, musical, dramatic, choreographic, pantomime, motion picture, or other audiovisual work); and (5) the right to display the work publicly. Of course, not every right applies equally to every work,[19] and, as this book is limited to comic books, the discussion of these five rights will be limited to how these rights affect that medium. For example, while it is possible for a comic book to be read in public or displayed in a gallery, this book will not discuss the intricacies of the performance right or the display right.

The first of these traditional rights is the right of reproduction. This is actually a copy right, as in, the right to make copies. This right is violated whenever anyone makes a copy of a work without permission. And unless some exception applies (e.g., fair use discussed below), the making of a single copy violates this right. Of course, this right is not as broad as it first appears as there are exceptions to the copy right. For example, libraries are allowed to make copies for preservation purposes or to provide their patrons with excerpts of works or works that are out of print. There are also some limitations that arise under the digital rules. For example, it is permissible to make back-up copies of computer software and copies of software in connection with computer maintenance and repair. As a result, any backups to comics downloaded to the device would be carved out from the copy right. Similarly, while not directly related to comics, and as discussed more fully in the fair use section, it is also permissible to draw or take pictures of protected architectural works provided they are visible from a public place. Finally, authorized entities are allowed to reproduce copies of published works in specialized formats for blind people or people with disabilities. So, if a qualified public and private nonprofit agency or organization such as a school, library, or a training program were to create a version of *Action Comics* without permission, this would not be considered improper copying under the statute.[20]

The second traditional right is the right of adaptation, which is the right to make a derivative work. To put this in relevant terms, only the owner of a comic book copyright has the right to create a screenplay based on the comic or to release a version of the comic in another language. This right overlaps the copy right in many respects as a derivative work, by definition, copies from the original work while adding new elements.

As described above, the owner of the copyright can transfer the right to make derivative works to someone else. What is important to note is that the purchaser of the derivative work is limited to the terms of the transfer. So, if someone is licensed to make a Cantonese version of a story, and also releases a Mandarin version, this would be considered copyright infringement as the licensee is limited to the terms of the license. Similarly, if a comic creator only licenses the rights to a toy property for a comic book adaptation, it then cannot release a prose novelization of the toys or write a screenplay based on the comic.[21]

The third traditional right is the right to distribute. In short, this is the right that makes the copyright owner the sole person allowed to disseminate copies to the public. Of course, many might wonder why there is a need for a separate distribution right when there is a prohibition to make unauthorized copies. The answer is simple: in many cases, the distributor is not the same as the printer. For example, assume an unknown person infringes a copyrighted work and a copy of this work is sold to bookstores and comic shops. The distribution right allows for the owner of the copyright to stop the book stores and comic shops from selling the illegal copies.

Once again, this right is not unlimited and there is one major limitation to the distribution right. This is referred to as the first sale doctrine. The first sale doctrine applies to situations where the owner of a legal copy of the work is entitled to sell, dispose of, or rent that copy without violating the distribution right of the original author. This allows comic collectors to sell their back issue collections to comic shops and for the comic shops, in turn, to sell the books to the public (most likely in quarter bins). It should be noted that illegal copies are not covered by this exception.[22]

The last two rights, performance and display, are beyond the scope of this book. In short, to "perform" a work is to recite, render, play, dance, or act it, either directly or by means of a device, and to "display" a work is to show a copy of it, either directly or by means of a film, slide, television image, or any other devices or process. Both of these rights are limited to public performance or display. So, if two people decide to act out the end of *Catwoman* issue 1 in the privacy of their bedroom, they are not performing the work. Similarly, if someone frames their near mint copy of *Superman Forever* issue 1 with an Alex Ross lenticular cover and hangs it in their living room, they are not violating the display right. However, if the first example is performed in a club on stage or the Alex Ross cover is hung on the wall of a restaurant, there is infringement of these rights as the action took place in public. Any further discussion on this topic is unwarranted.

Moral Rights

In recent years, more rights have been added to the copyright law as a result of changes in technology, especially the move to digital technology. First, beginning in 1990, with the passage of the Visual Artists Rights Act, the federal copyright law began to include protection for moral rights. The term moral rights comes from the French term *droit moral*, and refers to the right of a creator not to have the integrity of his work or reputation compromised. And while moral rights were commonly included as part of copyright law in Europe for nearly a century,[23] they are still relatively new in the United States. Moreover, moral rights under the federal law are quite limited. First, moral rights are only granted to works of visual art produced in either a one of a kind edition or in a limited edition of less than two hundred. Second, moral rights are independent from and different from copyright. This is because copyright protects property rights and allows owners to economically benefit from the copyright, where moral rights protect the personal and reputational rights of the creator. As a necessary conclusion, moral rights always belong to the author and it is important to note that moral rights can never be transferred or sold. However, moral rights can be waived.[24]

There are two primary types of moral rights under current law. First, there is the right of attribution. This means that creator has a right to say they are the creator of a work and can demand that they be credited for that work. On the other hand, an artist can also prevent the use of their name on work that they did not create. Similarly, an author can avoid being listed as the author of a work in the event of a distortion, mutilation, or other modification of the work which would be prejudicial to the author's reputation or honor. The second right is the right of integrity. Under the right of integrity, an author can prevent the intentional distortion, mutilation, or other modification to his work if such alteration would be prejudicial to his honor or reputation. In addition, the right of integrity gives an artist the right to prevent the destruction of the creator's work if the work is established to be of recognized stature. A few examples may be helpful. Assume that a creator named MPH creates pencils for an issue of *Spudman, the Potato Hero* for Tater Comics. Unless he waives his moral rights in writing, then Tater Comics must credit him for the work in the issue in which it appears. If it does not, it has violated his moral rights. If MPH is replaced on the second issue with a world renowned stick figure drawer, and the issue is credited to MPH, he has the moral right to request his name be taken off. Finally, assume that children's publisher Tater Comics is purchased by an adult film company who hires an inker to trace over the pencils in *Spudman* to add anatomical feature and changes the book to *Studman*. MPH has the right to have his name removed from the property. In the non-hypothetical world, Alan Moore could be seen as invoking his moral rights when he asked to have his name removed from the *Watchmen* and *V for Vendetta* feature films.

Duration of Copyright Under the Current Law

One would think that determining the length of a copyright would be simple. However, the differences between the 1909 Act, the 1976 Act, and a 1998 Term Extension Act, along with the need for transition rules necessary to implement the current law, complicate the issue. As a result, there are several different time periods depending upon when the work was created and/or published.

Under the current law, the general rule is that copyright protection in works created after January 1, 1978 lasts for the life of the author, plus 70 years after death of the creator.[25] This is fairly straightforward. This is true regardless of when the work is released. For example, if Kyle creates a comic in 1994 and then dies in 2014, the term of copyright will last until the year 2084 (2014 + 70). This example does not change if the book is delayed until 2016 or even if the book is never released.

For joint works, the term of copyright protection is seventy years from the last surviving creator. Once again, the date the work is released (or even if it is released at all) is not relevant to the time period. For example, if artist Steve and writer Hollis collaborate on a comic book that is released in 1980 and then Hollis is murdered in 1986 but Steve lives until 2050, the copyright of their joint work will last until 2120 (2050 + 70).

A different period applies if the creator is unknown. Obviously, the time period cannot be tied to the life of the creator of the work if it is anonymous. The same could be true for certain works for hire, where the creator of the copyright may be unknown. As a result, the publication date becomes more important. In these two circumstances, anonymous works and work made for hire, the duration of copyright is 95 years from publication or 120 years from creation, whichever comes first. For example, assume that a newspaper reporter named Clark writes a comic graphic novel entitled *Yellow Sun* under a work for hire agreement with Blaze Comics in 1990 and Blaze Comics publishes the book in the same year. The copyright would last until 2085, because this is the earlier of 95 years from publication (1990 + 95 = 2085) and 120 years from creation (1990 + 120 = 2110). However, if the hypothetical is changed and Blaze Comics does not put the book out until 2021, then the copyright would expire in 2110 because this is the earlier of 95 years from publication (2021 + 95 = 2116) and 120 years from creation (1990 + 120 = 2110).

Duration Under the 1909 Act and Termination Provisions

As previously mentioned, the time periods of protection under the current copyright law only apply to works created after January 1, 1978. However, given that a large quantity of works created prior to this date are still eligible for protection (and are featured in many of the chapters that follow), it is important to examine the 1909 Act and the transition rules that would apply to bridge the periods in the two Acts.

Prior to the 1976 Act, the 1909 Act covered the rules for the duration of copyright protection. When examining works created under the 1909 Act, it is important to take into account a fundamental difference between the two Acts as to when federal copyright protection applied. Under the current law, copyright protection arises the moment the work is completed. This was not the case under the 1909 Act. Instead, copyright protection under the 1909 Act only arose upon publication of the work with the correct copyright notice.[26] The importance of an adequate notice was very important in the *Shazam* case in chapter 4. Once a work was published, the copyright owner received a 28-year term. At the end of that term, the copyright creator could apply for renewal of the copyright and keep the work protected for another 28-year renewal period. This renewal was not automatic and the holder had to file an application to renew. If no application was timely filed, the work was no longer protected after the 28th year.[27] If the application was filed, the term was extended for another 28 years. To sum up, under the 1909 Act, a copyright creator could be protected for a total of 56 years. The purpose of the renewal period was to protect creators. The Congressional logic behind this renewal was that a creator may not know the value of his or her intellectual property when it is first sold. For example, if a creator was to sell or give away their property and it was to become immensely popular, someone else would reap the economic rewards of the initial creativity of the author. However, under the renewal system in the 1909 Act, the creator, as the only person who could renew the term, would be in a better bargaining position should the work become immensely valuable. In short, a creator under the 1909 Act gets two bites at the copyright apple.

When the law changed to take out the publication requirement and extend the time period in the 1976 Act, there were three types of works that had to be addressed. First, there were those works that were unpublished and therefore not covered by the 1909 Act but subject to state common law protection.[28] Second, there were works published in or before 1950 that were in their second renewal term. Third, there were works that were published after 1950 and were in their first term of copyright. Congress needed to address each one of these works to make sure the new law would be fairly applied. The result is a bit complicated.

For works that were unpublished on January 1, 1978, the effective date of the 1976 Act, the new law provided the normal copyright period of life of the author plus 70 years. However, given that the act was essentially revoking an unlimited term of common law copyright, the act also provided several additional safety nets. First, all work was guaranteed protection until December 21, 2002. Second, if the work was published prior to 2002, the protection of the work would be extended through 2047. For example, if Mickey were to write an unpublished manuscript in 1895, and the book was unpublished on January 1, 1978, it would be covered by this rule. This means as an unpublished work, the book would be for the life of Mickey plus 70 years. If he dies of yellow kid fever in 1963, the copyright would expire in 2033. However, the answer changes if he dies earlier. Assume the facts are the same except that Mickey is killed as the result of a mugging in Hogan's Alley in 1905. In this situation, the 70 year period would end in 1975, which is earlier than December 31, 2002. So the work would be protected until December 31, 2002. Assume further that Pulitzer Press decides to publish Mickey's book in 2000. In that situation, the protection would be extended until 2047.

Under current law, if a work was in the renewal term on January 1, 1978, the copyright protection expires 95 years from the date the work was first published. However, if the work was no longer protected (i.e., because the second term was never renewed) then the work would still not be protected.[29] For example, if Barnes were to publish a book called *Sidekick* in 1944, copyright protection would be automatic for the first 28 year period. If Barnes renewed the copyright in 1972, then the work would fit in this transition rule. As a result, the work would be entitled to protection for 95 years after publication or until 2039 (1944 + 95), which is longer than the original expiration date of 2000 (1944 + 56). However, if Barnes dies in a plane crash in 1945 over Germany and fails to renew the work in 1972, then there would be no copyright protection provided under the 1976 Act.[30]

Works that were in the first term of copyright on January 1, 1978, are protected for 28 years from publication, which is the same as the protection under the 1909 Act. The creator also gets a renewal right. However, when the copyright on the work is renewed, the renewal period now lasts for a second term of 67 years, which would make the total term of 95 years under the Act. Originally, the renewal was not automatic. This changed in 1992, and now the renewal is automatic.[31] For example, if Jones were to publish a book called *Sidekick* in 1969, the renewal period would not occur until 1997 under the 1909 Copyright Act. But, because the work was in its first renewal term on January 1, 1978, the transition rules would provide that when the copyright is automatically renewed in 1997, the renewal period will last for 67 years, until 2064.

The Transfer of Copyright

Given that it is the dream of nearly every independent comic creator to sell their story to a big time publisher, the transfer and sale of a copyright interest is an important issue. Once again, there are different rules based on when the work was published.

A copyright interest is a property. And because it is property, like a car or a house, it is freely transferable and can be sold. In fact, a creator can even transfer copyright in a work before it is created. Of course, selling the underlying object does not automatically transfer the copyright. For example, if Jonah buys a photograph from Parker, then he only gets ownership in the physical photo, and Parker would retain the copyright. That means Jonah would not be able to print it in his newspaper without permission.

In addition to being generally transferable property, copyrights are also considered to be divisible, which means that a creator can transfer portions of the copyright and retain others. For example, if Laurel publishes a book called *My Mother's Cry*, Laurel can separate her copyright interest and sell the license to make paperback books to one company named Distinguished Company, and then sell the license to make hardcover books to a different company named Bullet Heads. In short, the copyright in *My Mother's Cry* can be split into pieces in any feasible way (such as selling the license to one person to print the book in Atlantean, to have someone else make audio books, or to a third person to create a movie based on the work). Indeed, the transfer could even be nonexclusive. A nonexclusive license gives permission to someone to use the work but does not guarantee or promise that the same permission will not be given to someone else.

There are some requirements before a copyright can be validly transferred. For anything other than a nonexclusive license, the transfer must be in writing signed by the owner of the copyright. Nonexclusive licenses can be oral. In fact, nonexclusive licenses are sometimes imposed by courts because they are implied from course of conduct or from the dealings of the parties.

Once a copyright is transferred, the instrument of transfer (i.e., the contract) may be recorded in the copyright office. Of course, there is no requirement that the purchaser file the instrument with the copyright office. However, there is a major incentive to taking this action as the filing puts others on notice that the purchaser is the true owner of the copyright. It is also important if there are conflicting transfers (e.g., the same interest is sold to more than one person). If there is a conflict, the priority rules are straightforward. If there are two conflicting transfers for the same interest, the first one executed will win so long as it recorded within one month after it is signed or if it is recorded before the second transfer. If the first transfer is not filed within the grace period, and the second transfer is filed, then the second transfer takes priority so long as it was executed in good faith and for valuable consideration (i.e., they paid for it with the best of intentions).

Of course, as mentioned above, under the 1909 Copyright Act (and some transition rules in the 1976 Copyright Act) there is a renewal period in the copyright. The transferability of the renewal interest raises some issues that depend on whether the author survives. For example, assume that Sheldon creates a book of superhero photographs and publishes it in 1975 through MMMS Press, who buys the copyright to the book. Because this is prior to the enactment of the 1976 Copyright Act, the work would be subject to the coverage period in the 1909 Copyright Act. This means that MMMS Press owns, as assignee of the copyright, the rights to the work for the first 28 years. However, beginning in 2003, the renewal period begins and all rights revert back to the original creator. However, if Sheldon wanted to assign and sell off that renewal period to MMMS Press prior to 2003, he could.[32] But, that sale is considered to be a transfer of a contingency in the renewal term. This is because the author has the right to renew, but only if the author lives to the renewal date. If the author were to live to the renewal date, the transferee liability would vest and it could be conveyed or sold in accordance with the contingent contract. But, if the author dies before the 28th year, the transfer is considered null and void because the author transferred something he didn't own. Instead, as described above, the author's surviving heirs are the real owner. In our facts, if Sheldon transfers the renewal term in the work to MMMS Press as part of his contract in 1975, he has to survive past 2003 in order for MMMS Press to get those rights. So, if Sheldon dies of lung cancer in 2009, then the rights will pass to MMMS Press. However, if Sheldon is brought to ruin and killed by a virus he contracts from a fellow photographer in 1995, the rights will not transfer to MMMS Press and, upon renewal, will revert back Sheldon's heirs. This is made more complicated when derivative rights are considered. Assume that MMMS Press has a film division and Sheldon specifically assigns the rights to make the book into a movie (a derivative work). The movie is released in 1995 just before Sheldon's death. In executing Sheldon's will, his estate lawyer sells off the renewal period rights to Jameson Pictures. In a similar case, *Stewart v. Abend* involving the movie *Rear Window*, the Supreme Court has determined that if MMMS Press continues to exploit the film during the renewal period, then that would infringe on the copyrights owned by Jameson Pictures and be liable for damages.[33]

Under the current copyright law, there is the life plus 70 years period that can be freely transferred. As there is no renewal period, creators cannot obtain the second bite at the copyright that was available in prior acts, and the policy concern that a creator may transfer work at a cheap price before its true value is known and therefore lose the economic benefit of their work becomes more prevalent under the current law. In order to account for and remedy this concern, the law contains several provisions that allow individuals to terminate copyright transfers several years after the copyright has been granted. These termination rights, which allow a creator to recapture their creations, are at the center of the *Captain*

America, *Superman*, and *Kirby* suits described in this book. Of course, it goes without saying that these termination rights are only available for work that was transferred and not for works made for hire.

There are two provisions in the 1976 Act that provide for terminations; they are subtly different and arise based on the date of the transfer.[34] If the transfer is made after January 1, 1978, the basic rules are as follows. First, the termination is only available if the grant was made by the author. So, if the grant was made after the author has died then it cannot be terminated. Second, the grant of termination must be made in a specific five year time period. This five year window begins 35 years after the grant of rights is made and ends 40 years after the grant. Third, the termination can be initiated by the author. However, if the author is dead, then the termination can be initiated by majority vote of the author's spouse and children, if any.[35] Fourth, the author must give advance notice by mail to the transferee that the author is going to terminate the copyright at least two, but no more than ten, years before the selected termination date. Fifth and finally, if the transfer is terminated, the original transferee may continue to exploit any derivative works made during the period prior to termination.[36] For example, assume that Zatara writes a novel called *CIGAM* in 1980 and transfers all rights in the book to the Publishing House of Mystery in 1990 before he mysteriously dies at a séance in 1995 leaving behind Zatanna as his sole heir. First, it should be noted that the copyright will expire in 2065 (1995 + 70 years). This grant can be terminated between 35 and 40 years from the date of the transfer in 1990.[37] So, the termination period begins in 2025 and ends in 2030. This means that the work can be terminated any time during that period by Zatanna, his only surviving daughter. If she wants to terminate in 2025, she must serve written notice on the Publishing House of Mystery during the time period beginning in 2015 and ending in 2023. If the interest is terminated, then the Publishing House of Mystery must stop selling the book. Of course, if the Publishing House of Mystery was able to create a film version of the book and release a copy of it in the Interlac language before the rights were terminated, then the publishing company can continue to exploit these derivative works despite the termination.

If a work was transferred before January 1, 1978, the rules are different. As described above, works created before the enactment of the 1976 Copyright Act were protected by copyright for an initial first term, a 28-year period from publication. The protection could then be renewed for a second renewal period (initially 28 years and then increased in the 1976 Act). The right for an author to terminate only applies to transfers of the renewal term. This is because authors who only transferred the initial term did not need to terminate to regain their work after the first 28 year term—they could simply not transfer the renewal period. So, if in the example above, Zatara created his book *CIGAM* in 1970 and transferred the ownership for the initial term to the Publishing House of Mystery in 1975 when they published the book, the publisher would only own the book copyright until 2003. At that point, the copyright would revert back to Zatara for the renewal term (67 years) and there is no need to terminate. However, if Zatara were to have sold his rights in both the initial and the renewal period to the Publishing House of Mystery, then the 1976 Act would provide Zatara (or his family) with termination rights during the renewal period.

The termination rights for works transferred before January 1, 1978, work a little differently than for works transferred after January 1, 1978. First, there is no requirement that the author make the transfer. Another major difference is that termination dates for works transferred prior to the enactment of the 1976 Act are not measured from the date of transfer, but from the date of publication. Once again, there is a five-year window for termination, but this window begins 56 years after publication and closes 61 years after publication. And once again, advance notice must be provided to the transferee that the author is going to terminate the copyright at least two, but no more than ten, years before the selected termination date. Finally, the same rule applies as to the transferee's continued right to keep using derivative works developed in the first terms. So, taking the most recent Zatara example, because he transferred his renewal period he has termination rights. The window for the book to be terminated begins in 2031 and ends in 2036. If he chooses to reclaim the rights in 2031, he could provide notice any time from 2021 to 2029. If the Publishing House of Mystery made derivative works, they still retain the rights to them. Zatara will then be the owner of the work until 2070, when the work is no longer eligible for protection. As this calculation shows, the purpose of this termination right is to allow authors the chance to reclaim the 39 year period that resulted from the extension of the copyright that occurred when the 56 year period was increased to 95 years.[38]

Publication and How to Affix a Copyright

The current copyright law defines publication as the distribution of copies to the public by sale, other transfer of ownership, or by rental lease or lending. And while there has been a large amount of litigation on what this means for music and the performance arts, the concept is fairly straightforward in the comics industry. A book is published when it is printed and distributed to the public.[39]

Of course, as described above, under current law, the concept of publication is nowhere near as important as the predecessor law. This is because federal copyright protection now attaches the minute the work is created so publication and, for the most part, the protected period is tied to the life of the author. This is very different under the 1909 Copyright Act where publication ended the indefinite protection available under state law and started the federally prescribed period of protection.

To make matter worse, as can be seen in the District Court's opinion in the *Shazam* case, in chapter 4, DC Comics almost lost their most important property because publication without a proper notice affixed meant that the owner of the copyright waived protection under the 1909 Copyright Act. The notice needed to be put on all copies of the work. Without a proper notice, a creator did not fall under the federal statute and also lost the common law protection available to unpublished works. In fact, even if the failure to include the notice occurred by accident, this ended up being a waiver of copyright protection. This was referred to as a fatal publication.

Of course, publication is still important under the current copyright law. As described above, a number of limitation periods, such as the period of copyright protection for works created prior to 1976 and dates for renewal and termination, all flow from the date of publication. So while not as fatal as in the previous Act, failure to include proper notice when publishing a work can still affect things under the current law.

As a result of the importance of notice, it is important to discuss the mechanics of how proper notice is achieved. Luckily, achieving notice is fairly straightforward. Basically, when the book is published, the copyright owner has to include three components that are mandated in the statute to achieve proper notice First, the work must include either the word "copyright," an abbreviation of the word, or the copyright symbol ("©").[40] Second, the work must contain the name of the copyright owner. Third, the notice must contain the year of first publication. These three items must be placed on the comic in a location that is likely to come to the attention of the public.

The consequence of failing to include notice varies under the different copyright Acts. As described above, if a work was published before 1978, the effective date of the 1976 Copyright Act, failure to include notice would be fatal and the work would not be protected. If the work is published between 1978 and 1989,[41] then failure to include notice was not fatal to obtaining protection. While not having a notice endangered an author's right to protection, the failure could be cured after the fact.[42] Of course, after 1989, the notice requirement has no effect. In fact, notice has become completely optional.

Although notice is no longer mandatory under the current act, it is still important and highly recommended. This is because if there is no notice on a work and someone infringes that work, then the infringer can argue innocent infringement as a way to mitigate (i.e., lower) their damages. In short, the infringer can argue that because there wasn't notice they didn't know it was copyrighted. As a result, it is a very good idea for creators to include a copyright notice to help get them their damages.

Registration of Copyright

Under the present copyright law, which became effective January 1, 1978, registration in the Copyright Office is not required for copyright protection under the law.[43] There are, however, certain advantages to registration, including the establishment of a public record of the copyright claim. Copyright registration must generally be made before an infringement suit can be brought.[44]

As a result, any creator that is concerned about infringement and the ability to sue infringers should take advantage of the optional filing. And while it is true that registration can occur at any time (even after an infringement takes place) there are certain advantages to be gained via early and prompt registration. First, if registration is made within five years of creation, then that registration becomes prima facie evidence, which means that the other side must prove it wrong, that copyright is valid. Second, if registration is made before infringement, the copyright is entitled to recover statutory liquidated damages and attorney's fees. This damage remedy and cost recovery is unavailable if the property is registered after infringement.[45]

In order to register a book, the copyright owner needs to submit an application, a fee, and a copy of the work to the trademark office. Specifically, the copyright owner needs to submit one copy of unpublished works and two copies of published works. In addition, the law requires that copies of all published works must be submitted to the Library of Congress. This requirement does not affect the validity of the copyright and is not a prerequisite for filing. However, a failure to file the submitted works with the Library of Congress could result in a large fine.

More information on filing a copyright for comics is available in Circular 44.[46] That circular provides:

Copyright Registration

A cartoon or comic strip can be registered as a visual arts work or a literary work, depending on the nature of the work and the way it is presented. Generally, cartoons are considered works of the visual arts; however, if textual elements are preponderant in a cartoon or comic strip, it should be registered as a literary work.

An application for copyright registration contains three essential elements: a completed application form, a nonrefundable filing fee, and a nonreturnable deposit—that is, a copy or copies of the work being registered and "deposited" with the Copyright Office.

There are two ways to apply for copyright registration. Online registration through the electronic Copyright Office (eCO) is the preferred way to register basic claims for literary works; visual arts works; performing arts works, including motion pictures; sound recordings; and single serials. Advantages of online filing include a lower filing fee; the fastest processing time; online status tracking; secure payment by credit or debit card, electronic check, or Copyright Office deposit account; and the ability to upload certain categories of deposits directly into eCO as electronic files. To access eCO, go to the Copyright Office website and click on *electronic Copyright Office*.

You can also apply using paper forms. To access fill-in versions of Form VA (visual arts), Form TX (literary works), and Form CON (continuation sheet for paper applications), go to the Copyright Office website and click on *Forms*. Complete the form(s) on your personal computer, print them out, and mail them with a check or money order and a deposit. Blank forms can also be printed out and completed by hand or requested by postal mail (limit two copies of any one form by mail).

Note: Copyright Office fees are subject to change. For current fees, check the Copyright Office website at *www.copyright.gov*, write the Copyright Office, or call (202) 707–3000.

Deposit Requirements

The deposit requirements for cartoons and comic strips will vary in particular situations. The general requirements are as follows:

- If the work is unpublished, one complete copy.
- If the work was first published in the United States before January 1, 1978, two complete copies of the work as first published.
- If the work was first published in the United States on or after January 1, 1978, two complete copies of the best edition.
- If the work was first published outside the United States, whenever published, one complete copy of the work as first published.
- If the work is a contribution to a collective work and first published on or after January 1, 1978, one of the following: one complete copy of the best edition of the entire collective work, the complete section containing the contribution if published in a newspaper, the entire page containing the contribution, the contribution cut from the paper in which it appeared, or a photocopy of the contribution itself as it was published in the collective work. If first published before January 1, 1978, one complete copy of the issue as first published containing the contribution.

Registration of Collections and Contributions

A single registration can be made for cartoons published as a unit (for example, a comic book), provided that the copyright claimant is the same for all elements in the unit.

Two or more unpublished cartoons or comic strips can be considered for registration as a unit on a single application when submitted with a nonrefundable filing fee and a nonreturnable deposit of the work if the following four conditions are met:

- the selections are assembled in an orderly form;
- the combined selections bear a single title identifying the collection as a whole;
- the copyright claimant in all the selections and in the collection as a whole is the same; and
- all the selections are by the same author, or, if they are by different authors, at least one of the authors has contributed copyrightable authorship to each of the selections.

Works registered as a collection will be recorded in the records of the Copyright Office only under the collection title. *Copyright registration of cartoons and comic strips extends only to copyrightable selections deposited at the time of registration.* There is no blanket registration that will cover works to be produced in the future.

A cartoon or comic strip published as a contribution to a periodical (for example, a magazine or newspaper) may be considered for group registration if certain conditions are met. Contact the Copyright Office for information and instructions on group registration for contributions to periodicals.

Notice of Copyright

Before March 1, 1989, the use of copyright notice was mandatory on all published works, and any work first published before that date should have carried a notice. For works first published after March 1, 1989, the copyright notice is optional. For details, see Circular 3, *Copyright Notice*.

Effective Date of Registration

When the Copyright Office issues a registration certificate, it assigns as the effective date of registration the date it received all required elements—an application, a nonrefundable filing fee, and a nonreturnable deposit—in acceptable form, regardless of how long it took to process the application and mail the certificate.

You do not have to receive your certificate before you publish or produce your work, nor do you need permission from the Copyright Office to place a copyright notice on your work. However, the Copyright Office must have acted on your application before you can file a suit for copyright infringement, and certain remedies, such as statutory damages and attorney's fees, are available only for acts of infringement that occurred after the effective date of registration.

If a published work was infringed before the effective date of registration, those remedies may also be available if the effective date of registration is no later than three months after the first publication of the work.

The time the Copyright Office requires to process an application varies, depending on the amount of material the Office is receiving and the method of application. If you apply online for copyright registration, you will receive an email notification when your application is received. If you apply on a paper form, you will not receive an acknowledgment of your application, but you can expect a certificate of registration indicating that the work has been registered; a letter or a telephone call from the Copyright Office if further information is needed; or, if the application cannot be accepted, a letter explaining why it has been rejected.

The Copyright Office cannot honor requests to make certificates available for pickup or to send them by express mail. If you want to know the date that the Copyright Office receives your paper application or your deposit, use registered or certified mail and request a return receipt.

Infringement

Up until this point, there has been much discussion as to how to obtain copyright, how long protection lasts, and what an owner's rights are. The next important topic to discuss is what happens when there is an infringement of copyright. As a general matter, copyright infringement occurs when a copyrighted work is reproduced, distributed, performed, publicly displayed, or made into a derivative work without the permission of the copyright owner unless there is a limitation in the statute. Because the current copyright gives exclusive rights to the copyright owner, anyone else who takes advantage of those rights is an infringer. Of course, even if infringement occurs, the copyright owner must still sue the alleged infringer and prove their case in court.

If someone wants to sue for copyright violation, the case must be brought in the United States District Courts. This means that you cannot try a copyright infringement case in state court or small claims court. And as described above, a domestic copyright must be registered before a suit for infringement can be filed.

So, once a case for infringement is filed, what does a copyright holder need to prove? First, it is important to point out that there is absolutely no intent requirement under the statute. Innocent violation is equally liable under the copyright law. In fact, courts have held that subconscious copying is considered to be a copyright violation. For example, assume that a creator reads a low distribution small press comic book when he is 5 years old about a superhero that fights with a genie. Then 20 years later, he is working for a major comic book company and completely forgets about the original story. He is tasked with the creation of a new series and, without realizing it, ends up writing the same story word for word that he read as a child. This would still be considered copyright infringement and he would be liable to the original owner. Of course, the level of culpability of an infringer will affect the amount of damages a court is likely to impose. A willful infringer is more likely to be charged with a high level of damages, especially if the infringing behavior has gone on for a prolonged period of time for a commercial profit.

The next important point involves just how difficult it is to show that copyright infringement occurred. For example, it is not necessary for an infringer to copy every word, or image, or line in order to be held liable. So, it must be determined how much copying it takes before something is considered infringement. In fact, many infringement cases involve non-identical copies. The question in these cases is whether the infringer copied the expression, which is protected, or the underlying ideas, which are not protected. To further complicate matters, there is rarely an eyewitness to the process of infringement, so there is very little in the way of direct testimony. Instead, copyright infringement is usually proved through the use of what is known as circumstantial evidence. Circumstantial evidence is information and testimony that permits conclusions that indirectly establish the existence or nonexistence of a fact or event that the party seeks to prove. This is contrasted with direct evidence, which is information and testimony, if held credible, that proves existence of the fact in issue without inference or presumption.

In order to prove infringement, a copyright holder needs to present evidence to prove several elements. First, a copyright holder needs to show that the work at issue has actually been copied by the infringer. To show copying, most courts require the copyright owner to prove (1) that the infringer either had a copy of the work, or that it would have been easy for the infringer to have had access to a copy of the work; and (2) that probative similarity exists between the two works.[47] If a copyright holder can prove copying, the second element for the copyright holder to prove is substantial similarity between the two works. In other words, the copyright holder must show that the infringer took a substantial portion of the protected work so that, when viewed through the eyes of an ordinary observer, the works are considered similar. Of course, if only the ideas are the same, then there is no protection because the court is limited to considering the protectable elements of the two works. As can be seen in the stories in this book, the infringement analysis can be difficult when works have similar plots but different words and different details.

For example, the Ninth Circuit rejected a comic creator's infringement claim against the producers of the television series *Heroes*. In the facts of the case, Jason Barnes, the copyright holder, created a comic series called *Jazan Wild's Carnival of Souls*. When the NBC television show *Heroes* featured a carnival of lost souls and outcasts in its fourth season, Jason Barnes filed suit alleging copyright infringement of his book. The District Court found that two works "differ[ed] markedly in mood and setting," and weren't substantially similar works. The Ninth Circuit affirmed the case, holding the "comparable aspects of these scenes constitute nothing more than 'random similarities scattered throughout the works' that are insufficient to support a claim of substantial similarity."

In addition to the traditional notion of infringement described above, there are two other ways that a person can be held liable for infringement. First, is through what is known as vicarious liability, which is imposed when a person does not personally infringe a work, but has a right of supervision and a financial interest in the behavior of the direct infringer. For example, if the *Heroes* case described above was actually held to be infringement then NBC Universal could have also been vicariously liable for infringement if it supervised the producers of *Heroes* even though it did not personally have a hand in the infringement. The second type of nonconventional infringement involves contributory infringement. This occurs when a person has knowledge of another party's infringement and either induces the infringement or materially assists in the infringement. For example, a person who creates a machine or supplies a machine to an infringer, with the advance knowledge that it will be used for infringement.[48]

Remedies

People don't sue for copyright infringement because they want to be vindicated. Instead, they are looking for damages and other relief from the courts. The current copyright law provides several types of injunctive and monetary relief in the statute. First, a successful copyright owner is entitled to an injunction. Put another way, when the owner wins the lawsuit, he or she can make the infringer stop copying the work. Second, the copyright owner can also have the court impound the copies and the methods of making the copies while the case is pending. At the end of the case, the copyright owner can have the impounded material destroyed.

In addition, there are two alternatives for monetary damages under the current copyright law. First, a copyright owner can attempt to recover their actual damages plus any profits obtained by the infringer in excess of its actual damages. Alternatively, if the work has been registered prior to the infringement or within three months after publication, a copyright owner may request damages provided for under the statute that are unrelated to actual damages. These statutory damages allow the court to impose a range from $750 up to a maximum of $30,000 for each act of infringement. If the infringement is proved to be willful, the maximum amount is increased to $150,000. If the infringer can prove that the infringement was an innocent mistake, the courts can lower the minimum amount to $200.[49] In addition, if a copyright is registered before infringement or in the three month grace period after publication, the court can also award attorney's fees.

Finally, there are criminal liabilities that can be imposed if a party infringes a copyright willfully, and for purpose of commercial advantage or private financial gain, or by the reproduction of one or more copies with total retail value of more than $1,000. Criminal sanctions range from fines up to $2,000 and incarceration up to two years in jail depending on whether the criminal has multiple convictions.

Fair Use Exceptions

There are some defenses to copyright infringement. As described above, there are defenses available to government agencies, law enforcement, qualified braille printers, and libraries. Each of these defenses is rather specific. However, there is another general copyright infringement defense that is available to everyone—the fair use doctrine. As described above, there is a policy concern that underlies the entire theory of copyright that requires the need for flexibility. As a result, a strict copyright scheme would frustrate the free expression goals of the system. In response to this need, first courts, and later Congress, created an important limit on copyright protection known as the fair use doctrine, which allows people, in certain circumstances, to quote from or reproduce pieces of other people's work without infringing on their copyright. For example, people can quote a comic book in a book review or use excerpts in an academic analysis. The fair use doctrine originated in the court systems, but it was eventually codified (made into law) in the 1976 Copyright Act.

The current copyright law includes a list of the various purposes for which the reproduction of a particular work may be considered fair use, such as criticism, comment, news reporting, teaching, scholarship, and research. To further confuse things, the statute states that this is not an exclusive list. To make matters more complicated, courts have found that the fact that an item is on the list will not mean that it is automatically fair use and have also found that items that are not on the list could still be considered fair use. More comfort is provided in the fact that the copyright law also lists four factors to be considered in determining whether something is considered fair use. First, courts look to the purpose and character of the use. For example, if the use is for nonprofit educational purposes as opposed to those commercial in nature then it is more likely to be fair use. While courts have held that nonprofit uses are more fair that profit making uses, this is not dispositive. Similarly, courts have held that transformative uses, which use the original work to create something new, are arguably more fair than straightforward copying. Finally, the concept of parody falls into the category of transformative use that should be give greater weight under the fair use doctrine because it is usually transformative.[50]

The second factor to be considered in determining fair use is the nature of the copyrighted work. For example, some works, like factual works and data compilations, have what is known as thin copyright, which means that the work has few protected features. The use of these thin copyright works is more likely to be fair use. On the other hand, the use of a work that is unpublished is less likely to be considered fair use because courts have held that the original author should have the first opportunity to publish their work. Once again, it is important to note that none of these facts alone are dispositive under the statutes or case law.

The third factor to be considered in determining fair use is the amount and substantiality of the portion used in relation to the copyrighted work as a whole. This is fairly straightforward: the larger the percentage of work copied, the less likely it will be considered fair use. Similarly, if someone takes a small portion of the document, but that is the core of the work, then that can also be considered unfair and not protected by the fair use doctrine. In other words, the quality of the work taken is as important as the quantity of the book when determining fair use. On the topic, the Copyright Office warns, in FL-102, "The distinction between what is fair use and what is infringement in a particular case will not always be clear or easily defined. There is no specific number of words, lines, or notes that may safely be taken without permission."[51]

FL-102 also provides examples that have been considered fair use:

> The 1961 Report of the Register of Copyrights on the General Revision of the U.S. Copyright Law cites examples of activities that courts have regarded as fair use: "quotation of excerpts in a review or criticism for purposes of illustration or comment; quotation of short passages in a scholarly or technical work, for illustration or clarification of the author's observations; use in a parody of some of the content of the work parodied; summary of an address or article, with brief quotations, in a news report; reproduction by a library of a portion of a work to replace part of a damaged copy; reproduction by a teacher or student of a small part of a work to illustrate a lesson; reproduction of a work in legislative or judicial proceedings or reports; incidental and fortuitous reproduction, in a newsreel or broadcast, of a work located in the scene of an event being reported."

The fourth and final factor to be considered in determining fair use is the effect of the use upon the potential market for, or value of, the copyrighted work. And while it is the last factor listed, it is probably considered the most important. This factor not only looks at the economic effect of the copying by the person claiming fair use, but also considers what would happen if the copying became widespread. For example, one person copying a work may have minimal economic effect on the creator of the work, but if everyone behaved the same way as the copier, then the effect could be much greater. In addition, the effect must be measured in the current market for the work as well as the future markets of the work. For example, Rob owns the copyright to a comic book series about a dog that lives through a zombie apocalypse and Lucas, without Rob's permission, turns the book into a movie. In the ensuing infringement suit, Lucas might argue that the movie did not hurt the sale of Rob's comic and, in fact, increased the demand for the book. However, this is the wrong analysis. Instead, courts will look to how Lucas's conduct hurts Rob's future economic profit from potential movies despite the fact that Lucas's conduct boosted Rob's book sales.

The Digital Millennium Copyright Act

Given the importance of technology in the development of copyright law, it is perhaps important to end this chapter with the current protection against circumvention of technological measures that is included in the current law. In 1998, Congress enacted a new copyright provision called the Digital Millennium Copyright Act. The purpose of these provisions is to protect digital versions or copies of works. It stems from the battle between infringers and copyright owners. Over the years, many copyright owners have attempted to create anti-tamper and anti-copy technological measures to ensure that their work is not available to non-paying parties to either gain access to their works or make copies of their works. Of course, for each technological advance, hackers have found a way to circumvent the protection. The Digital Millennium Copyright Act was created to make it a crime to circumvent these kinds of technological safeguards under certain circumstances.[52]

The act provides that it is impermissible (1) to circumvent a technological measure that controls access to a copyrighted work; (2) to make a device that is primarily designed to circumvent either access controls or copy controls; or (3) to sell a device that is primarily designed to circumvent either access controls or copy controls. It should be noted that the Digital Millennium Copyright Act does not actually make it a crime to use software to circumvent copy control. Instead, it prevents users from circumventing access controls and prevents the design of devices that are primarily designed to circumvent access or copyright control. This is to permit individuals to access material that is fair use. Similarly, it is not a violation of the law to create a device that may as a secondary purpose be used to circumvent copyright.[53] Obviously, this is a new area of law and likely will be developing over the years.

In addition to imposing restrictions on copying, the Digital Millennium Copyright Act also provides for the treatment of copyright management information. Copyright management information is usually embedded in the digital work and contains contact information for the holder of the copyright. The purpose of the copyright management information is to provide legitimate users the ability to seek out the copyright holder to obtain a license. The Digital Millennium Copyright Act prohibits tampering with or removing copyright management information and imposes liability for anyone who provides or distributes false information.[54] For example, if an artist puts his art on his website that contains copyright management information and the next day, another artist downloads the image, strips out the copyright management information, and puts it on their website, the second person violated the Digital Millennium Copyright Act.

Conclusion

Hopefully, this chapter has provided the basic background that will help one understand many of the stories that follow. As can be seen, the copyright law has many complicated provisions. Moreover, the increasing pace at which technology advances will most likely further complicate the copyright law as it adapts and changes in the future.

CHAPTER 4

Don't Tug on Superman's Cape
DC Comics v. Bruns and Fawcett

Charles Caleb Colton is famous for saying that "imitation is the sincerest [form] of flattery." If that is true, then Superman should have felt very flattered in the 1940s and 1950s.

The Success of Superman

Action Comics issue 1 first appeared on newsstands in April 1938 with a cover date of June 1938. The book was published by National Comics, the predecessor to DC Comics[1] owned by publisher Harry Donenfeld. For a cover price of ten cents, the purchaser of the first issue of Action *Comics* was treated to 64 pages of stories and features: "Chuck Dawson in the A Gang" by H. Fleming and "Tex Thompson in Murder in England" by Bernard Baily were western stories; "Zatara Master Magician in The Mystery of the Freight Train Robberies" by Fred Guardineer introduced readers to a stage magician with real power[2]; "South Sea Strategy" by Captain Frank Thomas was a two page text featuring a war story; "Sticky-Mitt Stimson" by Alger was a humorous story about a thief; "The Adventures of Marco Polo" by Sven Elven was a historical tale about the explorer; "'Pep' Morgan in the Light Heavyweight Championship" by Fred Guardineer was a sports story; "Scooby the Five Star Reporter in The International Jewel Thief" by Will Ely was a mystery; and two one page stories entitled "Stardust" by "The Star-Gazer" and "Odds 'N Ends" were stories by Sheldon Moldoff. But, none of these other features were as important to comics history as the main cover story in the book. The cover featured a hero, dressed in blue and red with a red cape, lifting a car over his head as several thugs flee in panic.

The lead story was entitled, "Superman, Champion of the Oppressed," which was written by Jerry Siegel and drawn by Joe Shuster. In addition to the first appearance of a girl reporter named Lois Lane and her mild mannered partner, Clark Kent, the story also introduced the world to Clark Kent's alter ego, a character named Superman. Superman was the sole survivor of a dying planet, sent to Earth as an infant and raised by a kindly couple named the Kents. Superman possessed powers beyond those of normal men. He was invulnerable, could jump over buildings, lift enormous weights, and run faster than a freight train. After his parents died, Clark dedicated himself to serve humanity as Superman, the champion of the oppressed.

It would not be an understatement to say that comics would never be the same after DC Comics released *Action Comics* issue 1. The first issue had a print run of 200,000 copies, which promptly sold out. Jack Liebowitz, DC Comics' former Treasurer and Secretary, testified that by the end of 1938 the sales of *Action Comics* were half a million copies per month. The reason for this was Superman. *Action Comics* issue 4 offered twenty-five prizes in the amount of one dollar for the best letter received about *Action Comics*. Entrants were also required to rank in order of preference their favorite five features. DC Comics received 542 entries: 404 of these readers ranked the Superman feature as their favorite; 59 people picked it as their second favorite; 22 readers ranked it as third; 21 selected Superman as their fourth favorite; 17 people picked it as fifth; and 19 entries had no preference at all. Thus, Superman garnered almost 75 percent of the popular vote.

Based on Superman's popularity, DC Comics along with Siegel and Shuster entered an agreement with the McClure Newspaper Syndicate on September 22, 1938, to allow for a daily syndicated comic strip. The copyrights for these strips were taken out by the McClure Newspaper Syndicate in its own name and would revert back to DC Comics at the end of the agreement. The agreement further provided that Siegel and Shuster would draw the strips and be paid by DC Comics. After publication, the McClure Newspaper Syndicate would pay DC Comics an agreed upon share of the profits and agreed to return the strips to DC Comics.

The first strip appeared in the *Boston Transcript*, the *Milwaukee Journal*, and the *San Antonio Express* on January 16, 1939. More papers were soon added to the syndication so that, by 1944, at least 160 newspapers carried the strip. Very few of the strips published by the McClure Newspaper Syndicate contained copyright notices. When the stories did contain a copyright symbol (©) it was so small as to only be visible as a smudge without the aid of a magnifying glass.

As a result of the success of Superman in *Action Comics* and the newspaper strips, DC Comics released *Superman* issue 1 in 1939. And while the first issue mainly contained reprinted adventures, the book achieved greater sales than *Action Comics*. The first four issues of *Superman* were copyrighted by DC Comics. The stories in *Superman* issues 1 and 3 contained reprints from the first six issues of *Action Comics* along with other material originating from the *Superman* newspaper strip. Despite the fact that the original *Action Comics* stories were published from June to November 1938 and thus originally had a 1938 copyright, when DC Comics reprinted them, it gave them a 1939 copyright date because *Superman* 1 and 3 were released in summer and winter of 1939. After issue 4, the *Superman* copyright was obtained and held by Superman, Inc., an entity formed in October 1939.

According to an agreement dated January 18, 1940, DC Comics appointed Superman, Inc., as its

> exclusive agent to exploit "'Superman,' the trade-marks and copyrights and/or other rights therein in any manner whatsoever," except that Superman, Inc. should not have the right "to print, publish or distribute any pictorial or textual sequence containing the likeness of 'Superman,' other than through the magazine known as 'Superman.'"

Under the terms of the agreement:

all copyrights, trade-marks and/or other rights with respect to "Superman" now existing' should remain in Detective and continue to be owned by it, and that "when any further copyrights, trade-marks * * * or other similar rights are required to carry out the terms of this agreement," they should be obtained by Detective in its own name and the ownership of such rights should remain in it.

Superman, Inc., took out copyrights on *Superman* issues 5 and 6 despite the fact that the agreement did not authorize Superman, Inc., to take out copyrights in its own name. Apparently, someone at DC Comics discovered this error because, on August 14, 1940, DC Comics wrote Superman, Inc., and ratified (i.e., retroactively blessed) the prior copyright acquisition by Superman, Inc., and amended the January agreement to allow Superman, Inc., to obtain and hold copyrights in its own name.

In addition to appearing in *Superman*, the syndicated newspaper strips, and *Action Comics*, Superman also appeared in *New York World's Fair Comics*, which would later be known as *World's Finest Comics*. Superman also accepted an honorary membership in the Justice Society of America and appeared in their comic, *All Star Comics*.[3]

Wonder Man *Taken Down*

As a result of the undeniable commercial success of Superman, others attempted to recreate the character. The first of these was Bruns Publications, who released a superman clone called Wonder Man. In addition to being located in the same building as DC Comics (with Bruns Publications on the seventh floor and DC Comics on the ninth floor), half of Bruns Publication had been previously owned by DC Comics President Harry Donenfeld. While Victor Fox, the president of Bruns Publications, was publishing a magazine called *The World Astrology Magazine*, he came across the sales figures for *Action Comics* and decided to enter into the comics market. He contacted the Eisner-Iger Shop where Will Eisner, writing under the pseudonym Willis, delivered a comic featuring Wonder Man. Wonder Man was described as "Fred Carson, the Wonder Man, endowed with supernatural strength and pledged to be forever the champion of the oppressed, defender of the weak and relentless foe of all that is evil and unjust ... he is known to the world as Fred Carson a timid engineer and inventor."

Wonder Comics issue 1 appeared on the stand in May of 1939. There were numerous similarities between the characters of Wonder Man and Superman. Both characters had secret identities. Both characters possessed super strength, invulnerability, the power to leap tall buildings, and both wore skin tight uniforms (Superman dressed primarily in blue and red with a large "S" on his chest; Wonder Man wore red and yellow with a large "W" on his chest). Even the term "champion of the oppressed" was used to describe both characters in their first adventure. There were differences as well. Wonder Man's power came from a magical ring, whereas Superman's were based in science. Superman's alter ego, Clark Kent, was a mild mannered reporter whereas Wonder Man's secret identity, Fred Carson, was a timid engineer and inventor. In 1939, Will Eisner would testify that, at the time he created Wonder Man, he had never even read a *Superman* comic, and only did so after *Wonder Comics* issue 1 came out. Instead, Eisner said he based the character on the Phantom and classical literature like Hercules.[4]

The testimony reads:

Q. At the time you made the drawing [of Wonder Man] had you in any way known or heard of the plaintiff's character "Superman"?
A. No, Sir.

* * *

Q. And at the time you thought of the phrase or words "The Wonderman" had you at that time ever heard or had you ever known of "The Superman," which is the plaintiff's character?
A. No, sir.

* * *

Q. When for the first time did you ever read the comic strip "Superman"?
A. About several days after our book came out.
   THE COURT: Why did you read it then?
   THE WITNESS: Because I was informed by Mr. Fox that some sort of action was being taken.
Q. Referring to this lawsuit?
A. Referring to a lawsuit.
Q. And until you heard of this lawsuit you, the creator of "Wonderman," never read the strip "Superman," is that right?
A. That is true.

* * *

Q. Mr. Eisner, how long after you read "Superman" did you begin to use a W in a circle on the breast of "Wonderman"?
A. I used the W in a circle on the breast of "Wonderman" before I saw that "Superman." It was part of the original idea.
Q. In other words, Mr. Siegel has copied all of this from you, is that it??
A. I haven't claimed that.

After the publication of *Wonder Comics* issue 1, the similarities between the two characters incensed executives at DC Comics. In response, DC Comics filed suit against Bruns in the United States District Court for the Southern District of New York where it was heard before Judge Woolsey. The case went to trial on April 6 and 7, 1939. At trial, DC Comics put on evidence that Wonder Man infringed on their copyright in Superman. This was done by showing nearly identical panels in both books.

Bruns had two primary responses. First, as described above, through the testimony of Eisner, Bruns attempted to show that it did not infringe on the character because Eisner had never read the book. Second, Bruns argued that Superman was not subject to copyright protection because the various attributes of Superman have prototypes and analogies in literature and mythology.[5]

The court did not agree with either of Brun's arguments. First, the court determined simply by comparing the two comic books side by side that Wonder Man copied Superman.

Short of "Chinese copies" of the [DC Comics'] "Superman" strip, [Bruns] could hardly have gone further than it has done. E.g., the pictures shown in the moving papers on the preliminary injunction which came before one of the Judges in motion part and which may be referred to in the findings of fact to be hereinafter provided for, and the parallel column comparison of the text at pages 9–10 of [DC Comics'] brief.

The court also rejected Bruns' access argument because "access,—if it is not accepted as common ground—certainly has been established because the [DC Comics'] magazine was on all the newsstands for circa a year before the [Bruns'] magazine was published." As a result, Judge Woolsey awarded money damages, including reimbursement of costs and attorney's fees to DC Comics and ordered "[A] permanent injunction forbidding the further publication by the defendant Bruns Publications, Inc., of its cartoon character 'Wonderman,' in such form as will make that cartoon character trespass in any respect on the plaintiff's cartoon character 'Superman.'"

After the decision, Bruns appealed to the Court of Appeals for the Second Circuit where it was heard by Circuit Judges Learned and Augustus Hand (the two judges were cousins) and Judge Harrie B. Chase. As expected, Bruns made many of the same arguments as in the lower court. Augustus Hand wrote for the unanimous court in a decision affirming the trial court's decision. On the issue of whether the Wonder Man comic was copied from the *Superman* comics, Justice Hand provided much more detail on the nature of the infringement:

> We have compared the alleged infringing magazine of Bruns with the issues of "*Action Comics*" and are satisfied that the finding that Bruns copied the pictures in the complainant's periodical is amply substantiated. Each publication portrays a man of miraculous strength and speed called "Superman" in "*Action Comics*" and "Wonderman" in the magazine of Bruns. The attributes and antics of "Superman" and "Wonderman" are closely similar. Each at times conceals his strength beneath ordinary clothing but after removing his cloak stands revealed in full panoply in a skintight acrobatic costume. The only real difference between them is that "Superman" wears a blue uniform and "Wonderman" a red one. Each is termed the champion of the oppressed. Each is shown running toward a full moon "off into the night," and each is shown crushing a gun in his powerful hands. "Superman" is pictured as stopping a bullet with his person and "Wonderman" as arresting and throwing back shells. Each is depicted as shot at by three men, yet as wholly impervious to the missiles that strike him. "Superman" is shown as leaping over a twenty story building, and "Wonderman" as leaping from building to building. "Superman" and "Wonderman" are each endowed with sufficient strength to rip open a steel door. Each is described as being the strongest man in the world and each as battling against "evil and injustice."

The court next turned to the issue of whether Superman was an original creation or a compilation of prototypes and analogues. And while the court agreed that Bruns was correct in principle, it nonetheless found:

> But if the author of "Superman" has portrayed a comic Hercules, yet if his production involves more than the presentation of a general type he may copyright it and say of it: "A poor thing but mine own." Perhaps the periodicals of [DC Comics] are foolish rather than comic, but they embody an original arrangement of incidents and a pictorial and literary form which preclude the contention that Bruns was not copying the antics of "Superman" portrayed in "*Action Comics*." We think it plain that [Bruns] have used more than general types and ideas and have appropriated the pictorial and literary details embodied in [DC Comics'] copyrights.

However, Judge Hand refused to go as far as the district court, which ordered an injunction against the character of Wonder Man. The court found the lower court's ruling to be so sweeping as to give DC Comics a monopoly on all superheroes. Instead, Judge Hand ordered that Bruns be prevented "from printing, publishing, offering for sale or selling, or in any way distributing any cartoon or cartoons, or any periodical or book portraying any of the feats of strength or powers performed by 'Superman' or closely imitating his costume or appearance in any feat whatever."

Master Man Falls

With *Bruns*, Superman, and his handlers at DC Comics, had won the first battle against his pretenders.[6] But, as it turned out, the war was far from over. DC Comics next took on Master Man, a superhero drawn by Harry Fiske and released by Fawcett Comics that appeared in *Master Comics* issue 1 with a March 1940 cover date. Master Man was described as follows:

> Master Man! Stronger than untamed horses! Swifter than raging winds! Braver than mighty lions! Wiser than wisdom, kind as Galahad is Master Man, the wonder of the world! As a boy, young Master Man was weak until a wise old doctor gave the youth a magic capsule, full of vitamins, containing every source of energy known to man! The boy becomes the strongest man on earth! Upon the highest mountain peak he built a solid capsule made of solid rock! From there he sees all evil in the world and races to destroy it instantly!

Master Man wore a skin tight blue and red costume with the letter M emblazoned on his belt buckle. Like Bruns Publications, Fawcett decided to get into the comics business after discovering the success that DC Comics experienced with Superman and Batman. And while there were certainly differences between the Fawcett character and Superman—Master Man did not fly and his powers had a mystical origin—DC Comics nonetheless threatened to sue Fawcett if it did not stop publishing the character. Fawcett acquiesced and agreed to stop printing Master Man stories. However, unlike Wonder Man who only appeared in a single issue, Master Man's comic actually lasted six issues. Of course, the next time DC Comics would face Fawcett; it would be an even closer fight and would nearly cost DC Comics their most famous property.

The Power of Shazam

When Fawcett decided to enter the comics industry, the company hired writer Bill Parker to create several hero characters for their first comic title. This book was released in 1939 and alternatively called *Flash Comics* issue 1 and also *Thrill Comics* issue 1. The book, originally produced as an ashcan to generate advertising revenue and trademark filing, contained several stories written by Parker including Ibis the Invincible, Spy Smasher, Golden Arrow, Lance O'Casey, Scoop Smith, and Dan Dare. Of particular interest was a story featuring a new hero named Captain Thunder drawn by Charles Clarence "C. C." Beck. Captain Thunder, who was drawn to look like the actor Fred MacMurray, was originally intended to be a team of six superheroes, each possessing a different superpower given to them by a different mythological figure, before Ralph Daigh, Fawcett Comics' executive director, suggested the team be combined into a single character. Fawcett told his employees to create a character like Superman, only with a secret identity of a boy aged 10 to 12. Captain Thunder fit these requirements. Fawcett soon discovered, however, that the company could not trademark Captain Thunder, Flash Comics, or Thrill Comics, because all three names were already in use. As a result, the book was renamed *Whiz Comics*, and Captain Thunder became Captain Marvel.

Whiz Comics issue 2 was published in February 1940 with a cover price of 10 cents. The cover depicted Captain Marvel tossing a car, which mirrored the iconic cover of *Action Comics* issue 1. The story inside, however, featured a very different origin. In the story, an orphan newsboy named Billy Batson met a dying wizard named Shazam in a mysterious subway tunnel. The wizard names Billy as his champion and gives him great power. When Billy says the wizard's name, he summons magical lightning that transforms him into Captain Marvel, the world's mightiest mortal. The lightning imbued Billy Batson with the wisdom of Solomon, the strength of Hercules, the stamina of Atlas, the power of Zeus, the courage of Achilles, and the speed of Mercury. Captain Marvel wore a red military-looking uniform with gold trim and a yellow lightning bolt insignia on the chest. His costume also included a white collared cape trimmed with ceremonial gold. His visual appearance was still modeled after the actor Fred MacMurray. The first story also introduced Captain Marvel's greatest enemy, Doctor Thaddeus Bodog Sivana, a mad scientist out for revenge against a world that had rejected his greatness. *Whiz Comics* issue 2 also established Billy as a newscaster for radio station WHIZ, which (like Clark Kent's job at the *Daily Planet*), provided him with early access to information before the general public.

Whiz Comics issue 2 sold a half-million copies. As a result of the success of the series, Captain Marvel soon had his own solo series, *Captain Marvel Adventures*, which was created by Joe Simon and Jack Kirby. *Captain Marvel Adventures* would soon become the nation's highest circulated comic book magazine with sales of 1.4 million copies per issue. The character continued to star in *Whiz Comics* and was a guest star in numerous other titles, including the soon to be canceled *Master Comics*. In addition, Captain Marvel introduced many of the conventions present in modern comics. He was the first character to face a criminal group made up of members from past stories when several of his villains joined forces to form the Monster Society. In addition, Captain Marvel was the first superhero to be franchised with the creation of the Marvel Family, a collective of superheroes with powers and/or costumes similar to Captain Marvel's. In *Whiz Comics* issue 25, Freddy Freeman was given the power to become Captain Marvel, Jr., after being mortally wounded by an attack from Captain Nazi.[7] In 1942, Billy's long lost twin sister, Marvel Bromfield, became Mary Marvel by saying the magic word "Shazam."[8] *Whiz Comics* issue 21 introduced the Lieutenant Marvels, three boys, all named Billy Batson, who became Marvels when they said the word "Shazam!" in unison.

Mary Marvel starred in *Wow Comics*. Captain Marvel, Jr., took over as the lead feature (with Mary Marvel and Captain Marvel backups) in *Master Comics* after Fawcett was forced to discontinue using Master Man. Captain Marvel, Mary Marvel, and Captain Marvel, Jr., were featured as a team in a new comic series entitled *The Marvel Family*. Soon, there was also an Uncle Marvel, a Freckles Marvel, as well as Hoppy the Marvel Bunny, who first appeared in the 1942 *Funny Animals* comics, and was later given a series of his own.

Outside of comics, Captain Marvel became the first superhero to be adapted into film. On October 9, 1940, Republic Pictures entered into an agreement with Fawcett to produce a serial motion picture directed by William Witney and John English. These episodes were based on the comic stories. Filming commenced on December 23, 1940, and was completed January 30, 1941. The film debuted on March 28, 1941. The serial, which ran under the name *Adventures of Captain Marvel*, lasted for twelve chapters. Sadly, the film did not star Fred MacMurray. Instead, an actor named Tom Tyler appeared as Captain Marvel and Frank Coghlan, Jr., played Billy Batson in a plot based on the origin of Captain Marvel.

DC Comics Sues Fawcett and Loses It All

By the mid–1940s, Captain Marvel had become the most popular superhero in the country, far surpassing his DC Comics super rival. So, it should not come as a surprise that, in June 1941, DC Comics issued a cease and desist letter to Fawcett to stop publishing Captain Marvel–related comics. Given the popularity of the character, it should also come as no surprise that Fawcett did not comply. In response, DC Comics filed suit in September in the United States District Court for the Southern District of New York, alleging that Captain Marvel infringed on Superman. DC Comics also sued Republic Pictures for making *Adventures of Captain Marvel*.

After seven years of discovery, trial finally commenced in March 1948. At trial, DC Comics attempted to prove that Captain Marvel was merely a clone of Superman. Both had super strength, could fly, had a reporter alter ego, and wore similar costumes.[9] In response, Fawcett attempted to show that Captain Marvel was very different than Superman. They argued that Captain Marvel's powers were magic based, his alter ego was a child and not an adult like Superman, and there was no Lois Lane equivalent in Captain Marvel, and thus no romantic love triangle. Thus, Fawcett argued that Captain Marvel was an original character and not a Superman infringement. William Witney, the director of the serials, testified in his deposition that he believed that both Superman and Captain Marvel were, in fact, derivatives of Popeye. Fawcett also argued that DC Comics had not appropriately protected the Superman copyright and therefore put the character in the public domain by not including the required notices under the 1909 copyright law.[10]

At trial, several Fawcett employees testified that they received specific instructions from editors and management at Fawcett to imitate the Superman comics and make the Captain Marvel dialogue and scripts match Superman. In a specific example, Joe Simon, who created *Captain Marvel* issue 1, testified that he was told by Al Allard, Fawcett's art editor, that Captain Marvel was a "take-off of Superman." Simon was also shown several pages that he and Jack Kirby drew that were altered by a Fawcett employee named Bill Parker to look more like Superman panels. For example, Simon and Kirby drew a rifle that had been bent in half, but Fawcett changed the art to show the rifle being bent into the shape of a pretzel to look identical to a Superman panel from an earlier *Superman* story. Simon also stated that he was told by C.C. Beck, Fawcett's chief artist, that the artist copied Superman when he drew the first Captain Marvel comic. In response, Fawcett management testified and denied that they instructed employees to copy Superman. C.C. Beck denied that he ever told Simon he copied Superman. Both sides called experts, who debated the similarities and dissimilarities of the books.

The court issued its opinion on April 10, 1950. In an opinion written by Judge Coxe, the court determined that Fawcett had indeed infringed on Superman. First the court, citing the earlier Second Circuit *Bruns* decision, held that Superman was an original work and not a delineation of myths and legends. As such, it was subject to copyright. Next, the court determined that Fawcett had access to the book since Fawcett employees who were responsible for the creation, development, and portrayal of Captain Marvel all testified that they had at least seen and read Superman comics. On the issue of copying, the court noted the conflicting testimony but relied on common sense and visual inspection to see that there was evidence of copying. The court stated:

> Both "Captain Marvel" and "Superman" have the same athletic physique. Both have substantially the same clean-cut faces. Both wear the conventional regalia of the gymnast or circus acrobat—skin-tight uniforms, boots and a cape which is used in flying. The only real difference is in the color of their costumes, "Superman's" being blue and "Captain Marvel's" red. The incredible feats, performed by both, such as leaping great distances, flying through the air, exhibitions of marvelous strength and speed, and imperviousness to bullets, shells, explosions, knives and poisons, are identical, and the settings in which the feats are performed are often closely similar. Substantially all of the feats performed by "Superman" are later duplicated by "Captain Marvel." Identical phrases, expressions and dialogues are frequently found in the panels.
>
> "Superman" is represented as a normal human being, a meek newspaper reporter wearing eye glasses (Clark Kent), who, by throwing off his regular clothes, appears in his athletic costume and becomes a superhuman being and performs superhuman feats in the interests of justice and to overthrow evil. "Captain Marvel" is likewise represented as a normal human being, a radio reporter (Billy Batson), who, by uttering the magic word "Shazam," is transformed into a superhuman being, and, in that capacity, also performs superhuman feats in the interests of justice and to overthrow evil. There are villains in both stories, mad scientists who resemble each other in appearance, and who, by similar devices and methods, attempt to dispose of the hero ("Superman" or "Captain Marvel"), so that they can execute their plans of destruction without molestation.
>
> The stories depicted in the respective panels are much the same, as, for example, the experiences of both Clark Kent and Billy Batson in applying for jobs as reporters, being turned down, and finally being accepted as the result of having performed the same superhuman feat. In other instances they are different. For example, there is no romantic element in the "Captain Marvel" stories, such as Lois Lane, the girl reporter, who is a permanent member of the "Superman" cast; nor do the "Superman" stories have an ever-present evil enemy of the hero, like Sivana.

Despite the fact that the court found such clear evidence of infringement, it did not stop its analysis there. That is because Fawcett also made a second argument that DC Comics had given up its rights to the Superman copyright. Fawcett offered several grounds for this argument.

First, it pointed to the fact that when several of the stories in *Action Comics* were reprinted in *Superman Comics,* DC Comics did not copy the original copyright date from *Action*, but instead put the date of the reprint in violation of copyright law. The court rejected this argument and held the copyrights were valid because the *Superman* comics were not merely reprints of *Action Comics*, but also contained original material. As such, the copyright law provided that "publication of any such new works shall not affect the force or validity of any ... original works."

Next, Fawcett argued that Superman, Inc. improperly held the copyright to *Superman* starting with issue 6 because they were not given the authorization or power to do so in their agreement with DC Comics. DC Comics countered with the fact that it entered a later agreement, on August 14, 1940, that allowed Superman, Inc., to obtain copyright. The court held that the August agreement could not operate retroactively. Therefore, the agreement did not cover *Superman* issues 5 and 6. DC Comics executives also provided testimony that there was an earlier oral agreement made prior to May that was identical to the August agreement and would have covered issues 5 and 6. However, the court did not find this testimony credible (i.e., it didn't believe them). As a result, the court held that the copyright on *Superman Comics* issues 5 and 6 was invalid. As an ominous foreshadowing, the court added: "This finding is not to be construed as validating copyrights on such strips or stories as were reprints of those previously published without proper copyright notice."

Fawcett also argued that *Superman* issue 12 was published with an incorrect copyright notice. While the court pointed to the importance of following the notice compliance requirements, it held that DC Comics had substantially complied with the notice requirements of the law and the copyright was valid.

The court next turned to Fawcett's argument that McClure Newspaper Syndicate strips had waived copyright on Superman. In essence, Fawcett was arguing that because the strips did not contain the precise copyright language, McClure Newspaper Syndicate, on DC Comics' behalf, placed Superman into the public domain. Once again, DC Comics argued substantial compliance, as well as the fact that McClure Newspaper Syndicate, as their licensee, could not waive the copyright protection. Finally, DC Comics argued that the strips were mere prints or pictorial illustrations, rather than a book. In such a case, only the copyright symbol was required.

The court determined that each strip should be copyrighted as a book rather than print or pictorial illustrations. This is because "the panels are not used merely to illustrate the text, as the illustrations in a novel or other literary work do; rather, the panels themselves, together with the explanatory text, constitute the literary work—the story intended to be depicted."

As a result, the copyright needed to contain more than just the copyright symbol. The court explained this requirement as follows:

> [The 1909 Copyright Act] required that, in the case of books, the copyright notice should consist either of the word "Copyright" or of the abbreviation "Copr.," accompanied by the name of the copyright proprietor, and, if the work was a printed literary work, the year of publication, but that, in the case of prints and pictorial illustrations, the notice might consist of the letter "C," enclosed within a circle, accompanied by the initials, mark or symbol of the copyright proprietor. (There is no requirement in the latter case that the notice shall contain the year of publication.)

Using this higher standard, the court examined the McClure Newspaper Syndicate strips. It found them lacking:

> A very few of these strips as published in the newspapers carried the form of copyright notice required for a book. All the others carried no copyright notice whatever, or carried one of the following notices, viz.: (a) the words "McClure Newspaper Syndicate" alone, or (b) numerals representing the year, followed by the words "McClure Newspaper Syndicate," or (c) the letter

"C" within a circle, followed by numerals representing the year, and the words "McClure Newspaper Syndicate" (the letter "C" in many cases being so small, or so blurred, that it appears to be only a dot or is to be discernible only with the aid of a magnifying glass), or (d) the word "Copyright" (sometimes spelled "Copyrig"), followed by numerals representing the year.

The court also rejected DC Comics' licensee argument and determined that the strips were a joint adventure between the parties. A joint adventure is defined as a special combination of two or more persons, where in some specific venture a profit is jointly sought without any actual partnership or corporate designation. It is an association of two or more persons to carry out a single business enterprise for profit, for which purpose they combine their property, money, effects, skill, and knowledge. To support its conclusion, the court pointed to the fact that the agreement had all the hallmarks of a joint adventure.

> The agreement with McClure contains all the elements of a joint adventure. The subject matter of the joint enterprise was the use of the "*Superman*" strips for the sole purpose of newspaper syndication. The artists agreed to create and draw the strips, [DC Comics] agreed to pay them for their work and to furnish the strips to McClure, and McClure agreed to sell the strips to newspapers. Both the artists and [DC Comics] agreed to cooperate with McClure. The proceeds of the sales (there could be no losses) were to be divided between [DC Comics] and McClure. As the agreement was one of joint adventure, the errors and omissions of McClure are chargeable to [DC Comics], for the rights and obligations of joint adventurers are substantially those of partners, and each participant in a joint adventure is an agent for the others.

As a result, the court found that the copyrights upon the McClure Newspaper Syndicate syndicated newspaper strips were invalid. What this meant was that these strips have been dedicated to the public and did not have copyright protection. Put another way, the character of Superman was being printed largely unprotected under the law from January 1939 to April 1950. During this period, Superman appeared in at least 160 strips. As a comparison, in the same period, DC Comics only published 67 *Superman* comics. As can be expected, this was devastating. But, it did not compare with what would come next.

After finding that DC Comics, through the McClure Newspaper Syndicate, had inadequately protected the *Superman* strips, Judge Coxe next turned to what this meant for the case. Specifically, the court looked at whether the publication of so many uncopyrighted strips should be viewed as DC Comics abandoning the copyright on Superman. Under the 1909 copyright law, when an owner of a work deliberately authorizes or permits republication of its copyrighted material, it forfeits all rights to the copyrights. In examining the issue, the court not only found that the number of strips outnumbered the number of comics printed, but also acknowledged that, while the stories in the stories were not identical to the strips, they were so nearly similar that DC Comics could have successfully sued if the strips were published without their permission. As a result, the court held,

> [t]he same result must certainly follow in the present case, where [DC Comics] has permitted publication in the newspapers, without copyright protection, of stories which were the same in all material respects as its own copyrighted stories.
>
> I find, therefore, that the publication of the McClure syndicated newspaper strips without proper copyright notices resulted in the abandonment by plaintiff of the copyrights on the "*Action Comics*" stories. With this disposition it is unnecessary to consider any of the other instances in which the "*Superman*" stories or the "*Superman*" figure were published without proper copyright notices.

Put more simply, the court determined that Fawcett improperly copied the *Superman* comics. However, the court also found that DC Comics did not take the appropriate steps to protect its copyright, and therefore it waived any protection under the law making the copyrights invalid.[11] As a result, even though Fawcett was wrong, it did not have to pay DC Comics because DC Comics had waived its rights to sue Fawcett for its violation. Thus DC Comics lost their most valuable property because McClure Newspaper Syndicate, whom they had no control over, did not publish the correct copyright notices in their daily strips.

By this time of the court's decision, Superman was appearing in several comics magazines. In fact, DC Comics had changed its logo bullet to read, "A Superman-DC Publication." In 1940, the Superman of America fan club had over a million members. Superman sold all manner of products, including ray guns, cars, dolls, banks, gum, bread, milk, and even gas. Superman debuted on radio in 1940 and on film in cartoons made by the Fleischer Brothers. In 1948 and 1950, a live action Superman, played by Kirk Alyn, appeared on the big screen. Beginning in 1951, DC Comics was planning on bringing George Reeves to play Superman on the small screens. As a result, it should not be a surprise to hear that DC Comics appealed the decision to the Second Circuit in 1951.

The Appeal

And so, eleven years after its victory in the *Bruns* decision, DC Comics was once again presenting its *Superman* copyright arguments to the Second Circuit. Given that the Court of Appeals for the Second Circuit has 13 active seats, and numerous senior status judges that are assigned to hear cases, it is worth noting that DC Comics presented its cases to a nearly identical panel of judges as both Judges Learned Hand and Harrie B. Chase heard both *Bruns* and *Fawcett*. Although Judge Augustus Hand, who heard *Bruns*, was still sitting on the bench, the third judge on the Fawcett panel was Judge Jerome New Frank.

On August 30, 1951, the Second Circuit issued its decision reversing the lower court's decision and holding that there was no evidence of intent by DC Comics to abandon its copyrights and remanded the case for trial. Judge Hand wrote for a unanimous court. First, the court agreed with the lower court's decision on Fawcett's infringement of Superman. Judge Hand wrote:

> [The lower court] found that, in publishing the exploits of "Captain Marvel" in *"Whiz Comics"* and its other magazines, "Fawcett" copied from "strips"—a "strip" consists of a series of pictures, carrying legends—which had appeared in *"Action Comics,"* and had done so with the degree of detail which in [Bruns Publications], we found to infringe earlier copyrights of *"Superman"* by another plagiarist. The evidence does much more than show that this finding was not "clearly erroneous"; it leaves no possible doubt that the copying was deliberate; indeed it takes scarcely more than a glance at corresponding "strips" of "Superman" and "Captain Marvel" to assure the observer that the plagiarism was deliberate and unabashed. Whether "Fawcett" copied only from *"Action Comics"* in the end makes no difference, as will appear; but we shall assume arguendo that at times it also made use of [DC Comics'] other magazine, *"Superman."*

The court next turned to the issue of DC Comics' abandonment of the Superman copyright. Judge Hand distinguished between abandonment and forfeiture. Under copyright law, a publisher must show take steps to abandon a copyright through an overt act, which shows the intent or purpose to surrender rights in the work to the public at large. In light of this requirement, the Second Circuit determined that the District Court made a mistake when it held that DC Comics abandoned its copyright. Judge Hand wrote:

> There was no evidence in this case of any such an intent on the part either of [DC Comics] or "McClure"; indeed, although "McClure's" negligent omissions may have invalidated many of the copyrights in suit, the very fact that it continuously attempted to publish "strips" with some sort of copyright notice affixed, however imperfect that may have been, is conclusive evidence that it wished to claim a copyright upon them; and indeed it would have had no conceivable purpose in allowing its rights to laps.... In the case at bar [the confusion between forfeiture and abandonment] has led to the erroneous conclusion that because "McClure" with [DC Comics'] supposed acquiescence may have been negligent in protecting the copyrights upon many of the "strips" in suit, [DC Comics] abandoned its right to copyright all pictorial portrayals of the exploits of "Superman." Since it did nothing of the kind, the case can be disposed of only by determining the validity of the copyright on each "strip" separately, and we shall state what we deem the essential factors in such a determination.

Judge Hand also determined that the lower court may have mischaracterized the relationship between McClure Newspaper Syndicate and DC Comics as a joint adventure, commenting that the term was "one of the most obscure and unsatisfactory of legal concepts." Ultimately, Judge Hand determined that it didn't matter because the McClure Newspaper Syndicate was the holder of the strip copyrights. So, the court then looked at the effect of McClure Newspaper Syndicate publishing the copyrights without following the copyright law.

Initially, Judge Hand reiterated the general copyright principle that the absence of copyright on one work does not necessarily waive the copy of later works. Judge Hand specifically referred back to the *Bruns* case, where the Second Circuit limited the injunction to the specific exploits of Superman, rather than the Superman archetype. The same would apply to the *Superman* strips. As such, the Second Circuit completely disagreed with Judge Coxe's holding that the *Superman* strips were so similar that DC Comics could have prevailed in a copyright action against McClure Newspaper Syndicate. Judge hand wrote:

> To that test we cannot agree. There may indeed be limits to the protection that will be given to the variant of an earlier "work," even when the variations in it are plagiarized to the last particular. Added phrases in a written "work," or changes of a few lines or colors in a pictorial one, may be too trivial to be noticeable by an ordinarily attentive reader or observer; and we will assume arguendo that in such cases the variant cannot be copyrighted. But there were much greater variations than these between the different "strips," and each "strip" was an original "work," capable of independent copyright.

Next, the Second Circuit turned to the effect of the improperly displayed and filed copyrights on Fawcett's infringement.

> [Copyright Law] provides that when the "proprietor has sought to comply * * * with respect to notice, the omission by accident or mistake of the prescribed notice from a particular copy or copies shall not invalidate the copyright" as against an infringer who has "actual notice"; and "Fawcett" was such an infringer.... We are unwilling to allow a bare-faced infringer to invoke an innocent deviation from the letter that could not in the slightest degree have prejudiced him or the public.

Finally, the Second Circuit looked at the evidence and realized that, while it was clear that Fawcett infringed on DC Comics' copyright, there was not enough evidence to determine exactly what was infringed. As a result, Judge Hand wrote:

> [The lower court] made no findings except to say that Republic produced a serial motion picture photoplay, using the comic strips of "Captain Marvel" which had appeared in "Whiz Comics"; and that this was "exhibited in many theatres in the United States." "Republic" in its brief appears to suppose that, because its "photoplay" differed from "Superman" in essential details of plot and in general pattern, it did not infringe. Nothing could be more mistaken; a plagiarist can never excuse his wrong by showing how much he did not plagiarize.... On the new trial the court will have to decide what valid copyrights "Republic" did infringe, and we shall have findings to guide us. On this record we cannot dispose of the claim. Nor will we pass upon the merits of the cross-claim of "Republic" against "Fawcett" upon its agreement to hold "Republic" harmless for we have no findings.

After the ruling, DC Comics petitioned the Second Circuit to clarify its ruling and to enter an injunction against Fawcett from publishing *Captain Marvel*. On June 10, 1952, Judge Hand wrote a short opinion clarifying the earlier decision. First, he pointed out that the Second Circuit did determine that Fawcett infringed on some of the strips. However, the Second Circuit clarified that it did not find exactly which of the strips were copied. Instead it remanded the case to the lower court for trial for DC Comics to prove its case.

> That will demand a comparison of each strip put in suit by [DC Comics] the plaintiff with "Fawcett's" strip, which [DC Comics] asserts does so closely copy that particular strip. Each such comparison really involves the decision of a separate claim; there is no escape from it. The plaintiff may put in suit as many strips as it pleases, but it must prove infringement of each, or it will lose as to that strip. In saying that "Fawcett" was an "unabashed" infringer we meant no more than that there were some such instances. Whether the strips so copied were protected by a valid copyright we did not say.

The trial never happened. Instead, Fawcett decided to settle with DC Comics out of court for $400,000 and the agreement to stop publishing *Captain Marvel*. To be fair, Fawcett had already lost when Judge Coxe determined that Fawcett infringed DC Comics and the Second Circuit affirmed. The remanded trial was more about damages. In addition, anti-comics hysteria, described in chapter 20, was gaining momentum and some believed that comics were an endangered species. Of course, that raises the question of why DC Comics decided to accept the settlement when it had already won the case. That is not so clear. Presumably, in determining the settlement figure, the parties must have considered how much time it would have taken DC Comics, and, more importantly, the billable hours it would take its very expensive lawyers, to go through all the *Superman* comic books and strips and compare them to all the *Captain Marvel* comics to determine exactly which ones were infringed and how. Moreover, by eliminating Captain Marvel, DC Comics was getting rid of Superman's biggest (and some would argue more successful) competitor.

In accordance with the settlement agreement, Fawcett Comics discontinued all of its superhero comics and sold the reprint rights for *Hoppy the Marvel Bunny* to Charlton Comics, who re-lettered the artwork to identify the strip as *Hoppy the Magic Bunny*. L. Miller and Son, a small British publisher of black-and-white *Captain Marvel* reprints, adapted Captain Marvel into a derivative superhero named Marvelman. Of course, as will be seen

Marvelman became the subject of his own copyright and trademark dispute as discussed in the *Spawn* case in chapter 7.

Before leaving the subject of Captain Marvel, there is another event of legal significance surrounding the character that is important to point out. Initially, Fawcett had trademarked the name Captain Marvel. However, when Fawcett stopped publishing *Captain Marvel* comics, it abandoned the trademark on the name. After Marvel Comics began to gain prominence in the 1960s, they trademarked the name Captain Marvel.[12] In order to avoid losing the trademark, Marvel created a character named Captain Marvel for use in *Marvel Super-Heroes* issue 12. Marvel's Captain Marvel was a Kree warrior instead of a magical superhero. Soon, Marvel gave the character his own series, which continued until 1972. During this period, DC Comics managed to acquire the license to the original Captain Marvel (along with the rest of the Fawcett superheroes) from Fawcett (first on a per-use fee and then later by purchasing the character outright). However, because Marvel Comics owned the copyright to the name Captain Marvel, DC Comics could not use the word in the title, but instead named these books using the word Shazam! This may be the reason that DC Comics' version of the character has never returned to his 1940s level of popularity because DC Comics cannot sufficiently promote the book while Marvel Comics owns the trademark. In fact, DC Comics has officially renamed the character Shazam as part of its "New 52" line-up.

The last issue of *Marvel Family* shows Captain Marvel, Mary Marvel and Captain Marvel, Jr. fading into nothingness in a story entitled "And then there were none." A boy on the covers watches the vanishing heroes and exclaims, "Holey Moley! What happened to the Marvel Family?"

Apparently, they fell victim to the American legal system.

CHAPTER 5

When Captain America Throws His Mighty Shield
Marvel Comics v. Simon

By the end of 1940, Adolf Hitler and his Nazi Party had taken over Germany, aligned with Japan, and invaded Poland, Denmark and Norway as well as much of Western Europe. Across the pond, the United States had not yet officially joined the war effort. Despite this, America's newest superhero was featured on the cover of his comic book punching Hitler in the jaw. That superhero was Captain America and the book was *Captain America* issue 1 released by Timely Comics, the predecessor to Marvel Comics. One year after Captain America socked Hitler on the jaw, on December 7, 1941, Pearl Harbor would be attacked and America officially would enter World War II.

Captain America Is Born

Captain America Comics issue 1 contained several stories. The most important was the first story, "Meet Captain America," a simple origin story. After a series of terrorist attacks by fifth column spies disguised as United States Army soldiers, Franklin Delano Roosevelt instituted a program to create an American super soldier. At a secret laboratory, Steve Rogers, a draftee reject, received an injection. The serum took immediate effect and transformed Rogers into the perfect soldier. The doctor christened him Captain America and tells him that his duty is to protect the American shores from Nazi spies and saboteurs. However, before the process can be duplicated, a Nazi spy kills the doctor and destroys the serum that gave Captain America his powers. The story ends with Captain American adopting a teen sidekick named James Buchanan "Bucky" Barnes, who is also the mascot of Private Steve Rogers's unit. The comic contained three other Captain America comic stories. In "Case #2," Captain America faces villainous fortune tellers named Sando & Omar, who were actually Nazi saboteurs. In the "The Chess Board of Death," Captain America must solve a series of murders involving high ranking officers. In the final story, writer Ed Herron introduced the comic book world to one of Captain America's most infamous arch nemeses in "The Riddle of the Red Skull." The issue also featured a text story called "Captain America and the Soldier Soup." In it, the hero stops a Nazi spy from poisoning the mess hall soup.[1] The last two stories did not feature Captain America. "Murder, Ltd." featured a demi-god turned detective named Hurricane. "Stories from the dark age" told the story of Ak, the last of the shaggy ones, and his pet mammoth, Tuk, and their adventures in the prehistoric wilds of 50,000 BC.

It should be noted that Captain America was not the first patriotic hero. That honor belongs to The Shield, who first appeared in *Pep Comics* issue 1 in 1939 from MLJ (the predecessor to Archie Comics) and was created by writer Harry Shorten and artist Irv Novick. The Shield was soon followed by three other patriotic comic characters: Minute-Man in 1940, and then Captain America and Captain Battle, who both debuted in 1941. In fact, concerns about the similarities between The Shield and Captain America drew complaints from MLJ that Captain America's triangular shield looked a little too much like the chest symbol of their Shield character. In response, Marvel Comics traded the old shield for a newer more indestructible round shield starting in issue 2.

Captain America Comics issue 1, with a cover-date of March 1941, went on sale on December 20, 1940, and quickly sold over a million copies. Shortly after, Marvel Comics applied for and received registration of the copyrights in and to the first ten issues of "*Captain America* Comics," including the Captain America character. At the time of its creation, *Captain America Comics* issue 1 was governed by the Copyright Act of 1909. This meant that an author was entitled to a copyright in his work for twenty-eight years from the date of its publication. At the end of that term, the author could renew the copyright for a second twenty-eight year period by applying to the United States Copyright Office.

The True Origin of Captain America

While the origin of the character is undisputedly the Secret Soldier Serum, the origin of the concept is not as cut and dried. It is clear that Joe Simon and Jack Kirby collaborated on *Captain America Comics* issue 1 and were listed as the creators in the book; however, the details of that collaboration have been a matter of debate.

Joe Simon claimed that he created Captain America as an independent, freelance project before shopping it around to various publishers, including Martin Goodman at Marvel Comics. Simon said he was inspired by the spirit of patriotism that was surging through the nation. In response, he sketched out the idea for both Captain America and Bucky. He even came up with the idea of giving the character a shield based on his childhood memories and was inspired to create the Red Skull because of a hot fudge sundae with a cherry on top. Simon stated that he then sold the Captain America story to Marvel Comics for a fixed page rate of $12 per page plus a 25 percent share of the profits of the comic books. At that point, Simon turned to Jack Kirby to help him work on the first ten issues. Simon remembered that the second through tenth issues of Captain America Comics were created on a freelance basis. Simon consistently maintained that he orally assigned his interest in Captain America Comics and the Captain America character to Marvel Comics, that he was the sole creator of the character, and that all work for the first two issues was done in his studio without any involvement from Martin Goodman or Marvel Comics.

Jack Kirby's recollection of events differed from that of Simon. He stated that Martin

Goodman, the publisher of Marvel Comics, requested that Simon and Kirby create a character to compete with DC Comics' Superman. Kirby stated that he and Simon were aware of the Shield character, when they started out designing their patriotic character. Kirby wrote in a July 12, 1966, affidavit,

> This was the beginning of our partnership because we worked so well together. There was an exchange of ideas until we had a finished product that we believed would gain reader interest. In the course of the discussions we first evolved a main character and then began to build around him. I suggested the use of a side-kick whom we named Bucky. Joe designed the type of lettering to be used on the Captain America cover; it was the only thing I couldn't do. All my work for [Marvel Comics] was basically super-hero oriented. The general outlines for Captain America we worked out together. There were times when I would come up with a theme that we both thought would make a good story, and I worked it out in its entirety.

Stan Lee, who worked for Goodman in the early days of Marvel Comics, would later testify that Jack Kirby and Joe Simon had co-created Captain America.

> Q. To your recollection, were there any characters that Kirby had created before he was working with you or anyone at Marvel that he brought to Marvel and then were then [*sic*] published by Marvel?
> A. No, I don't believe so. I don't recall any. Oh, wait a minute. Wait a minute. Captain America, for God's sake. He and Joe Simon had created Captain America.

Captain America immediately became the most prominent and enduring of that wave of superheroes introduced prior to and during World War II, surpassing the popularity of his competitors like The Shield. The book regularly sold close to a million copies.

Simon stopped writing *Captain America* at the end of 1941 when he was allegedly fired from Marvel Comics. Simon, joined by his partner Kirby, then began to work for National Comics (the predecessor to DC Comics) where they created such memorable characters as Manhunter, the Newsboy Legion and the Boy Commandoes. Simon stated that Marvel Comics never paid him the full 25 percent of profits agreed to for Captain America.

After the departure of Simon and Kirby from Marvel Comics, the company continued to produce *Captain America Comics* with Al Avison and Syd Shores taking over on the title. In addition, the character of Captain America was also featured in several other comics, including: *All Winners Comics*; *Marvel Mystery Comics*; *USA Comics*; and *All Select Comics*. With *Captain America* issue 66, a wounded Bucky was replaced with a female sidekick named Golden Girl. Golden Girl was secretly Betsy Ross, Captain America's girlfriend, who had first appeared in *Captain America Comics* issue 1 and had a recurring role in the series. During this time, Captain America also led Marvel Comics' first super team, the All Winners Squad, which consisted of Captain America, the Human Torch, the Sub-Mariner, the Whizzer, and Miss America. Captain America was also the first Marvel Comics character adapted into another medium, with the release of the 1944 movie serial *Captain America*.

With the end of World War II, the popularity of superheroes began to dwindle. *Captain America Comics* initially ended with issue 73, when the title was converted into a horror style anthology called *Captain America's Weird Tales* in 1949. After a failed attempt by Atlas Comics (another Marvel Comics predecessor) to revive Captain America as a cold war "Commie Smasher," the title was again cancelled in 1954 with issue 78.

Captain America did not appear in any comics from 1954 until 1963.

Captain America Is Reborn

After the resurgence of superheroes in the Silver Age of comics, Marvel Comics released a story that appeared in *Strange Tales* issue 114 entitled, "Captain America." The story was written by Stan Lee and drawn by Kirby, who had since returned to Marvel Comics. The story starred the Fantastic Four's Human Torch as he faced off against Captain America, who had apparently come out of retirement. And while the Captain America in the story turned out to be an impostor, a message at the end of the stories hinted to readers that the character might return.

The real Captain America returned to comics in *Avengers* issue 4. In the story, the Avengers discovered that Steve Rogers had been trapped in suspended animation in a block of ice since the final days of World War II. In line with the rest of the new characters created by Marvel Comics, Captain America was recast as hero with feet of clay, who was a man out of time that suffered survivor's guilt over the death of his partner Bucky.

On this, Lee testified:

> Now, by the time in the 60s, Jack came to work for us, we weren't—there was no more Captain America. We weren't publishing it because Martin Goodman thought it was just a World War II character and people wouldn't be interested in it anymore.
>
> I always loved the character, so I decided to bring it back. And I tried to write a story where he had been frozen in a glacier for years, and they found him and he came back to life, and so forth. And I tried to give him some personality where he always felt—he was an anachronism. He was living in our day, but yet he had the values of 20 or 30 years ago. And I tried to make him a little bit interesting.
>
> And Jack would draw him. And Jack just drew him so beautifully, and the stories worked out so well that he became part of the Marvel superhero characters, the one that I did not create. Yeah. And he's a great character, and they'll be making movies of him soon.

The newly revived Captain America soon became leader of the Avengers and experienced resurgence in popularity and commercial success. After sharing a co-feature in *Tales of Suspense* with Iron Man, Captain America was eventually given his own title in 1968 with *Captain America* issue 100. Marvel Comics also released reprints of the early Captain America stories in *Fantasy Masterpieces*. In addition to making changes in art and story to receive approval from the Comics Code of America, Marvel Comics also removed the "art and editorial by Joe Simon and Jack Kirby" credits from the reprints. In other media, Captain America began to appear on *The Marvel Super Heroes* cartoon, a syndicated show that aired in September 1966. Perhaps as a result of this success, in 1966, two years before the end of twenty-eight year term of copyright for *Captain America* under the Copyright Act of 1909, Simon took steps to assert his ownership in Captain America.

The Early Lawsuits

Simon filed a complaint in an action captioned *Joseph H. Simon v. Martin Goodman and Jean Goodman*, individually and d/b/a/ Magazine Management Company, Krantz Films, Inc., R.K.O. General, Inc. and Weston Merchandising Corp. in the New York State Supreme

Court in November 1966. The New York State Court case sought an accounting, damages, and injunctive relief. As grounds for the relief, Simon argued that, because he was the true creator of Captain America, Marvel Comics' use of the Captain America character constituted unfair competition and misappropriation of his state law property right. In response, Marvel Comics denied that Simon was the sole creator of Captain America. Instead, Marvel Comics alleged in its answer that

> to the extent that the plaintiff, Joseph H. Simon, contributed to the origination, conception and creation of the "Captain America" episodes and the characters thereof, such work was done for and on behalf of Marvel, under the supervision and direction of Marvel, and as an employee for hire of Marvel whereby any rights arising out of such contribution by the plaintiff inured to Marvel.

A year later, in November 1967, Simon filed a second lawsuit in Federal District Court in the United States District Court for the Southern District of New York in *Joseph H. Simon v. Martin Goodman and Jean Goodman*, individually and d/b/a/ Magazine Management Company and Timely Comics, Inc. The federal action sought relief under the Copyright Act of 1909. Specifically, Simon requested that the court declare that he had the exclusive right to the renewal term of the copyright and asked the court to enjoin (i.e., stop) Marvel Comics from applying for renewals of the copyrights. As grounds, Simon once again alleged that he was the sole creator and owner of Captain America.

In support of Marvel Comics' position, Jack Kirby wrote, in a July 12, 1966, declaration, "I felt that whatever I did for [Marvel Comics] belonged to [Marvel Comics] as was the practice in those days. When I left [Marvel Comics], all of my work was left with them." It was later discovered that Kirby issued this declaration because Marvel Comics agreed to pay Kirby the amount of any future settlement with Simon. In addition, Marvel Comics timely filed for renewal in the Copyright Office to renew the Captain America copyright.

After more than two years of discovery and fact finding, a settlement agreement was reached between the parties on or about November 5, 1969, to resolve "all of the claims and areas of conflict between them, including these suits and all claims therein referred to or relating thereto." In exchange for a cash payment, Simon signed a settlement agreement that provided, among other things, that:

> Simon acknowledges and agrees that all his work on the Materials, and all his work which created or related to the Rights, was done as an employee for hire of [Marvel Comics].
>
> * * *
>
> Simon shall and hereby does assign ... any and all right, title and interest he may have or control or which he has had or controlled in and to the following (without warranty that he has had or controlled any such right, title or interest)....

On November 5, 1969, the parties in both the state and federal actions filed stipulations requesting that the court dismiss the cases with prejudice. The parties agreed that the dismissal would resolve "all claims and matters alleged, threatened or implied or set forth in any of the pleadings filed by Plaintiff...." Later, Simon would explain that although he initially retained counsel, he was forced to settle because he could no longer afford a lawyer to pursue his claims in litigation. He further stated that he did not understand what the term work for hire meant but signed the agreement with the understanding that he was giving up his remaining rights to the character under the Copyright Act of 1909.

Simon made no further claim to Captain America from 1969 to 1999. Over that thirty year period, Marvel Comics continued to produce *Captain America* comics and merchandise. The character not only continued to star in his own self-titled book and *Avengers*, but also appeared as a guest star in multiple other books produced by Marvel Comics. Outside of comics, Captain America made numerous appearances on television. In the '70s, the character starred in two made for television movies that aired on CBS, *Captain America* and *Captain America II: Death Too Soon*. In the 1980s, Captain America guest starred in episodes of Marvel Comics cartoons featuring *Spider-Man* and *Spider-Man and His Amazing Friends* as well as a public service announcement on energy conservation. In the 1990s, Captain America appeared as a guest in several animated episodes of *X-Men, Spider-Man,* and *Avengers: United They Stand*. In addition, the character has been featured in numerous video games including *Captain America in: The Doom Tube of Dr. Megalomann; Doctor Doom's Revenge; Captain America and the Avengers; Capcom's Marvel Super Heroes Series; Spider-Man and Venom: Maximum Carnage; Avengers in Galactic Storm; Spider-Man and Venom: Separation Anxiety;* and *Marvel Super Heroes: War of the Gems*. Finally, Captain America appeared in numerous prose novels including *The Avengers Battle the Earth-Wrecker* by Otto Binder in 1967, *The Great Gold Steal* by Ted White in 1968; *Captain America: Holocaust for Hire* by Joseph Silva in 1979; and *Captain America: Liberty's Torch* by Tony Isabella and Bob Ingersoll, published in 1998.

The Termination Lawsuit

While Captain America continued to fight for the rights of Americans in the comics, the American Congress continued to fight for the rights of creators in the real world. As described in chapter 3, the 1909 Copyright Act provided authors a second chance to benefit from their earlier works. One of the primary reasons for Congress to enact this provision for this was to allow for creators, who generally have a poor bargaining position, to be in a better position to renegotiate the terms of the grant once the value of the work has been tested. Despite this, in 1943, the Supreme Court, in *Fred Fisher Music Co. v. M. Witmark & Sons*, determined that the original creator could assign away the renewal rights during the initial copyright term. As a result, most publishers and copyright holders began to add terms to their contracts that required creators to assign away all renewal rights. The effect of this was to virtually eliminate the renewal period under the 1909 Act. In response, Congress enacted the Copyright Act of 1976.

Not only did this Act extend the length of copyrights by nineteen years, but it also allowed creators another opportunity to regain their rights through termination. Specifically, the Act provided:

> In the case of any copyright subsisting in either its first or renewal term on January 1, 1978, other than a copyright in a work made for hire, the exclusive or nonexclusive grant of a transfer or license of the renewal copyright or any right under it, executed before January 1, 1978, by any of

the persons designated [by statute], otherwise than by will, is subject to termination under the following conditions:

....

(5) Termination of the grant may be effected notwithstanding any agreement to the contrary, including an agreement to make a will or to make any future grant.

The 1976 Copyright Act further provided that the termination of the grant may be "effected at any time during a period of five years beginning at the end of fifty-six years from the date copyright was originally secured." Equally important, the language of the 1976 Copyright Act specifically stated that this termination provision was not available to material that was made as a "work for hire."

As a result of the provisions in the 1976 Copyright Act, Joe Simon recognized another opportunity to reclaim Captain America. On December 7, 1999, Simon filed Notices of Termination with the Copyright Office purporting to terminate his assignment of Captain America to Marvel Comics.

Simon maintained that he independently created the Captain America character and authored the first issue in the *Captain America* comic book series, and that he was "neither an employee for hire nor a creator of a work for hire." With regard to the 1966 settlement, Simon argued that he did not understand the legal significance of the words work for hire. Further, insofar as the Settlement Agreement refers to Simon as being an employee of Marvel Comics, the paragraphs were not true.

In 2002, Marvel Comics filed suit in the Southern District of New York seeking a declaratory judgment that established that it was the sole owner of the *Captain America* copyright. In response, Simon filed a counterclaim seeking a declaration that: (1) he was the sole author of the *Captain America* works; (2) the Termination Notices were valid; and (3) all copyrights in the *Captain America* works reverted to him on the effective date of the Notices of Termination. After extensive discovery was taken by both sides, Marvel Comics moved for summary judgment. The case was joined by The Authors Guild, Inc., the American Society of Journalists and Authors, the National Writers Union, Novelists, Inc., the Science Fiction and Fantasy Writers Association, the Society of Children's Book Writers and Illustrators and the Text and Academic Authors Association, all of which submitted papers as *amici curiae*.[2]

The court was asked to decide the case on a Motion for Summary Judgment. Summary judgment is only appropriate if the pleadings, depositions, answers to interrogatories, and admissions on file, together with the affidavits, if any, show that there is no genuine issue as to any material fact and that the moving party is entitled to a judgment as a matter of law. Because Marvel Comics filed the motion, the court was required to view any evidence in the light most favorable to Simon, the non-movant party, and to resolve all ambiguities and draw all reasonable inferences in Simon's favor. If there are material facts at issue, the court must deny summary judgment and let the case proceed to trial. A court is not permitted to resolve any disputed issues of fact on summary judgment.

Marvel Comics made three arguments in support of its argument that the termination notices were invalid: First, the doctrine of equitable estoppel required the court to accept the previous court's ruling on ownership. Second, the doctrine of res judicata and collateral estoppel prevented Simon from arguing that Captain America was not made as a work for hire. Third, under the principles of contract law, Simon had agreed that he had no further rights in Captain America as he agreed that it was made as a work for hire. Essentially, all three of Marvel Comics' arguments relied on the fact that Simon agreed that Captain America was created as a work for hire when he signed the settlement agreement in 1969.

Marvel Comics' first argument was based on the concept of equitable estoppel. Equitable estoppel is a defensive doctrine used by courts to prevent one party from taking unfair advantage over another party. It is invoked when one party relies on the language or conduct of another to act in a certain way to their detriment, which results in injury. To support its equitable estoppel argument, Marvel Comics argued that since it relied on the agreement signed thirty years prior, it had held itself out as the character's true owner and "invested in the exploitation of the Captain America." Moreover, most of the witnesses who could have supported Marvel Comics' position had the case not settled had since died. Therefore, Simon should be bound by the agreement because Marvel Comics relied on Simon's conduct to its detriment. In response to Marvel Comics' argument, Simon replied that he was merely exercising the right provided under the 1976 Copyright Act. Simon also argued that although Marvel Comics claimed it exploited Captain America, the company also profited by this exploitation whereas he did not. In short, Simon argued that the equitable considerations weighed in his favor. The court quickly dismissed Marvel Comics' argument, holding that:

> The plain language of the [1976 Copyright Act] envisions one exception to the termination right, for works for hire; it does not permit any exception for equitable considerations. It is not unimaginable that most holders of copyrights could fashion this type of an argument in response to the exercise of an author's termination rights. This would, however, contravene Congress's intent to permit authors an opportunity to benefit from ownership of their works. The Court therefore declines to grant summary judgment on these grounds.

Turning to Marvel Comics' second argument, the court examined the facts under the doctrines of res judicata and collateral estoppel, which are preclusion mechanisms that prevent the same lawsuit from being litigated more than once. In short, the doctrine of res judicata (claim preclusion) bars claims that have either been litigated or could have been litigated from being litigated again while the doctrine of collateral estoppel (issue preclusion) bars issues that have been litigated from being litigated again.

In examining the preclusion issues, the District Court found that, under New York law, collateral estoppel did not apply because it forecloses only those actions that have been actually litigated and determined in a prior action. As a result, the court had to determine whether the issue in the 2002 litigation was the same as the 1966 decision. It found that it wasn't. The court stated:

> As a preliminary matter, the Court is persuaded by the arguments by both Simon and amici curiae that the termination right is an entirely new and wholly separate right from the renewal right. Congress clearly intended to create a new property right for authors when it enacted the Copyright Act of 1976. Because the earlier lawsuits in the 1960s could not have resolved the legal question of whether Simon was entitled to the termination rights, the claims raised in both the sets of litigation are necessarily different.

As a result, the court concluded that, "[n]either res judicata nor collateral estoppel, however, preclude Simon from proceeding on his claim to the termination rights, even though it requires him to relitigate the issue of his authorship." However, the court clarified that while legally the case was different, whether the earlier litigation resolved the matter of Simon's authorship of Captain America was a different question. On that issue, the court examined the complaints in the two 1966 litigations and determined that the issue of ownership was central to the 1966 litigation. The court stated:

> In the present lawsuit, Simon's alleged authorship has been raised as a specific counterclaim, in which Simon requests this Court to provide declaratory relief stating that he is the author of the Works. None of the parties in the earlier litigation requested similar relief in the form of a declaratory judgment that Simon was or was not the author. But the Court notes that they could have.

The court determined that when the 1966 cases were dismissed with prejudice by stipulation, it was deemed a final adjudication on the merits for res judicata purposes on the claims asserted and the claims that could have been asserted. As a result, the district court found that res judicata barred Simon's claim that he was the sole author of the works because the parties' 1969 settlement agreement resolved the issue.

The final argument was based upon the basic concept that settlement agreements were contracts, and therefore are governed by contract law. In short, Marvel Comics argued that Simon made a clear admission that he created Captain America as an employee for hire when he entered into the Settlement Agreement. As a result, Marvel Comics argued the termination provision of the 1976 Copyright Act would not apply since Captain America was made as a work for hire. In response, Simon argued that whether Captain America was created as a work for hire is a question of fact that must be decided by a jury because he disputes that there was no meeting of the minds between the parties on the "employee for hire" language set forth in the Settlement Agreement. Moreover, Simon, along with the amici curiae, made a policy argument that by holding Simon to the for hire language would thwart congressional intent to protect authors since publishers, who are more sophisticated and have greater bargaining power than individual authors, would be able to avoid the termination provisions in the 1976 Copyright Act by including for hire language in every contract. The court rejected the policy argument on the grounds that Congress clearly intended to carve out an exception for work for hire arrangements. Instead, the court turned to "the ultimate issue in this case is whether the Works, including the Captain America character, are 'works made for hire' within the meaning of the statute."

In examining this issue, the court turned to the settlement agreement and found the terms to be unambiguous. The court found:

> By signing the Settlement Agreement, Simon, as well as all [Marvel Comics] in the earlier lawsuits, agreed to the terms contained therein. Specifically, the parties agreed that "Simon acknowledges and agrees that all his work on the Materials, and all his work which created or related to the Rights, was done as an employee for hire of [Marvel Comics]." ... Although the new protections provided by the Copyright Laws were not yet enacted at the time the parties entered into the Settlement Agreement, the term "work for hire" was a term of art in the copyright world.... Because the Settlement Agreement was a negotiated agreement between the parties, settling disputes initially raised and litigated by Simon and involving rights over which he claimed ownership; because Simon was represented by counsel at all times during the litigations and settlement of the previous actions; because the term "work for hire" was a negotiated part of

the contract which carries specific legal significance; [Simon's] argument that he was unaware of the legal significance of his actions at the time he entered into the Settlement Agreement has no legal merit.

Thus, the court found, based on the plain language of the settlement agreement, Simon created the works as an employee-for-hire and thus could not exercise the termination right and concluded:

> The Court will not interfere in this legally-binding agreement. Because [Captain America was] created for hire and all work done on the Captain America Works by Simon was done as an employee for hire, the protection offered by [Copyright Act of 1976] is unavailable to him. Accordingly, the Court holds that Simon's claims of ownership of [Captain America] in the Notices, and, therefore, the Notices themselves, are invalid and of no legal force and effect. In accordance with the Settlement Agreement, the Court awards Marvel declaratory judgment that Marvel is the sole owner of the copyrights in and to the Captain America Works.

Simon appealed the case to the Second Circuit Court of Appeals. Once again, the Authors Guild, Inc., the American Society of Journalists and Authors, the American Society of Media Photographers, Inc., the Graphic Artists Guild, and the Society of Children's Book Writers and Illustrators filed an *amicus curiae* brief. On June 3, 2002, the Second Circuit issued its unanimous opinion reversing the decision of the District Court and remanding the case back to the District Court to conduct a jury trial on the issue of ownership.

Because summary judgment orders are based on application of law and not determination of facts, appellate courts review summary judgment rulings on *de novo* basis. When a court applies a *de novo* review it is as if the appellate court were considering the question for the first time. *De novo* review allows the Second Circuit to substitute its own judgment about whether the lower court correctly applied the law. In this case, the Second Circuit reviewed all three of Marvel Comics' arguments with a fresh eye.

With regard to Marvel Comics' equitable estoppel argument, the Second Circuit stated:

> Marvel argues that if it knew that Simon would disavow the Settlement Agreement's admission that the Works were created for hire, it would have proceeded to trial in the Prior Actions and called both Martin Goodman and Jack Kirby as witnesses. As these two men have since died, Marvel contends that Simon should not now be able to raise the issue of his authorship of the Works in this action. We find Marvel's argument unpersuasive.

The Second Circuit also found Marvel Comics' equitable estoppel argument unpersuasive for three reasons. First, it agreed with the District Court that Marvel Comics' equitable estoppel arguments could easily be adopted by most copyright holders to circumvent the intent of the Copyright Act of 1976 in providing authors with a termination right. Second, the termination rights did not exist at the time of the settlement agreement and Simon should not be prevented from raising a claim that did not come into existence until almost a decade later. Third, the court determined that, "Marvel cannot establish detriment for equitable estoppel purposes. Marvel has received the full economic benefit of the Works' twenty-eight year renewal term." As a result, the Second Circuit rejected Marvel Comics' equitable estoppel arguments.

The Second Circuit also examined Marvel Comics' preclusion arguments. The Second

Circuit agreed with the District Court in its determination that the Doctrine of Res Judicata (claim preclusion) did not apply:

> On this appeal, Marvel contends that there is no meaningful distinction between the authorship issue raised in the Prior Actions and the termination right at issue in this case. Therefore, according to Marvel, res judicata bars Simon from asserting that he is the author of the Works in order to exercise his termination right under [the Copyright Act]. In contrast, Simon argues that the district court was correct in finding that neither res judicata nor collateral estoppel barred him from asserting that he was the Works' author because the factual issue of authorship was never fully and fairly litigated in the Prior Actions and is quite different from his present claim to termination rights in the Works. Simon is correct … it is clear that Simon is not precluded from claiming that he is the author of the Works for purposes of exercising the termination right under § 304(c). While Simon would be precluded from claiming that he was entitled to benefits flowing from the initial twenty-eight year renewal period, that is not his claim. He is claiming that he is entitled to terminate Marvel's copyright in the Works, a claim that did not exist when the Prior Actions were settled. Therefore, the district court was correct that res judicata does not bar Simon from asserting that the Termination Notices are valid.

On the issue of collateral estoppel, the Second Circuit looked to the stipulation of dismissal to determine that:

> [W]here a stipulation of settlement is "unaccompanied by findings," it does "not bind the parties on any issue … which might arise in connection with another cause of action." … Here, although the Settlement Agreement contained detailed findings on the authorship issue, neither of the stipulations filed in the Prior Actions contain any specific findings as to whether Simon authored the Works independently or whether the Captain America character was created as a work for hire. Nor do the stipulations reference the Settlement Agreement in any way. Therefore, the stipulations do not collaterally estop Simon from litigating the issue of authorship underlying his termination claim in this action.

The court also examined the lower court's ruling that Simon admitted that Captain America was created as a work for hire by signing the Settlement Agreement. The Second Circuit determined that the District Court applied the incorrect analysis. Instead, the Circuit Court examined something never discussed in the lower court's decision and turned "to the issue of first impression presented by this case: whether an agreement made subsequent to a work's creation that declares that it is a work created for hire constitutes an 'agreement to the contrary' under [the 1976 Copyright Act]."

After examining the plain language in the Copyright Act to determine that the term "any agreement to the contrary" did not clearly include settlement agreements. The court examined the legislative intent and purpose of the 1976 Copyright Act to determine that an agreement made after a work's creation, like the settlement agreement, that stipulates that the work was created as a work for hire constitutes an "agreement to the contrary" which can be disavowed under the 1976 Copyright Act. As a result, the Second Circuit concluded:

> In sum, we hold that an agreement made subsequent to a work's creation which retroactively deems it a "work for hire" constitutes an "agreement to the contrary" under [the 1976 Copyright Act]. Therefore, Simon is not bound by the statement in the Settlement Agreement that he created the Works as an employee for hire.

The Second Circuit then reversed the District Court's ruling and remanded the case back down to the District Court for a jury trial:

Because Simon has proffered admissible evidence that he did not create the Works as an employee for hire, the district court's grant of summary judgment to Marvel was erroneous. It will be up to a jury to determine whether Simon was the author of the Works and, therefore, whether he can exercise [termination rights under the 1976 Copyright Act].

While it is true that Second Circuit's decision was a major victory for Simon, it is important to mention that the appellate decision did not resolve the case. Most importantly, it did not resolve the issue of how Captain America was created and by whom. If things had continued, a trial would have been held and a verdict rendered. Only then, would there be a final decision on the creation of Captain America.

Instead, as most cases do, the matter settled. The parties filed a stipulation for dismissal on September 29, 2003. As Marvel Comics was in bankruptcy at this time, the settlement had to be approved by the bankruptcy court. As part of the agreement, once again, Simon assigned "to Marvel Comics of any and all copyrights he has in Captain America."

Simon died in New York City on December 14, 2011, at the age of 98.

Captain America still fights for truth in the pages of Marvel Comics.

CHAPTER 6

Atomic Batteries to Power and Turbines to Speed
DC Comics v. Mark Towle Replicas

The Batman made his first appearance in *Detective Comics* issue 27. In that story, the caped crusader drove a red coupe. Given that the Batman had a Batcave and a Batplane, it was only a matter of time until Batman's car would receive its own bat-identifier. Batman's red car, now depicted as a sporty convertible, was first referred to as the Batmobile twenty-one issues later in *Detective Comics* issue 48 in 1941. As readers know, the Batmobile was soon followed by other types of bat-vehicles, including the Batcopter, the Batcycle and the Batboat.

As the Batmobile continued to appear in the comics, it became more and more representative of its dark knight owner. For example, a large bat shaped hood ornament graced the long streamlined black Batmobile on the pages of *Batman* issue 5 in 1941.[1] As the car continued to appear in Batman stories, it evolved further. In *Detective Comics* issue 156 and *Batman* issue 20, the car added single large fin in the back. The Batmobile eventually received a permanent dark paint job and added bat like appendages, including the now famous large tailfins scalloped to resemble a bat's wings.

The Batman *TV Show*

In 1965, DC Comics entered into an agreement with the American Broadcasting Company ("ABC")[2] to create a 1966 *Batman* television series, which starred Adam West as Batman. As part of this agreement, DC Comics granted ABC the rights to use the Batman literary property to develop the Batman television show, including rights to "adapt, arrange, change, transpose, add to and subtract from said property" and "to secure copyright and renewals and extensions of copyright." As part of this agreement, DC Comics also reserved all merchandising rights, which were defined as:

> sole and exclusive right to produce and sell, license or grant to others the right to produce and sell or license or to enter into agreements with respect to the production, distribution and exploitation of endorsements, commercial tie-ups or manufacturing privileges under which a commodity, product or service is made, manufactured, or distributed under the name of "Batman" or any other character in the comic book series entitled "Batman," or under a name which incorporates any phrase, clause or expression used ... in the television series....[3]

For the show (as well as a companion feature film also released in 1966), Batman got a new Batmobile. The real world version of the comic book inspired car was the brainchild of George Barris, who hired Gene Cushenberry to modify a 1950s Lincoln Futura concept car into what would become one of Batman's most recognizable vehicles.[4] The car was manufactured by Barris's company, Barris Kustom City. Barris built the 1966 Batmobile pursuant to a September 1, 1965, agreement between 20th Century–Fox Television, Inc. and Greenway Productions, Inc. and Barris Kustom City. That agreement provided, in part:

> Any and all right, title and interest in and to the design of Batmobile I resulting from the application of the required Batmobile features in and to owner's prototype Lincoln chassis, save and except the name "Batmobile" and [certain specific] Batmobile features ... and of the completed Batmobile I provided for in Article 2 hereof, shall forever be vested in and owned jointly by [Barris Kustom City] and [20th Century–Fox Television, Inc. and Greenway Productions, Inc.], subject only to any and all right, title and interest of National Periodical Publications, Inc. ... in and to said Batmobile features in said design.[5]

On October 18, 1966, Barris obtained a design patent (Patent No. 205998) on the 1966 version of the Batmobile. Design patents last for 14 years. Thus, the 1966 Batmobile design patent expired in 1980.

The Batmobile that appeared in the comics also changed due to the popularity of the show. Soon, a version of the 1966 Batmobile worked its way into the pages of the comics until the show was cancelled in 1968. At that point, the original Batmobile reappeared in the comics. Over time, the Batmobile changed. Eventually, the car lost its bat shaped hood ornament and started to resemble a modern looking sports car. But things would change again as a result of real world intervention.

The Batman *Movie*

In 1979, DC Comics entered into an agreement with Batman Productions, Inc. (eventually assigned to Warner Bros., Inc.), in an effort to make a series of new Batman movies. Once again, DC Comics reserved all "merchandising rights" with respect to the new characters, additional characters, new elements, and additional elements, of any motion picture produced via the agreement. Under the agreement, the term "additional characters" was defined as

> any fictional character or characters newly created by [Batman Productions] and which, but for the operation of this agreement, would constitute an infringement of DC's copyright or trademark in or to any of the characters constituting the Property ... or any characters contained in the Property who are newly costumed or in any way altered by [Batman Productions] for any motion pictures.[6]

In 1989, Batman took to the silver screen again, this time played by Michael Keaton. The 1989 *Batman* film, directed by Tim Burton, was much darker in tone than its 1966 predecessor. To make the film, Burton turned to Anton Furst to create a noirish nightmare version of Gotham City. As part of this assignment, Furst designed and created another iconic version of the Batmobile.[7] The 1989 Batmobile incorporated two Chevrolet Impala chassis and a Chevy V8 engine covered by a custom body with custom wheels with Mickey Thompson tires. Furst obtained a design patent (Design No. 311, 882) on the 1989 Batmobile on November 6, 1990. Furst assigned the design patent to DC Comics.[8] This design patent expired in 2004.

As expected, the 1989 Batmobile became an immediate hit and soon became as recognizable and identifiable with the dark knight as its 1960s predecessor.[9] A version of the car was used in the comics, in *Batman the Animated Series,* as well as in several commercials for OnStar.

Mark Towle Replicas

As a result of the popularity of both the 1966 and 1989 version of the Batmobile, many car collectors, television and movie fans, and comic readers longed to drive their very own Batmobile. However, given that the 1966 Batmobile was valued at close to five million dollars and the 1989 version once sold for around $500,000, only someone with Bruce Wayne's disposable income could even get close to fulfilling the dream of owning the car.

Enter Mark Towle.

Since 2001, Towle has operated a business that manufactures replicas of vehicles that appear in famous movies and television programs. For example, he has sold replicas of Speed Racer's Mach 5, the Munsters' roadster, and Disney's Herbie the Love Bug. He also sold replicas of the 1966 and 1989 versions of the Batmobile. Not surprisingly, the Batmobiles were his most popular products and Towle estimated that about 60 percent of the replicas that he created were Batmobile replicas. Each replica cost around $90,000. Towle also produced replica car kits that allow others to customize their vehicles into the Batmobile.[10]

It probably goes without saying that DC Comics owns a number of Batman-related trademarks, including the Batmobile wordmark, the bat emblem design mark, the bat rep II design mark, the Batman wordmark, and other variations of the Batman symbol. The trademarks are registered in various classes, and appear on merchandise such as toy figurines and automobiles, apparel, and household goods.[11] DC Comics did not authorize Towle's Replicas to make Batmobiles. Instead, DC Comics licensed the manufacture and customization of full-size automobiles into the 1966 Batmobile vehicles to a company called Fiberglass Freaks, who makes replicas that range in price from $79,999 to $239,999. In addition, DC Comics had an agreement with Barris that allows him to produce replicas of the 1966 Batmobile and exhibit them in various locations around the world.

The Lawsuit

On May 6, 2011, DC Comics filed suit against Towle in the United States District Court for the Central District of California. DC Comics' complaint alleged copyright infringement, trademark infringement, unfair competition, trademark dilution, and declaratory relief.[12] In response, Towle argued that his replicas were not based upon the comic book versions of the Batmobile. Instead, his replicas were created from the public domain design patents of the two cars.[13] On the copyright issue, Towle further argued Congress specifically excluded automobile design as the subject of copyright protection as it serves a utilitarian purpose. Towle also pointed to the fact that there was no confusion in the marketplace between his cars and the licensed properties of DC Comics.[14] To support this argument, Towle submitted sworn affidavits from his customer, wealthy car collectors, to support their understanding that they did not believe that Towle's replicas are licensed or otherwise authorized by DC Comics.

In December 2011, Towle filed a motion to dismiss the copyright infringement claims on two grounds. First, Towle argued that DC Comics was not the owner of the copyright of the television show or the motion picture that depicted the Batmobiles on which Towle's replicas are based. Second, Towle argued that regardless of the pleadings, the Batmobile and all its variables were not copyrightable objects as a matter of law because they were useful objects. On January 26, 2012, the District Court denied Towle's motion. In an opinion written by District Judge Ronald S.W. Lew, the court rejected both of Towle's arguments. First, the court determined that the complaint for DC Comics properly alleged sufficient facts to support a claim of copyright infringement. This is because DC Comics' complaint contained sufficient facts to support the argument that: (1) DC Comics owned the copyrights to the Batmobiles and all Batman characters and their associated vehicles; and (2) Towle violated DC Comics' exclusive rights to reproduce and distribute properties based on its copyrights by making replica Batmobiles. Second, and perhaps more important, the court determined that Towle's "useful object" argument lacked merit because it ignored "the exception to the rule that grants copyright protection to nonfunctional artistic elements of an automobile design that can be physically or conceptually separated from the automobile." Thus, taking the facts in the best light to DC Comics, the court found that "the Batmobile and all of its relevant embodiments are not as a matter of law, excluded from copyright protection."

On February 14, 2012, Towle answered the complaint and raised several affirmative defenses, including laches, unclean hands, and fair use. The parties then conducted document discovery and took depositions.

On December 12, 2012, both sides moved for summary judgment. On February 7, 2013, the court issued an order on the motions. The court found that Towle was liable to DC Comics for unfair competition and trademark and copyright infringement. Once again, the court's opinion was written by Judge Lew.

First, the court determined that the replicas infringed on the trademarks owned by DC Comics. In reaching this conclusion, the court rejected Towle's argument that DC Comics did not have valid trademarks based on the fact that DC Comics was the registered holder of the Batman trademarks in other categories. Because it was clear that Towle was using DC Comics' trademarks, the court next looked at eight factors to determine that there was a likelihood of confusion between the trademark owned by DC Comics and the replicas made by Towle. The court determined: (1) the fact that DC Comics' trademark and the ones contained on the replicas were nearly identical increased the likelihood of confusion; (2) the strength of DC Comics' trademark as a fanciful mark would mean that the public would associate the replicas with DC Comics thus increasing the likelihood of confusion; (3) the fact that there was actual confusion that required Towle to inform customers that he was not affiliated with DC Comics weighed in favor of finding an increased likelihood of confusion; (4) the fact that DC Comics and Towle had the same customers increased the likelihood of confusion; (5) the fact that Fiberglass Freaks, who licensed from DC Comics, and Towle were direct competitors favored a finding of a likelihood of confusion; (6) the fact that Towle's customers were sophisticated buyers making a high dollar purchase weighed against finding a likelihood of confusion; (7) the fact that Towle was aware of DC Comics' ownership of Batman would lead to finding a likelihood of confusion; and (8) the fact that DC Comics licensed to sellers of Batmobiles indicated a strong possibility they would branch into the market and thus led to a finding of a likelihood of confusion. As a result of this analysis, the court granted DC Comics' request for relief on the trademark claims.

The court next turned to the unfair competition claim. Given that the unfair competition test and the trademark infringement test are primarily the same (i.e., whether there is a likelihood of confusion between the two products such that the public is deceived as to the source of the goods), the court had no trouble finding that DC Comics had prevailed in its claim and granted the partial summary judgment on the unfair competition claim.

The court then addressed the copyright argument. First, the court determined, over Towle's objection, that DC Comics could still bring suit even if it did not own the copyright to the Batmobile. The fact that DC Comics is the owner of all the literary copyrights related to Batman and, with regard to the 1966 and 1989 Batmobiles, specifically reserved the merchandising rights gave them standing to bring the copyright suit against Towle.[15] The court next determined that the Batmobile was entitled to copyright protection because it is a delineated character. Under the current law, copyright protection is given to characters[16] visually depicted in a television series or in a movie so long as they are distinctive and have displayed consistent, widely identifiable traits. The court concluded that the Batmobile satisfied this test because:

> It is undeniable that the Batmobile is a world-famous conveyance in the Batman franchise, exhibiting a series of readily identifiable and distinguishing traits. The Batmobile is known by one consistent name that identifies it as Batman's personal vehicle. It also displays consistent physical traits. The Batmobile, in its various incarnations, is a highly-interactive vehicle, equipped with high-tech gadgets and weaponry used to aid Batman in fighting crime. Even though the Batmobile is not identical in every comic book, film, or television show, it is still widely recognizable because it often contains bat-like motifs, such as a bat-faced grill or bat-shaped tailfins in the rear of the car, and it is almost always jet black. The 1989 and 1966 Batmobile iterations also display these physical qualities. In fact, the particular design of the Batmobile often reflects the car models of the time—for example, the Batmobile from the comic book Batman No. 5, which was released in 1941, has the shape of a 1940s Ford automobile, but contains a "bat" hood ornament and tailfins resembling a bat's wings. Regardless of the evolving design of the Batmobile, it retains distinctive characteristics.
>
> Other than its physical features, the Batmobile is depicted as being swift, cunning, strong and elusive. For example, in the comic book Batman #5, the Batmobile "leaps away and tears up the street like a cyclone." In the same comic book, the Batmobile is analogized to an "impatient steed straining at the reigns," shivering "as its supercharged motor throbs with energy ... and an instant later it tears after the fleeing hoodlums." The Batmobile participates in various chases and is deployed to combat Batman's enemies. The comic books portray the Batmobile as a super-

hero. The Batmobile is central to Batman's ability to fight crime and appears as Batman's side-kick, if not an extension of Batman's own persona.

As a result, the court found that the Batmobile was a character entitled to copyright protection and that Towle violated this copyright when he made a physical manifestation of the comic property as a derivative work.

Alternatively, the court also determined that the Batmobile was protected as a pictorial, graphic, and sculptural work. To reach this conclusion, the court addressed Towle's argument that the Batmobile is only a car, which is not protectable under the copyright law as a useful object. Once again, the court rejected the argument on two alternative grounds. First, the court determined that the Batmobile that appeared in the comic was not a useful object as defined in the statute and the fact that Towle created a derivative work that itself was useful did not change the copyrightability of the original. The court held: "[a] derivative work can still infringe the underlying copyrighted work even if the derivative work is not independently entitled to copyright protection." Alternatively, the court determined that the Batmobiles created for the movies themselves would be protected by copyright. This is because the court held that "The artistic features of the 1989 and 1966 Batmobile vehicles can be conceptually separated from their utilitarian features." As a result, those artistic features are entitled to copyright protection. Specifically, the court found:

> In all of the fictional works, the Batmobile is deployed as Batman's mode of transportation. However, the Batmobile is entirely distinguishable from an ordinary automobile. The Batmobile is a fictional character tied to the fictional Batman character. The Batmobile is a crime fighting weapon and used to display the Batman persona. The Batmobile, and the so-called functional elements associated with it, is not a useful object in the real world, and incorporates fantasy elements that do not appear on real-world vehicles. The "functional elements"—e.g., the fictional torpedo launchers, the Bat-scope, and anti-fire systems—are only "functional" to the extent that they helped Batman fight crime in the fictional Batman television series and movies. Thus, the Batmobile's usefulness is a construct. Additionally, [Towle's] argument that [the Batmobile] is merely a car wholly fails to capture the creativity and fantastical elements that stand apart from the fact that the Batmobile also happens to look like a car.... As such, all of the features that distinguish the Batmobile from any other car—the fantastical elements that feature bat design, such as the bat tailfin and the various gadgetry that identify the vehicle as the Batmobile—are protectable elements.

Once finding that the Batmobile was protected by copyright, the court had no problem finding that Towle had violated that copyright. Towle admitted he had access to the earlier Batmobiles and that the replicas are substantially similar to the originals.

Finally, the court turned to Towle's laches defenses. Laches is an equitable defense that comes into play when one side sits on their rights for so long that it would be unfair to enforce them. In other words, a failure to assert one's rights in a timely manner can result in a claim being barred by laches. In this case, Towle argued that DC Comics was aware of his Batmobiles for several years and took no steps to stop him. To prevail on a claim of laches, Towle needed to prove that (1) DC Comics' delay in bringing suit was unreasonable; and (2) Towle was prejudiced by the delay. Moreover, a laches defense would be prohibited if the court were to determine that Towle purposefully committed the infringing conduct. Because Towle admitted to intentionally copying the trademarks of DC Comics, the court found that the laches defense was inapplicable to the trademark or unfair competition claims and the court ruled in favor of DC Comics. However, the copyright issue was not as straight-forward as the record was not clear as to whether Towle knew that creating a Batmobile violated copyright. As a result, the court determined that it was unable to resolve the laches issue related to the copyright claims based on the undisputed material facts before it and denied summary judgment for both parties.[17]

On February 22, 2013, the court entered a judgment requiring Towle to pay DC Comics $70,000 in actual damages. On that same day, the court also entered an injunction that enjoined Towle from:

a. Infringing the Batman Properties, either directly or contributorily, in any manner, including generally, but not limited to, the manufacturing, producing, distributing, circulating, selling, marketing, offering for sale, renting, advertising, promoting, exhibiting, or otherwise disposing of any Unauthorized Products;

b. Using any simulation, reproduction, counterfeit, copy, or colorable imitation of any of the Batman Properties in the promotion, advertisement, display, sale, offer for sale, rental, manufacture, production, circulation, or distribution of Unauthorized Products in such fashion as to relate or connect, or tend to relate or connect, such products in any way to DC Comics or to any goods sold, manufactured, sponsored, or approved by or connected with DC Comics;

c. Making any statement or representation whatsoever, or using any false designation of origin or false description, or performing any act that can or is likely to lead the trade or public, or individual members thereof, to believe that any products manufactured, distributed, or sold by Defendant are in any manner associated or connected with DC Comics, or are sold, manufactured, licensed, sponsored approved, or authorized by DC Comics;

d. Engaging in any other activity constituting unfair competition with or an infringement of any of the Batman Properties or of DC Comics' rights in, or to use or to exploit the Batman Properties, or constituting any dilution of DC Comics' name, reputation, or goodwill;

e. Effecting assignments or transfers, forming new entities or associations or using any other device for the purpose of circumventing or otherwise avoiding the prohibitions set forth herein; and

f. Aiding, abetting, contributing to, or otherwise assisting anyone from infringing upon any of the Batman Properties.

Towle filed a Notice of Appeal on March 22, 2013. As of the writing of this book, the case is being briefed in the Ninth Circuit Court of Appeals.

CHAPTER 7

When Titans Tangle
Neil Gaiman v. Todd McFarlane

One is a world famous artist and a co-founder of Image Comics who revolutionized the creator-owned comic. The other is an award winning writer who revolutionized comics for a new generation of mature readers. But, for a short time in 2002 and 2010, these two extraordinary talents faced off against each other in a Wisconsin courtroom.

The Rise of Marvel Man

In order to gain a proper perspective of the lawsuit between Todd McFarlane and Neil Gaiman, it is important to go back in time before either man was born to another comic book lawsuit. As described more fully in chapter 4, DC Comics successfully sued Fawcett in the 1940s to stop the publication of Captain Marvel. Fawcett decided to settle with DC Comics and agreed to stop publishing Captain Marvel. In accordance with the settlement agreement, Fawcett Comics discontinued all of its superhero comics. By 1954, Captain Marvel (along with the entire Marvel Family) vanished from the American comics market.

But the popularity of Captain Marvel, whose exploits actually outsold Superman in his prime, was not limited to the United States. In fact, the character was very lucrative to L. Miller and Sons, who produced and sold black and white reprints of Captain Marvel's comics. Faced with the loss of Captain Marvel, Len Miller approached a creator named Mick Anglo from Gower Studios[1] about a new character to replace Captain Marvel.

Marvelman Is Born

Of course, it would be more accurate to say that Captain Marvel was reborn as there were many similarities between the two characters. In the new version of the character, a young Mickey Moran meets an astrophysicist named Guntag Barghelt. Guntag gives Mickey the ability to become a superhero with atomic based powers that allowed him to tap into the key harmonic of the universe. Like the transformation of young Billy Batson (who received his powers from a wizard by saying the word "Shazam") into the older Captain

Marvel, the adolescent Mickey Moran would transform into the adult Marvelman whenever he uttered the word "Kimota!" (Atomic spelled backward, more or less.)

The similarities between Captain Marvel and Marvelman did not stop at the main character. The supporting cast of the *Captain Marvel* family of books were also reworked and given mild makeovers. Captain Marvel Junior became Young Marvelman and the female heroine Mary Marvel was transformed into the male hero Kid Marvelman. The company even reimagined Captain Marvel's rogues' gallery of villains as Doctor Sivana was converted into Dr. Gargunza and Black Adam was given the moniker of Young Nastyman.

It should be noted that even though DC Comics had prevailed over Fawcett, L. Miller and Sons was apparently undeterred in their publication of a Captain Marvel clone. In fact, there were aspects of Marvelman that made the character even more derivative of Superman than the original Captain Marvel character. For example, while Billy Batson was a radio reporter, Mickey Moran was a mild mannered reporter for the *Daily Bugle*.[2] He even wore the same type of blue suit and red boots made famous by the Man of Steel, except the "S" symbol on the chest was replaced by the letters "MM." For some reason, perhaps because of the fact that Marvelman was published in England, DC Comics never brought action against L. Miller and Sons for the character.

Perhaps in an effort to retain its loyal Fawcett audience, L. Miller and Sons changed the title of issue 24, the final issue to feature Captain Marvel reprints, to *Captain Marvel: The Marvelman*. One month later, on February 23, 1954, the series was renamed *Marvelman* and continued with issue 25. In addition, L. Miller and Sons continued to use logos and trademarks that looked substantially similar to those used by Fawcett. Similarly, the publisher converted its remaining *Captain Marvel* family of titles into Marvelman titles and simply continued the numbering. *Captain Marvel, Jr.*, became *Young Marvelman* with issue 24. *Captain Marvel Family* and *Mary Marvel* became *Marvelman Family* and *Young Marvelman*, respectively, beginning with issue 25.

The new series continued to sell as well as its predecessor titles. The books were also printed in Italy, Australia, and Brazil (where the hero was named Jack Marvel). *Marvelman* and *Young Marvelman* each ran 346 issues and were published weekly until Mick Anglo ended his association with L. Miller and Sons in 1959 after writing 736 original issues of *Marvelman*, *Marvelman Family* and *Young Marvelman*. Thereafter, the last 36 issues of the series were released monthly and contained reprints of earlier *Marvelman* stories. A variety of *Marvelman* and *Young Marvelman* albums were also printed annually from 1954 to 1963. All of the *Marvelman* related books contained a copyright notice saying that the stories and illustrations belonged to L. Miller and Sons. The final issue of *Marvelman* was released in February of 1963.

In September 1974, L. Miller and Sons went out of business and sold their physical assets (including the printing plates to Marvelman) to Alan Class, Ltd.

After Mick Anglo left L. Miller and Sons, he attempted to reimagine the character of Marvelman again in his own imprint called Anglo Comics. In October 1960, Anglo Comics launched *Captain Miracle*, a series based on *Marvelman* reprints with changes to the artwork. This series starred Captain Miracle and his sidekick, Miracle Junior, and only lasted for only ten issues. In 1965 and 1966, Anglo again tried to recreate the character, this time as *Miracle*

Man, for Top Sellers publishers using the *Captain Miracle* stories from 1960, which, of course, themselves were altered *Marvelman* stories. These ultimately were sold with some success as *Mirakel Man* and *Super Hombre* in other countries, but were a commercial failure in the United Kingdom.

After this, Marvelman stories, in any form, would not be seen for nearly two decades.[3]

In 1982, Marvelman reappeared as the flagship character in the pages of a magazine-sized British comic called *Warrior*. *Warrior* was a black and white anthology series created by Dez Skinn, an editor working for Quality Communications, to compete with the British anthology magazine named *2000 AD*. Skinn wanted to feature the character of Marvelman. However, L. Miller and Sons was out of business. So, under the belief that no one owned the rights, Skinn contacted Mick Anglo to get his blessing before bringing the character back. Anglo had no objection and Skinn hired a relatively unknown writer named Alan Moore who was interested in writing the Marvelman revival with art by Garry Leach and, later, Alan Davis. Moore provided a much darker take on the character and featured a grown up Mickey Moran.

In exchange for their work on Marvelman, Skinn gave the creators an ownership interest in the title. Ownership was split between Alan Moore, Garry Leach, Alan Davis, and Dez Skinn.

The success of Marvelman led Quality Communications to release the *Marvelman Special* with a cover date of June 1984, which was composed of *Marvelman* reprints from the L. Miller days. Of course, the success of Marvelman and the publication of the *Marvelman Special* also attracted the attention of the legal department in Marvel Comics because the name Marvel was now a trademark of the company. As a result, Marvelman stopped appearing in *Warrior* with issue 19. Although originally envisioned by Moore as a multipart storyline, Marvelman ended abruptly and incomplete. After the book ended, Alan Davis gave his ownership percentage back to Garry Leach.

In 1985, Eclipse Comics released *Miracleman*, issues 1 through 5 which contained reprints of the Marvelman series from *Warrior* colored and resized for the American market. The books were re-lettered so that all references to Marvelman were changed to Miracleman. Issue 6 contained both reprinted stories and an all new Miracleman story by Alan Moore and artist Chuck Beckum (later known as Chuck Austen). For the most part, beginning with issue 7, *Miracleman* would feature new stories by Moore and several artists as Austen was eventually replaced by Rick Veitch and then John Totleben as artist on the book.[4]

In early 1986, Skinn and Leach decide to sell their ownership of the rights to *Miracleman* to Eclipse Comics. The contract reads, in part:

> Transfer of Rights: Eclipse shall not assign or otherwise dispose of its rights in the Ownership hereunder to any third party except to Rights Holder, or a new corporation or entity in which the majority stockholders of Eclipse are and remain the majority stockholders or managing partners.

In 1989, a new creative team was hired to take over the book beginning with *Miracleman* issue 17. The writing chores were taken over by Neil Gaiman.

Neil Gaiman was a voracious reader as a child and a fan of science fiction. In the early 1980s, Gaiman was influenced by Alan Moore's writing on *Swamp Thing* and became a comic book fan. After publishing several prose works (both in his own name and under pseudonyms such including Gerry Musgrave and Richard Grey), Gaiman began to write comics. His first published work was included in Future Shocks for *2000 AD*. He also wrote three graphic novels, *Violent Cases, Signal to Noise,* and *The Tragical Comedy or Comical Tragedy of Mr. Punch*. Soon after, he was hired by DC Comics where he wrote the limited series *Black Orchid* in 1987 and the critically acclaimed *Sandman*, which began in January 1989. The success of *Sandman* (along with *Swamp Thing* penned by Moore) led to the creation of DC Comics' Vertigo imprint, a line of comics for mature readers, in 1993. Gaiman's *Death: The High Cost of Living*, a limited series featuring a *Sandman* supporting cast member, became DC Comics' first book to bear the Vertigo imprint. *Sandman* would propel Gaiman into superstar status and help make him into a popular culture icon. His successes continued as a writer of novels, children's books, and comics. However, before this, in 1989, Neil Gaiman was selected to take over *Miracleman*.

Gaiman, who was joined on the book by artist Mark Buckingham, was handpicked by Alan Moore to continue his work on *Miracleman*. In March, Moore transferred his share in *Miracleman* to Gaiman, who, in turn, shared it with Mark Buckingham. The transfer agreement specifically stated that if Gaiman or Buckingham stopped working on *Miracleman* they could pass it on to the new creators, return it to Moore, keep it, or pass it on as they saw fit.

One month later, Gaiman signed a contract that provided he would be paid $60 per page as an advance against royalties[5] and receive a royalty of 3 percent for the first 50,000 copies sold, and a royalty of 4 percent for each book sold over 50,000 copies.[6] With regard to the ownership of the trademarks and copyrights, the contract provided:

> A. [Gaiman] and Eclipse acknowledges that [Gaiman] retains and is the sole and exclusive owner of all copyrights in and to the stories. Eclipse also agrees that a notice of copyright for the stories in the name of [Gaiman] shall appear in each and every issue of the series.
>
> B. [Gaiman] and Eclipse acknowledge and agree that all characters in the stories and all of the trademarks in and to the title *Miracleman* (and all characters featured in the Series except the Warpsmiths, the Quys and related characters owned by Alan Moore and Gary Leach), [Gaiman] and Artist shall, for the duration of their work on the series, jointly own One-third, and Eclipse shall own Two-thirds.[7] [The agreement between Gaiman and Moore was attached and incorporated]. All such rights shall include but not limited to:[*sic*]
>
> C. The exclusive right to secure trademarks in the Series and all characters in the United States, Canada, and throughout the world (unless [Gaiman] introduces new characters and [Gaiman] and Eclipse make separate arrangements for such characters.);
>
> (1) All allied, ancillary and subsidiary rights;
> (2) All film, television, video tape and dramatic rights of any kind in the Series;
> (3) Anthology and promotion rights therein;
> (4) The likeness of all characters and other elements of the Series; and
> (5) Reprint rights.

Alan Moore and John Totleben left *Miracleman* with issue 16 and Gaiman and Buckingham took over with issue 17 at the end of 1989. As expected, Gaiman and Buckingham receive critical acclaim for their work on the title.

Todd McFarlane's Spawn of the Image Revolution

Meanwhile in the United States, comics were changing. Specifically, more commercial and creative emphasis was being placed on the artist. For example, at Marvel Comics, sales of new comics were being driven primarily through the contributions of superstar artists like *X-Force* artist Rob Liefeld, *X-Men* artist Jim Lee, and *Spider-Man* artists Todd McFarlane and Eric Larsen. Eventually these artists became dissatisfied with the standard page rates and modest royalties in Marvel Comics' standard work for hire agreement as compared to the profits Marvel Comics was earning on merchandising the artwork and the new characters they created. After an unsuccessful meeting with Marvel Comics, the creators made their decision to leave the company and start their own company.

As a result, the comic world was amazed when eight well known Marvel Comic creators announced that they were breaking ties with the publisher and formed their own company called Image. Marvel Comics' stock fell $3.25 a share when the news became public.

Image's organizing charter had two key provisions:

1. Image would not own any creator's work; the creator would.
2. No Image partner would interfere—creatively or financially—with any other partner's work. Image itself would own no intellectual property except the company trademarks: its name and its logo.

Image initially had six partners, each with his own studio. Jim Lee, the former artist on *X-Men*, formed Wildstorm Productions; Rob Liefeld, who had gained fame through his work on *X-Force*, formed Extreme Studios. Marc Silvestri, a former *Wolverine* artist, founded Top Cow productions; Erik Larsen, the acclaimed artist on *The Amazing Spider-Man*, formed Highbrow Entertainment; Jim Valentino, writer/artist of *Guardians of the Galaxy*, formed Shadowline Studios; and Todd McFarlane, an artist on *Spider-Man,* formed Todd McFarlane Productions.[8] Each studio would publish its books as an imprint under the Image banner.

Although each of these imprints and creators would go on to great commercial and critical success, for the purpose of this chapter, the focus will be on Todd McFarlane, his company, Todd McFarlane Productions, and his creation: *Spawn*.

Todd McFarlane's first professional work appeared in a 1984 backup story in *Coyote*. Soon afterwards he began drawing for both DC Comics (where he worked on *Infinity, Inc.* and *Detective Comics*) and Marvel Comics (where he worked on *The Incredible Hulk*). In 1988, McFarlane became the regular artist on *Amazing Spider-Man* beginning with issue 298. The level of detail McFarlane brought to the book soon made him a fan favorite. During that time, McFarlane drew the first appearance of Venom and has been credited as the character's co-creator. In 1998, Marvel Comics gave McFarlane his own *Spider-Man* book, which he wrote and drew. McFarlane's *Spider-Man* issue 1 sold 2.5 million copies.

At the time McFarlane left Marvel Comics to form Image, he had an enormous fan base because of his work on Marvel Comics' books. In order to maintain that base and lure his fans away from Marvel Comics, McFarlane knew he needed to create an original character that was visually appealing with an engaging backstory that would appeal to comic audiences.

McFarlane succeeded on all counts with *Spawn*.

McFarlane first came up with the concept for *Spawn* when he was in high school. The idea was so compelling that he designed the hero's costume. Years later, McFarlane would return to that basic design when he introduced the first new, and what would become the most popular, title of his Image imprint. The first issue was released in 1992 and sold 1.7 million copies

Spawn tells the story of an assassin name Al Simmons and is a classic tale of love and redemption. Simmons was a ruthless soldier, who worked for the CIA, until he was murdered by his partner. His malicious past causes him to be sentenced to Hell. But, because of his love for his wife (named Wanda after McFarlane's own wife), Simmons makes a deal and sells his soul to the devil (more specifically, a demon named Malebolgia) to allow him to return to her.

Like most deals with the devil, the arrangement has a catch. Simmons is brought back as a demonic creature known as a Hellspawn. It turns out that Simmons was not the first Hellspawn to be created by Malebolgia. Instead, one is created every 400 years.[9] Each Hellspawn is given symbiotic living armor that bonds with its host. Each time a Hellspawn uses its power, it brings it closer to returning to Hell. Unfortunately for Simmons, his rebirth occurs five years after his death. In that time, his wife has married Simmons's best friend and had a child. Knowing he can no longer be part of their life, Spawn dedicates himself to fighting evil. His methods were emblematic of the dark antiheroes prevalent at the time. Spawn regularly and brutally killed his enemies. For example, in an early story, he carves up a pedophile masquerading as an ice cream vender.

Justice Posner eloquently summarized the character of Spawn's tragic history as follows:

> In 1992, shortly after forming his own publishing house, McFarlane began publishing a series of comic books entitled Spawn, which at first he wrote and illustrated himself. "Spawn," more precisely "Hellspawn," are officers in an army of the damned commanded by a devil named Malebolgia, who hopes one day to launch his army against Heaven. The leading character in the series is a man named Al Simmons, who is dead but has returned to the world of the living as a Hellspawn.
>
> Al's story is an affecting one. Born in a quiet neighborhood outside of Pittsburgh, he was recruited by the CIA and eventually became a member of an elite military unit that guards the President. He saved the President from an assassin's bullet and was rewarded with a promotion to lieutenant colonel. He was placed under the command of Jason Wynn, who became his mentor and inducted him into the sinister inner recesses of the intelligence community. When Al began to question Wynn's motives, Wynn sent two agents, significantly named Chapel and Priest, to kill Al with laser weapons, and they did, burning him beyond recognition. Al was buried with great fanfare in Arlington National Cemetery.
>
> Now Al had always had an Achilles' heel, namely that he loved his wife beyond bearing and so, dying, he vowed that he would do anything to see her again. Malebolgia took him at his word ("would do anything") and returned Al to Earth. But a deal with the devil is always a Faustian pact. Al discovered that he was now one of Malebolgia's handpicked Hellspawn and had been remade (a full makeover, as we'll see) and infused with Hell-born energy.
>
> Returned to Earth in his new persona, Al discovers that his wife has remarried his best friend, who was able to give her the child he never could. He absorbs the blow but thirsts for revenge against Jason Wynn. He bides his time, living with homeless people and pondering the unhappy fact that once he exhausts his Hell-born energy he will be returned to Malebolgia's domain and become a slave in an army of the damned with no hope of redemption. He must try somehow to break his pact with the devil.

And while the series was a commercial success, several reviewers were critical of McFarlane's writing. Perhaps in response to this criticism, McFarlane decided to approach several prominent comic book authors to take on the writing chores for early issues of *Spawn*. Specifically, McFarlane approached Dave Sim, Frank Miller, Alan Moore, and Neil Gaiman to write *Spawn* stories that would appear in issues 8 through 11 of the series. One of those writers, Gaiman, was featured in issue 9 of the series.[10]

There was no written agreement between Gaiman and McFarlane. There was no mention of compensation or copyright in the discussion between the two. Instead, there was only a promise that McFarlane would treat Gaiman "better than the big guys do." Later, McFarlane decided to pay Gaiman $100,000 for his work on *Spawn*.[11] At trial, Gaiman testified that the $100,000 payment was what he would have expected to receive had he written the script for *Spawn* for DC Comics as a work for hire.

Gaiman and McFarlane Co-Create Angela, Medieval Spawn, and Cogliostro

Gaiman's script for *Spawn* issue 9 introduced three new characters—Medieval Spawn,[12] Angela, and Count Nicholas Cogliostro. Gaiman wrote descriptions and dialogue and McFarlane drew the images for the issue.

In the script writing process, McFarlane told Gaiman to create a wise sage-type character to assist Spawn with his powers. Gaiman interpreted this as "a character who can talk to Spawn and tell him a little bit more about what's going on in the background and can move the story along." The script describes him as an "old man, who starts talking to Spawn and then telling him all these sort of things about Spawn's super powers that Spawn couldn't have known. And when you first meet him [Cogliostro] in the alley you think he's a drunken bum with the rest of them, and then we realize no, he's not. He's some kind of mysterious stranger who knows things." In his script, Gaiman described the appearance character of Cogliostro as "a really old bum, a skinny, balding old man, with a grubby greyish-yellow beard, like a skinny santa claus." However, McFarlane did not like the description and instead drew the character to be more like a wizened old warrior.

During the creation process, Gaiman asked McFarlane if there could have been previous Spawns.[13] Gaiman stated that McFarlane had no problem so long as there weren't a lot of them. The result was Medieval Spawn, who barely appeared in the story and was simply referred to as an old-time Spawn. The script states, "Spawn rides up on a huge horse. He's wearing a kind of Spawn suit and mask, although the actual costume under the cloak is reminiscent of a suit of armour." McFarlane stated that he drew this Spawn as "essentially Spawn, only he dressed him as a knight from the Middle Ages with a shield bearing the Spawn logo." Gaiman described Medieval Spawn as using archaic language. Gaiman also testified that to create the character he drew on many things, including: Barbara Tuchman's *A Distant Mirror*; childhood visits to various museums; Hever Castle; the Tower of London; and Thomas Malory's *Le Morte d'Arthur*. Although it was not thoroughly explored in the few pages on which Medieval Spawn appears, Gaiman stated that he made up a backstory for the character that involved being tricked by the devil to return to his sister and that, while he was dead, his sister married his worst enemy. This backstory is primarily told through the character's dialogue to another character, a maiden named Angela, who turns out to be more than she first appears.

Gaiman described Angela as a "warrior angel and villain." Gaiman assumed that if Spawn was a warrior of Hell, then he had to be fighting something. "So fighting Heaven seemed to make sense. And I thought, if you're warriors, you can't have nice angels, because you have to have somebody to fight—so, therefore, they have to be warrior angels." He then realized that he should make his angel a female character. McFarlane agreed and prepared a drawing of the character for the Previews catalog. Gaiman admitted that McFarlane's drawing of the character was not what he expected. However, he took what McFarlane had drawn (a woman wearing a dominatrix outfit and using a lance) and created Angela's backstory based on the design.

Gaiman wrote at the end of his script for the issue, "It's your playground. I'm just in for an afternoon on the swings."

Gaiman's s work appeared in *Spawn* issue 9, which was released in March 1993. In the story, which takes place 800 years in the past, Medieval Spawn is introduced and subsequently killed by Angela. The story then flashes forward to the present, where the current version of Angela hunts the latest incarnation of Spawn, Al Simmons. The story also introduced another character, a bum (and former Hellspawn) named Count Nicholas Cogliostro, who teaches Spawn how to draw power from his uniform. The remainder of the issue featured a fight between Angela and Spawn. The copyright in *Spawn* issue 9 stated that it was owned by Todd McFarlane Productions, Inc.

The Rise of Angela and the Fall of Miracleman

Spawn issue 9 sold over 1.1 million copies and Angela was an immediate hit—so much so that McFarlane asked Gaiman to write more about the character. Gaiman returned to write a three issue *Angela* mini-series (drawn by Greg Capullo and not McFarlane) that was released by Image in December 1994. Because Angela did not appear in the comics in over a year, McFarlane also asked Gaiman to write a few pages in in *Spawn* issue 26, which would serve as the lead-in to the mini-series.[14] McFarlane paid Gaiman $3,300 for his work on *Spawn* issue 26. Gaiman was not given any credits in *Spawn* issue 26 or any of the subsequent collections or trades that included reprints of the issue (including *Spawn Volume 6* and *Pathway to Judgment*). McFarlane paid around $30,000 to Gaiman for the *Angela* miniseries.

The miniseries gave Gaiman a chance to expand on Angela's backstory. Gaiman established that Angela was 100,000 years old and that there's an angelic host. Specifically, the series revealed that there are 330,000 beautiful warrior angels. These angels lived in a heaven named Elysium.

The *Angela* miniseries would later be collected in a trade paperback called *Angela* in 1995 (this trade was retitled *Spawn: Angela's Hunt* in later reprintings). Gaiman's name and biographical information were included in these trades. In all of the *Spawn* trades that included *Spawn* issue 26 as well as the *Angela* collections, the copyright statements clearly indicated that McFarlane was the sole copyright owner of the characters and material. Gaiman testified that he had not known about the trade until he saw it at a Texas comic convention in 2002. He also stated that is when he first discovered that his biography was prominently displayed on the back cover to market the book.

And while Medieval Spawn and Cogliostro were not as popular as Angela, they also continued to be featured in later issues of *Spawn* where the characters were expanded on. Unbeknownst to Gaiman, McFarlane filed for copyright protection for these characters, as well as for the comics and trade paperbacks that contained Gaiman's work.

In addition, Cogliostro, played by Nicol Williamson, was included as a supporting character in a live action *Spawn* movie released on October 31, 1997, starring Michael Jai White as Al Simmons. Laura Stepp also played Angela in an unnamed Easter egg cameo. The *Spawn* movie grossed an estimated $7.3 million in its first weekend and a total of $54 million in domestic box office receipts during its run. Later that year, *Todd McFarlane's Spawn* debuted on HBO. This Emmy award winning series starred Keith David as Spawn and Richard Dysart as Cogliostro. Angela, voiced by Denise Poroer, also appeared in the series.

Medieval Spawn, along with Angela, were also included in the licensed toy line based on the comics. It was estimated that these toys generated over $5 million in wholesale revenue. In addition, these characters were also featured in other products such as clothing, video games, books, trading cards, posters, and statuettes, which generated additional merchandising revenue. At one point, McFarlane sent a payment of $20,000 to Gaiman for royalties presumably on the sale of a Medieval Spawn statuette.

Meanwhile, Gaiman and Buckingham continued their work on *Miracleman*. They stayed on the book until issue 24, when the series was abruptly cancelled when Eclipse Comics ceased publication of all of its titles in August 1993.[15]

Eclipse Comics filed an application for protection under Chapter 7 of the Bankruptcy Code on December 21, 1994. As a bit of background, a Chapter 7 bankruptcy involves complete liquidation of a company's assets to pay its bills. This is different than a proceeding under Chapter 11, which involves the reorganization of a company into a new business. In short, this meant that Eclipse was closing shop. As a result, the assets of the company were auctioned off.

On February 29, 1996, an auction occurred in New York whereby Eclipse Comics sold off all of its copyrights, trademarks, characters, and other intellectual properties, in addition to some tangible assets including trading cards, film negatives and publishing agreements. Of particular note was United States Patent and Trademark Office registration number 1,447,456, which related to *Miracleman*, and the April 1989 contract between Eclipse and Gaiman over the ownership of the copyright to *Miracleman*.

The auction was won with a bid of $25,000 on behalf of McFarlane. The transfer agreement and letter of acceptance stated, "the onus is on you, as purchaser, to do your due diligence investigation." This meant that it was up to McFarlane or his lawyers to review the documents related to the items bought at auction. It is unclear what type of due diligence was done.

The Stage Is Set for Litigation

At some point in 1996, Gaiman learned that McFarlane might sell his business and asked for a written contract from McFarlane to protect his interests in the characters he co-created. McFarlane agreed and, in 1997, a series of lengthy negotiations took place related to Gaiman's work on *Spawn*.[16] The main focus of these negotiations was McFarlane's promise that he would treat Gaiman better than Marvel Comics and DC Comics, collectively referred to as the big two.[17] Given that Gaiman was primarily working for DC Comics, that company served as the basis for the discussion of compensation and rights. In litigation that eventually ensued, McFarlane testified that he repeatedly requested that Gaiman provide copies of his contracts but was never provided with them. This testimony was contradicted by Larry Marder, the executive director at Image, who stated that he had reviewed Gaiman's DC Comics contracts and provided a summary to McFarlane. On cross examination, Gaiman's lawyers produced the summary and McFarlane admitted to reviewing them.

Once agreement was reached, the negotiations were memorialized in a faxed agreement sent to McFarlane by Gaiman. Under the agreement that was reached, McFarlane would pay royalties to Gaiman for Angela, Medieval Spawn, and Cogliostro. After these payments were to be made, Gaiman would transfer rights in Medieval Spawn, and Cogliostro to McFarlane in exchange for McFarlane's giving rights in Miracleman to Gaiman. This transfer was supposed to take place on July 31, 1997. Afterwards, several payments and tangible property in the amount of $110,000[18] were provided to Gaiman. And while McFarlane sent some of the *Miracleman* materials to Gaiman, the exchange of rights never took place. Instead, in October 1997, McFarlane filed trademark applications for the use of the Miracleman name and also filed an "intent to use" application for the character.

Although negotiations continued well into 1999, they were fruitless. It appeared that McFarlane's side believed that Gaiman overstated his rights under his DC contract related to royalties on derivative characters. It appeared that Gaiman's side, on the other hand, believed that McFarlane was taking credit for Gaiman's work without providing him with compensation.

On February 14, 1999, McFarlane sent Gaiman a letter that stated that he was "officially rescind[ing] any previous offers I have placed on the table." Instead, McFarlane presented a take it or leave it offer to exchange all rights for Angela for all rights for Miracleman. The letter closes with McFarlane's belief that "all rights to Medieval Spawn and Cogliostro shall continue to be owned by Todd McFarlane Productions." Based on this correspondence, it appeared that Medieval Spawn and Cogliostro were no longer on the table. In February 2001, *Hellspawn* issue 6 featured a character named Mike Moran, Miracleman's secret identity. Later, it was announced that Miracleman would be appearing in issue 13. But, because Gaiman, as part copyright owner, objected to the character's inclusion, Miracleman never appeared in the book.[19]

It is important to note that, according to law, McFarlane's February 14, 1999, letter started the running of a three year statute of limitations in which Gaiman could sue McFarlane under the Copyright Act because it was an unambiguous denial of his ownership rights in Medieval Spawn and Cogliostro. In other words, if Gaiman intended to take McFarlane to court to prove that he was the co-owner of these characters, he needed do it by February 15, 2002.

The battle lines were clearly being drawn and it appeared the only way to resolve the issue was through litigation. In the words of Marder, "a jury will have to decide if it believes an Englishman or a Canadian."

Soon, however, Gaiman would get a Marvelous ally in the fight.

Marvel's Miracle Move

On October 24, 2001, Marvel Comics held its regularly scheduled conference call press briefing. On the call, Marvel Comics' Editor in Chief Joe Quesada and President Bill Jemas were joined by Gaiman. Together they announced a new upcoming project between Gaiman and Marvel Comics to be released in 2002 that would feature a unique take on the characters of the Marvel Universe.[20] Perhaps more relevant to this discussion, it was announced that all the profits from this project would be donated to Marvels and Miracles, LLC, a new company formed by Gaiman and his lawyer, Kenneth F. Levin. The purpose of Marvels and Miracles was to serve as a Marvelman property fund. Specifically, the Marvels and Miracles, LLC, Fund would be used to collect money to pay for Gaiman's legal efforts in acquiring the Marvelman property from McFarlane. All other monies raised by the fund would go to comic charities such as the free speech champion known as the Comic Book Legal Defense Fund and the charity established to help out of work comic creators, the Hero Initiative (formerly known as ACTOR).

Also on this call, Quesada stated, should Gaiman prevail, Marvel Comics no longer would object to the use of the name Marvelman for the character.

With this move, Marvel Comics officially joined the fight on the side of Gaiman.

The Lawsuit Commences

On January 24, 2002, three weeks before the statute of limitation expired, Gaiman filed a complaint with the United States District Court for the District of Wisconsin. The case was captioned as *Neil Gaiman and Marvels and Miracles, LLC v. Todd McFarlane, Todd McFarlane Productions, Inc., TMP International, Inc., McFarlane Worldwide, Inc., and Image Comics, Inc.* The suit alleged nine counts against McFarlane. In short, Gaiman sued McFarlane for: (1) the copyright infringement of Angela, Cogliostro, and Medieval Spawn[21]; (2) the breach of the oral agreement in 1992; and (3) the breach of the agreement in 1997. Of course, underlying the lawsuit was the ownership of Miracleman, which was the subject of the agreement.

McFarlane counterclaimed and argued that Gaiman's suit was untimely, the characters were not copyrightable, and alternatively, that McFarlane should be acknowledged as the sole owner if the court decided the character could be copyrighted.

A jury trial was held over four days in October 1992. Judge John C. Shabaz presided and jury selection resulted in an all-female seven person jury ranging in age from their 20s to their 60s. Testimony was heard from both McFarlane and Gaiman on the first day. Both McFarlane and Gaiman appeared very professional during the trial and their testimony demonstrated that there was a mutual respect between the two creators.

Gaiman testified and described his inspiration for the story. During the testimony, Gaiman became agitated when he described how he discovered the Angela trade after the lawsuit was filed. His anger increased as he explained that the Angela trade did not simply represent a loss of royalty, but was being sold by capitalizing on his fame without his control or his permission,

McFarlane also took the stand and described the creation of Spawn. A particularly emotional part of the trial involved the testimony of McFarlane as he described how devastated he was to discover that he might not be the sole owner of all versions of the Spawn character that he created while in high school. He became upset when he described how, if Gaiman was held to own a portion of Medieval Spawn, then there would have been a portion of Spawn's world that he no longer owned.

A large percentage of the second day's trial was spent going through Gaiman's writing contracts since it was agreed that there was a promise to treat Gaiman at least as well as DC Comics. Gaiman's contracts for *Black Orchid*, *Books of Magic*, *Sandman* and *Sandman* trademarks were entered into evidence to show that Gaiman's percentages were consistent with the numbers that he shared with McFarlane during the settlement talks.

The first phase of trial, regarding liability, ended with closing arguments. Gaiman's counsel argued that Gaiman was more credible than McFarlane. He further argued that McFarlane's argument that there was no agreement was contradicted by the statements of his employees that showed they thought there was a deal and the fact that Larry Marder expressed surprise that deal had fallen through. McFarlane's counsel argued that Gaiman was trying to steal credit from McFarlane and also attacked Gaiman's credibility. Image's attorney gave a separate closing argument, which similarly attacked Gaiman's credibility.[22]

At the end of the trial, the jury was instructed how to apply the law, given a jury form that contained several numbered paragraphs, and sent to the jury room to deliberate at around 3:30 p.m. on Wednesday, October 2. The questionnaire consisted of 18 questions and the jury had to be unanimous in reaching their answer to each question. After several hours, the jury adjourned for the day and returned the next morning. The jury filled out the jury form on October 3, 2002, and found as follows:

1. Does plaintiff Neil Gaiman have a copyright interest in the following? (answer yes or no to each).

    Medieval Spawn: *YES*
    Cogliostro: *YES*
    Spawn Issue 26: *YES*

2. Would a reasonable person in plaintiff Gaiman's position have discovered prior to January 24, 1999 that the McFarlane defendants were claiming to be sole owners of copyright interests in the following? (answer yes or no to each).

    Medieval Spawn: *NO*
    Cogliostro: *NO*
    Angela: *NO*
    Angela issues 1, 2, and 3: *NO*

Spawn issue 9: *NO*

Spawn Issue 26: *NO*

3. Did the plaintiff and McFarlane defendants enter into a contract in 1992?

Answer: *YES*

(Yes or No)

IF YOU ANSWERED QUESTION 3 "YES" ANSWER QUESTION 4. OTHERWISE PROCEED TO QUESTION 5.

4. Did the McFarlane defendants breach the 1992 contract?

Answer: *YES*

(Yes or No)

5. Did the plaintiff and the McFarlane defendants enter into a contract in 1997?

Answer: *YES*

(Yes or No)

IF YOU ANSWERED QUESTION 5 "YES" ANSWER QUESTION 6 AND PROCEED TO QUESTION 13. OTHERWISE PROCEED TO QUESTION 7.

6. Did the McFarlane defendants breach the 1997 contracts?

Answer: *YES*

(Yes or No)

IF YOU ANSWERED QUESTION 6 PROCEED TO QUESTION 12.

7. Did the McFarlane defendants make a promise to plaintiff Gaiman which they should have expected would induce action or forbearance by him?

Answer: _____ NOT ANSWERED

(Yes or No)

IF YOU ANSWERED QUESTION 7 "YES" ANSWER QUESTION 8. OTHERWISE PROCEED TO QUESTION 10.

8. Did the promise by the McFarlane defendants induce such action or forbearance by plaintiff Gaiman?

Answer: _____ NOT ANSWERED

(Yes or No)

IF YOU ANSWERED QUESTION 8 "YES" ANSWER QUESTION 9. OTHERWISE PROCEED TO QUESTION 10.

9. Can injustice be avoided only by enforcing the McFarlane defendants' promise?

Answer: _____ NOT ANSWERED

(Yes or No)

10. Did defendant accept or retain benefits from plaintiff under circumstances where it would be inequitable to retain them without paying plaintiff the value thereof?

Answer: _____ NOT ANSWERED

(Yes or No)

11. Did plaintiff Gaiman accept and retain benefits from the McFarlane defendants under circumstances where it would be inequitable to retain the benefit of them without paying defendant the value thereof.

Answer: _____ NOT ANSWERED

(Yes or No)

12. Was defendant's failure to identify plaintiff Gaiman as a co-author of *Spawn* issue 26, *Spawn* volume 6 or *Pathway to Judgment* a false description of the origin of the work?

Answer: *YES*

(Yes or No)

IF YOU ANSWERED QUESTION 12 "YES" ANSWER QUESTION 13. OTHERWISE PROCEED TO QUESTION 14.

13. Does Plaintiff Gaiman believe that defendant's failure to identify him as a co-author of *Spawn* issue 26, *Spawn* volume 6 or *Pathway to judgment* is likely to damage him?

Answer: *YES*

(Yes or No)

14. Did plaintiff Gaiman consent in writing to the use of his name and biographical information on *Angela's Hunt*?

Answer: *NO*

(Yes or No)

15. Did plaintiff Gaiman make misrepresentation or omissions of material fact to defendant concerning his DC Comics contract during the negotiation of the 1997 contract?

Answer: *NO*

(Yes or No)

IF YOU ANSWERED QUESTION 15 "YES" ANSWER QUESTION 16. OTHERWISE PROCEED NO FURTHER.

16. Did plaintiff Gaiman make the misrepresentation knowing it was untrue or recklessly without caring whether it was true or untrue?

Answer: _____ NOT ANSWERED

(Yes or No)

IF YOU ANSWERED QUESTION 16 "YES" ANSWER QUESTION 17. OTHERWISE PROCEED NO FURTHER.

17. Did plaintiff Gaiman make the misrepresentation with the intent to deceive and to induce defendant to act on it?

Answer: _____ NOT ANSWERED

(Yes or No)

IF YOU ANSWERED QUESTION 17 "YES" ANSWER QUESTION 18. OTHERWISE PROCEED NO FURTHER.

18. Did defendants believe such misrepresentation to be true and justifiably rely upon it to their pecuniary damage?

Answer: _____ NOT ANSWERED

(Yes or No)

An analysis of the jury form leads to the conclusion that Gaiman won the first phase of the trial on all counts. More specifically, the jury ruled:

1. Gaiman was co-owner of Medieval Span, Cogliostro and Angela;
2. A reasonable person would not have understood McFarlane was claiming a full ownership from the copyright notice.
3. McFarlane had entered, and subsequently breached, contracts with Gaiman in 1992 and 1997.
4. Image Comics' failure to identify Gaiman on books caused damage.
5. Image Comics did not have the right to use Gaiman's information in the *Angela* trade.

The Effect of the Decision

After the jury reached its decision in favor of Gaiman, the only thing that remained was the calculation of damages. Prior to trial, the parties agreed that, if it were decided that Gaiman had a copyright interest in any of the characters he created, he had the option of either keeping his ownership of the characters or enforcing the 1997 contract, under which he would relinquish his rights on the characters in exchange for the *Miracleman* interest. After a very short recess at the conclusion of the trial, Gaiman decided that he would keep his copyright in Medieval Spawn, Cogliostro, and Angela. As a result, McFarlane would continue to possess the Miracleman interest he purchased as part of the Eclipse bankruptcy proceeding.[23] The court ordered an accounting to determine Gaiman's share of the profits earned by McFarlane as a result of the exploitation of the characters.

The only matter left for the jury to decide was the amount of damages to award based on the ruling that McFarlane used Gaiman's name on the *Angela* trade improperly and without authorization. Gaiman's attorneys asked for $45,000 based on a similar contract entered into with Big Entertainment in 1993.[24] In response, McFarlane argued that Gaiman had done much more work for Big Entertainment than he had for McFarlane. On October 3, the jury awarded Gaiman the full $45,000 requested, which was to be paid by Image.

The most interesting thing about this trial was that the issue of Miracleman was never resolved despite the fact that evidence was presented concerning ownership of the characters.

Post-Trial Activity

Several things happened after the trial.

First, the parties both filed a few procedural motions. Second, McFarlane appealed to the Seventh Circuit. Third, McFarlane entered into bankruptcy. Fourth, McFarlane continued to produce comics, which inadvertently led both creators back to Madison, Wisconsin, and into the witness chairs again.

Procedural Motions

McFarlane and his counsel immediately moved to overturn the decision, for a new trial, to amend the judgment, and for attorney fees on one side. On the other side, Gaiman moved for an amended judgment and for attorney fees.

As grounds to overturn the decision, McFarlane argued that Gaiman's suit was untimely because McFarlane had claimed sole ownership more than three years before Gaiman filed his suit. As can be seen above, the jury found that Gaiman was unaware of this. The judge sustained this holding, pointing to the fact that if McFarlane had really owned the sole rights, he would not have continued negotiating with Gaiman over the rights. "[McFarlane's position does not consider] the contradictory behavior whereby defendants repeatedly recognized plaintiff's ownership interest." Additionally, McFarlane argued that the jury was wrong when it awarded co-ownership of *Spawn* Issue 26 because Gaiman only contributed notes for three pages out of twenty-six. The court rejected this, stating "Gaiman's contribution provided an important promotion for the *Angela* mini-series." Finally, McFarlane argued that the court should reverse the jury's decision because Medieval Spawn and Cogliostro were not copyrightable characters as a matter of law. The court dismissed this claim. "Comic book characters have physical and conceptual qualities and, unlike literary characters which lack a distinct visual image, are generally subject to copyright protection," and highlighted that "In support of their position that the characters are not subject to copyright defendants cite not a single case where a comic book or cartoon character was denied such status."

Next, McFarlane argued for a new trial based on alleged inconsistencies in the jury form. The judge admitted that there may have been literal inconsistencies, but denied that a new trial was necessary because the jury addressed the issues in the case. "Defendants are not in a position to complain that in pursuing their remedies plaintiffs chose to disregard the jury's answers to the contract questions, because defendants have consistently denied the existence of the contract."

The court next ruled on the cross motions for attorney fees. The court denied fees for the copyright claim. "The principal litigants, plaintiff Gaiman and defendant McFarlane, are highly successful as author and artist both financially and artistically. The underlying dispute arose from divergent expectations of the parties at the time the works were created and their inability to reduce an agreement on copyright ownership to writing. Each pursued the action vigorously motivated by the conviction that each was right in principle rather than for the potential for economic gain. The trial provided an opportunity for the vindication each sought."[25]

The Appeal to the Seventh Circuit

After losing his motions for a new jury and to overturn the ruling, McFarlane made a decision to appeal the case and have the Seventh Circuit review the lower court's decision. A case can only be appealed if there is a final judgment. Consequently, because the accounting of McFarlane's profits from the three characters was not yet complete, the appeal was limited to the injunction that required McFarlane to acknowledge Gaiman's co-ownership in the three characters. Of course, if McFarlane had prevailed on these claims an accounting would not have been necessary.

McFarlane made several arguments on appeal. First, he contended that a reasonable jury would not have rejected his statute of limitations defense. He also argued that two of the characters (Cogliostro and Medieval Spawn) were not copyrightable. In response, Gaiman cross-appealed to preserve his win, and subsequent voluntary dismissal of his auxiliary claim for breach of contract. Thus, if he prevailed on ownership, the circuit would not need to decide the issue.

Oral argument in the case was heard on January 5, 2004, in front of Circuit Judges Posner, Kahnne, and Rovner. The circuit court issued its opinion on February 24 and affirmed the trial court's decision.

The court rejected McFarlane's statute of limitations arguments first:

> McFarlane's argument [that the suit is not timely], however, reflects a misunderstanding of both the function of copyright notice and the nature of the copyright in a compilation. The function of copyright notice is to warn off copiers..., not to start the statute of limitations running.
>
> * * *
>
> The copyright notices in the paperback books, however—notices that claim copyright for McFarlane in "all related characters"—might seem to be an example of our earlier point that there may be cases in which a copyright notice denies a contributor's copyright. But unless there

is a duty of authors to read the copyright pages of works containing their copyrighted materials—and there is not—then since as we said the purpose of copyright notice is not to affect the time within which the victim of an infringement can sue (which is why there is no duty of authors to study copyright notices), the notice can affect the accrual of the cause of action only if the victim reads it. The jury was entitled to believe Gaiman's testimony that he had never seen the paperback books in which the suspicious notices appeared.

In addition to the copyright notices, McFarlane registered copyright on the issues and the books. But to suppose that by doing so he provided notice to Gaiman of his exclusive claim to the characters is again untenable. Authors don't consult the records of the Copyright Office to see whether someone has asserted copyright in their works; and anyway McFarlane's registrations no more revealed an intent to claim copyright in Gaiman's contributions, as distinct from McFarlane's own contributions as compiler and illustrator, than the copyright notices did.

The existence of a dispute over the terms of a publication contract does not alert the author to a challenge to his copyright. Quite the contrary, it presumes that he owns the copyright. If his work is in the public domain, the publisher could publish it without the author's permission, so would hardly be likely to have promised to pay him for the "right" to publish it—he would already have (along with the rest of the world) the right to publish it.

There was other evidence that right up until McFarlane's 1999 letter, receipt of which clearly did start the statute of limitations running, he acknowledged or at least didn't deny Gaiman's ownership of copyrights in the three characters. There was the reference in the royalty reports to Gaiman's being the "co-creator" of the characters, the fact that McFarlane let pass without comment Gaiman's claim in the demand letter to have created the characters, and the payment to Gaiman of royalties on the statuettes, payment that would make most sense if they were derivative works of copyrighted characters—with Gaiman the (joint) owner of the copyrights. McFarlane argues that he could have given Gaiman these royalties pursuant to contract, and he points out that under Gaiman's work-for-hire agreement with DC Comics Gaiman received payments denominated as "royalties" even though he had no copyrights. But McFarlane also contends that DC Comics would not have paid Gaiman royalties on the statuettes, so what would have been Gaiman's entitlement to such royalties from him unless Gaiman had a copyright interest?

In reaching its decision on copyrightability Judge Posner first ruled out that the characters written by Gaiman were created as a work for hire. Under the 1976 Copyright Act, in order to prove that Gaiman was creating a work for hire, McFarlane had to show either (1) that Gaiman was working as an employee of McFarlane, or (2) that Gaiman's work was identified in writings as work for hire. Justice Posner quickly disposed of the issue pointing out that, first, it was not argued that Gaiman was an employee acting within the scope of his employment as defined in the 1976 Copyright Act and, second, looking to the fact that there was no written agreement, the court held that Gaiman's creations did not qualify as work for hire. Consequently the relationship between Gaiman and McFarlane was not a work for hire. Thus, the court concluded that McFarlane could not be the sole and exclusive author and owner of all rights created by Gaiman.

The court next turned to McFarlane's argument that Gaiman's contributions to the creation of Medieval Spawn and Cogliostro were merely ideas and could not be protectable by copyright until after McFarlane drew the characters.[26] Thus, Gaiman did not have a claim to joint ownership. McFarlane argued that someone can't copyright an idea and all that Gaiman contributed was the ideas for the characters. Instead, McFarlane likened Gaiman to a research assistant or a secretary. Although the court agreed with the underlying premise that there needs to be some original independently copyrightable contribution in order for a contributor to be considered a co-author, it disagreed as to McFarlane's characterization of Gaiman's role in the creation of these characters and stated:

> Had someone merely remarked to McFarlane one day, "you need a medieval Spawn" or "you need an old guy to move the story forward," and McFarlane had carried it from there, and if later a copyeditor had made some helpful editorial changes, neither the suggester nor the editor would be a joint owner. Otherwise almost every expressive work would be a jointly authored work, and copyright would explode.
>
> But where two or more people set out to create a character jointly in such mixed media as comic books and motion pictures and succeed in creating a copyrightable character, it would be paradoxical if though the result of their joint labors had more than enough originality and creativity to be copyrightable, no one could claim copyright. That would be peeling the onion until it disappeared. The decisions that say, rightly in the generality of cases, that each contributor to a joint work must make a contribution that if it stood alone would be copyrightable weren't thinking of the case in which it *couldn't* stand alone because of the nature of the particular creative process that had produced it.

The court went on to point out that the creation process of the comic's medium naturally lends itself to joint copyright ownership. Justice Posner wrote:

> The contents of a comic book are typically the joint work of four artists—the writer, the penciler who creates the art work (McFarlane), the inker (also McFarlane, in the case of Spawn No. 9, but it would often be a different person from the penciler) who makes a black and white plate of the art work, and the colorist who colors it. The finished product is copyrightable, yet one can imagine cases in which none of the separate contributions of the four collaborating artists would be. The writer might have contributed merely a stock character (not copyrightable, as we're about to see) that achieved the distinctiveness required for copyrightability only by the combined contributions of the penciler, the inker, and the colorist, with each contributing too little to have by his contribution alone carried the stock character over the line into copyright land.

The court next turned to McFarlane's argument that Gaiman's creations of Medieval Spawn and Cogliostro were merely stock characters and therefore not copyrightable.[27] Specifically, McFarlane argued that Gaiman couldn't prove his copyright because the attributes he created were so rudimentary, commonplace, standard, or unavoidable that they did not serve to distinguish one work within a class of works from another.

The court rejected McFarlane's argument and found that Gaiman's creation was a "character that has a specific name and a specific appearance. Cogliostro's age, obviously phony title ('Count'), what he knows and says, his name, and his faintly Mosaic facial features combine to create a distinctive character. No more is required for a character copyright."

As a result, the court held:

> Although Gaiman's verbal description of Cogliostro may well have been of a stock character, once he was drawn and named and given speech he became sufficiently distinctive to be copyrightable. Gaiman's contribution may not have been copyrightable by itself, but his contribution had expressive content without which Cogliostro wouldn't have been a character at all, but merely a drawing. The expressive work that is the comic-book character Count Nicholas Cogliostro was the joint work of Gaiman and McFarlane—their contributions strike us as quite equal—and both are entitled to ownership of the copyright.

In short, the court found that since there was no work made for hire relationship and that the work of Gaiman was copyrightable, as a result Gaiman and McFarlane were joint authors on all the characters.

McFarlane's lawyers filed a petition for rehearing, asking that the entire Seventh Circuit hear the case, on March 9, 2004. The petition was denied on March 31, 2004.

McFarlane had lost his appeal.

McFarlane's Financial Trouble and Derivatives Multiply

Shortly before the *Gaiman* case was filed, McFarlane was also sued by hockey player Tony Twist. On December 11, 2004, a jury awarded a $24.5 million judgment against McFarlane in favor of Twist.[28] Soon after, McFarlane's company declared bankruptcy under Chapter 11 of the Bankruptcy Code. When a company goes into bankruptcy the court imposes an automatic stay, which prevents the company, for the most part, from paying creditors and protects the bankrupt entity by not allowing creditors to collect from the bankrupt entity. Instead, people owed money must file proofs of claim in the bankruptcy proceeding, assert what they are owed, and become creditors in the bankruptcy. As a result of the bankruptcy procedure, Gaiman became one of the largest creditors in the bankruptcy proceeding. According to papers filed in the bankruptcy, McFarlane was required, in July of 2008, to place $382,000 of insurance proceeds into an interest bearing escrow account to offset potential losses in the *Gaiman* suit. The amounts in this escrow account were released to Gaiman on February 24, 2012.

The bankruptcy was a reorganization and not a liquidation, which meant that McFarlane intended to stay in business. As a result, McFarlane continued to produce cards, toys, and comics, including those based on *Spawn*. As a result, new stories were created, which required new plots and new characters. Three of these characters, Tiffany, Domina, and Dark Ages Spawn, would cause further complications in the *Gaiman* case and bring everyone back in to court.

Tiffany and Domina

Tiffany and Domina first appeared in *Spawn* issue 44 in March 1996. Tiffany and Domina were two members of the 330,000 heavenly host warrior angels that Gaiman introduced in the *Angela* miniseries and referred to as "female, kick-ass warrior angels, who are hunters, merciless and not very nice." Because McFarlane created the art designs for the characters, Tiffany and Domina were visually similar to Angela. All three characters shared similar physical traits—they had long hair, mask-like eye makeup, and voluptuous physiques, highlighted by battle uniforms consisting of thong bikinis, garters, wide weapon belts, elbow length gloves, and very tight fitting armor bras. All three warrior angels also wore masks designed to be the opposite of the Spawn mask; all had blank eyes and wings.[29] The characters were described as warrior angels who fight in the war between Heaven and Hell. The backstories for Tiffany and Angela established that each has failed to kill only one of their targets: Al Simmons, the modern day Spawn. Domina's backstory was not as developed, but she had superpowers substantially similar to Angela's. She was described, like Angela, as being headstrong and not inclined to obey Heaven's commands.

Dark Ages Spawn

Spawn: The Dark Ages introduced Lord Covenant, a 12th century knight killed in a holy crusade far from his homeland, who returns to Earth as a Hellspawn. As a plague of violence and turmoil cover the English countryside, the dark knight must choose whether to align himself with the innocent inhabitants of the once-thriving kingdom or with the malevolent forces of evil and corruption. The series ran for 28 issues.

Spawn: The Dark Ages was written by Brian Philip Holguin and drawn by Liam McCormack-Sharp.[30] Prior to his work on *Spawn, the Dark Ages*, Holguin had written *Kiss: Psycho Circus, Aria, Cyberforce, Mr. Majestic, More Than Mortal* as well as issues of the main *Spawn* title—his first *Spawn* work appeared in *Spawn* issue 72. Holguin said that he co-created Dark Ages Spawn with artist McCormick-Sharp and based the character on McFarlane's Spawn. He testified that he did not consider Medieval Spawn when he worked on the character. Holguin said he wanted the character of Lord Covenant to have similarities to Al Simmons, such as the fact that both were assassins, but also some differences.

Holguin said he went with the dark ages because he was a big fan of the fantasy genre and a history buff. Similarly, McCormack-Sharp, his co-creator, loved Celtic and Norse mythology.

The Parties Go Back to Court

Because of the potential liability raised by the creation of Tiffany, Domina, and Dark Ages Spawn, the parties were back into court for an evidentiary hearing in front of Senior Judge Barbara B. Crabb on June 14, 2010.[31] Gaiman appeared as the only witness for his side and McFarlane and Holguin appeared on behalf of McFarlane's side.

At the hearing, Gaiman's attorneys argued that Dark Ages Spawn, Domina and Tiffany were derivative of Medieval Spawn and Angela. In response, McFarlane's attorneys argued that Dark Ages Spawn was only derivative of the original Spawn and that Tiffany and Domina had elements similar to Angela, but those elements were generic to the comic book industry.

During his testimony, Gaiman explained his creation of Angela and the writing process behind *Spawn* issue 9. He was then shown drawings of Tiffany and Domina (from *Spawn* issue 100 and *the Spawn Bible*). Gaiman noted that they looked very similar to Angela. Gaiman pointed out that McFarlane did a lot of variant action figures of Angela in various outfits. He assumed that Tiffany and Domina were simply two more variants. He was also shown pictures of Dark Ages Spawn and assumed it was Medieval Spawn because of McFarlane's rule that there was a Spawn only once every 400 years. On cross examination, Gaiman admitted that Medieval Spawn was a derivative of Spawn and that he drew in creating the character from other works and history.

In the afternoon, Holguin, the creator of Dark Ages Spawn, took the stand. He testified about the origins of Dark Ages Spawn. He admitted that he had read *Spawn* issue 9, but was unaware of the backstory Gaiman had created. He said he did not base Dark Ages on

Medieval Spawn. He also said that he was quite a fan of Gaiman and would have loved to work with the Medieval Spawn character in any way, but stressed that was not what he was asked to do.

Then, McFarlane took the stand. He explained the history of Spawn, describing it as a love story. He testified that Dark Ages Spawn took from the original Spawn and not Medieval Spawn. He also distinguished how the visuals of Tiffany varied from the original design of Angela. For example, McFarlane testified that Tiffany had different hair, wings, and a gun, whereas Angela was wingless and had a spear. He also testified that the statement that a Spawn comes once every 400 years was neither a rule nor consistently applied because of the needs of the story or the marketing opportunities that presented themselves.[32]

After the hearing, both sides submitted briefs reiterating their positions. Gaiman argued that Dark Ages Spawn was derivative of Medieval Spawn and Tiffany and Domina were derivative of Angela and since Gaiman was the co-owner, he was entitled to a share of the profits. McFarlane argued that these characters were stock characters that were derivative of the original Spawn, which was owned solely by McFarlane. Therefore, Gaiman would be owed nothing.

On July 29, 2010, the court ruled in favor of Gaiman. The order stated:

IT IS ORDERED that plaintiff Neil Gaiman's motion for an order to compel discovery relating to the money earned from derivative characters Dark Ages (McFarlane) Spawn, Domina and Tiffany is GRANTED. Defendants Todd McFarlane, Todd McFarlane Productions, Inc. and TMP International, Inc. are to produce the requested information promptly and in no event later than September 1, 2010.

In the memorandum supporting the court's decision, Senior Judge Crabb wrote:

[McFarlane] contend[s] that these characters are not subject to plaintiff's copyright because they were based solely on plaintiff's ideas and not on any physical expression of those ideas. I conclude that the newer characters are derivative and that plaintiff is entitled to his share of the profits realized by these characters and to the immediate production of all documents and other information material to the calculation of the profits.

Specifically, the court rejected the argument that Dark Ages Spawn was merely another derivative of Spawn and not derivative of Medieval Spawn. The court found that while the differences between the two characters were sufficient to show that Dark Ages Spawn was individually copyrightable (just as Posner found with Medieval Spawn), they were not sufficient to show that Dark Agents Spawn was not derivative of Medieval Spawn.[33] The court stated:

The small differences in the two knights do not undermine a finding of derivation. Dark Ages (McFarlane) Spawn is substantially copied from Medieval (Gaiman) Spawn. It is not, as defendant claims, a simple borrowing of an idea but a borrowing of the expression of ideas of the copyright owners. It would be considered infringing if it had been developed by anyone not working for defendant.

Interestingly, the court went even further and suggested several original plot devices that would not be derivative of Medieval Spawn:

Much as defendant tries to distinguish the two knight Hellspawn, he never explains why, of all the universe of possible Hellspawn incarnations, he introduced two knights from the same century. Not only does this break the Hellspawn "rule" that Malebolgia never returns a Hellspawns [*sic*] to Earth more than once every 400 years (or possibly every 100 years, as suggested in *Spawn*, No. 9, exh. #1, at 4), it suggests that what defendant really wanted to do was exploit the possibilities of the knight introduced in issue no. 9. (This possibility is supported by the odd timing of defendant's letter to plaintiff on February 14, 1999, just before publication of the first issue of *Spawn The Dark Ages*, to the effect that defendant was rescinding their previous agreements and retaining all rights to Medieval [Gaiman] Spawn.)

If defendant really wanted to differentiate the new Hellspawn, why not make him a Portuguese explorer in the 16th century; an officer of the Royal Navy in the 18th century, an idealistic recruit of Simon Bolivar in the 19th century, a companion of Odysseus on his voyages, a Roman gladiator, a younger brother of Emperor Nakamikado in the early 18th century, a Spanish conquistador, an aristocrat in the Qing dynasty, an American Indian warrior or a member of the court of Queen Elizabeth I? It seems far more than coincidence that Dark Ages (McFarlane) Spawn is a knight from the same century as Medieval (Gaiman) Spawn.

The court next turned to Tiffany and Domina. Based on the similarities between the characters, the court determined:

> They are not identical to Angela, but substantially similar. Certainly they are similar enough to be infringing if they had been produced and sold by someone other than the copyright owners. The totality of their attributes and traits, that is, their visual appearance, their costumes, their manner of speaking, their activities and their common origin (Heaven's angelic phalanx), mark them as derivative of Angela. Domina and Tiffany capture the "total concept and feel" of Angela, and are recognizable immediately by Spawn fans as warrior angels destined to fight Hellspawn.
>
> In summary, for the same reasons that Dark Ages (McFarlane) Spawn is derivative of Medieval (Gaiman) Spawn, Domina and Tiffany are derivative of Angela. Therefore, plaintiff is entitled to an accounting of the profits earned by all three of the derivative characters.

Miracleman Activities

While the ownership of Miracleman/Marvelman was not resolved in any of the trials or hearings, there was some additional activity that bears noting. First, in April 2003, McFarlane released a Miracleman statue through McFarlane Toys. Gaiman released his own version of the statue in January 2005. On July 24, 2009, Marvel Comics announced that it had purchased Mick Anglo's copyright in Marvelman. A year later, on July 11, 2010, McFarlane attempted to register the name Miracleman in the Patent and Trademark Office. Gaiman opposed the registration.

Settlement

In January 2012, the parties finally settled their long standing dispute.[34] The terms were confidential.[35] On February 3, 2012, Judge Crabb entered final judgment in the case. It read:

> IT IS ORDERED AND ADJUDGED that judgment is entered in favor of plaintiffs and against the McFarlane defendants declaring that plaintiff Neil Gaiman is a joint 50 percent owner of the copyrights to the publications *Spawn* issues 9 and 26 and *Angela* issues 1, 2 and 3 and the content of those publications, with the respective future rights and obligations of the parties with respect hereto being resolved under the terms of their settlement agreement.
>
> IT IS FURTHER ORDERED AND ADJUDGED that judgment is entered dismissing all remaining claims and counterclaims with prejudice, the parties having waived in their

settlement agreement any right of appeal with respect to any such claims or counterclaims. All parties are to bear their own attorney fees and costs.

In 2012, Gaiman formed the Gaiman Foundation with the proceeds of the settlement. The Gaiman Foundation is described as supporting a range of causes, particularly those to do with free speech and the arts. The Gaiman Foundation is a non-profit benefit corporation founded to grant gifts to selected charitable and educational organizations that have demonstrated dedication and excellence in their respective missions.

Spawn still continues his fight against injustice in the pages of Image Comics under the guidance of Todd McFarlane.

CHAPTER 8

Trademark
An Overview

Trademark law came about as a result of the federalization of the state common law right of misappropriation. Simply put, a trademark is a word, name, device, phrase, logo, other designation or a combination of such designations that is distinctive of persons, goods or services and is used to distinguish persons, goods or services from those offered by others. Trademarks are prevalent in the modern world and consumers are surrounded by them. The role of trademark law is threefold. First, it provides incentives for merchants to create and maintain quality goods and services by protecting their trademark from free riders; second, it protects consumers who can be sure they can choose quality products and services by their trademark; and third, it prevents unfair competition and trade practices. Of course, there are some downsides to trademark law. For example, strict enforcement of trademark can act as a barrier to entry. This can partially be seen by the fact that only DC Comics and Marvel Comics have the right to use the word superhero to avoid consumer confusion. In addition, the use of trademark can be viewed as increasing the need for advertising because most consumers are drawn to the trademark and not the product. Moreover, limiting trademarks may restrict free speech and communication. This is especially true when a trademarked term becomes common in everyday vernacular (such as the Pepsi generation, an e-ticket attraction or when someone Googles themselves).

Source of Law

As described in chapter 2, the trademark law is the successor to the passing off doctrine, which prevented one merchant from taking credit for another's goods or services. And, unlike federal copyright law, in which the Copyright Act of 1976, a federal law, replaced state common law, the trademark law exists simultaneously at both state and federal levels. Due to the background nature of this chapter, it will focus on trademark law as promulgated in the Lanham Act, which is the primary federal trademark statute of law in the United States[1] and the common law of trademark.

The Lanham Act was passed on July 5, 1946, and signed by President Harry Truman a day later.[2] The effective date of the act is July 6, 1947. For disputes that occurred prior to this effective date, courts applied the state common law. Congress has updated and amended the Lanham Act several times since its enactment, but many of the basic protections and rules remain.

Items Protected by Trademark

There are several items that could qualify for trademark protection. These are referred to as marks. Traditionally, a mark has been defined as a word, name, phrase, symbol, or device or other designation or combination of such designations that is distinctive of a person's goods or services and that is used in a manner that identifies those goods or services and distinguishes them from the goods or services of another.

Technically, there is a distinction between a trademark, which is used to identify goods and products, and service marks, which are used to describe services. There is also a third type of mark called a certification mark, which relates to a word, name, phrase, symbol, or device or other designation or combination of such designations signifying that certain goods or services have certain characteristics. The owners of these certification marks allow others to use these marks if certain standards are met, such as a level of quality, a certain geographical origin, or the involvement of union workers. An example of this in the comics industry is the now-defunct Seal of the Comics Code Authority. As described more fully in chapter 20, the Comics Code Authority was formed by the Comics Magazine Association of America in an effort to self-regulate the comics industry. Members submitted comics to the Comics Code Authority to make sure that they satisfied the requirements of the Comic Book Code. If the book was acceptable, the Comics Code Authority authorized the use of their seal on the cover of the book. This seal would be considered a certification mark.[3] Finally, there is the fourth type of mark, called a collective trademark, which is used by organizations to identify their members or the fact that goods or services were made or performed by that organization. Collective trademarks differ from certification marks because collective trademarks can be used by the members of the organization which owns them, whereas certification marks may be used by anybody who complies with the standards defined by the owner of the particular certification mark. This overview chapter will refer to all of these different marks as trademarks.

Another type of trademark includes the concept of trade dress. A trade dress generally refers to characteristics of the visual appearance of a product or its packaging.[4] Basically, this rule covers a situation where the uniqueness of a product is apparent because of a unique combination of features. Taken together, this combination makes a recognizable image in the mind of the public. Trade dresses are protected under both the common law and the Lanham Act. In 1994, the United States District Court for the Southern District of New York found that the Mighty Morphin Power Rangers were protected as a trade dress. The Power Rangers were made up of several costumed action heroes, each represented by a color, that have power zords that morphed into a single giant robot. When 222 World Corp, and others,[5] sold similar items, Sabaan, the owner of the Power Rangers' intellectual property rights, sued for infringement. In granting an injunction, the court found that the trade dress of the Power Rangers was inherently distinctive and that "Trade dress involves the total image of a product and may include features such as size, shape, color, or color combinations, texture, graphics, or even particular sales techniques." As a result, trade dress can be registered if it is distinctive and nonfunctional.[6] This means characters can be trademarked.

Requirement for Distinctiveness

As described above, marks can take many forms. Words and terms are the most common type of marks. That being said, a mark can also be made up of symbols or numbers or a combination of all of the above. Slogans are considered protected marks under the trademark law. Drawings are also considered to be marks as well. In addition, packaging, trade dress, and colors of the product can also serve as a mark. So, although there are many types of marks, there is one key requirement before protection will be provided under the trademark law.

This key requirement to achieve trademark status is distinctiveness. Unless a mark has distinctiveness it will not be given trademark protection. Distinctiveness is measured by classifying the mark into one of four groups: (1) arbitrary/fanciful marks; (2) suggestive marks; (3) descriptive marks; and (4) generic words or symbols. Marks falling into the first two categories (arbitrary/fanciful marks and suggestive marks) are automatically considered distinctive. Marks in the third category, descriptive marks, are not judged to be inherently distinctive. However, if the owner of the mark can demonstrate that the descriptive term has achieved distinctiveness through its use in commerce so as to achieve a secondary meaning, then the mark can be eligible for a protected trademark. The fourth category, generic marks, are incapable of being distinctive and therefore are not eligible for copyright protection. Each will be discussed in turn.

The first category, arbitrary and fanciful marks, are always considered to be distinctive. An arbitrary mark refers to a term that has meaning but is not descriptive of the product or service. For example, a comics publisher with the name Vertigo[7] can trademark the name as an arbitrary mark. Similarly, Diamond qualifies for an arbitrary mark for a comic book distributor. A fanciful mark, unlike an arbitrary mark, has no meaning at all other than the company. Keeping with the company name theme here, Markosia is a fictitious name based on the name of its founder, Harry Markos. Markosia would be considered a fanciful mark. The same would apply to the word Google. Neither of these words has a plain English meaning. All arbitrary or fanciful marks are considered distinctive. The same would hold true for the former publisher known as Crossgen.

The second category is a suggestive mark. A suggestive mark provides an indirect description of the product or service to which it refers. This means that there needs to be some work on the part of the consumer to figure out the connection. A good example of this kind of a name would be the Canadian publisher Drawn and Quarterly or Timely comics. It takes extra thought to realize the connection between the name and the comics industry. Like the first category, suggestive marks are inherently distinctive.

The third category of marks is descriptive marks. These marks directly describe the products or services.[8] These types of marks include several types: (1) those that appear to describe the type of product they identify (Quality Comics); (2) those that appear to describe the geographic location from which the product comes (Texas Comics); and (3) those that are a person's surname (Harvey Comics). These are generally not considered distinctive unless they have acquired secondary meaning.[9] The policy reasoning behind this is that other companies in the same business should be able to use these same marks to describe their goods or services. If protection were permitted for these terms, then the first person who enters the market could prevent others from competing. Different spellings of common words will not save the mark. So, naming a comic book company reallygudcomix will not make the mark any more acceptable.

The fourth category is generic terms. A generic term is a word or symbol that is the common descriptive name of the product. In short, a synonym for the product or service. For example, a generic term would be to call a comic company Comics. The generic term can never serve as a valid mark under trademark law. The way to determine whether a term is generic is whether the primary significance of the term, when looked at through the eyes of the public: (1) is the common name for a class of service or products or (2) is the indicator of origin. The flip side of this category is the fact that some formerly trademarked names have become generic over time as a result of common use in the marketplace.[10] Examples would include kerosene, yo-yo, pogo stick, Phillips head screwdriver, zipper, heroin, thermos, trampoline, and aspirin. Ironically, the companies that have spent the most making their products a household name lost the right to hold the trademark when the terms grew so popular they became generic terms.[11]

Finally, the Lanham Act also lists several marks that are precluded from registration. Such a mark

> (a) Consists of or comprises immoral, deceptive, or scandalous matter; or matter which may disparage or falsely suggest a connection with persons, living or dead, institutions, beliefs, or national symbols, or bring them into contempt, or disrepute; or a geographical indication which, when used on or in connection with wines or spirits, identifies a place other than the origin of the goods....
>
> (b) Consists of or comprises the flag or coat of arms or other insignia of the United States, or of any State or municipality, or of any foreign nation, or any simulation thereof.
>
> (c) Consists of or comprises a name, portrait, or signature identifying a particular living individual except by his written consent, or the name, signature, or portrait of a deceased President of the United States during the life of his widow, if any, except by the written consent of the widow.
>
> (d) Consists of or comprises a mark which so resembles a mark registered in the Patent and Trademark Office, or a mark or trade name previously used in the United States by another and not abandoned, as to be likely, when used on or in connection with the goods of the applicant, to cause confusion, or to cause mistake, or to deceive: [unless certain exceptions apply].
>
> (e) Consists of a mark which (1) when used on or in connection with the goods of the applicant is merely descriptive or deceptively misdescriptive of them, (2) when used on or in connection with the goods of the applicant is primarily geographically descriptive of them, except as indications of regional origin may be registrable [under the statute] when used on or in connection with the goods of the applicant is primarily geographically deceptively misdescriptive of them, (4) is primarily merely a surname, or (5) comprises any matter that, as a whole, is functional.

Categories (a) and (e) refer to misdescriptive terms. Category (a) refers to deceptive marks, which can never be registered or enforced in any circumstances. And Category (e) refers to deceptively misdescriptive marks, which may be registered upon a showing of secondary meaning. To determine whether a mark is deceptive or deceptively misdescriptive, courts will look at the misrepresented fact to see whether it would be believed by the consumer or influence their buying decision. For example, a company that produces shrink-wrapped black and white books and calls themselves Full Color Comics would fit into this category.

Category (d) above refers to previously used marks. This is similar to the common law, in cases where courts would not enforce the use of a mark confusingly similar[12] to previous used marks. The reasoning behind this is common sense. Two companies should not be able to use the same mark to identify the same or similar products.

Obtaining Trademark

In the United States, the method by which a merchant obtains trademark protection is more complex than in other areas of intellectual property law. This complexity arises from the fact that federal trademark law (statutory law in the Lanham Act) runs concurrent with state law (the common law developed through cases). Trademark protection can be obtained through either type of trademark law, or under both federal and state law.

In addition, many states have passed statutes that mirror the Lanham Act. The United States Patent and Trademark Office provides the following list of states with trademark laws and a link to where further information can be found.[13]

State	Website Address
Alabama	http://www.sos.alabama.gov/BusinessServices/Trademarks.aspx
Alaska	http://www.commerce.state.ak.us/occ/tmark.htm
Arizona	http://www.azsos.gov/business_services/tnt/
Arkansas	http://www.sos.arkansas.gov/BCS/Pages/default.aspx
California	http://www.sos.ca.gov/business/ts/ts.htm
Colorado	http://www.sos.state.co.us/pubs/business/forms_main.html#Trademarks
Connecticut	http://www.sots.ct.gov/sots/cwp/view.asp?a=3177&q=392124&SOTS Nav_GID=1844#trade
Delaware	http://corp.delaware.gov/trademark.shtml
District of Columbia	Use of a mark solely within the District of Columbia qualifies for federal registration. There is no D.C. trademark law. The District's trade name registry can be found at: http://brc.dc.gov/planning/requirements/tradename.asp
Florida	http://form.sunbiz.org/cor_t.html
Georgia	http://sos.georgia.gov/corporations/trademarks.htm
Hawaii	http://hawaii.gov/dcca/areas/breg/registration/trade/
Idaho	http://www.sos.idaho.gov/tmarks/tmindex.htm
Illinois	http://www.cyberdriveillinois.com/publications/business_services/trademark.html
Indiana	http://www.in.gov/apps/sos/trademarks/
Iowa	http://sos.iowa.gov/business/FormsAndFees.html#TradeServiceMarks
Kansas	http://www.kssos.org/resources/resources_faq_trademark.html

State	Website Address
Kentucky	http://sos.ky.gov/business/trademarks/
Louisiana	http://www.sos.louisiana.gov/tabid/500/Default.aspx
	Application for Registration of Mark (PDF 42kb):
	http://www.sos.louisiana.gov/Portals/0/309TradeNameTradeMark
	andServiceMarkRegistration.pdf
Maine	http://www.maine.gov/sos/cec/corp/trademarks.html
Maryland	http://www.sos.state.md.us/registrations/trademarks/Trademarks.aspx
Massachusetts	http://www.sec.state.ma.us/cor/corpweb/cortmsm/tmsmfrm.htm
Michigan	http://www.michigan.gov/dleg/0,1607,7-154-35299_35413_35431---,
	00.html
Minnesota	http://www.sos.state.mn.us/home/index.asp?page=18&dc_id=101
Mississippi	http://www.sos.ms.gov/business_services_trademarks.aspx
Missouri	http://www.sos.mo.gov/business/trademark.asp
Montana	http://sos.mt.gov/business/Trademark/index.asp
Nebraska	http://www.sos.ne.gov/business/corp_serv/corp_form.html
Nevada	http://nvsos.gov/index.aspx?page=246
New Hampshire	http://www.sos.nh.gov/corporate/trademarkleader.htm
New Jersey	http://www.state.nj.us/treasury/revenue/dcr/geninfo/corpman.
	shtml#TMSM
New Mexico	http://www.sos.state.nm.us/sos-Trademarks.html
New York	http://www.nysl.nysed.gov/tradmark.htm
North Carolina	http://www.secretary.state.nc.us/trademrk/
North Dakota	http://www.nd.gov/sos/businessserv/registrations/trademark.html
Ohio	http://www.sos.state.oh.us/SOS/Businesses/businessServices.aspx
Oklahoma	https://www.sos.ok.gov/trademarks/default.aspx
Oregon	http://sos.oregon.gov/business/pages/business-registration-forms.aspx
	Oregon Trade and Service Mark law: http://www.leg.state.or.us/ors/
	647.html
Pennsylvania	http://www.dos.state.pa.us/corps/cwp/view.asp?a=1093&q=431231
Rhode Island	http://www.sec.state.ri.us/corps/trademark/trademark.html
South Carolina	http://www.scsos.com/Library_of_Forms_and_Fees#Trademarks
South Dakota	http://sdsos.gov/content/viewcontent.aspx?cat=corporations&pg=/
	corporations/trademark.shtm
Tennessee	http://tennessee.gov/sos/bus_svc/trademarks.htm
Texas	http://www.sos.state.tx.us/corp/trademark.shtml
Utah	http://corporations.utah.gov/business/tm.html
Vermont	http://www.sec.state.vt.us/corps/tmkhome.htm
Virginia	http://www.scc.virginia.gov/srf/bus/tmsm.aspx
Washington	http://www.sos.wa.gov/corps/Trademarks.aspx
West Virginia	http://www.sos.wv.gov/business-licensing/trademarkservicemarks/Pages/
	default.aspx
Wisconsin	http://www.sos.state.wi.us/trademark.htm
Wyoming	http://soswy.state.wy.us/Forms/FormsFiling.aspx?startwith=Business
	Wyoming Trademark and Service Mark Law: http://legisweb.state.
	wy.us/statutes/statutes.aspx?file=titles/Title40/T40CH1.htm
Puerto Rico	http://www.estado.gobierno.pr/ (in Spanish)

Whether protection is sought under the Lanham Act or the state common law, a prerequisite for trademark is the requirement of use. The most important requirement in obtaining trademark is that a merchant must be the first to use the mark in trade and then continue to use it on a regular basis thereafter in achieving sale to the general public. Courts have varied on just how much use is sufficient. Some courts have found that a single use is sufficient so long as it is ongoing and systematic. Other courts have found the use to be sufficient only when it is pervasive enough to notify competitors of the product. Still other courts have held that use requires that a product obtain sufficient market penetration so that there would be market confusion if someone else were to use the mark. What is clear from the cases is that a merchant that places its mark on their goods (either through labelling or packaging of its goods) and then sells those goods to the public should be able to prove use under both the Lanham Act and the state common law.

Obtaining State Common Law Protection

At common law, a merchant could not receive protection for a mark unless that merchant has begun to associate that mark with goods or services. Only active use allows consumers to associate the mark with the product. This would also provide notice to competitors that the mark is associated with the merchant's product. In short, a merchant uses his or her mark to educate consumers and build good will towards the product. If two merchants decide to use the same mark at the same time, then the court will grant trademark protection to the senior user (i.e., the one who used it first). In these circumstances, it is important to determine who used the mark first. For this purpose, token uses are insufficient. Instead, the mark must travel with the goods, meaning that: (1) the mark must directed to the goods or services for which trademark protection is sought[14]; and (2) the type and scope of the use must be reasonable, substantial and in the ordinary course of trade. This means that use of the mark cannot be on samples, but directed to the products intended to be sold to the public. In other words, courts look to sales to the public to see who used the mark first. To put this in the comic book context, a low print run of a book sent to prospective publishers and friends for editorial comment would probably not be sufficient to generate trademark protection. However, if the book were listed for sale with a small press publisher, sold at shows, and sold on consignment in comic shops, it would be eligible for protection under the common law.

Obtaining Federal Trademark Protection
through Registration

While ownership of the mark arises automatically under the common law when the mark is used in trade and requires no registration to claim trademark, federal protection for trademark is based on a registration system. And while registration is completely optional, as more fully described below, there are advantages to federal registration. First, federal registration guarantees trademark protection in all of the United States, including areas where the product is not sold, which is greater than the protection provided under common law. Second, federal registration permits users to use the Trademark Symbol (®). This puts potential infringers on notice that the mark is protected. Third, registration allows the merchant to obtain assistance from the United States Customs Service in preventing the importation of infringing products. Fourth, as discussed below, registration creates a presumption of ownership in lawsuits and, after five years of registration, will prevent certain challenges from being made against the mark. Fifth, registration protects against dilution claims.[15] Sixth, federal registration means that the claims will be heard in the United States District Courts. And seventh, federal registration can be used as a basis for obtaining registration in foreign countries. Given the importance of registration, it is important to understand how to register a mark. Under current law, there are two alternative ways in which to apply for registration of a mark: (1) Use Applications and (2) Intent to Use Applications.[16]

Use Applications Procedures

Under the Use Application procedure, a person who has used the mark in trade of interstate commerce may apply to register by filing application papers with the United States Patent and Trademark Office. Under the statute, the concept of use is defined as "the bona fide use of a mark in the ordinary course of trade, and not made merely to reserve a right in a mark."[17] This change was made to eliminate token use, which is the common law view.[18] However, there is a major distinction from the state common law. Because the Lanham Act gets its power from the Commerce Clause of the United States Constitution, the federal law use requirement for registration requires the mark be used in commerce.

The procedures for registration of a Use Application are fairly straightforward.[19] The first step is to fill out an application with the Patent and Trademark Office. This form is short and merely requires disclosure of the mark and the categories of goods in which the mark has been used. The applicant must also swear that he or she (or it in the case of corporate registrants) knows of no one with a superior right to use the mark in question.[20] An applicant must also submit a drawing of the mark to be registered[21] and specimens of use of the mark to show how it is actually being used in commerce. As of the writing of this book, the filing fees[22] for a trademark application were:

- $325 per class for an application filed electronically using the Trademark Electronic Application System (TEAS);
- $275 per class for a TEAS Plus application[23]; or
- $375 per class for an application filed on paper.

Once the application is complete, it will be assigned to a Trademark Examining Attorney, who will review the application to determine if registration is proper. During the examination process, the examiner will communicate questions to the applicant in writing through what is referred to as an Office Action. Once an Office Action is issued, an applicant has six months to respond. If the applicant cannot convince the examiner that the problem raised would not interfere with registration, the applicant has the right to amend the application to cure the defect.

If the examiner determines that the mark is not eligible for trademark registration, the applicant will receive a notice of final denial. At that point, the applicant may appeal the examiner's decision to the Trademark Trials and Appeals Board. In the proceeding that follows, the Trademark Examining Attorney will explain why the trademark was rejected and the applicant can argue its case for registration. Once the Trademark Trials and Appeals

Board decides, the case is appealable, by the unsuccessful party, to the United States Court of Appeals for the Federal Circuit.

If the examiner determines that the mark deserves to be registered or the applicant prevails in the Trademark Trials and Appeals Board, the proposed mark will be published in the *Official Gazette of the Patent and Trademark Office*, a periodical that lists marks seeking trademark approval. The purpose of the *Official Gazette of the Patent and Trademark Office* is to allow the public to come forward and make objection to pending registrations. If someone wishes to object to the approval of a mark, they have thirty days to file an objection, officially referred to as an Opposition.

If an Opposition is filed, the matter will be referred to the Trademark Trials and Appeals Board. The opposing party will be allowed to explain why it believes the mark should not be allowed to be registered, and then the applicant will have a chance to respond. Based on these arguments, the Trademark Trials and Appeals Board will render its decision. The unsuccessful party may appeal the ruling to the United States Court of Appeals for the Federal Circuit.

If no Opposition is filed, or if the applicant successfully defeats an Opposition challenge in the Trademark Trials and Appeals Board, the registration process is considered complete and the Patent and Trademark Office will issue a registration certificate, which is good for ten years. An applicant may renew the registration certificate an unlimited number of times provided that the mark is still being used.[24]

Intent to Use Application Procedures

While the Use Application procedure is effective for merchants using marks, it certainly has some drawbacks. For example, some companies spend an enormous amount of money developing their marks and even more money to advertise them. Yet, these companies may find that before they use the mark, another company is already using the mark. As a result of this concern, the trademark law was changed in 1989 to allow for Intent to Use applications. This provision provides for an alternate registration method, which allows an applicant, who is not currently using a mark, to file application papers with the Patent and Trademark office setting forth the applicant's bona fide intention to use the mark for trade and interstate commerce.[25]

The application materials and examination process are substantially similar to the procedure listed above for the Use Application. However, there are some differences. Obviously, an Intent to Use Application need not provide any specimens of how the mark is being used. In addition, when an application is filed based on a bona fide intent to use the mark in commerce, additional documents and fees will be required at a later time.[26] If no Oppositions are filed, or if an Opposition is filed and the applicant prevails, the Intent to Use applicant will receive a Notice of Allowance. Within six months of receiving the Notice of Allowance, the applicant must begin using the mark.[27] After the applicant begins using the mark, the applicant must file a Statement of Use with the Patent and Trademark Office (along with $100 fee per class). Only after the applicant submits the Statement of Use will the federal trademark registration be issued. If the mark is never used, there can be no trademark protection. What this means is that, despite the fact that an application can be filed before use, obtaining trademark protection ultimately requires use. In essence, the Intent to Use process allows the applicant to reserve trademarks while they get their product to market. In the event someone else uses the same mark after the registration date, but before the use date, the applicant will have priority over the infringing competitor.

Trademark Rights

As described above, federal and state law concurrently protect trademark rights. As a result, it is necessary to look at the rights under both the state common law and the federal statute. Each will be addressed separately.

Under state common law, trademark protection provides the trademark holder the ability to prevent others from using the same mark, or a similar mark, in such a way that creates a likelihood of confusion. This trademark protection does not extend beyond the market in which the trademark owner's products are sold or in which the mark is known. Similarly, the protection does not extend into geographical areas where the trademark owner's mark is not known.[28] This means that a later user of the mark after the trademark owner might actually be able to continue to use the identical mark if the later user shows (1) that he or she used the mark in good faith (e.g., without knowledge of the trademark owner's use of the mark) and (2) that he or she operates in a remote geographical area. For example, assume that Samantha creates and sells a superheroine comic with the trademarked name *Argent* in Ravenscroft, North Carolina, in 1994. In 1996, Toni creates a superheroine comic with the trademarked name *Argent* in Metropolis, Illinois, a geographically remote location from Ravenscroft, North Carolina. So long as Toni acted in good faith, Samantha will not have a common law infringement claim against Toni. Samantha was not selling in Illinois so there is no likelihood of consumer confusion. In fact, if Samantha wanted to release her *Argent* book in Metropolis, Toni could block the sale as infringing on her copyright, even though she came later. Note, given the countrywide notice assumed under the federal statute, if Samantha had registered *Argent*, she would have a claim against Toni, even though she had never sold in Metropolis.

Under the federal statute, a trademark holder has all of the rights under the common law as well as some additional protections. First, registration provides prima facie evidence of the registered mark's ownership and validity during litigation.[29] This is a fancy way of saying that the owner will be considered the owner unless someone can prove that they aren't. Second, under the federal law, there is nationwide constructive notice of the mark as of the filing date of the application, which means that the scope is broader than the common law. Third, federal registration provides nationwide constructive use as of the date of the application.[30] Fourth, a federally valid trademark is protected against the importation of infringing goods, which means that the owner can ask the United States Custom Service to block imports of foreign goods that bear the registered trademark. Fifth, only federally registered marks may bear the trademark symbol, the letter R inside a circle ("®"), which provides notice to the public and other merchants that the mark is protected, which is the equivalent of putting a security alarm sign in the window of a car to deter theft.

Infringement

One of the primary rights of a trademark owner is to prevent his goods and services from being confused with others. In other words, a trademark owner prevents their own trade from being diverted to competitors through the use of similar marks. This is called infringement. As a result, the crucial question to ask when assessing the possibility of infringement is whether there is any likelihood that an appreciable number of average consumers would be misled or confused as to the source of the good in question.[31]

There are numerous tests to apply to determine the likelihood of consumer confusion. The leading tests involve eight factors[32]: (1) the strength of the mark; (2) the degree of similarity between the original mark and the potentially infringing mark; (3) the proximity of the products; (4) the likelihood that the prior owner will bridge the gap; (5) actual confusion; (6) good faith; (7) quality of the product with the infringing mark; and (8) the sophistication of the buyers. Of course, a side by side comparison between the two marks is not appropriate because it is highly doubtful that a customer will see the items side by side. Instead, the courts will look more generally to gauge whether the consumer is confused. For example, a product named Tornado was found to be infringed by a product named Cyclone.

The first factor is the strength of the trademark. Put simply, the more recognizable the trademark, the more likely it is that members of the public will be confused. For example, Batgirl is much more recognizable than Sky Girl.[33] Therefore it is more likely that someone would be confused by two heroines named Batgirl than two heroines named Sky Girl. The strong, highly recognizable Batgirl trademark will obtain broader protection than the lesser known Sky Girl trademark.

The second factor is the degree of similarity of the two trademarks. Courts will look at the sight, sound and meaning of the two marks when comparing the two trademarks. In the sound test, the spelling of the trademark doesn't matter. For example, a creator who creates a book named *Axshun Comix* that stars a character named Sooperman would still be liable to DC Comics, the holder of the *Action Comics* and Superman trademarks. In the sight test, the similarity in visual appearance between the two marks is measured. For example, if a character named Sam has an S symbol in a triangle as his trademarked symbol, it is highly likely that a court would find infringement of the DC Comics trademarked Superman symbol. The meaning test looks at whether the two marks convey the same expression. For example, and keeping with the Superman example, the following titles may be infringing: Superdude, Superguy, or SuperiorMan.

The third factor is the proximity of the two products. Historically, this was the most important factor as trademark protection extended only to competing goods in the same industry and, in early decisions, courts would not block trademarks if they were on goods not offered by the original owner. Today, the courts will extend the reach of the trademark protection to goods and services other than those to which the owner has applied the mark.

The general rule looks at whether the consumer would confuse the two merchants. For example, if the goods are in the same section of a store or marketed to the same demographic in the same types of media, the likelihood of infringement is increased. It may help to examine the facts of a real case involving a comic book trademark applied outside of comics. As readers know, Kryptonite is a green meteorite created by the destruction of the planet Krypton and is one of the only substances that can weaken Superman. DC Comics owns the copyright to the word Kryptonite. Ingersoll-Rand Kryptonite Corp., a lock company, attempted to patent and trademark Kryptonite Locks.[34] In July 2000, DC Comics sued Ingersoll alleging infringement, unfair competition and dilution[35] of the trademark and state law claims that Ingersoll was using the word Kryptonite to confuse consumers into believing there was a connection between its products and Superman. Judge Richard Owen of the Southern District of New York determined that the word Kryptonite was a protectable symbol under the Lanham Act. Ingersoll argued that there was no actual confusion between the products because they were in different industries. The court rejected this argument and set the matter for trial to determine whether there was a likelihood of confusion at the consumer level between goods of a manufacturer of bicycle locks and accessories and goods of a comic book publisher. A joint stipulation of dismissal was filed on March 23, 2006, before the case could be tried.

The fourth factor is the likelihood that the trademark owner will bridge the gap between the industries. This comes into play when the goods and services are not directly competitive. The courts will look at whether the owner may sell goods in the new industry at a later date. There need be no existing plans to expand into that market. For example, it is completely foreseeable that the trademarked logo of a comic book character would be placed on mugs, t-shirts, and other similar products and therefore the court would consider this when examining whether there is infringement.

The fifth factor is actual confusion. This occurs when an owner can prove that customers were confused between the two trademarks. Evidence of this could include complaints or correspondence sent to a comic company about another character because there are similarities between that character and the trademarked character owned by the comic company. The more confusion, the more likely a finding of infringement.

The sixth factor is the good faith of the accused infringer. In this, the court will look at whether that party intended to capitalize on the trademark owner's trademark. Intent is not necessary for trademark infringement; innocent infringement is still infringement. This is something more; it's the situation where someone knows they are infringing.

The seventh factor is the quality of the infringing goods.[36] If the accused infringer uses the trademark on goods of lesser quality than the original goods, then it is more likely that the use of the mark on the goods will be considered infringement. This is because the substandard goods would hurt the original owner's reputation.

The eighth, and final, factor is the sophistication of the buyer. Basically, the smarter the buyer, the less likely it is that they will be confused. Similarly, if the cost of the goods is higher, then courts reason that it is more likely that people will take time to closely examine the goods and it would be less likely that they would be confused.

Fair Use

Fair use is a defense against infringing registered marks, including those that are incontestable. The concept of fair use is the same under state and federal law. Fair use occurs when the trademark is used fairly and in good faith only to describe the goods and service that are covered by the trademark. In essence, trademark doesn't provide owners with the right to prohibit all use of the trademark.[37] When looking at fair use, courts first apply the infringement factors, then, after determining that infringement has occurred, the court will look at the following three factors to determine whether there is fair use. First, does the accused infringer use the trademark only to describe the product or services or do they go further and display the mark as if they owned it? Second, is the alleged infringer using the trademark in good faith or are they trying to take advantage of the mark's popularity? Third, are members of the public likely to be confused by the potential infringer's use of the mark? For example, if someone were to write a hypothetical book on comic book law and that book were to use the trademarks of several comic companies in an effort to provide examples of how those trademarks are protected, that would be considered fair use since no one is likely to think the author owns those marks. Fair use arises in three contexts: (1) parody cases; (2) comparative advertising cases; and (3) reconditioned goods cases. As can be seen, each of these uses is collateral to the main use of the product. Of course, given that this book focuses on comic book law, it will only focus on the parody and comparative advertising as the matter of reconditioned goods is not likely to arise in the comic book context.

As can be seen in music, movies, comics, and television, there is certainly a market for products that humorously spoof recognized trademarks. As can be guessed, the original owner of the trademark may not like to be mocked and sometimes brings suits for infringement against these parodies. In these cases, courts will examine the facts and circumstances using the standards described above. While parody by its nature relies on the recognition and success of the original trademark, it does not create brand confusion. It is the differences that create the humor.

For an example of parody in comic books, one need look no further than the comic master of parody, *Mad Magazine*. *Mad* premiered as a comic in August 1952 from EC Comics and has been lampooning pop culture since its debut. Over the course of the magazine's history the comic, and later the magazine, has been involved in numerous lawsuits and threats of lawsuits. For example, when SuperDuperMan appeared in issue 4 of the comic, DC Comics threatened, but never filed, a suit for trademark infringement. In 1961, however, a group of music publishers, representing songwriters such as Irving Berlin, Richard Rodgers and Cole Porter, did sue the publisher claiming $25 million in infringement damages as a result of parody versions of 25 songs contained in a "Sing Along with *Mad*" segment. In 1963, Judge Charles Metzner of the U.S. District Court for the Southern District of New York ruled on motion in *Mad*'s favor for 23 of the 25 songs and held they were parodies. However, the court believed that two of the songs, "Always" and "There's No Business Like No Business," were a closer call and required a trial because they relied on the same verbal hooks as the originals ("Always" and "There's No Business Like Show Business"). On appeal, the United States Court of Appeals for the Second Circuit not only affirmed *Mad*'s right to publish the

23 songs, but also ruled for *Mad* on the remaining two songs. Circuit Judge Irving Kaufman wrote, "We doubt that even so eminent a composer as plaintiff Irving Berlin should be permitted to claim a property interest in iambic pentameter."[38]

A second context for which fair use of trademark comes up is with comparative advertising. Simply put, the best way to describe a product is by using a more established product. As a result, the general rule is that a person can refer to a trademark of a competitor without trademark infringement so long as the statements and the comparisons are true.

In addition to the three classic examples of fair use, the concept of nominative fair use is also important to a comic creator. Nominative fair use comes into play when someone wants to use the mark without authorization for a commercial purpose that would not capitalize on market confusion. The Ninth Circuit Court of Appeals, in *New Kids on the Block v. News America Publishing, Inc.*, has held that allowable nominative fair use occurs if: (1) the unauthorized user's product is readily identifiable with the use of the trademark; (2) The unauthorized user only uses so much of the mark as to identify the product; (3) the unauthorized user does nothing else that would suggest sponsorship or endorsement of its product by the original trademark holder. For example, assume that Chris was hired as a freelance writer on a comic with the trademarked name *M-Dudes*. His run generates a fan base before Chris leaves the title over creative differences. Chris would be allowed to identify himself on his website, his promotional material, and on a sign at comic conventions as "Chris, writer of *M-Dudes*."[39] As will be seen in the Ghost Rider case in chapter 13, Chris could not, however, photocopy the cover of *M-Dudes* issue 1, sign the copies, and sell them.

Abandonment

An additional defense against trademark infringement is that the owner of the trademark has abandoned it. Under federal trademark law, there are two ways to abandon a mark. First, a mark will be deemed abandoned when the owner of the mark discontinues the use of the trademark and has no intent to resume the use of the trademark in the foreseeable future. Under current law, failure to use a mark for three consecutive years is prima facie evidence of an intent to abandon.[40] For example, when Fawcett lost their lawsuit to DC Comics, the company stopped selling *Captain Marvel* comics. As a result, it abandoned the trademark, which ultimately ended up with Marvel Comics. As a result, when DC Comics ultimately acquired the rights to the Captain Marvel character, they could not call the book *Captain Marvel* because the trademark belonged to Marvel.[41] The second way to a cause a mark to be abandoned is through act or omission that causes the mark to lose its significance as a mark. This can occur if a vendor does not take adequate steps to protect their mark after it is assigned.

Damages for Violation of Trademark

The federal trademark law imposes several types of damages against infringers. These range from stopping future use of the trademark, to reimbursement of actual losses caused by the infringement to even a taking of all the profits of the infringer.

First, the owner of a trademark can move for an injunction against future infringement. Basically, the infringer will no longer be able to use the trademark. Injunctions are regularly granted in trademark cases. In some cases, courts will issue a qualified injunction, which will usually require the second user to issue a disclaimer that they are unrelated to the holder of the trademark. For example, assume that Sam Marvel wants to create a comic and call it *Marvel's Comics*. It is likely that the consumers will confuse Sam's book with that of Marvel Comics, a longtime trademark. In this case, a court may require that Sam print a disclaimer that his book is unaffiliated with the Marvel Comics brand. This is especially true if the infringement is innocent and there is no likelihood of confusion. For example, assume that *Marvel's Comics* makes a single product that is distributed solely to the five employees in Sam's office. As there can be no confusion, the court would likely limit the use of *Marvel's Comics* to this limited purpose (since it is his surname). In other cases, the trademark owner can move to have a permanent injunction imposed, which would preclude the use of the mark forever by the infringer. In order to obtain a permanent injunction, a trademark owner must show (1) it has suffered an irreparable harm; (2) the remedies at law are inadequate to compensate from the injury; (3) equity is warranted when the court balances the hardships between the infringer and the owner of the trademark; and (4) the public interest would not be harmed by issuance of a permanent injunction. The federal trademark law also allows for the destruction of the infringing items. The trademark statute specifically provides courts with the power to issue orders calling for the destruction of goods, advertisement, packaging, and other depiction of the trademarked property.

Second, the trademark law allows for the imposition of monetary damages against an infringer. Both the common law and the federal rely on two possible measures of damages. First, the owner can collect the actual damages suffered because of the infringement of the original mark. In order to obtain actual damages, the owner must show, in court, that but for the infringer's wrongful use of the trademark, the owner would have achieved a specific amount of sales. This could be difficult to prove given that most trademark infringement results in reputational harm, which is hard to quantify.[42] As a result, there is a second category of damages whereby the trademark owner can collect the profits earned by the infringer as a result of the infringement. In this situation, the trademark owner would only need to put forward evidence of the infringer's sales. Then the burden of proof shifts to the infringer to show that they had expenses or costs that would have reduced those sales figures.[43] Of course, courts differ on what measure should be used in each situation. For example, some courts limit the availability of the second calculation (the infringer's profits) to cases where the trademark violation was willful, while other courts routinely allow damages to be calculated under either method. As a general matter, courts are hesitant to issue any damages if the infringer has acted in good faith.[44] Finally, the federal trademark law allows for the imposition of attorney's fees in a reasonable amount in cases when there is willful or bad faith conduct.

One final topic should be discussed related to damages. This occurs in the case where the owner of the trademark does not adequately display the designations related to the trademark.[45] In this situation, damages will not be awarded unless the owner can prove that the infringer had actual notice of the registration.

Dilution

Up until now, the discussion of trademark infringement has been focused on whether there is a likelihood of confusion between the trademark owner and the infringer. Dilution is a cause of action[46] that extends trademark protection beyond the likelihood of confusion standard. Dilution is based on the theory that the continued use of an infringing mark on noncompeting goods may erode the original trademark. The dilution cause of action eliminates the requirements of competition and confusion and allows a trademark owner to enforce the mark against a wide range of products and services even if the owner is not active in those markets.[47] As a result of free speech concerns under the First Amendment, several types of activities are exempt from liabilities under the dilution cause of action: (1) fair use of a trademark by another person in comparative commercial advertising or promotion to identify the competing goods or services of the owner of the trademark; (2) noncommercial use of the trademark; and (3) all forms of news reporting and news commentary.

Dilution is a controversial doctrine and not always applied by the courts. It should be noted that courts would be more likely to find a cause of action for dilution if there has been tarnishment. Tarnishment arises when the infringer's use of the same, or similar, mark associates the trademark owner with illegal or unwholesome activities. For example, if the name of a wholesome comic book icon of truth and justice were to be depicted on products sold in the adult entertainment industry, there would certainly be an argument for dilution.

Trademark on the Word Superhero

No discussion of comic trademark and comic books would be complete without a discussion of the word superhero. The word superhero has appeared as early as 1917.[48] However, on April 12, 1966, DC Comics and Marvel Comics jointly trademarked the term super heroes along with its variations as a registered typography-independent "descriptive" trademark. These trademarks have been renewed several times.[49]

What this means is that comic book creators cannot include the word superhero as part of their title. Of course, this does not limit a creator from using the word superhero inside the book, merely within the title.

Both DC Comics and Marvel Comics have diligently defended their super hero trademark. In every case but one, DC Comics and Marvel Comics have managed to protect their trademark.[50] For example, the comic *Superhero Happy Hour* was changed to *Hero Happy Hour* after a cease and desist letter. Similarly, Ray Felix, founder of the Bronx Heroes Con, created a comic called *A World Without Superheroes*. In September 2010, Marvel Comics and DC Comics sent him a cease and desist letter after he registered a trademark *Cup O Java Studio Comix a World Without Superheroes*. (U.S. Trademark Serial No. 85098521). In March 2012, DC Comics and Marvel Comics filed a formal opposition with the Trademark Trial and Appeal Board. According to the U.S. Patent and Trademark Office, this mark was abandoned on June 16, 2014.

CHAPTER 9

What's in a Name?
Stan Lee v. Stan Lee Media v. Marvel Comics

Stanley Martin Lieber was born on December 28, 1922. He graduated from DeWitt Clinton High School in 1939 at the age of 16. Lieber loved to write. Growing up, he had part time jobs writing obituaries for a local paper, press release articles for the National Tuberculosis Center, and plays for the WPA Federal Theatre Project before finally getting a job as an editorial assistant at Timely Comics in 1939.

In May of 1941, Lieber released his first comic story—"Captain America Foils the Traitor's Revenge," a text filler in *Captain America Comics* issue 3, in May 1941.[1] In the story, Captain America and Bucky fight to stop a dishonorably discharged soldier from taking revenge against Army Colonel Stevens. This story is best remembered as the first time that Captain America performed his signature ricocheting shield-toss.

But, Lieber also had a dream. He was going to write the great American novel. Because of this, he was very careful to protect his name and didn't want to waste his real name on silly kids' things like comics. That's why, when Lieber published his first comic story, he used a pseudonym.

The name he chose was Stan Lee.

Stan Lee continued to write comics through the 1940s and 1950s. During that period, Lee helped create several comic-book characters such as The Witness, The Destroyer, Jack Frost, Whizzer, and Black Marvel. And while he never left Timely, the company's name would change from Timely Comics to Atlas Comics and from Atlas Comics to Marvel Comics. Lee would rise in the ranks. He became an editor in 1942. By the late 1950s, however, Lee was dissatisfied with the comics medium and looking to change careers.

The Marvel Age of Comics

At the time, DC Comics, Marvel Comics' competitor, had reinvented many of its classic superhero characters, including the Flash and Green Lantern, and was having great success with a team book starring the Justice League of America. In response, Lee was assigned to create a team book for Marvel Comics to compete with DC Comics. At the suggestion of his wife, and because he felt he had nothing to lose as he was planning on changing careers,

Stan Lee experimented with a more realistic type of comic story where the heroes were not merely one dimensional ideological archetypes, but complex naturalistic characters with real world problems and personalities.

The result was the creation of the Fantastic Four with Jack Kirby in 1961. This was followed a year later by the debut of the Amazing Spider-Man, co-created with Steve Ditko, in the pages of *Amazing Fantasy* issue 15. Soon, these characters were joined by other Lee/Kirby creations, including the Incredible Hulk, Iron Man, Thor, the Avengers, and the X-Men, as well as Daredevil (co-created with Bill Everett) and Doctor Strange (co-created with Steve Ditko). These stories with iconic characters possessing both amazing powers as well as human insecurities and emotions helped Lee usher in a new age of comic book storytelling. Far from a writer, Stan Lee had become the architect of a new universe: the Marvel Universe. Lee had become one of the fathers of modern comics. He eventually abandoned the name Stanley Lieber and legally changed his name to the moniker that had made him famous: Stan Lee.

Lee stayed at Marvel Comics throughout the next several decades. In 1972, Lee became publisher and editorial director of the group. From there, Lee became editor-in-chief and art director of the comics division. He continued in his career at Marvel Comics for more than 60 years. During that time, Lee worked as a writer, editor, publisher, president, and chairman at Marvel Comics. Over that time, Lee created and co-created numerous characters and storylines for the company. In addition, at the time of this writing, he's made cameo appearances in 18 films based on his creations, as well as numerous television and direct to video productions.[2] A sharp eyed rider will also find him at the end of the Amazing Adventures of Spider Man ride in Islands of Adventure at the Universal Studios Orlando theme park.

Marvel Comics Branches Out

Although Marvel Comics started as a comic book company, it was clear that Lee and Marvel Comics both recognized that their characters could be worth so much more. The first character to escape the printed page was Captain America in 1944 when the character starred in a motion picture serial produced by Republic Pictures.

Based on the popularity of its books in the 1960s, Marvel Comics began to license its properties for use in consumer products. By 1966, *The Marvel Superheroes* cartoon series was playing in homes around the country. The show featured Captain America, The Incredible Hulk, The Invincible Iron Man, The Mighty Thor, Prince Namor the Sub-Mariner as well as guest appearances from the Avengers and the original X-Men.[3] By 1970, these characters were joined by both *The Fantastic Four* and *Spider-Man*, each of which received their own Saturday morning cartoon on the ABC television network.

Marvel Comics had also begun merchandising many of its characters, who appeared on dozens of types of consumer products. In fact, by the late 1970s, licensing became a principal line of Marvel Comics' business. As a result, in 1980, Stan Lee decided to move from New York to California and help establish and operate Marvel Comics' animation studio and exploit Marvel Comics' characters in television and motion pictures.[4] And while there was some success on television such as the *Incredible Hulk* and cartoons, for the most part, Marvel Comics and Lee had failed to make an impression on mainstream Hollywood prior to the late 1990s. It was worse for the movies, as Marvel Comics' publishing competitor, DC Comics, presented Superman and Batman in major motion blockbusters with record breaking box office receipts, whereas Marvel Comics was only able to release lackluster films, such as George Lucas' big budget commercial and critical failure *Howard the Duck* in 1986 and a 1989 direct to video Punisher movie starring Dolph Lundgren.[5]

Stan Lee's Contracts

In 1994, Stan Lee and Marvel Comics entered a lifetime exclusive Employment Agreement providing Lee with $1 million a year salary for life and 10 percent of movie and TV profits.

The court summarized how this agreement worked:

In 1995, pursuant to this agreement, Marvel paid Lee a 10 percent participation, which was based on revenue received by Marvel under an arrangement with Danchuk Productions. The payments to Marvel were characterized as "profit participation." Marvel remitted 10 percent ($4,994) to Lee without any deduction for costs. Marvel stated to Lee that this sum "represent[ed] your 10 percent of the profits." The executory portion of this prior agreement was rejected by Marvel during the bankruptcy.

Marvel Comics declared bankruptcy on December 27, 1996. As part of that bankruptcy, Marvel Comics attempted to void Stan Lee's 1994 agreement. In September 1998 Stan Lee retained Counsel Arthur Lieberman to negotiate a new contract. A new contract was entered on November 17, 1998, after Marvel Comics emerged from bankruptcy.[6] The agreement[7] reads:

Dear Stan:

Confirming the various discussions between your attorney Arthur Lieberman and Tuck Hardie of Marvel, this letter when accepted and agreed to by you constitutes an agreement between you and Marvel Enterprises, Inc. ("the Company"), the parent company of Marvel Characters, Inc. ("Marvel"), represented by us to be the survivor after bankruptcy of Marvel Entertainment Group, Inc.

1. You will serve as an employee of Company, or one of its affiliates as may be designated by the Company, based in Los Angeles for a term commencing as of the date hereof and terminating on your death. Notwithstanding such death, the compensation provided for in Section 4 hereof shall continue until the last to occur of (i) your death (ii) the death of your present wife, Joan Lee (provided that she is still your wife upon your death) or (iii) five years after the death of both you and Joan Lee, provided that your daughter Joan C. Lee survives both of you.

2. Your services shall be non-exclusive but your work for Marvel shall be on a preferential basis. You shall not, however, be required to put in more time on Marvel's behalf than you have averaged in the last two years, which shall be approximately 10–15 hours per week. Any time in excess of that shall be at your option but without additional compensation. It is agreed that you can engage in and be compensated for any activities outside those performed for the Company or Marvel including activities that are competitive to those of the company or its affiliates, so long as that competition does not violate any of the intellectual property or other rights of the Company or Marvel or result from the unauthorized disclosure of the Company's proprietary or confidential information, if you are so advised of the proprietary or confidential nature of such

information (at the time of disclosure) in writing. Your services to Marvel will consist of the following:

(a) Serve generally as a spokesman for Marvel, including giving speeches and interviews and visiting conventions on Marvel's behalf, as Marvel may from time to time reasonably request;

(b) Conferring on a regular basis with the creative staff at Marvel's various operations, guiding and advising the editorial and art personnel and the like in existing Marvel characters; and

(c) Work with motion picture and television producers and distributors to stimulate their licensing of Marvel characters and supervise movie and television projects of Marvel Characters on Marvel's behalf and be named executive producer or co-executive producer of such productions.

3. You will continue to serve as Publisher of Marvel Comics and your name and likeness shall be non-exclusively licensed to Marvel in the manner it has traditionally appeared on Marvel Comics as more specifically provided for in paragraph 5 below. At your option, Marvel shall name you as Chairman Emeritus of the movie or television company as listed in the Hollywood Creative Directory and/or Publisher or Publisher Emeritus of Marvel Comics, a division of the Company.

4. As compensation to you for your life notwithstanding any disability, Joan Lee, your current wife, and Joan C. Lee, your daughter, the Company agrees to provide the following compensation:

(a) Base Salary

(i) from the date hereof, through October 31, 2002, you are to be paid a base salary (the "Base Salary") of $810,000 per year;

(ii) from November 1, 2000 through October 31, 2001 the Base Salary shall be $850,000;

(iii) from November 1, 2001 through October 31, 2002, the Base Salary shall be $900,000; and

(iv) from November 1, 2002 until death the Base Salary shall be $1.0 million dollars.

All amounts of Base Salary shall be paid in accordance with customary payroll policy on a biweekly or semi-monthly basis. You may elect to have all or any portion of the Base Salary paid to S.L. Productions or any company you so designate in lieu of making the payments to you individually.

(b) Survivor Payments

(i) Upon your death, your current wife Joan Lee (provided she is your wife at the time of your death) shall be entitled to receive, for the balance of her life, an amount equal to 50 percent of the Base Salary in effect on the date of your death. Such amounts to be paid in accordance with customary payroll policy as provided in paragraph (a) above.

(ii) Upon your death and Joan Lee's, Joan C. Lee, your daughter, shall be entitled to receive, for a period of five years, the sum of $100,000 (payable in accordance with customary Marvel payroll practices) provided that Joan C. Lee does not predecease either you or your wife Joan Lee. In such case, no amounts would be due by the Company.

(c) Stock Options

(1) The Company agrees to issue to you, in accordance with the Company's 1995 Stock Option Plan (the "Plan"), a total of 150,000 options to purchase shares of the Company's common stock. Such options shall be, if possible be within the employee plan and are, granted as follows: (I) 100,000 options shall be granted at a price equal to the market bid price as of the date of grant, such grant to be made as promptly as practicable following execution on this Letter Agreement, but not later than November 20, 1998; (II) 25,000 options shall be granted not later than the first anniversary of the execution of this Letter Agreement at a price then

equal to the market bid price and (III) 25,000 options shall be granted at a price then equal to the market bid price not later than the second anniversary of the execution of this Letter Agreement, each of the above options to vest in the year of granting and be for five years from date of issuance.

(d) Set-Off

If, after November 1, 2002, you personally receive, or any company wholly owned or wholly controlled by you receives revenue from competing business activities, then the Company shall be entitled to set-off from the amounts due as Base Salary hereunder an amount equal to 25 percent of such competing business revenue (before deduction of expenses and on a pre-tax basis) to a maximum of $190,000 in any contract year (i.e., November 1, through October 31). You agree each year after November 1, 2002 to furnish a certified accountant's statement (with appropriate support) to the Company detailing the computation of said Set-Off. Where the maximum set-off of $190,000 is being permitted a simple statement shall be sufficient.

(e) Expenses/Fringe Benefits

(i) You are to receive prompt reimbursement for all ordinary and necessary business expenses incurred by you in connection with your activities on behalf of the Company upon presentation of appropriate documentation (included expenses shall be a cell phone) in accordance with Company policy, except that you shall be permitted your customary style of business travel (which shall be first class with limousine and stay in luxury hotels).

(ii) You also continue to have the benefit of a single full-time assistant. (f) In addition, you shall be paid participation equal to 10 percent of the profits derived during your life by Marvel (including subsidiaries and affiliates) from the profits of any live action or animation television or movie (including ancillary rights) productions utilizing Marvel characters. This participation is not to be derived from the fee charged by Marvel for the licensing of the product or of the characters for merchandise or otherwise. Marvel will compute, account and pay to you your participation due, if any, on account of said profits, for the annual period ending each March 31 during your life, on an annual basis within a reasonable time after the end of each such period.

(g) You will have the right to continue to author the syndicated newspaper comic strip "Spider Man" and receive the same extra compensation therefrom that you have been receiving, to wit, $125,000 annually pursuant to your agreement with Marvel. All such comic strips shall continue to be published as is done in the current circumstances.

5. Subject to paragraph 5(f) below, in express consideration for and expressly dependent upon the faithful performance of the foregoing obligations of Marvel, you, Stan Lee, residing at XXX agree as follows:

(a) Except for your name, likeness and the integration of either your name or likeness with a specific phrase, such as "Stan's Soap Box," "Stan Lee presents," and except for the term "Excelsior" (as to which Marvel shall have non-exclusive rights of use, in accordance with the terms hereof, the "Non-Exclusive Rights"), you hereby assign, convey and grant (without representations or warranties of any kind except as set forth herein) to Marvel forever throughout the universe all right, title and interest solely and exclusively which you may have or control or which you may have had or controlled in the following: Any and all ideas, names, titles, characters, symbols, logos, designs, likenesses, visual representations, artwork, stories, plots, scripts, comic books or comic strips, episodes, literary property, and the conceptual universe related thereto which will or have been in whole or in part disclosed in writing to, published, merchandised, advertised, and/or licensed by Marvel, its affiliates or their predecessors and successors in interest and licensees (which by agreement inures to Marvel's benefit) or any of them (the "Property") and any copyrights, trademarks, statutory rights, common law, goodwill, moral rights and any other rights whatsoever in the Property in any and all manner and media and/or fields, including all rights to renewal or extensions of copyright or trademarks and to recover for past infringement and make application or institute suits therefor (the "Rights"). With respect to the Non-Exclusive Rights, the foregoing rights of Marvel shall extend solely to the uses heretofore utilized by Marvel; changes thereto may be made with your permission. Such prior uses may continue in perpetuity. Specifically excepted from above, you have represented that you have been receiving royalties on a number of publications to Marvel's knowledge directly from third-party publishers. Specifically excepted from the above is the right during your life to continue receiving such royalties unimpeded. You have also represented that Marvel has heretofore assigned to you the character(s) The Femizons. You may continue forever in perpetuity to so own and exploit the Femizons character(s) for your own benefit. Notwithstanding what is set forth herein, you may, for publicity, advertising, public relation, historical and any related purposes (but excluding any use coupled o commercial usage) refer to or hold yourself out as founder and/or creator of whatever characters and images you created or founded on behalf of Marvel, provided such uses do not confuse ownership or source of origin. Such image uses may not be story-related, must be substantially identical to prior Marvel uses and must give full attribution of trademark and copyright to Marvel and the use of the images must be substantially minor in context.

(b)   You hereby warrant that you have not assigned, licensed, pledged or otherwise hypothecated, nor attempted to do so any of the Property and Rights to anyone other than Marvel, its affiliates, predecessors or their designees and will not do so in the future.

(c)   Subject to a material breach of this agreement, you hereby agree to execute upon request from Marvel any documents it deems reasonably necessary to effect the purposes of this assignment.

(d)   Subject to a material breach of this agreement, you will never file with the U.S. Copyright Office or the U.S. Patent and Trademark Office or any governmental or public agency throughout the world, and will never assert or assist on your behalf or cooperate with others in asserting on your behalf or in claiming rights through you, any claim to ownership (except to Non-Exclusive Rights, subject to Marvel's license) of the Rights in the Property, or in making any objection to Marvel's complete and unrestricted right to use and exploit said Property or Rights throughout the world in any form, manner or medium Marvel may desire now or hereafter known or devised.

(e)   Subject to a material breach of this agreement, you agree not to contest either directly or indirectly the full and complete ownership by Marvel, its affiliates, designees, or successors in interest, of all right, title and interest in and to the Property and Rights or the validity of the Rights, which may be conferred on Marvel by this Agreement, or to assist others in so doing. Examples of such prohibited contestation would be, without limitation, applying for copyright, renewal copyright, trademarks, service marks, patents, etc. for the Property and/or Rights herein specified or the publication by you or your assigns or agents of literary property which would infringe upon, violate or be confusingly similar to such Property and/or Rights.

(f)   It is agreed that the failure to pay pursuant to Paragraphs 4(a)—4(c) hereof for any reason, after notice and a thirty (30) day cure period, shall be a material breach which shall permit you at your option to vitiate Paragraphs 5(a)—(5(e) (the Assignment) above and place the parties to the "Assignment" in the condition that existed between them just prior to the date of execution of this Agreement and nothing contained herein, including the existence of the conveyances contained herein, shall be used as evidence in any subsequent proceeding nor shall it prevent the parties from taking any position with respect to the ownership of the Property or the Rights. It is further agreed that as to all other breaches of this agreement, you shall be relegated exclusively to a suit for either specific performance or money damages or both, if appropriate, at your option.

(g) It is acknowledged and agreed that so long as the Company continues to make the payments required in paragraphs 4(a)—4(c) and upon full payment of the amounts required by Paragraphs 4(a)—4(c) none of the heirs, executors, estates, or other successors-in-interest of any of Stan Lee, Joan Lee, or Joan C. Lee shall be entitled to make any claim for payments under Paragraphs 4(a)—4(c) and neither Joan Lee nor Joan C. Lee shall have the right to contest, challenge or otherwise dispute the grant of Rights in the Property (or Assignment) hereunder or the rights to the Non-Exclusive Rights.

6. This Agreement, including the assignment set forth herein, shall be binding upon the parties hereto, their affiliates and subsidiaries, legal representatives, successors and predecessors in interest, and assigns.

7. The invalidity of any provision or part hereof or obligation hereunder, or the contravention thereby of any law, rule or regulation of any State, the Federal Government or any agency, shall not relieve any party from its obligation under, nor deprive any party of the advantages of, any other provision or part of this Agreement.

8. Other Provisions. This Agreement will constitute the entire understanding between the parties in connection with Stan Lee's relationship with Marvel from the date hereof, shall supersede any and all previous agreements and may not be amended or modified except by a writing signed by the party to be charged. This agreement will be governed by and construed in accordance with the laws of the State of New York, N.Y. jurisdiction. All notices to Marvel shall be given by you at the above address and all notices to you shall be given to you at, with a copy to Arthur M. Lieberman at 461 Fifth Avenue, New York, New York 10017, or to such substitute address as a party otherwise designates in writing.

9. Marvel and the Company agree to submit this agreement together with appropriate supporting papers to the court overseeing Marvel's bankruptcy prior to November 25th, 1998 and to obtain court's approval of this agreement prior to December 5th, 1998. Should the court fail to act on this agreement, it shall be binding between the parties. Should the court disapprove this agreement, then paragraph 5(f) shall control and place the parties in the condition that existed between them just prior to the date of execution of this agreement.

10. The Company agrees to pay your reasonable legal fees and expenses in connection with the negotiation of this agreement.

Stan Lee Branches Out with Stan Lee Media

After working for Marvel Comics in an official capacity for nearly sixty years, Lee began to pursue other projects. In 1998, he formed Stan Lee Entertainment with a former lawyer, Peter F. Paul.

Paul had a very different career path than Lee. Paul was born on September 2, 1948. In the seventies, he was working as a lawyer in Miami and served as president of the Miami World Trade Center. Shortly thereafter, Paul pled guilty to federal conspiracy charges for fraud and to possessing cocaine with intent to distribute. Paul received an eight year sentence for the cocaine and a three year concurrent sentence for the fraud, but he only served three years before he was paroled.[8] By the end of the eighties, Paul had been released from prison again and permanently relocated to Los Angeles, where he established himself as a business manager for several celebrities. In 1998, Paul and Lee joined together to form Stan Lee Entertainment.

On October 15, 1998, Lee signed an employment agreement/rights assignments with Stan Lee Entertainment, Inc. The agreement reads:

Dear Stan:

Confirming our discussions, this letter, when accepted and agreed by you, shall constitute an agreement-between you and Stan Lee Entertainment, Inc. (the "Company") relating to the terms of your employment with the Company as set forth below:

1. Stan Lee will serve as Chairman and Chief Creative Officer of Company, based in Los Angeles, for a term commencing as of the date hereof and terminating on the death of Stan Lee.

2. Stan Lee's services shall be exclusive with the exception of those services provided under a lifetime agreement with Marvel Enterprises, Inc., which shall require no more than an average of 10–15 hours per week on its behalf. All other services performed and intellectual property created for the Company, or for any other entity, which entity shall be approved in writing by the Company, shall inure to the benefit of the Company to the entire extent your participation provides. Your services to Company shall include, but not be limited to, the following:

    (a) Serve, and be listed in all directories and publications, as Chairman, Publisher and Chief Creative Officer of the Company, including attending corporate meetings, developing and supervising development and production of intellectual property in any and all media, directing and guiding the creative staff or staffs of the Company, all subsidiaries and affiliates as reasonably requested by the company.

    (b) Act as Executive Producer or Co-Executive Producer for all media productions and receive customary fees accordingly.

    (c) Apply your good faith, best efforts to enhance the brand and good will of the company, support and stimulate strategic alliances, joint ventures, sponsors, production partners and all direct and ancillary business of the company.

    (d) Serve as spokesman for the company to all media and assemblies as reasonably requested by the company.

    (e) Take all actions and contribute all creative talents within your reasonable capability, pursuant to your good faith determination of your schedule, as may reasonably be required to advance the interests of the company.

3. As compensation to you for all rights and services contributed by you, to the Company hereunder, notwithstanding any disability, the Company agrees to provide the following compensation for your life:

    a) Base Salary—You shall receive a base salary of $250,000 (Two Hundred Fifty Thousand Dollars) per annum payable in equal monthly installments commencing February 1, 1999, payable to you or any company you so designate in lieu of making payments to you individually.

    b) Bonuses—You shall receive bonuses on those projects you personally initiate and/or accomplish with approved entities from your participation as assigned to the company. You shall also receive ten per cent of all net profits after taxes reported by the Company on its Federal Tax Return. The Company will compute, account and pay to you your participation due, if any, on account of said profits, for the annual period ending each January 31 during your life, on an annual basis within a reasonable time after the end of each such period.

    c) Stock Options—The Company agrees to issue to you, in accordance with the Company's Stock Option Plan, as and when it may be adopted, the highest number of options offered to Company executives.

    d) Expenses/Fringe Benefits—You are to receive prompt reimbursement for all ordinary and necessary business expenses incurred by you in connection with your activities on behalf of the Company upon presentation of appropriate documentation, and you shall be permitted your customary style of business travel, which shall be first class with sedan limousine and stay in deluxe hotels.

    e) Insurance—The company shall no later than December 31, 1998, secure a term life insurance policy in the minimum principal sum of two million dollars, providing your designated heir as co-beneficiary with the company on the event of your death.

4. In express consideration for the performance of the foregoing obligations of the Company, you agree as follows:

 a) I assign, convey and grant to the Company forever, all right, title and interest I may have or control, now or in the future, in the following: Any and all ideas, names, titles, characters, symbols, logos, designs, likenesses, visual representations, artwork, stories, plots, scripts, episodes, literary property, and the conceptual universe related thereto, including my name and likeness (the "Property") which will or have been in whole or part disclosed in writing to, published, merchandised, advertised, and/or licensed by Company, its affiliates and successors in interest and licensees (which by agreement inures to Company's benefit) or any of them and any copyrights, trademarks, statutory rights, common law, goodwill, moral rights and any other rights whatsoever in the Property in any and all media and/or fields, including all rights to renewal or extensions of copyright and make applications or institute suits therefor (the "Rights").

 b) Subject to a material breach of this agreement, I hereby agree to execute upon request from Company any documents it deems reasonably necessary to effect the purposes of this agreement,

 c) Subject to a material breach of this agreement, I will never file with the U.S. Copyright or Patent and Trademark Office or any governmental or public agency, and will never assert or assist others in asserting on my behalf or in claiming rights through me, any claim to ownership of the Rights in the Property, or in making any objection to Company's complete and unrestricted right to use and exploit said Property or Rights in any form, manner or medium Company may desire.

5. This Agreement, including the assignment set forth herein, shall be binding upon the parties hereto, their affiliates and subsidiaries, legal representatives, successors and predecessors in interest, heirs and assigns.

6. The invalidity of any provision or part hereof or obligation hereunder, or the contravention thereby of any law, rule or regulation of any State, the Federal Government or any agency, shall not relieve any party from its obligation under, nor deprive any party of advantages of any other provision of this Agreement.

7. This Agreement will constitute the entire understanding between the parties in connection with Stan Lee's relationship with the Company from the date hereof and may not be amended or modified except by a writing signed by the party charged. This agreement shall be governed by and construed under the laws of the State of California.

One month after signing the employment agreement/rights assignments with Stan Lee Entertainment, Inc., Lee and Marvel Comics entered the contract described above.

In April 1999, Lee and Paul took steps to get their private company publicly traded. First, Stan Lee Entertainment merged with Stan Lee Media, Inc., of Delaware. Later that year, in July, Stan Lee Media of Delaware acquired Boulder Capital Opportunities, Inc., a publicly traded company, which permitted Stan Lee Media to become traded on the stock market under the symbol SLEE. At the same time, a different stock for Stan Lee Media appeared on the New York Stock Exchange under the symbol SLM.

Stan Lee Media was an internet entertainment company that would feature original content created by Lee. The company's first project, an animated online series called *7th Portal*, featured the first new team of superheroes to be created by Stan Lee in thirty years and was very successful when it started.

7th Portal was a series of animated features that told the story of six beta testers turned superheroes that band together as the Data Raiders to stop Lord Mongorr from entering the 7th Portal (the internet).[9] The show premiered on Shockwave, a new online animation hub, on February 29, 2000. The launch was so popular that it overloaded Macromedia's servers. And while the show was originally only available on the web, it was eventually picked up by Fox for distribution on television in South America and Europe. The property was eventually adapted into a 3D ride attraction in four Paramount theme parks and was developed for a $150 million movie by Paramount with producer Mark Canton, though the film was never made. *7th Portal* lasted for twenty-two episodes.[10]

7th Portal was followed by several other less successful series that were also created by Lee. *The Drifter*, which was co-developed by Steve Gerber and Taylor Grant, told the story of a time traveler. *The Backstreet Project* featured the Backstreet Boys as costumed adventurers. *The Accuser* was co-developed by Roy Johansen, Taylor Grant and Steve Gerber and starred a science fiction based vigilante. *Evil Clone* featured a failed experiment to clone Lee into a cartoon character with humorous results. Lee provided his own voice for the project.

Stan Lee Media also explored several projects that never manifested. In June, the company entered into a joint venture with Venture Soft, a leading anime and manga company in Japan. In addition, Stan Lee Media purchased the company that owned the rights to *Conan the Barbarian* for $4.3 million worth of Stan Lee Media stock.[11]

As a result of its early successes, Stan Lee Media was awarded the Best of Show Web Award in November 2000, as the best entertainment portal on the internet.

Despite this initial success, Stan Lee Media was out of business by December 19, 2000. In February 2001, Stan Lee Media filed for bankruptcy protection. By this time, Paul had left the country and moved to Brazil. In June 2001, Paul was extradited back to the United States after a federal grand jury in New York indicted Paul on two felonies in connection with trading of Stan Lee Media stock.[12] Paul pled guilty and was sentenced to ten years in jail.

In November 2001, Lee, Gill Champion, and Arthur Lieberman formed POW! Entertainment, LLC. During the bankruptcy, Lee assigned the major character franchises he created to his new company. On June 9, 2007, Stan Lee Media sued Lee, POW! Entertainment, and others regarding the transfer. On January 20, 2009, Judge Stephen Wilson, in the United States District Court for the Central District of California Los Angeles, ruled that POW! had transferred assets of Stan Lee Media, including *The Drifter* and *The Accuser*, to POW! without the knowledge or approval of the bankruptcy court and therefore in violation of the bankruptcy court's order.

Blade *Kills at the Box Office but Not for Marvel Comics*

At the same time as Lee was forming and working with Stan Lee Media, Marvel Comics continued its attempts to create a viable film license. Their first attempt resulted in *Howard the Duck* in 1986, a critical and commercial failure. However, things turned around in 1998, with the release of *Blade*, starring Wesley Snipes as the title character. *Blade* was loosely based on the Marvel Comics character created by Marv Wolfman for the *Tomb of Dracula* series.[13] In the film, a half-vampire who can walk in daylight protects the human race from evil vampires. The movie spawned two sequels (*Blade II* and *Blade Trinity*) as well as a television series (*Blade: The Series*). However, despite the fact that *Blade* grossed over $70 million and had an estimated budget of only $45 million, Marvel Comics did not receive any of these profits as a result of the profit-participation provision of the production agreement.

The court explained how this was possible:

> This profit-participation provision, which Marvel has characterized as a "Hollywood accounting" provision, entitled Marvel to a share of *Blade*'s "net profits," as that term was defined by the language of the production agreement. Marvel's [representative] stated that "Hollywood accounting" can be interpreted "to mean that you will never see anything—you will never see— the company would not see any revenues from the studio...." Marvel's chief creative officer, Avi Arad, testified that "Hollywood accounting is—is the term used to—studios deduct everything possible out of film revenues, from cost of the movie to getting a star flowers to—you name it and it's in there. And it's expensive and it's hard to monitor, and therefore I'm allergic to it."

The court further explained Hollywood accounting in a footnote:

> 1. One commentator has provided the following description of the typical provisions of a "Hollywood accounting" deal: [T]he basic net profits formula subtracts from the studio's (distributor's) adjusted gross receipts the production costs, distribution expenses, and distribution fees.... Production costs are all costs directly attributed to the particular film (plus overhead). Production costs include the payments to all other participants in a film including the contingent compensation of gross participants. So, for example, [if a given actor] had fifteen gross points for [a given movie] (that is, he received 15 percent of the gross receipts), every dollar of revenue that the film generated pushed the net profits breakeven point back fifteen cents. Thus, if a film has significant gross participants, the breakeven point quickly recedes. Almost all the box office smashes that failed to produce net profits had significant gross participants.

No More Hollywood Accounting

As a result of not receiving any money from *Blade*, Marvel Comics made a business decision to avoid Hollywood accounting treatment for the use of the Marvel Comics characters. And that is precisely what they did when Marvel Comics contracted with Sony for use of the character Spider-Man. Consequently, the Spider-Man contract contained a gross-profit participation provision. This turned out to be an excellent decision as the May 2002 release of *Spider-Man: The Movie* earned $114.8 million in its opening weekend and more than $800 million in worldwide box-office gross. In turn, Marvel Comics earned more than $50 million under its agreement with Sony.[14]

Marvel Comics' licensed movies continued with two more *Spider-Man* films, as well as a trilogy based on the *X-Men* franchise, two *Fantastic Four Films*, and several solo films featuring Daredevil, Elektra, the Punisher, the Hulk, and Wolverine. The contracts for each of these films provided for gross profit participation.[15]

The court concluded;

Between November 17, 1998 and today, Marvel has entered into over a thousand merchandising agreements pursuant to which it has licensed to third parties the right to use its characters in connection with various toys, games, collectibles, apparel, interactive games, arcade games and electronics, stationery and school products, health and beauty products, snack foods and beverages, sporting goods, party supplies, and amusement destinations. Merchandising has generated hundreds of millions of dollars in revenue to Marvel during this period.

But Lee wasn't being paid for it.

The Lawsuit

Given the longstanding relationship between Marvel Comics and Lee, it came as a surprise when the legendary comic creator filed a lawsuit against Marvel Comics on November 12, 2002. The case was filed in the United States District Court for the Southern District of New York where the case was assigned to Judge Sweet.

In his complaint, Lee raised several claims. First, Lee alleged that Marvel Comics violated paragraph 4(f) and paragraph 2(c) of his employment agreement, which Lee contended entitled him to be named executive producer or co-executive producer of any movie or television production utilizing Marvel Comics' characters. Second, Lee sought damages against Marvel Comics caused by the company's alleged breach of a duty of good faith and fair dealings. Third, Lee asked the court to order that Marvel Comics pay him the amounts owed under his contract and provide for an accounting. Fourth, Lee asked the court to determine what he would be owed under the participation agreement.

Marvel Comics moved for partial summary judgment asking the court to dismiss the claims in the complaint that sought any profits from licensing of its characters for merchandising. At or around the same time, Lee moved for partial summary judgment on the grounds that, under his contract, Lee was entitled to a 10 percent participation in profits "derived by Marvel Comics from television or movie productions, not limited by so-called Hollywood Accounting, including film/television merchandising when the profits do not result from a fee for licensing."

In addressing these arguments, the court examined paragraph 4(f) of Lee's contract that provides:

[Lee] shall be paid a participation equal to 10 percent of the profits derived during [his] life by Marvel (including subsidiaries and affiliates) from the profits of any live action or animation television or movie (including ancillary rights) productions utilizing Marvel Characters. This participation is not to be derived from the fee charged by Marvel for the licensing of the product or of the characters for merchandise or otherwise....

The court summarized it as follows:

This deceptively simple language, drafted by a company and an executive both skilled and experienced in the industry, has given rise to a multimillion dollar controversy because of changes in the way Marvel has conducted business since the execution of the Agreement in November 1998.

Basically, Marvel Comics argued that paragraph 4(f) only entitled Lee to 10 percent participation in only those television and motion picture production deals where Marvel Comics was afforded rights of net profit participation and that the second sentence of paragraph 4(f) barred Lee from any profits from merchandising. In response, Lee argued that paragraph 4(f) entitled him to 10 percent of all profits regardless of whether they were gross profits or gross proceeds and that he was entitled to participate in all revenue from film/television merchandising with the exception of profits resulting from fees from licensing for merchandise.

Turning to the first issue, the court rejected Marvel Comics' reading of the contract and found:

> In short, the first sentence of paragraph 4(f) is not ambiguous. It provides that Lee is entitled to share in the results of Marvel's arrangements for movie and television productions involving Marvel characters, however those arrangements may have been characterized as between Marvel and the third party, as long as there is a valuable gain or return, a benefit to Marvel.

With regard to the second issue, the court found that the term ancillary rights included merchandising. The court, relying on expert testimony, held that "[b]ased on this expert testimony proffered by Lee and Marvel concerning common usage in the relevant industries, it is determined that the phrase 'ancillary rights,' as used in the first sentence of paragraph 4(f), necessarily includes merchandising rights."

The court also concluded that the agreement excluded fees from licensing from the profit participation calculation but ruled that a trial was necessary to determine the specifics.

Lee and Marvel Comics resolved their remaining issues and settled the case out of court.

Stan Lee Media Wants In

Later, Lee's former company, Stan Lee Media, attempted to intervene in the Lee/Marvel Comics dispute as the real party of interest. The court did not allow the intervention because Stan Lee Media was in bankruptcy and could not prove who was authorized to bring suit. After the Colorado bankruptcy approved a new board of directors, Stan Lee Media appealed to the Second Circuit. The Second Circuit issued a summary order dismissing the appeal as untimely. The court held "that Stan Lee Media's management was in an extended period of disarray does not excuse its more than five-year delay in filing its [motion to intervene]."

Of course, this was not the first, nor the last, attempt by Stan Lee Media to obtain Marvel Comics' characters. There have been several unsuccessful challenges in various state and federal courts in New York, California, Colorado, and in a securities class-action settlement.[16] Most recently, Stan Lee Media filed suit against the Walt Disney Company, which purchased Marvel Comics in 2009, in the United States District Court for the District of Colorado seeking profits from $5.5 billion it claimed Disney has made from Marvel Comics movies and merchandise.

Disney moved to dismiss. On September 5, 2013, U.S. District Judge William J. Martinez granted Disney's motion to dismiss. The court stated:

Plaintiff has tried time and again to claim ownership of those copyrights; the litigation history arising out of the 1998 Agreement stretches over more than a decade and at least six courts.... Taking its cue from the Southern District of New York and the Central District of California, this Court holds that Plaintiff is precluded from re-litigating the issue of its ownership of copyrights based on the 1998 Agreement....

On October 2, 2013, Stan Lee Media appealed to the Tenth Circuit Court of Appeals. The case is still pending as this book goes to print.

CHAPTER 10

A Lack of Curiosity Killed the Pussycats
Dan DeCarlo v. Archie Comics Publications

Long before Josie and the girls wore long tales and ears for hats, they were figments in the imagination of Dan DeCarlo inspired by his wife, Josie. DeCarlo had met Josie Dumont during World War II. She was a French citizen and the two met on a blind date in Belgium not long after the Battle of the Bulge. They were married within a year and Josie was soon pregnant with their first child. In order to support his new family, DeCarlo started a career in the comics industry. After the war, DeCarlo took a job working for Stan Lee at Timely Comics (the predecessor to Marvel Comics).

While at Timely Comics and later at Atlas Comics (another Marvel Comics predecessor), DeCarlo worked on numerous teen and humor books like *Jeannie, Millie the Model,* and *My Friend Irma*. He even co-created, with Stan Lee, a mailman named Willie Lumpkin for use in a syndicated newspaper strip.[1] DeCarlo's art also appeared in the *Saturday Evening Post, Argosy* and several pin-up digests released by Martin Goodman (the owner of Timely and Atlas).

In the late 1950s, DeCarlo left Marvel Comics and began to work for Archie Comics. Over the course of his first decade at the company, DeCarlo modernized the look of Archie Comics and created a new house style for the books. He also introduced several lasting characters to the Archie Comics line of teen books like Sabrina the Teenage Witch and Cheryl Blossom. Eventually, DeCarlo began working for Archie Comics as a full time freelancer. That was when DeCarlo came up with the concept for Josie.

Here's Josie; She's Josie

DeCarlo has said he came up with the idea for *Josie and the Pussycats* while on a cruise. His wife Josie wore a cat costume to an event on the boat and DeCarlo became inspired. From there, DeCarlo developed a syndicated comic strip called *Here's Josie* and tried to sell it to United Features, a newspaper syndicate in New York. United Features ultimately rejected *Here's Josie*.

DeCarlo then pitched the idea for *Here's Josie* to Richard Goldwater at Archie Comics in 1961. He said he showed the original strip, which contained Josie, Melody, and Pepper.

Archie Comics decided to release it as a comic book and purchased the concept. Archie Comics disputes this version of the facts and retorts that *Josie* was created as a freelance work for hire. Archie Comics paid DeCarlo $23 per page for his work on the *Josie* comic books. In addition, the company paid him a 5 percent royalty on revenues earned from June 1966 through October 1969. Archie Comics also sent DeCarlo a check for $1,406.25 in 1998 without any explanation.

What is undisputed is that the character of Josie was introduced in the pages of *Archie's Pals 'n' Gals* issue 23. The story called "Tongue Twister" focused on Josie's friend Melody who has trouble learning Spanish. Luckily, Josie and Pepper are there help her out. Eventually, Josie got her own series with *She's Josie* in 1963 with a February cover date. Like other Archie Comics books at the time, *She's Josie* featured a joke cover. On the cover, a pretty red-haired Josie works out with her bookish brunette friend Pepper while her friend Melody, a perfectly proportioned blond bombshell, flirts with the boys of Riverdale High in the background. Pepper strains as she is lifting weights and asks "Josie! How's Melody making out with the dumbbells?" Josie looks over at the boys fawning over her flirtatious blond friend and replies, "Just fine, Pepper.... JUST FINE!"

For a cover price of twelve cents, the readers of *She's Josie* issue 1 were treated to several interrelated stories featuring Josie and her friends, the aforementioned Pepper and Melody, as well as Josie and Pepper's boyfriends, Albert and Sock; Albert's rival, Alexander Cabot III; and Alex's twin sister, Alexandra. The plot of the first issue had to do with fitness. In one story ("a Gym Dandy") Melody is banned from gym class because she is distractingly attractive. The story continues in "Neat Workers" in which Josie and Pepper try to get their boyfriends to participate in President Kennedy's nationwide physical fitness program by cleaning the garage.[2] Next, their boyfriends refuse to exercise, but love to dance and fight in "Muscle Hustle." The issue ends with a twist in "Track Down," whereby Melody, who was accused of being a distraction in the first story, is revealed to be the motivation for the boys to exercise as they chase her around the track spurred on by her short shorts. This issue also featured a self-caricature of DeCarlo. In the story, he was portrayed as one of the boys chasing Melody. This tradition of self-caricature would continue until issue 44. Throughout the publication of the comics, DeCarlo did very little to challenge Archie Comics' treatment of *Josie* as its own. For example, in 1963, an Archie Comics subsidiary claimed sole ownership and registered the copyright in *She's Josie* issue 1. DeCarlo testified he "didn't think it was right" but still never challenged the claim at the time.

Josie Rises in Popularity

She's Josie was renamed to a simpler *Josie* with issue 17. Beginning with issue 22, released in 1966, the creator credits changed. Instead of listing DeCarlo and Richard Goldwater separately on the cover, the credit just read "by Dan 'n Dick"—a combination of the names of the two Archie Comic creators. With the exception of one issue, this pseudonym hybrid credit appeared on all books through issue 47, which was released in 1970.

In 1969, the book was once again renamed, to *Josie and the Pussycats*, with issue 45. In that issue, Josie and Melody decide to start a band called the Pussycats with new girl Valerie Smith playing bass. The Pussycats donned their now-famous leopard print band uniforms and performed at a school dance. For some reason, Albert, Sock, and Pepper vanished from the book, never to be seen again.[3] *Josie and the Pussycats* lasted until 1982 and ended with issue 106. The characters and the band, however, continue to appear in one shots and as guest stars in other Archie Comics to this day.

Outside the comics, Josie was becoming famous. Spurred on by the success of *The Archie Show* cartoon produced by Filmation, Hanna-Barbera Productions acquired and adapted *Josie and the Pussycats* into a successful Saturday morning cartoon.[4] The show lasted for sixteen episodes and ran from 1970 until 1972. In 1972, the show was re-conceptualized as *Josie and the Pussycats in Outer Space*, which lasted sixteen episodes on CBS from 1972 through 1974. Reruns of the original series aired through 1976 and alternated between CBS, ABC, and NBC. This means that the cartoon ran on all three networks during its run. Not only has the show become ingrained in pop culture, but Valerie is credited as the first regularly appearing female black character in a Saturday morning cartoon show.

Once again, DeCarlo did little to protect his property. Although he knew that Archie Comics licensed the *Josie* property to Hanna-Barbera, he did nothing. In fact, DeCarlo said that he knew Archie Comics was "making a fortune" from the cartoons. Despite this, DeCarlo neither received nor even asked for any money. The artist also knew that Archie Comics had later allowed the *Josie and the Pussycats* cartoons to be released on videocassette and even licensed the production of *Josie* underwear. In fact, he later learned, in 1993, that Archie Comics had authorized the Cartoon Network to play *Josie and the Pussycats*. DeCarlo said he was "pretty much hardened that … [t]hey're doing anything they want with the show, the character. And they were." Despite this, DeCarlo, by his own testimony, reported that he never said anything to Archie Comics about his ownership of *Josie and the Pussycats*. Instead, DeCarlo remained quiet about Archie Comics' use of the *Josie* characters until he filed suit in 2000.

The Agreements Between DeCarlo and Archie Comics

Not only did DeCarlo fail to express his ownership rights in Josie, but he arguably took steps to affirmatively waive them on several occasions. On October 25, 1988, DeCarlo and Archie Comics entered into a Newsstand Comic Independent Contractor's Agreement. The agreement provided:

> [Archie Comics] is the publisher of comic strips and comic books … of which [Archie Comics] is the sole and exclusive owner,
> [Archie Comics] seeks to supplement its own existing comic strips and comic books (hereinafter the "Existing Archie Works") by the purchase of the entire right, title and interest in existing third party comic strip and pages for its comic books (hereinafter the "Existing Third Party Works"),
> [Archie Comics] desires to retain third parties to modify or otherwise work with the Existing Archie Works and/or the Existing Third Party Works … on a work made for hire basis, to create modified comic strips and pages for its comic books (hereinafter the "Modified Works"), and

The Contractor [i.e., DeCarlo] desires to confirm the assignment to [Archie Comics] of the Contractor's entire right, title and interest in and to whatever comic strips and pages for comic books the Contractor may have heretofore provided [Archie Comics] in furtherance of this project and further desires to work with [Archie Comics] in the future under the terms and conditions hereinafter expressed.

The agreement then set forth covenants in relevant part as follows:

1. (a) The Contractor hereby assigns and conveys to [Archie Comics] all of its rights, title and interest in the Existing Third Party Works heretofore submitted to [Archie Comics].

   (b) The Contractor further agrees to work with [Archie Comics] on a work for hire basis to:

   (i) create and develop for [Archie Comics] exclusive use Additional Works, and

   (ii) perform modifications of Existing Archie Works, Existing Third Party Works (including Existing Third Party Works of others) and Additional Works...

* * *

2. (a) The Contractor hereby assigns to [Archie Comics] all right, title and interest in and to all Works submitted under this Agreement as well as to any patent rights, copyrights, trademark rights and/or applications therefore which relate thereto. The Contractor agrees to execute all documents which are reasonably required to perfect such assignment. It is agreed and understood that such Works shall constitute Works Made for Hire and shall be the sole and exclusive property of [Archie Comics]. To the extent any work of Contractor shall not be deemed under law to constitute subject matter which may be treated as work made on a Work Made for Hire basis, then Contractor hereby assigns and conveys to [Archie Comics] all of its rights, title and interest in any such work.

   (b) The Contractor hereby expressly waives all claim of right which it may have to any ownership interest in such Works and/or the ARCHIE property.

In 1996, DeCarlo and Archie Comics signed another agreement entitled a Work for Hire Agreement between DeCarlo and Archie Comics. Once again, the agreement began with a series of introductory recitals:

[Archie Comics] is in the business of producing and/or publishing comic strips and comic books that include characters, artwork, stories, plots, trademarks, logos, and other creative expressions ("Properties"). All references to "Properties" in this Agreement will include existing and future-created Properties that are commission by [Archie Comics] and/or used in any of [Archie Comics'] publications or licensed products.

All past, pending and future uses of all Properties, including uses by [Archie Comics] licensees, will be collectively referred to in this Agreement as "Works."

The 1996 Agreement then set forth several provisions that defined the relationship between DeCarlo and Archie Comics: compensation, job duties, etc. For example, the agreement provided:

5. Contractor's full and complete compensation for each assignment ... will be a fixed sum based on a rate to be mutually agreed upon.... Contractor will not be entitled to royalties, to income derived from licensing or merchandising, or to additional compensation for the creation of new Properties....

19. To the extent that any past, pending or future contributions by Contractor to the Works or Properties do not qualify as a Work for Hire, Contractor will and hereby does assign to [Archie Comics] any right, title and interest that he/she has or may obtain therein, including all copyrights, patents, trademarks and other proprietary rights. Contractor will sign, upon

request, any documents needed to confirm that any specific Works or Properties are Works for Hire, to effectuate the assignment of his/her rights in any Works or Properties to [Archie Comics] and/or to obtain copyright, trademark and/or patent protection for any of the Works or Properties.

The Live Action Josie Movie

In the late 1990s, Universal City Studios began negotiations with Archie Comics to acquire the licensing rights for a *Josie and the Pussycats* movie. Because DeCarlo never mentioned that he had an interest in the property, Universal did not negotiate with him. In 1998, Universal wrote to inquire whether DeCarlo ever had made any claim to ownership or co-ownership in the property. Archie Comics responded that he had not. They stated, based on DeCarlo's silence, that Universal's "concerns vis-a-vis the copyright issue ... are without any merit" and a "non-issue." In fact, after Universal acquired the rights, Archie Comics agreed to indemnify Universal against the consequences of any dispute that might arise as to ownership of the *Josie* characters.

In 2001, Universal and Metro-Goldwyn-Mayer released the live action movie, *Josie and the Pussycats*, starring Rachel Leigh Cook as Josie, Tara Reid as Melody, and Rosario Dawson as Valerie. The film was not anywhere near as successful as the cartoon or the comic. Instead, the film only grossed $14,866,015 at the U.S. box office, which was much less than its production budget, an estimated $39 million.[5]

The State Court Lawsuit

On March 8, 2000, perhaps spurred on by the mistaken belief that the *Josie and the Pussycats* movie would be a hit, DeCarlo sued Archie Comics in the New York State Supreme Court. The complaint contained five causes of action. First, DeCarlo alleged that he created the Josie, Melody and Pepper characters and that any agreements with Archie Comics, including the 1988 and 1996 contracts, were limited to comic strips and books. As a result, Archie Comics was improperly using and licensing the characters for any other purposes, such as toys, clothing, comics and movies. Thus, DeCarlo requested a declaration that he was the sole owner of the characters and had the exclusive right to use or license them for purposes other than comic books and comic strips. Second, DeCarlo claimed that Archie Comics had breached its oral and written contracts with him by failing to pay certain royalties and by licensing the characters for unauthorized uses. The third and fourth claims were substantially identical to the second, but also sought relief for alleged breaches of an implied covenant of good faith and fair dealing and of fiduciary duty; i.e., they should have treated him better. Finally, the fifth cause of action sought to impose a constructive trust on assets derived from the allegedly improper use of the characters. In other words, DeCarlo wanted the court to rule that all the movie and television money Archie Comics made on Josie, in fact, belonged to him, but was being held for him by Archie Comics in a trust.

Archie Comics filed a counterclaim in the state action. Specifically, Archie Comics alleged that DeCarlo was violating the terms of the 1996 Agreement, which prevented him from taking actions inconsistent with Archie Comics' exclusive rights in *Josie*. As a result, Archie Comics alleged that DeCarlo violated this agreement when he claimed ownership in his complaint.

The State Court Matter Becomes a Federal Case

On March 28, 2000, Archie Comics removed the case from state court to federal court. After discovery, both sides moved for relief. DeCarlo requested the court send the action back to state court or find as a matter of law that he was the owner of *Josie and the Pussycats*.[6] In response, Archie Comics moved for summary judgment on the grounds that the undisputed facts show as a matter of law that Archie Comics was the true owner of *Josie and the Pussycats* and requesting the court to grant its counterclaim, which, of course, DeCarlo opposed.

As grounds for the move to federal court, Archie Comics argued that DeCarlo's first argument was based on federal copyright law of 1909. As a result, only the federal court could hear the action. They also argued that federal court had the ability to hear the rest of the arguments in the complaint, even though they were technically state law claims. In response, DeCarlo argued that the case was not about copyright law, but instead arose under New York state law.

The case was heard by United States District Judge Lewis A. Kaplan, who refused to send the case back to New York state court and ruled in DeCarlo's favor on Archie Comics' counterclaim related to the breach of contract, but ruled in Archie Comics' favor on the ownership of *Josie*.

In reviewing the matter, Judge Kaplan first looked whether the court had jurisdiction over the case, which means that he determined whether federal court was the proper place for the case to be decided. To support his position, DeCarlo relied on a 1921 case called *Fisher v. Star Co*, which involved the comic strip *Mutt and Jeff*, and which the court summarized as follows:

> The plaintiff in Fisher, a comic strip cartoonist, sued a newspaper publisher for printing purported versions of his comic strip drawn by another after its contract to publish the real thing had expired. Fisher held that this was tortious under New York unfair competition law on a "passing off" theory: Where "figures and names have been so connected with ... the originator or author, ... the use by another of new cartoons exploiting the characters ... would be unfair to the public and the plaintiff. No person should be permitted to pass off as his own the thoughts and works of another."

The court disagreed and pointed out that the real problem in *Fisher* was not based on a property right, but rather on the fact that the newspaper passed off the source of the strip as the original creator. That was not the situation with the *Josie* comics because there was no confusion since Dan DeCarlo was not associated with the movie or the cartoon.

The court next turned to see if copyright law applied. As an initial matter, the court observed that DeCarlo's original *Josie* pitch documents would not be covered by the 1909

Copyright Act. This is because copyright protection under the Act was only available once the work was published with the proper copyright notice.[7] The court also recognized that while the 1976 Copyright Act eliminated all state law copyright in unpublished works, it specifically provided that it covered unpublished works created before January 1, 1978, until December 31, 2002. As a result, the court determined:

> In consequence, if DeCarlo ever had any common [state] law rights in these characters by virtue of his long unpublished original drawings, they were transformed by the 1976 Act into federally protected copyrights.

> * * *

> DeCarlo's first cause of action alleges that he is the creator of the Josie characters.... Thus, it is authorship that forms plaintiff's only alleged basis for rights in the Josie characters. Since the effective date of the Copyright Act of 1976, the exclusive source of rights arising from authorship of a work fixed in tangible form is that statute.

DeCarlo also argued that federal copyright law didn't apply to comic book characters. Once again, the court rejected the argument. Although it agreed that "the copyrightability of literary characters can present a troublesome question," the court pointed out that several courts have held that copyright protection is available for characters portrayed in comics and cartoons:

> This is so ... because the difficulties of distinguishing distinct attributes of a literary character from its embodiment of more general ideas and themes do not arise, at least to the same degree, with visual images. "While many literary characters may embody little more than a protected idea, a comic book character, which has physical as well as conceptual qualities, is more likely to contain some unique elements of expression." Such elements have been held to include "what the character thinks, feels, says and does and the descriptions conveyed by the author through the comments of other characters in the work," as well as "the visual perception ... [which] tends to create a dominant impression...." Moreover, the protectable attributes in an animated character "extend ... not merely to the physical appearance of the animated figure, but also to the manner in which it moves, acts and portrays a combination of ... characteristics." In consequence, DeCarlo's contention that cartoon characters are not protectable under the Copyright Act is, at best, a vast oversimplification.

As a result, the court determined that it had the right to decide the case.

The court next turned to the arguments in support of DeCarlo's sole ownership of the property. The court analyzed the case by looking at the three types of ownership rights asserted by DeCarlo in the case: (1) the underlying work, consisting of the original Josie sketches from which the comic strips were derived; (2) the illustrated comic book series; and (3) the comic book periodicals, a compilation of the illustrated series. Basically, DeCarlo was arguing that he was the owner of the underlying work and he never transferred those rights. And while DeCarlo admitted that, by signing the 1988 and 1996 contracts, he gave Archie Comics limited rights in the illustrated series, those rights were limited to the compilation of material released by Archie Comics and not the underlying material. Of course, these arguments all assumed that the work was not for hire. For some reason, DeCarlo's lawyers did not address the issue in the case or state why DeCarlo believed he was sole originator of the work. The court stated:

The basis for DeCarlo's claim to rights in the series is unclear. His brief states that "only one [level of rights] is factually disputed," and it is clear from the brief that plaintiff is referring to the dispute as to who created the original characters that form the "underlying work." But his attorney's declaration asserts that "the illustrated stories remained unquestioned as the separate property of Mr. DeCarlo ... independently for many years, until [Archie Comics] claims they were transferred to [Archie Comics] under agreements signed in 1988 and 1996." It is unclear whether plaintiff asserts independent ownership in the series or ownership based on his rights in the underlying work. If the former is the case, then it appears that plaintiff disputes that the illustrated series constituted a work made for hire. It is impossible to ascertain plaintiff's position in regard to this issue, as he has refused to make any arguments applicable to the copyright issues in this case.

However, even assuming that DeCarlo did not make the original creation as a work for hire, the court found that the case was not timely filed under the statute of limitations. A statute of limitations is a time limit in which someone can bring suit. Basically, the statute of limitations period exists to enforce the notion that if a person sits on their rights, they will lose them. For the 1909 copyright law, the statute of limitations was three years. The Copyright Act of 1976 similarly provides, "no civil action shall be maintained under the provisions of this title unless it is commenced within three years after the claim accrued." As a result, the court looked to the period of time when DeCarlo knew, or reasonably should have known, that Archie Comics was infringing on his rights to Josie. Of course, DeCarlo knew all along what Archie Comics was doing with Josie. As a result, the court held that his claims were time-barred. The court stated:

> As there is no meaningful distinction between an action seeking a declaration of co-ownership and one seeking a declaration of sole ownership, the same result follows here. And the result is sound for the same reason—the interest in repose after all these years is compelling, particularly after DeCarlo silently watched [Archie Comics] claim ownership in these characters literally for decades.

The court then turned to the rest of the counts in DeCarlo's complaint: breach of contract; breach of fiduciary duty; and breach of the implied covenant of good faith. The court determined that all of these claims were based on the same premise:

> [T]hat DeCarlo's original sketches are the works underlying all subsequent iterations of the Josie characters and that he owns those sketches and the literary property inherent in them. Everything else—such as the licensing of merchandise, animated cartoons and live-action motion pictures—he contends, is derivative of those sketches. Accordingly, he maintains that all of [Archie Comics]'s exploitation of the characters violated plaintiff's rights except to the extent that plaintiff licensed [Archie Comics]'s actions by the parties' agreements.

The court did not reach the issue of whether this was true because it instead held that DeCarlo was equitably estopped from prevailing on his claims. Much like the statute of limitation, equitable estoppel arises when someone sits on their rights so long that it would not be fair for them to enforce them. Equitable estoppel is a fairness principle that prevents one party from being harmed by the other party's voluntary conduct. As the court put it, "Equitable estoppel applies in both law and equity to deny a litigant the right to plead or prove an otherwise important fact because of something he has done or omitted to do [and it] applies in actions for breach of contract and fiduciary duty as well as for copyright infringement."

Before turning to the court's application, perhaps an example of equitable estoppel could be helpful. Assume Bruce and Selina decide to get married and have a ceremony in Corto Maltese. They stay married for more than 30 years and have a daughter named Helena. Years later, Selina finds out that, while they were married, Bruce had a child named Damian with another woman named Talia. She moves for divorce and, because of the infidelity, she asks for everything in the divorce: the stately manor, the cave, the boat, and even the shark repellant. In response, Bruce argues that she can't get these things because marriage is not legally recognized in Corto Maltese and therefore they were never married in the first place. Because Bruce had held himself out as being married to Selina for all those years, the divorce court, in fairness, would not allow him to make that argument. In other words, he would be equitably estopped from claiming the marriage wasn't valid because for years and years he said that it was.

In order for the court to find that equitable estoppel barred DeCarlo's remaining claims, the undisputed facts needed to show: (1) DeCarlo knew Archie Comics was infringing his work; (2) He either (a) intended that Archie Comics rely on his acts or omissions or (b) acted or failed to act in such a manner that Archie Comics had a right to believe it was intended to rely on DeCarlo's conduct; (3) Archie Comics was ignorant of the true facts; and (4) Archie Comics relied on DeCarlo's conduct to its detriment. The court had no problems finding that DeCarlo's action met the prongs of the test. First, the evidence was overwhelming that DeCarlo knew of the infringement:

> He admits that in 1963 he read the copyright notice in She's Josie # 1, which claimed sole copyright in "cover and content" in [Archie Comics] subsidiary, Radio Comics. He admits that he understood in 1963 that [Archie Comics], claimed sole ownership of the copyright; he testified in fact that he "didn't think it was right" for it to do so. He knew that the covers of Josie # 22 (published in 1966) through Josie and the Pussycats # 47 (published in 1970) bore the creator credit "by Dan 'n Dick," in reference to plaintiff and Richard Goldwater, then the managing editor and now co-owner of [Archie Comics]. He learned of [Archie Comics'] license of the Josie property to Hanna-Barbera for the production of animated programs which aired on CBS from 1970 to 1974, and admits he knew [Archie Comics] was "making a fortune" from the shows although he received no compensation. He learned "a long time ago" that some of the Josie cartoons had been released on videocassette and that there had been a Josie underwear license. DeCarlo testified at his deposition that he "had heard some talk about 'Josie' merchandising ... maybe ten years ago." He knew in 1993 that Josie and the Pussycats cartoons were being aired on The Cartoon Network, and testified in his deposition, "I was pretty much hardened at that point. This is it. They can do—They're doing anything they want with the show, the character. And they were."

Second, DeCarlo's inaction was enough to show that he conducted himself in a manner that gave Archie Comics the right to think it owned the Josie Copyrights. The court stated: "In short, DeCarlo's failure ever to voice a complaint or make a competing claim in the face of numerous opportunities to do so—not least, at the point where he signed the 1996 Agreement with which he was 'very unhappy'—gave [Archie Comics] the right to rely on his silence."

Third, the court found that Archie Comics was ignorant of DeCarlo's claim to the characters because he never mentioned his concerns.

Fourth, the court held that Archie Comics relied on DeCarlo's silence to its detriment. The court found:

Based on DeCarlo's silence throughout decades of [Archie Comics'] use of the characters as well as two written agreements, [Archie Comics] also took the position that Universal's "concerns vis-a-vis the copyright issue ... are without any merit" and "a non-issue which is being over-lawyered." It decided not to investigate any potential claims to ownership DeCarlo might have had and urged Universal to execute the licensing agreements without further delay. Indeed, [Archie Comics] agreed to indemnify Universal should any dispute arise as to ownership of the Josie characters.

As a result, the court had no trouble finding:

In these circumstances, DeCarlo is equitably estopped from claiming that [Archie Comics] has violated his rights in the Josie property and characters, whether those claims are couched in terms of copyright, contract or some other legal theory. [Archie Comics] is entitled to summary judgment dismissing the second through fifth causes of action.

The court did grant summary judgment in favor of DeCarlo on one issue—attorney fees. Archie Comics argued that it was entitled to attorney's fee and costs of litigation because DeCarlo breached the clause of the 1996 agreement that provided: "Contractor will not take any action that is inconsistent with or that limits or challenges Archie's exclusive right to exploit the Works and/or the Properties...."

The court found that the paragraph did not clearly provide for the payments of attorney fees and therefore it found no basis for enforcing the paragraph against DeCarlo. And while DeCarlo did prevail on this one issue, this probably provided little consolation to him on the loss of his beloved characters.

The Appeal

DeCarlo moved for summary reversal, which was denied on March 1, 2001. Shortly after, DeCarlo appealed to the United States District Court for the Second Circuit where the case was heard by Circuit Judges Joseph M. McLaughlin and Rosemary S. Pooler, and District Judge John S. Martin, who sat by designation. The Second Circuit affirmed the case on January 22, 2001.

First, the Second Circuit addressed the holding of the lower court that it could hear the case. It agreed that Count One was really a copyright claim for the same reasons, including distinguishing the *Fisher* case. The Second Circuit stated:

DeCarlo would only have a viable *Fisher* cause of action if he sought an injunction against the use of the Josie characters' names, or the use of an all-girl rock band performing in pussycat costumes, for example, because the public might be tricked into thinking DeCarlo sponsored the product. DeCarlo's complaint, however, raises no such cause of action. Instead, it seeks an injunction against the "wrongful use" of and defendant's profit from, DeCarlo's creation of the Josie characters. This is not a *Fisher* claim.

The Second Circuit also agreed with Judge Kaplan that the copyright claim in Count I of the complaint was time barred as the suit was filed after the close of the three year statute of limitations. In addition, the Circuit court also addressed a new argument brought up by DeCarlo. On appeal, DeCarlo argued that even if his ownership suit was held to be not filed within the three year statute of limitations, he nonetheless could still have filed a copyright suit for infringement. The Circuit did not address the merits of this argument because it found a procedural technicality that prevented it from hearing the issue. The Copyright Law of 1976 provides, "no action for infringement of copyright in any work shall be instituted until registration of the copyright claim has been made." As a result, the Second Circuit determined that "DeCarlo cannot maintain a suit for copyright infringement because he never registered the copyrights in accordance with the statute, a necessary first step to instituting a lawsuit based on those rights. Thus, his infringement argument fails."

The Circuit Court then summarily resolved the remaining claims finding no clear error in Judge Kaplan's holding. Specifically, the court found that:

> The district court correctly found DeCarlo pled a copyright claim, properly asserted federal subject matter jurisdiction and correctly found the action barred by the statute of limitations. Further, primarily for the reasons given by the district court, we find the district court properly dismissed DeCarlo's state law claims.
>
> We have examined DeCarlo's remaining claims and find them without merit.

The Supreme Court denied DeCarlo's petition for writ of certiorari on December 3, 2001, which means that the fight for Josie was over.

Or was it?

Remember that the court did not exactly reach the issue of whether Josie was created as a work for hire, it just assumed that it was for the purposes of granting summary judgment. As a result, DeCarlo filed termination notices for the Josie character as well as for Sabrina the Teenage Witch and Cheryl Blossom.

But that is another story.

CHAPTER 11

Whose Witch Is What?
Archie Comics v. Dan DeCarlo

As previously mentioned, Dan DeCarlo was a comics artist who worked for Archie Comics in the 1950s. Not only did he revolutionize their comics by creating a new house style for their teen line, but DeCarlo was instrumental in creating or co-creating several new original characters like Josie and the Pussycats, Sabrina the Teenage Witch, and Cheryl Blossom.

Josie, as discussed in chapter 10, was first pitched as a syndicated comic strip before eventually being picked up by Archie Comics as a regular strip in 1963. Eventually, the name of the book was changed to *Josie and the Pussycats* with issue 45 and the plot changed from following ordinary teens in high school to following a group of touring famous teen rock stars. This iteration of the characters would go on to spawn two successful Saturday morning cartoon series, a plethora of tie-in merchandise, and a less than successful big budget live action movie.

Sabrina the Teenage Witch

Sabrina the Teenage Witch also became famous outside her four color world of comics in the world of television. Her success is indisputable; her origins are more a matter for debate.

Sabrina first appeared in the pages of *Archie's Madhouse* issue 22, which debuted in October 1962, in a five page story entitled "Sabrina the Teen-Age Witch" written by George Gladir. In the story, readers were introduced to Sabrina, a very special teenager. Although Sabrina's mother was a normal mortal human, her father was a magical warlock. This combination made Sabrina a magical half-witch, which gave her the ability to perform spells. Sabrina lived with her two aunts, Hilda and Zelda Spellman, who were both full witches, and a cat named Salem, who was, in fact, a transmogrified warlock named Saberhagen who was being punished for his failed world domination attempts.

Conveniently, the three witches and Salem lived in Greendale, which was the neighboring town of Riverdale, the home of Archie Andrews and his famous friends. This allowed the cast of one Archie comic book to interact with one another. They frequently guest starred in each other's books. Sabrina's primary romantic interest was her mortal boyfriend named

Harvey Kinkle who, like nearly all the other mortals in Sabrina's world, was unaware his girl-friend was a witch.

Sabrina was the creation of DeCarlo and writer George Gladir. DeCarlo stated that in or about 1962 he worked with Gladir to create *Sabrina the Teenage Witch*. Specifically, DeCarlo stated that he "created the physical appearance, mannerisms, personality and 'look' of Sabrina." He claimed he was responsible for the "[t]he entire visual 'look' of the *Sabrina* comic books" as he not only created the original model sheet for Sabrina, but he also personally prepared all of the original design and creative art work for her and various supporting characters. Archie Comics began publishing the *Sabrina* comic books in 1971 and continued until 1983, during which period DeCarlo did all of the art work on a fixed page rate payment basis.

The initial run of *Sabrina the Teenage Witch* lasted for 77 issues from 1971 to 1983. Archie Comics revived the series again in 1997, and it ran through 1999. In 2000, Archie Comics introduced a new, more modern version of the character in a series called *Sabrina*. This *Sabrina* series lasted for 37 issues before being retitled *Sabrina, the Teenage Witch* in 2002. The series changed again when it converted to a Japanese manga style after issue 54 in 2004. The series ended with issue 100 in 2010.

Outside the comics, Sabrina proved to be more marketable than Josie. Based on the success of the *Archie* cartoon, Filmation created a *Sabrina* Saturday morning cartoon, which debuted in 1970. The show ran for four seasons. In addition, one of the short segments, which featured Sabrina's cousins the Groovie Goolies, was spun off into its own series in 1971. However, the character would have even bigger success as a live action property.

In 1996, a young actress named Melissa Joan Hart starred as Sabrina in a live-action made-for-TV film called *Sabrina the Teenage Witch*. If the television movie was a test to see if Sabrina would work as a show, it must have been a success because in September 1996, the *Sabrina, the Teenage Witch* television series premiered. The sitcom ran for seven seasons and included two television movies, a soundtrack release, and a video game. Sabrina also appeared in over 60 tie-in prose books related to the series.

Sabrina, the Animated Series came in 1999. Melissa Joan Hart also starred in this version, but she now provided the voice of Sabrina's two aunts. This series lasted one season and produced 65 episodes, the television/direct-to-video movie *Sabrina: Friends Forever*, and the continuation-spinoff series *Sabrina's Secret Life*. In 2011, Archie Comics announced plans to produce a new animated series based on *Sabrina the Teenage Witch* to be released in late 2012. The show became *Sabrina: Secrets of a Teenage Witch*, a 3D computer-animated series, airing on the Hub Network, which premiered on October 12, 2013.

In April 2012, Sony pictures announced that they would be producing a live-action film based on the comic. No information was available about this movie at the time this book went to press.

Once again, as with the *Josie* properties, DeCarlo never made a claim of ownership for *Sabrina* until he filed suit.

Cheryl Blossom

Cheryl Blossom was never as popular as Sabrina. The character was introduced in 1982 in *Betty and Veronica* issue 320 in a story titled "Dare to Be Bare." Betty and Veronica have been pining for Archie since the beginning.[1] In an effort to raise the stakes, DeCarlo added Cheryl Blossom as a third love interest for Archie. However, due to her sexy nature, she was removed from the book. Eventually, Cheryl returned. Since then, Cheryl has appeared in several comic book stories over the years and has even enjoyed her own series. Recently, it was revealed that Cheryl was being treated for breast cancer in a story that focused on the affordability of, and the right to, healthcare.

The creation of Cheryl Blossom is not as clear. As the court summarized.

> DeCarlo admitted in his deposition that Goldwater approached him with the idea of creating Cheryl and her family. Goldwater explained to DeCarlo that he wanted to create a "real sex symbol," a rich and snobby character, and he asked DeCarlo to draw her and her family. DeCarlo drew a model sheet depicting a family as Goldwater had requested, chose the name Cheryl Blossom, and created Jason, Cheryl's twin brother, a girlfriend of Cheryl's and her parents. There is some evidence that DeCarlo did the drawings for one or two stories written by another for the Cheryl Blossom family. With limited exceptions, [Archie Comics] has made little use of this property.
>
> There is some debate as to who drew the first Cheryl Blossom stories. [Archie Comics'] records indicate that DeCarlo's son, Daniel S. DeCarlo, Jr., was paid for illustrating the stories, although DeCarlo testified at his deposition that he thought the work looked like his own. DeCarlo, Jr., as well as all the other first hand witnesses to the matter, have passed away, making it unlikely that evidence will surface that can shed light on the matter. In the end, though, this is immaterial to the ownership of the copyright in Cheryl Blossom

What is clear is that as with the *Josie* and *Sabrina* properties, DeCarlo never made a claim of ownership on Cheryl Blossom until he filed suit.

The Agreements and Check Endorsements

As described earlier, Dan DeCarlo and Archie Comics entered into a Newsstand Comic Independent Contractor's Agreement on October 25, 1988, which provided:

> [Archie Comics] is the publisher of comic strips and comic books ... of which [Archie Comics] is the sole and exclusive owner,
> [Archie Comics] seeks to supplement its own existing comic strips and comic books (hereinafter the "Existing Archie Works") by the purchase of the entire right, title and interest in existing third party comic strip and pages for its comic books (hereinafter the "Existing Third Party Works"),
> [Archie Comics] desires to retain third parties to modify or otherwise work with the Existing Archie Works and/or the Existing Third Party Works ... on a work made for hire basis, to create modified comic strips and pages for its comic books (hereinafter the "Modified Works"), and
> The Contractor [i.e., DeCarlo] desires to confirm the assignment to [Archie Comics] of the Contractor's entire right, title and interest in and to whatever comic strips and pages for comic books the Contractor may have heretofore provided [Archie Comics] in furtherance of

this project and further desires to work with [Archie Comics] in the future under the terms and conditions hereinafter expressed.

The agreement then set forth covenants in relevant part as follows:

1. (a) The Contractor hereby assigns and conveys to [Archie Comics] all of its rights, title and interest in the Existing Third Party Works heretofore submitted to [Archie Comics].
(b) The Contractor further agrees to work with [Archie Comics] on a work for hire basis to:
   (i) create and develop for [Archie Comics'] exclusive use Additional Works, and
   (ii) perform modifications of Existing Archie Works, Existing Third Party Works (including Existing Third Party Works of others) and Additional Works...

* * *

2. (a) The Contractor hereby assigns to [Archie Comics] all right, title and interest in and to all Works submitted under this Agreement as well as to any patent rights, copyrights, trademark rights and/or applications therefore which relate thereto. The Contractor agrees to execute all documents which are reasonably required to perfect such assignment. It is agreed and understood that such Works shall constitute Works Made for Hire and shall be the sole and exclusive property of [Archie Comics]. To the extent any work of Contractor shall not be deemed under law to constitute subject matter which may be treated as work made on a Work Made for Hire basis, then Contractor hereby assigns and conveys to [Archie Comics] all of its rights, title and interest in any such work.
(b) The Contractor hereby expressly waives all claim of right which it may have to any ownership interest in such Works and/or the ARCHIE property.

DeCarlo and Archie Comics signed another agreement entitled a Work for Hire Agreement between DeCarlo and Archie Comics in 1996. This agreement stated:

[Archie Comics] is in the business of producing and/or publishing comic strips and comic books that include characters, artwork, stories, plots, trademarks, logos, and other creative expressions ("Properties"). All references to "Properties" in this Agreement will include existing and future-created Properties that are commissioned by [Archie Comics] and/or used in any of [Archie Comics'] publications or licensed products.

All past, pending and future uses of all Properties, including uses by [Archie Comics] licensees, will be collectively referred to in this Agreement as "Works."

The 1996 Agreement then set forth several provisions that defined the relationship between DeCarlo and Archie Comics: compensation, job duties, etc. For example:

5. Contractor's full and complete compensation for each assignment ... will be a fixed sum based on a rate to be mutually agreed upon.... Contractor will not be entitled to royalties, to income derived from licensing or merchandising, or to additional compensation for the creation of new Properties....

19. To the extent that any past, pending or future contributions by Contractor to the Works or Properties do not qualify as a Work for Hire, Contractor will and hereby does assign to [Archie Comics] any right, title and interest that he/she has or may obtain therein, including all copyrights, patents, trademarks and other proprietary rights. Contractor will sign, upon request, any documents needed to confirm that any specific Works or Properties are Works for Hire, to effectuate the assignment of his/her rights in any Works or Properties to [Archie Comics] and/or to obtain copyright, trademark and/or patent protection for any of the Works or Properties.

In addition to the agreements, when DeCarlo and Archie Comics eventually went to court, a copy of the back of a check from the late 1970s was produced by DeCarlo during discovery that showed the following endorsement from Archie Comics:

This check is accepted as payment in full for all the undersigned's right, title and interest in and to the strip, copy, art, continuity, characters, story or manuscript entitled or used in (as listed below) and the undersigned affirms that the maker of this check and/or its assigns are given the full rights to use said property for publication, movies, talkies, radio, television, broadcasting, advertising, or for any other use. Permission is hereby granted to make editorial changes. Endorser is the autor [*sic*] or accredited agent in this sale and guarantees [*sic*] that the work is free from libel or infringement.

In addition, Archie Comics produced voucher agreements during discovery as well as copies of cancelled checks. The form of voucher agreement provided:

KNOW ALL MEN, that I, _____ residing at _____ in consideration of the sum of $1 (One Dollar) paid by _____..., herein called "the Assignee," hereby sell, assign, and transfer to the assignee all my right, title and interest in and to the name, title, trade mark and comic strip, including the character or characters portrayed therein, entitled _____ together with the world copyrights therein, and in all renewals and extensions of said copyright, which may be secured under the laws, now or hereafter, in force and effect in the United States, or in any other country or countries.

The endorsement on the back of the checks produced by Archie Comics stated:

This check is accepted in full payment for all the undersigned's right, title and interest in and to the strip, copy, art, continuity, characters, story or manuscript entitled _____ and the undersigned agrees that the maker of this check and or its successors assigns [*sic*] are granted the full ownership rights to said work for publication, transcription by dramatization, movies, radio, television, broadcasting, advertising, or for any other uses including copyright. Permission is hereby granted to make editorial changes. Payer/Endorser is the author or accredited agent in this outright transactions [*sic*] and guarantees that the work is free from libel or copyright or other infringement.

According to the evidence, freelance artists working for Archie Comics were required to sign documents similar to, or substantially the same as, the form agreement and endorsements referred to above at least as early as 1954.

Notices of Termination Are Sent

On July 19, 2000, DeCarlo sent a cease and desist letter to Archie Comics. In September 2000, DeCarlo served purported notices of termination of the grant and licenses of copyrights, including to derivative works made in the 1988 and 1996 Agreements, for *Josie, Sabrina* and *Cheryl Blossom*. In response, Archie Comics filed suit in the United States District Court for the Southern District of New York. In its complaint, Archie Comics requested several items related to *Josie, Sabrina* and *Cheryl Blossom*.

First, Archie Comics sought a ruling from the court that would bar DeCarlo from ever challenging

[Archie Comics'] exclusive ownership of all right, title and interest in and to the so-called Josie property, which was the subject of the DeCarlo case, as well as the so-called Sabrina and Cheryl Blossom Properties, other comic strips that defendant has drawn for plaintiff over the years, as well as a determination that he is barred from pursuing any action against plaintiff, its licensees or anyone else based on any claim that he owns any interest in this properties [*sic*].

As support for its first claim, Archie Comics relied on numerous legal arguments. First, it argued that any claims would be untimely under the statute of limitations, laches, and estoppel because DeCarlo sat on his rights too long.[2] Alternatively, Archie Comics argued that DeCarlo signed away the rights to these characters when he signed the agreement.

In addition, and relevant to this discussion, Archie Comics' fourth cause of action sought a declaration from the court that the copyright termination notices sent to Archie Comics and filed in the Copyright Office in the Josie and Sabrina properties were invalid.

Fifth, Archie Comics sought an injunction barring DeCarlo from ever serving or recording any notice of termination of copyright with respect to Josie, Sabrina or Cheryl Blossom.

Sixth, Archie Comics argued that DeCarlo violated the terms of paragraph 20 of the 1996 Agreement between DeCarlo and Archie Comics.

In short, Archie Comics wanted a court order that said they were the owners of these properties and that DeCarlo could not say otherwise.

DeCarlo filed a very complicated counterclaim against Archie Comics. The counterclaim had three separate parts, which were each named a counterclaim. Each counterclaim had its own facts and up to five parts designated as claims in each counterclaim with separate legal theories supporting each. In an effort to simplify, the basic core of DeCarlo's arguments was as follows:

The first counterclaim stated that he was the proper owner of the *Sabrina the Teenage Witch* comic strip and characters and that Archie Comics violated the Copyright Act because it wrongfully transferred control over the strip when Archie Comics licensed *Sabrina* for use in the TV movies and show, the animated cartoons, video games and other uses. Specifically, the first part of DeCarlo's first counterclaim asked for the court to impose a constructive trust because Archie Comics breached a duty owed to the artist when it transferred the properties because they all "assumed a position of special trust and confidence with regard to" DeCarlo and his creations, "including a duty not to use such creations in any way other than in accordance with the terms of their agreements." The second part of his first counterclaim argued that using his character of Sabrina in a television show was causing him to unfairly compete against his own creation. The third part of his first counterclaim stated that Archie misappropriated his work on *Sabrina*. The fourth part of his first counterclaim argued that there was a wrongful conversion, i.e., theft, of *Sabrina* by ABC when they aired the *Sabrina* television show. Finally, DeCarlo's fifth part of his first counterclaim stated that Archie had unjust enrichment through their use of his characters.

The second counterclaim was identical to the argument DeCarlo made about Josie and the Pussycats, and lost, in the earlier case. Basically the second counterclaim asserted that Archie Comics had incorrectly credited themselves by saying that *Sabrina* was "the creation and property of" Archie Comics by airing the television show with a credit line that stated, "Based on Characters Appearing in Archie Comics." As a result, DeCarlo said this violated trademark law and he wanted credit and money for what he contended was his character.

The third counterclaim was very similar to the first but expanded it in scope and included claims against Archie Comics Online, the owner and operator of the Archie Comics short-lived web site. Once again, DeCarlo argued that he owned "a property interest in the principal and supporting comic book characters in the comic book series *Sabrina the Teenage*

Witch, Josie and the Pussycats, and the character of Cheryl Blossom." As a result, he argued Archie Comics and Archie Comics Online violated the copyright act by unlawfully licensing, selling, or otherwise using the characters. Once again DeCarlo asserted breach of fiduciary duty, unfair competition, misappropriation, conversion and unjust enrichment.

Procedural Fights

What followed next was a series of procedural motions and rulings that helped narrow the case. Equally important, Judge Kaplin's comments and statements in these orders not only provide an excellent analysis of the current state of copyright law and proper procedure for terminations, but also give a clear indication of just how much of an uphill battle DeCarlo was facing against Archie Comics in the fight for these characters.

Archie Comics next filed a motion to dismiss DeCarlo's counterclaims. On April 27, 2001, Judge Kaplan ruled dismissing the counterclaims. First, the court ruled, relying on its earlier decision in *Josie,* that the majority of DeCarlo's claims were improper because they were preempted by the Copyright Act. This meant that the only way DeCarlo could win the case was to prove his case under copyright law and not the variety of other arguments raised in DeCarlo's second through fifth claims for relief in the first and third counterclaims. The court held:

> Each of DeCarlo's challenged claims for relief is based on the common allegation that [Archie Comics] and its principals "wrongfully transferred control" over DeCarlo's "property in the ... characters" in violation of the Copyright Act. Moreover, the crux of each of the challenged claims, even considered without regard to the express violations of the Copyright Act that DeCarlo alleges, is copyright infringement. The second claims for relief complain of the use of the characters allegedly owned by DeCarlo in other works without his permission. The essence of the third, fourth and fifth claims for relief—misappropriation, conversion and unjust enrichment—is that the counterclaim defendants are said to be exploiting rights that allegedly belong to DeCarlo by virtue of authorship—in other words, exploiting and thus infringing rights that are those of a copyright holder. Finally, none of these claims requires proof of any element "instead of or in addition to the acts of reproduction, performance, distribution or display"— each complains of the benefit to the counterclaim defendants derived from their infringement of the exclusive rights of a copyright holder. Accordingly, all of these claims are within the general scope of copyright and preempted by the Copyright Act.

Second, Judge Kaplan stated that there could be no breach of fiduciary claims because "The express and implied obligations assumed by a publisher in an exclusive licensing contract are not, as a matter of law, fiduciary duties." As a result, Judge Kaplan determined:

> DeCarlo's allegations that there were agreements between the parties and that [Archie Comics] and its principals exploited the characters in ways not contemplated by those agreements alleges, at most, breach of contract. The allegations do not set forth a basis sufficient to conclude that there was a fiduciary relationship among the parties. The breach of fiduciary duty claims therefore are legally insufficient.

Finally, the court dismissed DeCarlo's Lanham Act (trademark) claims because "the credit line at issue here does not speak to the origin of the characters. It simply (and truthfully) states that the characters, whoever created them, appear in Archie comics. There are no allegations suggestive of confusion as to the source of the Sabrina programs."

As a result, the court granted the motion to dismiss filed by Archie. However, Judge Kaplan allowed DeCarlo to resubmit the first claim for relief (i.e., the copyright claim) in the first and third counterclaim.

DeCarlo filed his amended counterclaims.[3] He also added two new counterclaims for copyright infringement. Soon afterwards, Archie Comics asked the court to dismiss the reasserted counterclaims and the new counterclaims because DeCarlo did not prove that he registered its copyrights.[4] In response, DeCarlo asked the court to stay the case to allow time for his registrations to process in the copyright office. In other words, after the court's earlier ruling, DeCarlo's lawyers began the paperwork to register for copyrights on his characters. Now, he was asking the court to wait until he was done before ruling on Archie Comics' request to dismiss the case. In the alternative, DeCarlo asked the court to dismiss his claim, "without prejudice to permit Mr. DeCarlo to pursue his breach of contract and any other available state law remedies in the New York State courts and to permit him to reinstate his amended counterclaims in due course after the copyright technicalities have been dealt with." Under this argument, the result would be the same. Judge Kaplan would take the issue out of the case by dismissing them. But, because the dismissal was "without prejudice," DeCarlo would be allowed to file the claims again, when his copyright ducks were in a row.

The court disagreed with both arguments and dismissed the new counterclaims on July 23, 2001. The court's reasoning for this was that it would be unfair to make Archie Comics wait to resolve its copyright issues because "the resolution of factual or legal issues ... as a practical matter would be dispositive of defendant's copyright infringement claims." Alternatively, if Archie Comics lost its case, then DeCarlo "would be no worse off than if a stay were entered because he then could pursue his infringement claims, assuming of course that he obtains certificates of registration." Judge Kaplan also found that there was no reason to make the dismissal without prejudice because it "would not preclude either a supplemental pleading in this action or an independent complaint (assuming arguendo that that would be appropriate) once certificates of registration were obtained."

In the next battle in the case, DeCarlo moved to dismiss several of Archie Comics' claims. Specifically, he asked the court to get rid of the following claims by Archie Comics: the first claim (a ruling that DeCarlo cannot challenge ownership of the properties); the fourth claim (that the notices of termination are not valid); the fifth claim (a ruling that DeCarlo can never challenge ownership again); and the sixth claim (the money requested for breach of contract).

With regard to the first claim, DeCarlo took issue with the precise wording of the declaration requested by Archie Comics and argued that it was not supported by the law.[5] Judge Kaplan rejected this argument commenting that DeCarlo "misconceive[d] the nature of a declaratory judgment action and a court's role in passing on a motion to dismiss such a complaint." The court explained that all that is necessary for a party to receive declaratory relief (i.e., an injunction) is "the existence of a live, definite and concrete controversy between adverse parties and circumstances making a binding judicial declaration useful in establishing their rights." Moreover, the court explained the concept of notice pleading, which means that when a party files suit it need only present facts to support its case and the fact that judicial intervention is warranted. As a result, the precise wording of requested relief is unimportant and will be decided by the court. Instead, Archie Comics must show the propriety of relief.

Looking at the facts, Judge Kaplan had no problem finding that Archie Comics' first claim was warranted:

> In this case, the existence of an actual controversy between adverse parties with respect to ownership of rights in the Josie, Sabrina and Cheryl Blossom properties is undisputed and obvious. Further, notwithstanding the prior decision in the DeCarlo case, that controversy appears to extend to the Josie property because there is every reason to believe that defendant, whose litigiousness is patent, will seek to assert claims against third parties with whom plaintiff has contracted or with whom it seeks to contract in the future for exploitation of its claimed rights in the property.

The court next turned to DeCarlo's request to dismiss the fourth cause of action based on the timing of the notices of termination sent by DeCarlo to Archie Comics. Under copyright law, a creator can terminate the transfer during a five year period. Both Archie Comics and DeCarlo disputed when that five year period started. In its complaint, Archie Comics argued that, at the very least, DeCarlo's termination notices were premature because copyright law proved that this period begins thirty-five years from the date that DeCarlo signed the 1988 and 1996 agreements. DeCarlo moved to dismiss this argument on the ground that copyright law requires, in the case of the grant of a publication of a work, that the five year period begins at the earlier of 35 years from publication or 40 years from the signing of the grant. Therefore, because the underlying works involved in the 1988 and 1996 Agreements were published in the fall of 1967, the grants effected by those Agreements could be terminated in the fall of 2002—thirty-five years after publication.

The court denied DeCarlo's request because the rule invoked by DeCarlo applied to situations where the execution of the grant came first. In this case, the grant came many years later.

> He relies on [the language that allows for termination the earlier of thirty-five years from the date of publication of the work under the grant or forty years from execution of the grant.] As plaintiff contends, however, he is mistaken because he overlooks the significance of the phrase "under the grant" in that clause. As explained in House Report No. 94–1476, "the alternative method of computation is intended to cover cases where years elapse between the signing of a publication contract and the eventual publication of the work." [This alternate form of computation] therefore does not apply where, as here, the copyrights in previously published works are assigned. In consequence, any right that [DeCarlo] may have to terminate rights transferred pursuant to the 1988 and 1996 Agreements must be exercised during the five year period beginning at the end of thirty-five years from the date on which the relevant grants were executed. There is, accordingly, no merit to [DeCarlo]'s motion insofar as it is addressed to the fourth cause of action.

The court next moved to DeCarlo's claim that it should dismiss the fifth cause of action of Archie Comics. In this claim, Archie Comics requested an injunction that barred DeCarlo from "making any ... claim premised on the assertion that [he] has and/or ever has had any rights in the copyrights to [the Josie, Sabrina, and Cheryl Blossom properties] based on the fact that that any such claims were barred by the statute of limitations based on the court's earlier *Josie* reasoning. In response, DeCarlo argued that the ruling would not be binding in the new case. The court found that it didn't matter. It stated:

In the [earlier *Josie*] case, this Court held ... that [DeCarlo's] contention that he rather than [Archie Comics] owned the copyright in the Josie characters was barred by the statute of limitations. At least as far as the Josie characters are concerned, DeCarlo conclusively determined the issue.

Although [DeCarlo] devotes some energy to the assertion that the ruling is not binding in this case, the point is academic. Regardless of whether it is binding as a matter of principles of former adjudication, this Court would reach the same result for the same reasons here.

As a result, DeCarlo's motion to dismiss was limited to the three year period that arose between the *Josie* decision and the filing of Archie Comics' complaint. Even then, the court was not impressed with DeCarlo's argument:

[DeCarlo's] position on this issue makes little sense and is against the great weight of authority. In order to make out a case for copyright infringement, a plaintiff must establish ownership of a valid copyright plus copying. At least as between [DeCarlo] and [Archie Comics] and, in all likelihood, those claiming by, through or under [Archie Comics], [DeCarlo] cannot possibly establish ownership of a valid copyright with respect to the Josie property because, as between [Archie Comics and DeCarlo, DeCarlo] has lost that argument. [DeCarlo] therefore cannot possibly establish the elements of a claim for copyright infringement against [Archie Comics] and its mesne and ultimate licensees and assignees with respect to the Josie characters. If [Archie Comics] can establish the other prerequisites to injunctive relief, it would be entitled to the injunction it seeks by the fifth cause of action. There is, of course, more to the fifth cause of action and to [DeCarlo's]. The extent to which any injunction to which [Archie Comics] might be entitled properly should affect [DeCarlo's] right to bring claims against strangers to this litigation, for example, is an open question. The point, however, is that this Court may not now dismiss the fifth cause of action unless it now is clear that [Archie Comics] cannot prove any facts that would entitle it to any relief on this claim. The foregoing discussion demonstrates that this is not the case. There is no need at this juncture to accept [DeCarlo's] invitation to attempt to formulate a decree even in advance of [Archie Comics]'s establishing that it is entitled to one.

Finally, the court denied DeCarlo's motion to dismiss Archie Comics' sixth cause of action, which sought damages, other than attorney's fees and litigation costs. Archie Comics argued that DeCarlo owed these amounts because he breached paragraph 20 of the 1996 Agreement in which [DeCarlo] covenanted that he "will not take any action that is inconsistent with or that limits or challenges [Archie Comics'] exclusive right to exploit the Works and/or the Properties..." when he sent a July 19, 2000, cease and desist letter to [Archie Comics] and recorded notices of termination for the *Sabrina* and *Josie* properties. DeCarlo moved to dismiss this claim based on the court's earlier decision in the Josie case. However, as the court explained, that earlier case was based on the request for attorney's fees and it found that argument to be "entirely frivolous [because] the issues raised here were neither actually litigated nor necessarily decided in [the *Josie* case]." Moreover, the court found because the cease and desist letter and termination notices occurred after the *Josie* decision, they could not have been part of the earlier case. As a result "Any claims in the instant action that arise out of the three letters or DeCarlo's interposition of counterclaims could not have been filed on March 6 or April 3, 2000 as the events giving rise to the claims had not yet occurred. [Archie Comics'] sixth cause of action therefore is not barred...."

The next round of procedural motions came after the close of discovery. First, DeCarlo sought to amend his counterclaim again to reassert several copyright infringement claims that were dismissed because DeCarlo did not show that he had obtained certificates of registration for Josie, Sabrina, and Cheryl Blossom. Although DeCarlo alleged that these were "entirely new claims, based on very recent tortuous [*sic*] actions taken by [Archie Comics] in 2001 during the pendency of the case," the court denied the motion. A court has discretion in determining whether to allow a party to amend their complaint and will usually do so to promote economic or judicial efficiency, especially when the amendment will not cause undue delay. Weighing these factors, Judge Kaplan found that amendment was inappropriate. First, the court observed that discovery was already completed and that the case was "on the eve of disposition, either by motion or by trial" and introducing these new claims would have unnecessarily delayed the process. Second, the court found that "the reassertion of the copyright infringement claims at this juncture almost surely would be futile." This was because DeCarlo had still not alleged that he ever obtained the certificates of registration. Third, perhaps in a bit of foreshadowing, the court reiterated its view that the specific issues in the new counterclaims could be resolved in the current litigation. "Finally, as the Court has noted previously, it is entirely possible that the litigation of [DeCarlo's] claim may result in the resolution of factual or legal issues that as a practical matter would be dispositive of [DeCarlo's] copyright infringement claims."

As a result, the court denied the motion on December 10, 2001. A month later, Archie Comics moved to amend its complaint to remove the sixth cause of action, which requested money damages for DeCarlo's alleged breach of the 1996 Agreement. As a result of removing this claim, Archie Comics also requested the court to change the trial from a jury trial to a bench trial.[6] DeCarlo agreed to the amendment but opposed the jury issue, arguing that this was really a copyright case and therefore eligible for a jury trial. In response, Archie Comics argued that it did "not agree that a suit for a declaration of non-infringement would be triable as of right to a jury absent a counterclaim for monetary damages."

Judge Kaplan found a middle of the road position:

> There is no reason to decide this issue now. The Court will empanel a jury in this case and submit to it any factual issues as to which [DeCarlo] even arguably has a right to a jury trial. If the Court and the jury are in accord, the issue will be moot. Only if the Court and the jury disagree will there be any need to determine whether [DeCarlo] is entitled to have the jury find the facts. Should the Court then decide that it is the proper trier of any disputed facts, it will treat the jury's verdict as that of an advisory jury.

Substitution

Sadly, DeCarlo died on December 18, 2001, at the age of 82.

On February 1, 2002, the court allowed Josette Dumont DeCarlo, the widow of DeCarlo and executrix of DeCarlo's estate, to substitute herself for him in the case. Not only was Josette the widow of DeCarlo, but she was also the inspiration for Josie.

On January 3, 2003, in a bit of foreshadowing, the court also decided to separate, or bifurcate, the liability and damage phases of DeCarlo's counterclaims and to put on hold, or stay, any proceedings relating to damages. The effect of this allowed the parties to focus on arguing who would win. After the court decided that, it would turn to the issue of hearing evidence about calculating damages. In other words, he court would only have to

consider DeCarlo's evidence on damages if it decided he won. If DeCarlo lost, then bifur-
cation would save time and money because the evidence would never need be presented.

On April 23, 2003,[7] DeCarlo lost in a ruling written by Judge Kaplan. First, the court
addressed the *Josie* properties.[8]

> As noted, *DeCarlo I* was decided on the ground that DeCarlo was equitably estopped to
> challenge [Archie Comics]'s ownership. [Archie Comics] makes precisely that claim here. The
> question whether [Archie Comics] was ignorant of DeCarlo's claim of ownership in the Josie
> property was essential to the decision in DeCarlo I, actually litigated and necessarily decided.
> DeCarlo had a full and fair opportunity to litigate it. The estate therefore is collaterally
> estopped by the finding in DeCarlo I from contesting [Archie Comics]'s ignorance of DeCarlo's
> claim of ownership in the Josie property.
>
> The recent production of the form of agreement and the check endorsements does not alter
> this conclusion. Res judicata and collateral estoppel apply even in the face of a claim that the
> prior judgment was erroneous as long as that judgment stands. In any case, DeCarlo had his copy
> of the check endorsement used in 1970 and access to Messrs. Boiling and Edwards and the docu-
> ments they possessed at the time DeCarlo I was litigated. He has offered no explanation for his
> failure in that case to raise the contention he now makes. In all the circumstances, defendant is
> precluded by DeCarlo I from asserting any claim of ownership in the Josie property.

The court next turned to the *Sabrina* properties. Given its earlier ruling, the court
applied two separate analyses. First it examined whether the works done prior to January 1, 1978, were works for hire. In finding they were, the court held:

> First, the lynchpin of DeCarlo's contention that there indeed was an agreement or agree-
> ments to the contrary is the form of voucher agreement and the check endorsements to which
> reference already has been made. But he has produced no such agreement with respect to any
> *Sabrina* contributions. Rather, he has adduced evidence that there were, or perhaps were,
> voucher agreements and check endorsements relating to his *Sabrina* contributions—all of which
> have been lost—and that their terms were "similar" or "identical" to the forms that he has prof-
> fered, at least so far as a couple of witnesses remember decades later.... The evidence before the
> Court does not permit a reasoned, logical decision as to the terms of any voucher agreements
> and check endorsements during the relevant period.
>
>   * * *
>
> Second, even if one were to assume that the check legends and voucher agreement forms
> used from 1960 through the end of 1977 were the same as the endorsement DeCarlo copied
> down in 1970, the assumption would not permit an inference (under either a clear and convinc-
> ing or a preponderance standard) that [Archie Comics] and DeCarlo agreed that DeCarlo
> would retain copyright in his contributions to the Sabrina property. The 1970 endorsement con-
> firms that [Archie Comics'] "check is accepted as full payment for all the undersigned's right,
> title and interest in and to the strip, copy, art, continuity, characters, story or manuscript entitled
> or used in" the story identified on the check. It "affirms that the maker of this check and/or its
> assigns are given the full rights to use said property for publication, movies, talkies, radio, televi-
> sion, broadcasting, advertising, or for any other use" and have the right to make editorial
> changes. And it represents that the "endorser is autor [*sic*] or accredited agent in this sale and
> guarantees [*sic*] that the work is free from libel or infringement." Thus, the endorsement, far
> from suggesting that DeCarlo retained copyright in the contribution for which the endorsed
> check was issued, supports the view that [Archie Comics] was the sole owner of all rights.
>
>   * * *
>
> Third, the 1988 Agreement assigned to [Archie Comics] all of DeCarlo's "rights, title and
> interest in the Existing Third Party Works heretofore submitted to Archie" and conveyed to

[Archie Comics] any rights that DeCarlo had in any of the comic strips and pages that he previously had "submitted to Archie," which included all of his *Sabrina* artwork.

The court next ruled that DeCarlo had no rights to the *Sabrina* property after January 1, 1978. The court determined:

> Between January 1, 1978, the effective date of the 1976 Act, and October 25, 1988, the date of the 1988 Agreement, DeCarlo illustrated only three short stories, three short gags, some covers and a fashion page involving *Sabrina*. [Archie Comics] contends that none of these projects contained any new *Sabrina* material.... In view of the fact that DeCarlo's minimal contributions to the *Sabrina* property in the 1978–1988 period contained no new delineation of the property or characters, [Archie Comics] owns those works.
>
> In any case, *Sabrina* works created after October 25, 1988, the date of the 1988 Agreement, qualify as works for hire owned by [Archie Comics]. Works created on or after January 1, 1978 are governed by the 1976 Act.... The *Sabrina* works fall within the periodical categories covered by the 1976 Act. All were specially ordered or commissioned by [Archie Comics]. Moreover, the 1988 Agreement expressly provided that all works DeCarlo submitted to [Archie Comics] would constitute works for hire, and the 1996 Agreement further stated that "[t]his is a Work for Hire agreement between Archie Comic Publications, Inc. ... and Daniel S. DeCarlo." In consequence, any contributions by DeCarlo to the *Sabrina* property created after October 25, 1988, the date of the 1988 Agreement were works for hire.

Finally, the court turned to *Cheryl Blossom* and determined that the properties belonged to Archie Comics, the court held:

> The *Cheryl Blossom* works are part of the Archie property. Paragraph 2(b) of the 1988 Agreement provides that DeCarlo "hereby expressly waives all claims of right which [he] may have to any ownership interest in such works and/or the ARCHIE property." In consequence, [Archie Comics] also is the owner of any copyright interests in the *Cheryl Blossom* property. Moreover, for reasons discussed above, DeCarlo assigned any rights he may have had to any such works in the 1988 and 1996 Agreements.

As a result, the court issued the following ruling:

> [Archie Comics'] motion for summary judgment is granted to the extent that [Archie Comics] shall recover judgment:
>
> (1) declaring that [DeCarlo] is equitably estopped from challenging [Archie Comics'] exclusive ownership of all rights, title and interest, including copyrights, in and to the *Josie* property;
>
> (2) declaring that [DeCarlo]'s testator's contributions to the *Sabrina* property were works for hire owned ab initio by [Archie Comics] and, in any case, that any right, title and interest therein, including copyrights, which he ever had were assigned by him to [Archie Comics];
>
> (3) declaring that all right, title and interest of [DeCarlo]'s testator's contributions to the *Cheryl Blossom* property, if any, were assigned by him to [Archie Comics];
>
> (4) declaring that the Notices of Termination of Transfer of Copyright and Related Licenses and Rights referred to in the complaint are null and void; and
>
> (5) enjoining [DeCarlo] from:
>
>   (a) commencing any action against [Archie Comics], its successors, its licensees and its licensees' successors which challenges [Archie Comics]'s ownership of the *Josie*, *Sabrina* and/or *Cheryl Blossom* properties, and/or any character or characters depicted therein, which challenges [Archie Comics]'s ownership thereof, including without limitation, copyrights therein, premised on the assertion that [DeCarlo]'s testator has and/or ever has had any rights therein; and (b) serving and/or recording any notice of termination of transfer of copyright pursuant to 17 U.S.C. § 203 with respect to the *Sabrina* property,

and/or any character or characters depicted therein, premised on the assertion that [DeCarlo]'s testator has and/or ever has had any rights therein.

A final judgment was entered on June 11, 2003, granting summary judgment in favor of Archie Comics and permanently enjoining DeCarlo's estate from challenging Archie Comics' ownership of intellectual property associated with Josie, Sabrina or Cheryl Blossom. Josie DeCarlo appealed to the Second Circuit, which affirmed in a summary order (i.e., no analysis or discussion) on March 3, 2004. After losing in the Second Circuit, Ms. DeCarlo filed for a writ of certiorari to the Supreme Court. The Supreme Court declined to grant certiorari on October 4, 2004.

The case was concluded. No one could make a claim on the properties against Archie Comics. Ironically, not even Josie herself could claim ownership to Josie, the character based on her.

CHAPTER 12

Contracts in Brief

Contracts are a way of life. Every day, people enter into numerous contracts. From employment contracts to mortgage contracts to the purchase of consumer goods to fee for service contracts, contracts permeate every aspect of modern society. For the comic creator, contracts take on a particularly significant meaning.

As will be seen, if creators are not careful, they could limit the use of their creations or, even worse, outright lose all rights to their characters. Similarly, the failure to have a clear written contract that adequately explains the expectations of the parties can, at best, create unnecessary legal expenses and, at worst, lead to long protracted litigation.

As a background, it may be helpful to explain what a contract is and explain the requirements of a valid contract.

Types of Contracts

A contract is an enforceable agreement. Basically, what this means is that if one side of the agreement doesn't hold up their end, the other side can take them to court to enforce the contract.

A contract can be written or oral.[1] Both are equally enforceable. Despite this, when dealing in business transactions, it is always better to have a written contract. This is because a written contract memorializes the terms of the contract, which helps prevent confusion at the time, and helps refresh recollection at a later date should issues arise or relationships fail.[2]

Contracts are either unilateral or bilateral. A unilateral contract involves a promise for an act. Once the act is completed then the promise must be satisfied. They are one sided and there is no liability owed if the act never occurs. For example, if Barry tells Jay, "If you build a cosmic treadmill, I will take you to an alternate earth." Once Jay builds the treadmill, Barry must take him to the alternate earth. If Jay never builds the treadmill, Barry has no recourse against him, he just is not obligated to take him to the alternate Earth.

A bilateral contract, on the other hand, works very differently. A bilateral contract is a promise for a promise. The contract is formed when the promises are made and are enforceable by both sides. For example, if Barry says to Jay, "if you promise to build me a cosmic treadmill, I promise to take you to an alternate Earth." This is a bilateral contract. If Jay accepts and promises to build the machine, both sides are obligated to perform under the contract. This means that if Jay decides not to build the treadmill, Barry can sue him for nonperformance.

Requirements for a Valid Contract

In order for a contract to be enforceable, it must satisfy several basic requirements.

First, the people entering into the contract must actually be able to enter into the contract. This means that everyone needs the legal capacity to bind themselves. For example, a minor is not able to enter into a contract.

Second, there must be a valid offer. This means there needs to be a clear or definite request to contract. For example, "will you draw pencils for a three issue limited series for a hundred dollars a page?" is much more definitive than "It would be cool to do something together."

Third, there must be an unqualified acceptance that shows understanding of the terms. Again, "Yes, I will draw pencils for a three issue limited series for a hundred dollars a page" is more definitive than, "yeah, cool."[3]

Fourth, a contract needs consideration. This is a legal term that means each party has to promise or provide something of value to the other. Without this exchange, there is no contract. Of course, consideration does not always have to mean money. For example, if an offer states, "If you pencil my book, I will give you five copies," then the five copies are the consideration.[4]

Fifth, there also needs to be a meeting of the minds (referred to as mutual assent). This means that both sides to the agreement must agree on the essential terms and must intend to be bound by their agreement. This is precisely what Siegel and Shuster argued was lacking in their Superman agreement with DC Comics in their New York State lawsuit, discussed in chapter 15.

Sixth, a contract cannot violate the law. This is called legal purpose. Obvious examples of this would involve hit men and bank robbers. However, the same logic would apply to a contract that attempts to transfer moral rights (chapter 3) or to one transferring a termination right (chapter 17).

As can be seen, a contract can be as simple as a few sentences.

This Agreement is made on (date) by (Party One) and (Party Two). For valuable consideration consisting of (Consideration), Party One agrees to (Promise One), and Party two agrees to (Promise Two). Additional terms include (Conditions). Signed, this date. (Signatures).

At the other end of the spectrum a contract could be several hundred pages with introductory material, recitals, representations, whereas provisions, definitions, key terms, conditions, a statement of purpose, assurances, warranties, covenants, boilerplate provisions, and many exhibits.

Conclusion

A comic creator can expect to encounter several different types of contracts. These include, but are not limited to: Publishing Contracts; Distribution Contracts; Work for Hire Contracts; Non-Disclosure Agreements; Licensing of Rights; Transfers of Intellectual Property (Trademark or Copyright); Consignment Agreements, Translation Contracts; Website Maintenance Agreements; Appearance Contracts; and Employment Contracts.[5] Detailed discussion about these types of contracts is beyond the scope of this book. Needless to say, if a creator is in a position to negotiate these contracts, the assistance of a lawyer up front can avoid many problems in the future. If money is an issue, many law schools and other organizations offer free clinics to assist artists and creators in these types of situations.

CHAPTER 13

Riders in the Storm
Gary Friedrich v. Marvel Comics

In the early seventies, comics were changing. Restrictions in the Comics Code were loosened allowing companies to have more flexibility. In response, many introduced darker characters. One such character sprang from the imagination of Gary Friedrich and onto the pages of Marvel Comics in *Marvel Spotlight* issue 5, which appeared in 1972. Friedrich named his creation Ghost Rider, a supernatural alter ego of stunt motorcyclist Johnny Blaze, who, in order to save the life of his mentor, agreed to sell his soul to Satan. Now, whenever evil was present, Blaze would become engulfed by hellfire, which caused his head to become a flaming skull and gave him the power to ride a fiery motorcycle, gaze with a soul-piercing stare, and shoot fire from his skeletal hands.

The Original Ghost Rider

Johnny Blaze was not the first character to be called Ghost Rider. In fact, Marvel Comics had previously published several stories featuring a western character named Ghost Rider.[1] Moreover, the very first Ghost Rider was not a Marvel Comics creation at all. Instead, the original Ghost Rider debuted in 1949 in the pages of *Tim Holt* issue 11 from Magazine Enterprises.

The original Ghost Rider character was the creation of writer Ray Krank and artist Dick Ayers. This version of Ghost Rider appeared in horror-themed Western stories like *Tim Holt*, *Red Mask*, and *A-1 Comics*, which were put out by Magazine Enterprises in the 1950s.[2] The hero known as Ghost Rider was, in reality, a federal marshal named Rex Fury who wore a white outfit covered with phosphorus and had a cape that had a phosphorescent covering on one side and black cloth on the other. Rex used the black side of the cape to cover parts of his body to give the illusion that he was merely a floating head or pair of hands. To further his ghostly illusion, he wielded a black lariat and a black bullwhip so that he could appear to grab things at a distance. Even his twin six-guns and his horse, Spectre, used the same phosphorescence to appear to glow in the dark.

The original Ghost Rider's reign lasted until the institution of the Comics Code. As described more in chapter 20, the Comics Code Authority, among other things, greatly restricted the amount of violence, crime, and horror that could be shown in the pages of a comic. As a result, a character like Ghost Rider no longer had a place in mainstream comics and faded into publishing obscurity. Magazine Enterprises did not even bother to maintain the copyright or trademark on the name. The original Ghost Rider, along with the other Magazine Enterprise characters, has entered the public domain.[3]

But Magazine Enterprises' loss was Marvel Comics' gain. Marvel Comics' first Ghost Rider debuted in February 1967 after Magazine Enterprises abandoned the trademark and the copyright expired. Although heavily based on the original Ghost Rider, this version of the character was named Carter Slade and was a cowboy who battled evil while dressed in a virtually identical phosphorescent white costume as the original, complete with a full-face mask. There was another major difference between the two characters. Unlike the Magazine Enterprises version of the character, the stories featuring Marvel Comics' version of Ghost Rider were horror-free and therefore permitted under the Comics Code Authority. The Marvel Comics version of the character first appeared in *Ghost Rider* issue 1 in 1967 and was co-written by writers Roy Thomas and Gary Friedrich (the original Ghost Rider artist, Dick Ayers, returned to draw the story). Marvel Comics' first *Ghost Rider* series only lasted seven issues. However, the character went on to appear in several stories in a 1970 *Western Gunfighters* series.[4]

The Origin of Gary Friedrich

The one thing that tied both versions of Marvel Comics' Ghost Rider together was the involvement of Gary Friedrich. Friedrich was born and raised in Jackson, Missouri, and that is where he met Roy Thomas. Friedrich and Thomas became close friends in their teenage years. After high school, Thomas moved to New York to pursue a career in comics. Friedrich stayed in Missouri, where he got married and had a child. While in Missouri, Friedrich held several jobs, including as a writer/editor of a bi-weekly newspaper and a union job at a factory making waffle irons. Friedrich also testified that he struggled with alcoholism.

Sometime in the mid-sixties, Friedrich's friend Thomas contacted him and suggested Friedrich pursue a career in comics. At the time, Thomas worked for Marvel Comics as a staff writer. He suggested Friedrich move to New York to try to get freelance writing work. Friedrich took a Greyhound bus the following day and moved in with Thomas. With the help of Thomas, Friedrich began writing romance and superhero stories for Charlton Comics. Eventually, Friedrich began working for Marvel Comics writing western comics such as *Kid Colt, Outlaw*; *Two-Gun Kid*; *Rawhide Kid*, as well as the aforementioned cowboy version of *Ghost Rider* (co-plotted with Thomas) in 1967. By the beginning of the 1970s, Friedrich's freelance work had expanded and he was regularly writing several issues of mainstream Marvel Comics titles, including *Sgt. Fury and His Howling Commandos*; *The Incredible Hulk*; *Uncanny X-Men*; *Captain America*; *Captain Marvel*; *Daredevil*; *Nick Fury, Agent of S.H.I.E.L.D.*; and the Black Widow feature in *Amazing Adventures*. But Friedrich is most remembered for the creation of the supernatural character known as Ghost Rider that premiered in 1972.

The Origin of Ghost Rider

The facts surrounding the specific creation of Ghost Rider have become quite controversial. Friedrich claims that he alone came up with the concept. As far back as the 1950s, Friedrich said he had the idea for a motorcycle-riding superhero who wore black leather. Then, after Evel Knievel became popular in the late 1960s, Friedrich's hero transformed into a motorcycle stuntman. According to Friedrich, but heavily disputed by Marvel Comics, in 1968, Friedrich remembered seeing a bony-faced and red-headed friend driving a motorcycle. This was the sight that gave him the idea for the look of his character and inspired the motorcycle stuntman's flaming skull head. Once this new character was completed, Friedrich says he created an origin story in which his flaming skull motorcycle riding hero became a demon after making a deal with the devil.

Here the stories diverge further. Friedrich remembers that, in 1971, he decided to try to pitch a comic book starring his flaming-skulled hero after the Comics Code Authority relaxed its standards to permit comic books to contain more adult-themed and supernatural content. Friedrich took his original concept, refined the story, and created a character design. Then, at his own expense, Friedrich created a written synopsis for the Ghost Rider, which detailed the character's origin story and the main characters' appearances. Friedrich then pitched his written synopsis to his friend Thomas. By this time, Thomas had been elevated to assistant editor at Marvel Comics. Thomas liked the idea so much that he gave it to Stan Lee, Marvel Comics' Chief, and arranged a meeting so that Friedrich could pitch the idea to Lee. After this meeting, Lee and Marvel Comics agreed to publish the Ghost Rider comic book as part of a series Marvel Comics had developed to try out untested characters called *Marvel Spotlight*. And while there was no discussion about renewal rights or even a written agreement, Friedrich agreed to assign his rights in the Ghost Rider characters solely to Marvel Comics. Friedrich understood that Marvel Comics would own the rights to the character and the work for comic books—but, without any articulation on his part, let alone acknowledgment on the part of Marvel Comics management, he assumed that he would personally retain rights to exploit the character and the work in other, non-comic mediums. At the time, he was considering the possibility of a television show, but never discussed this fact or obtained any agreement from Marvel Comics that even television rights would be left out of the bundle of rights that Marvel Comics would own. Specifically, Friedrich testified:

> Q. Were you aware that the copyright for Marvel Spotlight Number 5 and Number 6 and
> several other Marvel Spotlight publications featuring the motorcycle Ghost Rider character were claimed in the name of either Magazine Management or Cadence?
> A. Yes.
> Q. Did you ever have a discussion with anyone at Marvel about that?
> A. No.
>
> * * *
>
> Q. What is your understanding of how the copyright was transferred or is supposed to be
> transferred from any of those companies or their successors to you?
> A. I—I thought that I was giving Marvel the right to use any character for comic book use
> only. If they began to use it for movies and other things, then I thought that I had a

right to the copyright, to—well, that I had the copyright to the character for movies and anything other than comic books.

* * *

Q. What did you do to make your intent to utilize the characters in Marvel Spotlight Number 5 known since 1968?

A. Roy and I talked about, after the deal with Marvel was cooked that, you know, what might happen with the character down the road if it were successful, there might be—at that time we thought it might be made into a TV series.

At Marvel Comics' instruction, Friedrich then gave the synopsis to a freelance artist named Mike Ploog. Ploog drew the story under Friedrich's supervision. Friedrich was very specific and advised Ploog on how the characters should look and what to draw in the story.

Marvel Comics' version of the creation of Ghost Rider is very different. Marvel Comics alleges that, in 1971, Friedrich was working on an issue of *Daredevil* when he had an idea for a villain. Friedrich then met with his editor, Thomas, and suggested that he include a motorcycle-riding villain named Ghost Rider in the Daredevil story he was currently working on. After hearing the idea, Thomas thought that the Ghost Rider might be better if he was a superhero in his own comic book. Soon after, Thomas arranged a meeting with Lee to discuss the concept. At the meeting, Lee agreed to publish the concept, but decided that Ghost Rider's alter ego would be named "Johnny Blaze." Both Friedrich and Thomas disliked the name, but started work on the book.

According to Marvel Comics, it was only after this meeting that Friedrich began writing Ghost Rider's origin story. Soon after the meeting, Thomas arranged a meeting with Ploog to create a design for the character. Friedrich did not attend the meeting and, thus, could not provide any instruction on what Ghost Rider should look like before Ploog created his design. Ploog stated that he modeled the look of the new character after the original cowboy version of the character, but also incorporated suggestions by Thomas that Ghost Rider should wear an Elvis-like leather jump suit and have a skull for a head. While drawing the skull, Ploog spontaneously decided to add flames in an effort to successfully frame the skull.

Marvel Comics, at the time, utilized what was known as the Marvel Method to create their books. Under the Marvel Method, the first step was to initiate the project through either the purchase of an independently developed character or synopsis or the assignment of a creator to either create a new or utilize an existing character in a new story. And while Marvel Comics and Friedrich disagree as to what happened in this first step of the method, they do agree that the rest of the book's creation was produced using the Marvel Method. After the first step, the Marvel Method proceeded as follows: (2) an artist (not the writer) illustrated a work based on the synopsis, (3) the artist then provided the illustrated panels to the writer for text to be written, (4) a letterer placed the text in the appropriate spot on the illustration (sometimes in consultation with the writer), (5) the pages were inked and colored, and (6) finally, the book was printed and distributed. In this case, Ploog drew the story; Friedrich wrote the story; John Costanza lettered the story.[5] All of this work was done in accordance with and at the direction of Lee and Thomas, the editors employed by

Marvel Comics. Marvel Comics paid for the work, including a page rate for Friedrich's contributions as a freelance writer, as well as all the cost of publication and distribution.

In spring and summer of 1972, Marvel Comics published several issues of its comics that contained a promotional segment called Marvel Bullpen Bulletin, which announced the Ghost Rider character and told readers to look out for *Marvel Spotlight* 5. This segment stated that Friedrich had "dreamed the whole thing up" and encouraged people to read it.

Marvel Spotlight issue 5 appeared on the stands in April 1972. In the story, Johnny Blaze, to save the life of his mentor and the man who has become like a father to him, makes a deal with the devil and is transformed into the spirit of vengeance, Ghost Rider. The issue bore a copyright notice that said that "Magazine Management Co., Inc. Marvel Comics Group" owned the rights and the first page assigned the Marvel Comics brand to its wholly-owned subsidiary Magazine Management. The credit box in the issue read that the story was:

> Conceived and Written
> Gary Friedrich

Ghost Rider *Gains Momentum*

The book became an overnight success. Ghost Rider stories continued to appear in the next six issues of *Marvel Spotlight*. By May 1973, Marvel Comics launched a separate *Ghost Rider* comic book series. Friedrich continued to write these stories for several issues on a freelance work for hire basis. In October 1974, Marvel Comics included a reprint of *Marvel Spotlight* issue 5 as part of *Ghost Rider* issue 10 (along with a new first and last page). *Ghost Rider* 10 still contained Friedrich's "Conceived & Written" credit. The *Ghost Rider* comic book series continued to run even after Friedrich left the title from 1973 to 2002 and Marvel Comics published over 300 comic book stories starring Ghost Rider. In fact, Marvel Comics reprinted *Marvel Spotlight* issue 5 five times, including as late as 2005. Marvel Comics never removed Friedrich's "Conceived & Written" credit from any of the *Marvel Spotlight* issue 5 reprints. Marvel Comics promptly filed registrations for several of these subsequent *Ghost Rider* comic books, even though it had not filed a registration for *Marvel Spotlight* issue 5.

Throughout the 1970s, Friedrich continued his work and worked as both an employee and freelance comic book writer for Marvel Comics. When he worked as an employee, Marvel Comics paid Friedrich with a payroll check. When he worked as a freelancer he was paid separately by check. Friedrich remembers that those checks, like the checks issued to all of Marvel Comics' freelance workers, had a legend on the back that "said something about by signing over the check I gave over my rights to [Marvel Comics]." The checks paid to Friedrich for his work on Ghost Rider all contained this language. The checks issued to Friedrich for his work on *Ghost Rider* and *Marvel Spotlight* issue 5 also had this legend on the back of his freelance checks. He signed all of them. At some point in the 1970s, Friedrich decided to move back to Missouri where he continued to write freelance comics for Marvel Comics.

In 1976, the copyright law changed. The change in the law permitted companies to renew their copyrights longer, but also permitted creators a chance to get their intellectual property back for the renewal period unless it was made by an employee or as a work for hire. Under the 1976 Copyright Act, a work created outside the scope of employment would only be considered a work for hire if the creator and purchaser executed an express written agreement that specifically identified the relationship as work for hire. Obviously, these changes forced a lot of comic companies to enter into more formal arrangements with their creators. As part of this, in 1978, Marvel Comics created a work for hire agreement and required all of its freelance artists and writers to sign it if they wished to continue working for Marvel Comics. The agreement was a page long and read:

> Agreement made this _____ day of _____, 19__ by and between _____ at _____ (herein "Supplier") and the Marvel Comics Group... [herein "Marvel"].
>
> MARVEL is in the business of publishing comic and other magazines known as the Marvel Comics Group, and SUPPLIER wishes to have MARVEL order or commission either written material or art work as a contribution to the collective work known as the Marvel Comics Group. MARVEL has informed SUPPLIER that MARVEL only orders or commissions such written material or art work on an employee-for-hire basis.
>
> THEREFORE, the parties agree as follows:
>
> In consideration of MARVEL's commissioning and ordering from SUPPLIER written material or art work and paying therefor, SUPPLIER acknowledges, agrees and confirms that any and all work, writing, art work material or services (the "Work") which have been or are in the future created, prepared or performed by SUPPLIER for the Marvel Comics Group have been and will be specially ordered or commissioned for use as a contribution to a collective work and that as such Work was and is expressly agreed to be considered a work made for hire.
>
> SUPPLIER expressly grants to MARVEL forever all rights of any kind and nature in and to the Work, the right to use SUPPLIER's name in connection therewith and agrees that MARVEL is the sole and exclusive copyright proprietor thereof having all rights of ownership therein. SUPPLIER agrees not to contest MARVEL's exclusive, complete and unrestricted ownership in and to the Work.
>
> This agreement shall be binding on and inure to the benefit of the parties hereto and their respective heirs, successors, administrators and assigns.
>
> IN WITNESS WHEREOF, the parties hereto have executed this Agreement as of the date first above written.

On July 31, 1978, Friedrich filled in his name and address by hand as the "Supplier" and signed the agreement. He admitted that he had read the complete agreement when he signed it, and even discussed it with other freelancers. Friedrich stated that Marvel Comics said that this agreement only covered future work and that he had to sign it without alteration if he wanted to obtain further freelance work from them. However, Friedrich also stated that he discussed the proposition of giving up preexisting rights which the freelancers may have had in exchange for the possibility of additional work from Marvel Comics. Friedrich was not paid anything for signing the agreement but did so for the possibility of future work.

Friedrich also testified that after he signed the agreement, he vanished from the comics scene for a year. Friedrich, an alcoholic, relapsed and spent the year traveling with a friend. At his deposition, Friedrich described:

> In 1978 my alcoholism got completely out of control, my wife left me and took my child with her, left me with no furniture or anything, just left me an empty house, so I moved out of the

empty house and stayed with a friend in Missouri for a while and then I wound up running around the country with another friend of mine who was a truck driver, and I spent most of 1978 riding around the country in a truck with him.

As a result, Friedrich did not seek any freelance work and could not be found by Marvel Comics after he signed the 1978 Agreement.

Under the 1976 Copyright Act and absent a specific agreement, the renewal copyright for *Ghost Rider* would have vested in Friedrich twenty-eight years after *Marvel Spotlight* issue 5's original publication date in 1972, which would have been at the end of 2000. After this date, Marvel Comics continued to profit from the Ghost Rider character by publishing reprints of *Marvel Spotlight* issue 5 in 2001, 2004, and 2005; publishing six issues of a new Ghost Rider comic series that ran from August 2001 to January 2002; offering a single Ghost Rider toy for sale in catalogs in 2003 and 2004; having Ghost Rider make cameo appearances in other characters' video games released in 2000 and 2006; filming the *Ghost Rider* movie in 2005 and releasing it (pursuant to a licensing agreement entered into in 2000)[6]; and releasing a *Ghost Rider* video game, based on the movie, in 2007. The reprints of *Marvel Spotlight* issue 5 each contained the "Conceived & Written by Gary Friedrich" language and Marvel Comics paid him royalties with checks labeled "roy," meaning royalties. Most of the other items did not credit Friedrich at all for the creation of Ghost Rider and none of the other items earned him royalties.

Friedrich was generally unaware of Marvel Comics' use of the Ghost Rider character until he first learned that Marvel Comics was going to release a *Ghost Rider* movie. On April 6, 2004, Friedrich hired an attorney to write a letter to Sony Pictures, the company producing the movie, and assert Friedrich's rights to the *Ghost Rider* copyright. The letter simply stated:

> I represent Gary Friedrich, the creator of the character "Ghost Rider."
> My client is informed that Sony Pictures intends to release a film based on the character and has asked me to intercede to determine his legal rights related to the use of the character. Please call me to discuss this matter at your earliest convenience.

Marvel Comics responded in a letter dated April 14, 2004, and advised Friedrich that Ghost Rider was a work-for-hire. Marvel Comics wrote:

> Marvel's position is that Ghost Rider was created as a work for hire under the copyright laws and that Marvel is the owner of all right, title, and interest in the copyright and trademark. We are unaware of any agreement with Mr. Friedrich that would give him any interest in the character or its merchandising. If you are in possession of such an agreement or have information you believe to be contrary, please let me know.

After counsel was unsuccessful in obtaining Friedrich's participation rights, there was a several year hiatus in his pursuit of legal action. Friedrich said he first learned about the concept of renewal rights in 2005 or 2006.

Columbia Pictures released the *Ghost Rider* feature film on February 18, 2007. The movie starred Nicolas Cage and Eva Mendes. The film version of *Ghost Rider* tells the story of a stunt cyclist named Johnny Blaze. Many years ago, in order to save his dying father, Blaze sold his soul to Mephistopheles and sadly parts from the love of his life, Roxanne Simpson. Years later, Johnny meets Roxanne again. Unfortunately, Mephistopheles also returns and offers to release Johnny's soul if Johnny becomes the fabled, fiery Ghost Rider, a supernatural agent of vengeance and justice, to defeat Mephistopheles's nemesis and son, Blackheart. *Ghost Rider* took first place at the box office with $52 million in ticket sales. The film would go on to gross approximately $229 million worldwide and spawn a sequel, *Ghost Rider, Spirit of Vengeance*, which did not fare as well with the public or the critics.

In 2007, Friedrich retained new counsel and, in February, he filed for, and received, a Renewal Copyright Registration in *Marvel Spotlight* issue 5 and *Ghost Rider*, which he assigned to his company, Gary Friedrich Enterprises, LLC. On April 4, 2007, Friedrich filed suit against the Marvel Comics and their licensees. Friedrich alleged copyright infringement and various state law claims. Although the case was originally filed in the Southern District of Illinois, the case was eventually transferred to the Southern District of New York where it was assigned to Judge Jones. Judge Jones dismissed plaintiffs' state law claims because they were either preempted by the Copyright Act[7] or, even if true, would not have allowed Friedrich to legally prevail. The remaining claims survived.

Marvel Comics answered the complaint on the grounds that *Ghost Rider* was a work for hire on May 17, 2010. On December 15, 2010, Marvel Comics brought three counterclaims against Friedrich alleging copyright infringement, trademark infringement, and a violation of the Lanham Act on the basis of false description, false representation, and false designation of origin.

Extensive discovery was taken by both sides. After discovery on the ownership issues, both sides moved for summary judgment. In essence, both sides argued that the court could rule for them without the need for a trial. As previously explained, when a court decides a case on summary judgment it gives every reasonable inference to the nonmovant. What this means is that, if there is any reasonably possible way of interpreting a fact against the side moving for summary judgment, it will.

For example, assume that Lex sues Kal for damages to his battle suit caused by Kal's dog. Lex moves for summary judgment arguing that Kal let his dog roam free unsupervised. Kal also moves for summary judgment arguing that his dog is always locked up in his fortress when he isn't around. If, in her deposition, Kal's cousin, Kara, testifies that she can't remember if she closed the gate in the fortress, then the court will assume that it was left open when deciding Kal's motion and that it was closed when deciding Lex's motion. Most likely, both sides would lose and a jury (or fact finding judge) will have to decide whether the gate was open.

Friedrich argued that he was the sole author, or at least a joint author, as a matter of law. On the other hand, Marvel Comics argued that Friedrich's ownership claim was barred by the statute of limitations. But, if the claim was valid, Marvel Comics also argued that Friedrich had assigned any renewal rights to Marvel Comics with the later agreements. Although the District court concluded that there were disputes of the material facts surrounding the authorship of the work, it still ruled in Marvel Comics' favor by granting Marvel Comics' motion and denied Friedrich's motion. The court determined that even if Friedrich were found to be the sole creator of Ghost Rider, he had given up his rights to the character by signing the agreements and conveying all his rights to Marvel Comics forever. The District Court also noted that its conclusion would be reinforced because each time Friedrich was paid for his work on *Marvel Spotlight* issue 5, the checks contained legends that assigned all of his rights to Marvel Comics. .

The District Court reasoned that the term "forever" clearly indicated the parties' intent to convey the renewal term to Marvel Comics. The court wrote: "Language in a contract that includes 'general words of assignment can include renewal rights,' including words such as 'forever,' 'hereafter,' and 'perpetual' effectively convey renewal rights."

The language of the 1978 Agreement could not be clearer:

SUPPLIER [i.e., Friedrich] expressly grants to MARVEL forever all rights of any kind and nature in and to the Work, the rights to use SUPPLIER's name in connection therewith and agrees that MARVEL is the sole and exclusive copyright proprietor thereof having all rights of ownership therein.

By this assignment, in 1978 Friedrich undoubtedly conveyed whatever renewal rights he may have retained, if any.

The court concluded:

As a result, this Court finds that there is no triable issue of fact regarding whether the 1978 Agreement conveyed whatever rights Plaintiffs may have had at that time or would have acquired in the future, including renewal rights.

* * *

[Marvel Comics] October 17, 2011 motion for summary judgment is GRANTED. [Friedrich's] October 17, 2011 motion for summary judgment is DENIED. The claim of ownership over the Character and the Work (Count I) is resolved in [Marvel Comics'] favor, which necessarily disposes of [Friedrich's] claims for infringement.... Accordingly, [Friedrich's] remaining claims in the First Amended Complaint ... are dismissed.

Of course, this left open Marvel Comics' counterclaim for copyright infringement because Friedrich signed photocopies of *Ghost Rider* covers at trade shows. After the court issued its order, the parties stipulated that Friedrich earned $17,000 from the distribution and sale of goods depicting the Ghost Rider character appearing in *Marvel Spotlight* issue 5. In addition, Marvel Comics also agreed to voluntarily dismiss their trademark counterclaims without prejudice, pending appeal. On February 6, 2012, the District Court entered final judgment dismissing all outstanding claims, awarded the $17,000 in damages to Marvel Comics, and enjoined Friedrich from using the Ghost Rider copyright.

Friedrich appealed to the Second Circuit.

On appeal, the Second Circuit reversed the lower court decision that dismissed the lawsuit.

Specifically, the Second Circuit stated that the lower court's ruling that the 1978 renewal agreement relinquished Friedrich was incorrect. Instead, the Second Circuit determined that "The agreement is ambiguous on its face." Moreover, the court concluded that "The contract contains no explicit reference to renewal rights."

The court added that Friedrich's argument that he thought the 1978 contract only covered his future work was a matter for a jury to decide. The circuit court stated:

It is doubtful the parties intended to convey rights in the valuable Ghost Rider copyright without explicitly referencing it.... It is more likely that the agreement only covered ongoing or future work. Hence, there is a genuine dispute regarding the parties' intent for this form contract to cover Ghost Rider.

The court added that the contract was "ungrammatical and awkwardly phrased" and the language wasn't clear "whether it covered a work published six years earlier" or "whether it conveys renewal rights."

As a result, the court determined:

> We conclude that the district court erred in granting summary judgment because the Agreement is ambiguous and there are genuine disputes of material fact regarding the parties' intent to assign renewal rights in that Agreement, the timeliness of Friedrich's ownership claim, and the authorship of the work.
>
> Accordingly, the judgment is Vacated and the case is Remanded for trial.

Of course, this did not mean that Friedrich was going to win at trial, as the court noted:

> When construed in Marvel's favor, the record reveals that Friedrich had nothing more than an uncopyrightable idea for a motorcycle-riding character when he presented it to Marvel because he had not yet fixed the idea into a tangible medium. [Ghost Rider was created] through the collaborative efforts of Friedrich, Thomas, Lee, and Ploog, all of whom were paid by Marvel. If this is accepted as true, a jury could easily conclude from these facts that Ghost Rider was a "work made for hire" and thus that Marvel was the sole statutory author.

On remand, the District Court set trial for November 4, 2013. However, on September 6, 2013, the parties informed the court the case was settled.

Ghost Rider still seeks vengeance in the pages of Marvel Comics.

CHAPTER 14

The King Deposed
Marvel Comics v. Jack Kirby

No one can deny the contributions of Jack Kirby to the world of comics. And no other case in this book has been the subject of as much heated debate as this one. As a result, it is important at the outset to quote District Court Judge Colleen McMahon, who described exactly what the *Kirby* case is, and more importantly, what it is not:

> At the outset, it is important to state what this motion is not about. Contrary to recent press accounts and editorials, this case is not about whether Jack Kirby or Stan Lee is the real "creator" of Marvel characters, or whether Kirby (and other freelance artists who created culturally iconic comic book characters for Marvel and other publishers) were treated "fairly" by companies that grew rich off the fruit of their labor. It is about whether Kirby's work qualifies as work-for-hire under the Copyright Act of 1909, as interpreted by the courts, notably the United States Court of Appeals for the Second Circuit. If it does, then Marvel owns the copyright in the Kirby Works, whether that is "fair" or not. If it does not, then the Kirby Heirs have a statutory right to take back those copyrights, no matter the impact on a recent corporate acquisition or on earnings from blockbuster movies made and yet to be made.

With that caveat, the background of this groundbreaking decision can be explored.

The Fall of the Superhero

When most people outside of the industry think of comic books, they think of superheroes. What many people don't realize is that comic books are much more than a single genre. There are nonfiction comics, war comics, jungle comics, romance comics, western comics, horror comics, and science fiction/fantasy comics. In fact, after World War II, the public's interest in superheroes began to wane. In response, superhero publishers, like Marvel, swapped out their previously bestselling costumed crusaders for macabre tales of the supernatural. For example, Marvel Comic's top rated Captain America had to vacate his own title in 1949, when the book turned into *Captain America's Weird Tales* with issue 74. Similarly, DC Comics were forced to cut their line down to its core heroes, Superman, Batman and Wonder Woman.

It appeared that superheroes were doomed. But salvation came in the form of censorship.

After the enactment of the Comics Code of 1954, very few golden age publishers survived. Those that did longed for something new that could reinvigorate a sagging industry.

The Silver Age of Comics and the Rebirth of the Superhero

That change came in the form of the Silver Age of comics and a new twist on the classic superhero. And like the Golden Age, which began with the appearance of DC Comics' Superman, the Silver Age started with DC Comics leading the charge.

Most comic historians agree that the Silver Age began not with a flash, but with the Flash in *Showcase* issue 4, which was released in 1956.[1] However, this new Flash had nothing to do with the Golden Age version. Instead, editor Julius Schwartz, writer Gardner Fox, and artist Carmine Infantino created an entirely new Flash, with a modern science-based origin and a new secret identity in the form of police forensics scientist Barry Allen. After the success of the Flash, DC Comics reworked several other Golden Age characters, including Green Lantern, the Atom, and Hawkman. Eventually, several of these characters banded together as the Justice League of America in the pages of *Brave and the Bold* issue 28.

The success of the Justice League of America prompted Martin Goodman, publisher of Marvel Comics, to approach his editor, Stan Lee, and ask him to create a new team to compete with DC Comics. In response, Stan Lee called upon artist Jack Kirby to work on the project.

In 1962, Marvel Comics released *Fantastic Four* issue 1. With the introduction of the innovative Fantastic Four, comics changed forever. Unlike the near-perfect superhero archetypes that existed at the time, Lee and Kirby introduced a more relatable stable of characters with human failings and real world problems. These characters had hopes and fears. They fought with each other and worried about real world problems like trying to pay the rent.

The Fantastic Four were soon joined by several other characters that followed the same feet of clay hero mold, including the Amazing Spider-Man, the Incredible Hulk, the Mighty Thor, Daredevil, the X-Men, and the Avengers. Jack Kirby's dynamic artwork combined with Lee's irreverent prose became popular with college students, who identified with the struggles of Marvel's characters.

Thus began the Marvel Age of Comics. This also was the genesis of the 2010 lawsuit between Kirby's heirs and Marvel Comics.

Jack Kirby Becomes the King

The subject of Kirby's contributions to comics and comic book storytelling and his role in the early days of Marvel Comics is beyond the scope of this book. In fact, several very good books and magazine articles have focused on this topic. Instead, this chapter will focus on presenting the facts found by the United States District Court and the United States Court of Appeals as gathered in the discovery phase of the case in the fairest light possible. Some will obviously disagree with the portrayal as being pro–Marvel; others will no doubt say that it is anti–Marvel. But, at the risk of repetition, it is important to remember the words of Judge McMahon:

> This case is not about whether Jack Kirby or Stan Lee is the real "creator" or Marvel characters, or whether Kirby (and other freelance artists who created culturally iconic comic book characters for Marvel and other publishers) were treated "fairly" by companies that grew rich off the fruit of their labor.

Jacob Kurtzberg (Jack Kirby's real name) was born on August 28, 1917, in New York City. Jack Kirby's love of drawing led him to first to the Pratt Institute and the Educational Alliance, but he didn't last long at either. Instead, Jack Kirby taught himself to draw.

After drawing comic strips for the Lincoln Newspaper Syndicate, and *Popeye* cartoons for the Fleischer Animation studios, Jack Kirby began writing and drawing for the comic-book packager Eisner & Iger. While at Eisner & Iger, Kirby worked on numerous comics including science fiction (*The Diary of Dr. Hayward*), westerns (*Wilton of the West*), swash-buckling (*The Count of Monte Cristo*), and humor (*Abdul Jones*). He also created his Jack Kirby pseudonym while at the company.

Eventually, Kirby left Eisner & Iger to work at Fox Feature Syndicate, where he began to draw superhero comics with *The Blue Beetle*. During this time, Kirby met and began collaborating with Joe Simon.

Simon and Kirby left Fox and began working for Martin Goodman at Timely, Marvel Comics' predecessor. At Timely, Simon and Kirby created Captain America. After the success of Captain America, Martin Goodman and Simon asked Kirby to join the Timely staff as the company's art director.

Stan Lee Becomes the Man

While employed as Timely's art director Kirby worked with Stan Lee. Stanley Martin Lieber (Stan Lee's real name) was born in New York City on December 28, 1922. After working as a part time obituary and press release writer, a delivery boy, an usher, an office boy and a door to door salesman, Stan Lee joined Marvel Comics in 1939 to work for Martin Goodman, who was his cousin's husband. As an editorial assistant, Lee said his job consisted of sharpening pencils, erasing pages, and fetching lunch.

Captain America continued to be a huge success. When Simon felt that Goodman was not paying the promised percentage of profits, he and Kirby began to look for work at other comic publishers. When Goodman found out that Simon and Kirby had agreed to work for Marvel Comics' competition, National (later known as DC Comics), he allegedly fired them.

After the departure of Simon and Kirby from Marvel Comics, Lee took over as art director and writer. In 2010 Lee described it as follows:

> Joe Simon and Jack Kirby were really the only two people there producing the comics, and for some reason they left, and I was the only guy left in the department. So Martin asked me if I

could sort of function as the editor and art director and writer until he hired someone, a grown up. And I said, Sure, I can do it. And I think he forgot to hire a grownup, because I was there ever since.

Simon and Kirby's Non-Marvel Comics Work

Meanwhile, Kirby went on to work for several other comics publishers, where he worked on and created several notable characters, including Captain Marvel, Sandman, the Newsboy Legion, Manhunter, and the Boy Commandos, before going off to fight in World War II.

Upon his return from the war, Kirby and Simon teamed up once again to create what would become known as the romance comics genre with the creation of *Young Romance* for Crestwood Publications. They also tried to recreate Captain America with less success in the form of Fighting American. They ultimately formed their own comic company, Mainline Publications, which dissolved when Simon left the comics industry to pursue a career in advertising.

Of note is that before Joe Simon left the comics industry, he and Kirby did a story about Thor that appeared in DC Comics' *Adventure Comics* issue 75 in 1942. In the story, Thor faces off against the Sandman and Sandy in a story called "Villain from Valhalla." Thor has a magic hammer named Mjolnir, a winged helmet, and strapped boots. At the end of the story Thor is defeated by the heroes and revealed to be a metallurgy professor/robber with an invisible bullet-proof suit and a mechanical hammer.

Kirby would later introduce another Thor to the DC Comics audience in the pages of *Tales of the Unexpected* issue 16, which appeared in 1957 in a story entitled "The Magic Hammer." Like the earlier version, this Thor also wore a horned helmet and wielded a magic hammer. This version of the Norse god had a beard, cape, and circular designs on his chest.

After dissolving Mainline Publications, Kirby continued to create memorable comics, including work on *Green Arrow, Yellow Claw, Sky Masters of the Space Force,* and *The House of Mystery.*

While at DC Comics, he created the *Challengers of the Unknown* with Dave Wood. The Challengers of the Unknown were four acquaintances that miraculously survive a plane crash unscathed. They conclude that since they are living on borrowed time, they should band together for hazardous adventures. The members of the group are the pilot Kyle "Ace" Morgan, a daredevil named Matthew "Red" Ryan, strong and slow-witted Leslie "Rocky" Davis, and scientist Walter Mark "Prof" Haley.

The Marvel Age

Ultimately, Kirby ended up back at Marvel Comics, where he drew most genres, but became popular for drawing monsters such as Groot, the Thing from Planet X; Grottu, King of the Insects; and Fin Fang Foom.

He was working at Marvel Comics when Lee approached him about Martin Goodman's request for a super team to compete with Justice League of America. Stan Lee explains what happened next in his deposition:

Q. And let's start with the Fantastic Four. You actually referenced them earlier. Tell me to the best you can recall, how did the idea for the Fantastic Four come about, and who they were, and what was the back story with regard to the Fantastic Four.

A. Well, as I mentioned, Martin Goodman asked me to create a group of heroes because he found out that National Comics had a group that was selling well. So I went home, and I thought about it, and I—I wanted to make these different than the average comic book heroes. I didn't want them to have a double—a secret identity.

And I wanted to make it as realistic as possible. Instead of them living in Gotham City or Metropolis, I felt I will have them live in New York City. And instead of the obligatory teenager Johnny Storm driving a whiz bang V8, he would drive a Chevy Corvette.

I wanted everything real, and I wanted their relationship to be real. Instead of a girl who didn't know that the hero was really a superhero, not only did she know who he was, but they were engaged to be married, and she also had a superpower.

So, you know, things like that. And I thought I would try that. So I wrote up a very brief synopsis about that, and naturally I called Jack, because he was our best artist, and I asked him if he would do it. He seemed to like the idea. He took the synopsis, and he drew the story and put in his own touches, which were brilliant.

And it worked out beautifully. Books sold, and that was the start of the Marvel success, you might say.

Q. Tell us what was your thinking with regard to or the idea behind these specific four characters.

A. Well, I wanted them to be a team, but I wanted them to act like real people. So they didn't always get along well. I wanted one of them to be—we called him The Thing, to be kind of a very powerful ugly guy who would be pathetic because—they all got their superpowers by being in a spaceship that was hit by cosmic rays. And Mr. Fantastic got the ability to stretch his limbs. The girl Sue Storm had the ability to become invisible and surround herself with the force field. And the boy Johnny Storm, her brother, was able to burst into flame and fly.

I took that from an old Marvel book, one of Timely Comics' first books called The Human Torch. I always loved that character who had been an android, a robot or something. But I felt I'm going to give Johnny Storm that power. He can fly and burst into flame.

So we had a guy who can stretch, a girl who could be invisible, a man who was an ugly monster. And again, to go against type, I thought I'd make the ugly monster kind of a funny guy. He's pathetic, but he's also the comedy relief. And he was always arguing and fighting with The Human Torch, who was always trying to give him a hot foot. And he was always trying to grab him and throttle him.

They all loved each other, but they never got along well. The more they fought amongst themselves, the more the readers loved it. And that was the way I envisioned them.

Q. And then it says, Story No. 1, Introduction, "Meet the Fantastic Four." Is that the synopsis that you wrote back in 1961?

A. This is the original synopsis that I wrote, and I gave it to Jack. And of course, after that we discussed it, and we embellished it, and we made little changes. But this was the beginning of it. Yeah.

Mark Evanier, a Kirby historian who was hired as an expert for the Kirby family, disputes the account:

Q. Well, I'm asking for your understanding as to, first of all, what did Mr. Kirby tell you about that, which characters, when did he do that, and whether or not this was one of the versions you chose to believe.

A. Okay. Mr. Kirby told me that he brought in sketches for knew [*sic*] characters, including rough sketches of The Fantastic Four that he did on his own. Brought them in.

His version of the creation of Fantastic Four was that when Mr. Goodman asked for a superhero book to parallel DC Comics' Justice League of America, Stan's initial idea was to revive the characters from the 1940s The Human Torch, The Submariner, Captain America, and certain others. And Mr. Kirby then went out and said, no, we need new characters. And he came up with some sketches. And he took them in, and The Fantastic Four was born out of those discussions.

On August 8, 1961, *Fantastic Four* issue 1 appeared on the newsstands with a cover price of 10 cents. The fact that the comic was meant to compete with the Justice League of America was apparent from the cover, which had a similar layout to *Brave and the Bold* issue 28. That *Brave and the Bold* cover, drawn by Mike Sekowsky and Murphy Anderson, featured Green Lantern, the Martian Manhunter, Wonder Woman, Aquaman, and the Flash attacking a large starfish-shaped monster. A caption box announced, "The world's greatest heroes team up to battle 'Starro the Conqueror!'" Similarly, the cover to *Fantastic Four* issue 1, penciled by Kirby and inked by Dick Ayers, featured a monster breaking through a city street. In this respect, it was very similar to the Kirby covers created for other Marvel Comics books like *Amazing Adventures, Strange Tales, Tales to Astonish, Tales of Suspense,* and *World of Fantasy.* However, in addition to the city's citizens cowering in terror in the background, the cover to *Fantastic Four* issue 1 also featured four unique individuals attacking the creature. In the upper left part of the cover the monster's huge grotesque hand clutched a pretty blonde teen girl, who was fading from view. She exclaimed, "I—can't turn invisible fast enough!! How can we stop this creature Torch?" To the reader's right, another character, engulfed in flames, flew across the center of the page and announced, "Just wait and see sister! The Fantastic Four have only begun to fight." The bottom right corner featured a strangely elongated man stretching free from the ropes that bind him while saying, "It will take more than ropes to keep Mister Fantastic out of action." Finally, a hideous orange monster charged at the creature from the bottom left and exclaimed, "The three of you can't do it alone! It's time for the Thing to take a hand!" The caption box proudly proclaimed; "Featuring, 'The Thing!' 'Mr. Fantastic!' 'Human Torch' 'Invisible Girl!' Together for the first time in one mighty magazine." And, while this cover implies that the readers had seen these characters before, they were all new creations.

Of course, the other interesting thing about this cover is that it has nothing to do with the story inside. Instead, *Fantastic Four* issue 1 featured three chapters. In "Fantastic Four" the team gathers together to face an unknown entity as the team's origin is told a flashback story. In order to help the United States win the space race, four individuals break onto a military base and steal a prototype space ship. After being bombarded by cosmic rays, the four discover they have developed amazing abilities and powers. Reed Richards, a stuffy scientist who designed the rocket, became Mister Fantastic with the ability to stretch his body. Test pilot and college football star Ben Grimm became the Thing, a misshapen brute made of rock. Teenage Sue Storm, complete with schoolgirl crush on Reed, transformed into the Invisible Girl with the power to make herself vanish. The last member of the team was Sue's kid brother, Johnny, a hot-rodding hothead who gained the ability to burst into flame and become the Human Torch.[2] In the second chapter, "The Fantastic Four Meet the Mole

Man!" the team flies off to face a mysterious island to determine who has been attacking atomic power plants. The team fights a three headed monster before meeting the villainous Mole Man. In the final chapter, "The Mole Man's Secret!" the team faces off against the Mole Man and stops his plans to invade the surface world.

Evanier, in his capacity as an expert witness, pointed to the similarities between this story and Kirby's *Challengers of the Unknown*.

> Like Fantastic Four, Challengers of the Unknown depicted the adventures of four people who form a team after surviving an air crash. The members of the Challengers had personality traits similar to the Fantastic Four. Pilot "Ace" Morgan, like the Fantastic Four's Reed Richards, was the decisive leader of his group. "Rocky" Ryan, like Benjamin Grimm, aka "The Thing," was the group's strongman. Daredevil "Red" Ryan was the resident firebrand, much like Johnny Storm. "Prof" Haley was, like Sue Storm, the bland and nondescript member of the group. The Challengers team, like the Fantastic Four, confronted science fiction enemies in a wide variety of fantastic settings.

Stan Lee was asked about these similarities:

> Q. To your knowledge, was anything in The Fantastic Four based on a previous work by Kirby called "Challenges of the Unknown"?
>
> A. No. I had never—to this day I've never read "Challenges of the Unknown," and I really know nothing about it, except that there is or was a book of that title.

After the success of the Fantastic Four, Marvel Comics sought to expand its superhero line. As a result, it offered several new characters that would soon become part of the Marvel Age of Comics. The next was the Incredible Hulk. Once again, Lee turned to Kirby. Lee explains:

> Q. Okay. Let's go now to the Incredible Hulk. And could you tell us how The Incredible Hulk came about? What was your idea for him?
>
> A. Well, same thing. I was trying to—it was my job to come up with new characters and to expand the line as much as I could. So I was trying to think again what can I do that's different. I liked the thing very much, and I thought, what if I get somebody who is a real monster? And I remembered I had always in the old movie Frankenstein with Boris Karloff I had always thought that that monster was the good guy because he didn't want to hurt anybody, but those idiots with torches who were always chasing him up and down the hills.
>
> Q. He was a misunderstood monster.
>
> A. A mis—you said it better than I could have. So I thought it would be fun to get a monster who is really good but nobody knows it, and they fight him. But then the more I thought about it, I figured it could be dull after awhile just having people chasing a monster. And I remember Dr. Jekyll and Mr. Hyde. I thought, why not treat him like Jekyll and Hyde? He's really a normal man who can't help turning into a monster, and it would make a very interesting story if when he needs his monstrous strength the most, the poor guy turns back into a normal man. I could get a lot of story complications. So I thought that would be good.
>
> I needed a name. Years ago I remember there was a comic book called The Heap, H-E-A-P. I don't remember even what he was, but I always thought that was some real crazy name. And somehow or other I thought I will call him The Hulk. It's a little like The Heap, and it has that same feeling. But I love adjectives like the Fantastic Four, the Uncanny so-and-so. So I decided I'll call him The Incredible Hulk. And that's what happened.
>
> Q. And how come The Hulk is green?

A. That's a long story. When I did the Fantastic Four, we started getting a lot of fan mail. And the fan—remember, I told you I didn't want them to have costumes. And the fan mail said, We love the book. It's great. Oh, it's the best new thing we've seen. But if you don't give them costumes, we'll never buy another issue. And I realize there's something unique about the comic book reader. They love—the superhero fan. They love costumes.

   Well, I couldn't figure out a way to give a monster a costume. I couldn't see a monster, The Hulk, walking into a costume store or making one for himself. So I figured I'll do the next best thing. I'll give him a different skin color. That will always look like a costume.

   You may not know this, but originally I made him gray. I thought that a gray skin would look spooky and scary and dramatic. But when the book was published, the printer apparently had a problem with the color gray. On one page he was light gray. On one page dark gray. On one page black. On one page almost white. I said, This will never do. So I decided on another color. See, you can do that when you're a comic book editor. You can do anything.

   So I will change the color of his skin. So I looked around for a color that wasn't being used. I couldn't think of any green hero. I said, I will make him green. And it turned out to be a good choice, because I was able to come up with little sayings like, The Jolly Green Giant, or the Green Goliath, and so forth. And that's how it happened. I could have thought of pink or blue or any other color.

Q. Now, after you came up with the character, who did you ask to draw the character?

A. My best guy, Jack Kirby.

Q. And do you remember giving Kirby directions as to what you wanted with regard to what he was to draw?

A. I remember the first thing I said to him. I said, Jack, you're going to think I'm crazy, but I want you to draw a sympathetic monster. And he came up with The Hulk.

Q. And did you, as part of that direction, give him a back story and a story line?

A. Oh, yeah. We had to figure out how The Hulk would be—how he came to be The Hulk. So I decided he's a scientist named Bruce Banner. And I'm not very scientific. All I know are the names of things. I don't really know how they work or anything. But I had used cosmic rays for the Fantastic Four to get them their powers. So I heard the expression "gamma ray" somewhere. So I said let's let Bruce Banner be subjected to a gamma ray, and that turns him into The Hulk. But it had to be in a heroic way. So I said let's get a teenage—they're doing a test for a new kind of gamma ray bomb somewhere. The military is doing that. And some idiot teenager is riding his bike past the no trespassing sign onto the test area. And Bruce Banner in his cubicle sees the kid, and he runs out to save the kid, say, "Get out of here. There's going to be a gamma ray explosion."

   But Bruce Banner had a rival scientist who was jealous of him, and when the scientist sees Bruce Banner run out, he says, "Quick. Start the explosion." And the gamma ray explodes, and Bruce throws himself on top of the kid to save the kid, and he gets subjected to the gamma ray. That's how he becomes the Hulk, and that's how we know he's really a hero at heart.

* * *

Q. —as The Hulk progressed, did you follow the same process that you previously testified to in terms of how you directed and edited The Hulk stories?

A. Yeah. Well, I told Jack essentially what I told you. And he just drew it any way, you know, the best way he could. And it turned out great.

The Incredible Hulk debuted on May 10, 1962. For 12 cents, readers were promised "The strangest man of all time!!" and "Fantasy as you like it!" and were asked, "Is he man or monster of is he both?" The iconic cover, with pencils by Kirby and inks by George Roussos, showed a meek scientist standing in front of a large gray hulking monster as a beautiful woman and army men in the background looked on in horror. The story introduced Bruce Banner, a military scientist trying to develop a gamma ray bomb. In order to protect a teen named Rick Jones, who sneaks onto the test site, Banner is bombarded by gamma rays when his experiment is sabotaged. Later it is discovered that the gamma rays have caused Banner to transform into a large hulking gray monster when the sun goes down. By the end of the story, however, the Hulk has saved the base and defeated the saboteur.

Marvel's next hero debuted in the pages of *Journey into Mystery*, a 1952 horror anthology created by Marvel Comics' predecessor Atlas Comics. With issue 83, *Journey into Mystery* joined Marvel Comics' superhero lineup with the appearance of the Mighty Thor. Once again, Lee and Kirby worked together on the concept. However, the task of writing the script for the story was given to Larry Lieber, Lee's brother. Lee testified:

Q. Let's talk next about Thor.
A. Mm-hmm.
Q. And how Thor was created and what was your idea behind Thor.
A. Same thing. I was looking for something different and bigger than anything else. And I figured what could be bigger than a god? Well, people were pretty much into the Roman and the Greek gods by then, and I thought the Norse gods might be good. And I liked the sound of the name Thor and Asgaard and the Twilight of the Gods' Ragnarok and all of that.

And Jack was very much into that, more so than me. So when I told Jack about that, he was really thrilled. And we got together, and we did Thor the same way.
Q. And what was the idea behind Thor? What was his deal?

* * *

A. I wanted him to be the son of Odin, who is the King of the Gods, like Jupiter. And I wanted him to have an evil brother, Loki. And just like the Fantastic Four were always fighting Dr. Doom, and Spider-Man was usually fighting the Green Goblin, I figured Loki would be the big villain. He's Thor's half brother. He's jealous of Thor. He has enchantment powers. So in a way he's a good foe. Thor has strength, but Loki is like a magician and can do all kind of things. So that seemed good to me.

And then Thor had a girlfriend from legend called Sif, S-I-F. And I would have her involved in the stories and have jealousy.

And then I wanted some comedy relief, so it wasn't—I don't think it was until the strip had been going for a while, but I decided there were three guys. I called them The Warriors 3 that I wanted to include, a very fat guy named Volstag, The Voluminous Volstag, I called him, who acts like a real hero. "Come on, let's go get them." But when the fights start, he's cowardly and always holds back.

Another guy like Errol Flynn called Fandral the Dashing. And a guy like Charles Bronson in Death Wish. I think I called him Hogan the Grim. And the three of them, Fandral the Dashing, Hogan the Grim, and Volstag the Voluminous I thought they could be Thor's friends, and they would provide comedy relief. And I'm happy to see they're using them in the movie, I think.

And it was something that we both enjoyed doing very much. And Jack was wonderful with the costumes that he gave them. I mean, nobody could have drawn costumes like he gave them.
Q. The character Thor, how did—what idea did you have to come up to give him his powers?
A. Well, he had—
Q. What was the back story?

* * *

A. Oh, yeah. He had mainly a hammer, an enchanted hammer. The back story was I decided to make him a guy here on Earth, Dr.—I forgot his name. But whatever his name was, he was lame and he walked with a cane. And for some reason he went to Norway, and there he—I think—the Stone-Men from Saturn or somewhere. Some aliens who were stone men had landed in Norway and they wanted to kill our doctor.

And he rushes into a cave somewhere to hide from them. And they're coming toward him, but he sees a hammer in the ground, and some kind of a sign that said—I don't remember the exact wording, but, Whoever is worthy would be able to lift this hammer, sort of like the King Arthur legend. And he grabs the hammer, and he's able to lift it up. And it seems that destiny had prepared that for him over the centuries. The minute it lifts it up, he turns into The Thunder God Thor, and wielding the hammer he takes care of the Stone-Men. And then he can always become Dr. Don Blake. That was his name. I believe Don Blake. If he hits the hammer on the ground, it turns back into the cane that he always had because he was lame. He walked with a cane as Don Blake, Dr. Don Blake.

Journey into Mystery issue 83 debuted on August 10, 1962, for 12 cents and featured several different stories including a crime drama ("The Perfect Crime") and a story about an atomically super powered lion ("When the Jungle Sleeps"). The most important tale was the cover feature, "The Power of Thor." The cover boldly announced, "Introducing the Mighty Thor! The most exciting superhero of all time!!" and told readers to "Begin the Saga of Thor in this issue!" Inside, the comic introduced Dr. Donald Blake, an American tourist in Norway, who witnesses an invasion by aliens from Saturn. When Blake is trapped in a cave, he finds a magic walking stick that transforms him into the mighty Thor.

Once again, there are obvious similarities between this character and the previous incarnations of Thor created by Kirby. Expert Evanier points out:

> Thor is another creation that reflects earlier Kirby work but which has no precedence in the thousands of comic books that Stan Lee had worked on prior to its inception in Journey into Mystery No. 83 in 1962.... Kirby's lifelong interest in mythology continued after the creation of Thor when, working for DC Comics again in the 1970s, he created his own pantheon of mythological deities in his New God~ comic book and his "Fourth World" saga.

Next came Spider-Man. Lee tells the story of his creation:

Q. Now, did you discuss the idea that you had for Spider-Man with Mr. Goodman?
A. Spiders. Secondly, you can't make him a teenager. Teenagers can just be sidekicks. And finally, problems? Don't you know what a superhero is? They don't have problems. They're superheroes.

So I had a feeling I hadn't hit pay dirt with that one as far as Martin was concerned, but I always liked the idea. So sometime later we had a magazine we were going to drop. It was called Amazing Fantasy. Strangely enough, Steve Ditko had drawn all the stories in that one, now that I remember. Anyway, it wasn't selling well, and we were going to drop it.

Now, when you drop a magazine, nobody cares what you put in the last issue because you're dropping it anyway. So just to get it out of my system, that's when I asked Jack to draw it. Then I asked Steve to draw it. And we did a little, I don't know, 10- or 12-page story. And we threw it in Amazing Fantasy in the last issue. And just for fun, I put him on the cover.

And the book sold fantastically. So a couple months later when the sales figures were in, Martin came to me and he said, "Hey Stan, you remember that Spider-Man idea of yours that we both liked so much? Why don't we make a series of it."

And while Kirby did the original design, Lee rejected it. After Kirby's design was not used, the task of creating Spider-Man was given to Steve Ditko. Lee explained:

> A. With Spider-Man, that was kind of an interesting thing. I thought Spider-Man would be a good strip, so I wanted Jack to do it. And I gave it to him. And I said, Jack, now you always draw these characters so heroically, but I don't want this guy to be too heroic-looking. He's kind of a nebbishy guy.
>
> Q. Would we call him a nerd today?
>
> A. I would say so. Yeah.
>
> Anyway, Jack, who glamorizes everything, even though he tried to nerd him up, the guy looked still a little bit too heroic for me. So I said: All right, forget it, Jack. I will give it to somebody else.
>
> Jack didn't care. He had so much to do.
>
> Q. Who did you give it to?
>
> A. I gave it to Steve Ditko. His style was really more really what Spider-Man should have been. So Steve did the Spider-Man thing. Although, again, I think I had Jack sketch out a cover for it because I always had a lot of confidence in Jack's covers.

* * *

> Q. And you mentioned that you thought that Kirby actually did the cover on Spider-Man. What was—the cover that he did was based on his original drawing or was it based on what Ditko had done?
>
> A. Oh, it would have had to have been based, I think, on what Ditko did because it would have to look like the Spider-Man.
>
> Q. The nerdy Spider-Man?
>
> A. I would think so. Well, as Spider-Man he didn't look nerdy. He looked nerdy as Peter Parker, yeah.

Once again, Kirby's heirs presented a different story:

> Kirby also played an important role in the creation of Spider-Man. In 1962. As Marvel cast about for new super-hero ideas, Kirby and Lee devised Spider-Man, which Kirby said was based on an idea that he has developed with Joe Simon in the mid-fifties.
>
> It had originally been conceived as a character called The Silver Spider, then rebranded as Spiderman. In 1959 in one of their last collaborations, Simon and Kirby had refashioned it as a character called The Fly and sold it to John Goldwater, who was still publishing it through his company, Archie Comics.

When asked about this, Lee testified:

> Q. And to your knowledge, was the idea for Spider-Man something that Kirby brought to you based on his previous work on something called "The Fly"?
>
> A. No.

Spider-Man first appeared in *Amazing Fantasy* issue 15. Ditko also drew the first version of the cover. However, when Lee asked for another angle, Ditko ended up collaborating with Kirby on a new cover. Since its debut, on August 15, 1962, the cover image of Spider-Man carrying a would-be robber as he swings on his web line has been duplicated numerous times. The original cover had Spider-Man taunting the reader, "Though the world may mock Peter Parker, the timid teenager.... It will soon marvel at the awesome might of Spider-Man." The book also promised "An important message to you, from the editor—about the new Amazing!" Spider-Man soon transitioned into his own title, *The Amazing Spider-Man*, and soon became Marvel Comics' biggest and most lucrative property.

Next, Lee and Kirby brought the story of Ant Man to readers. Ant Man first appeared in *Tales to Astonish* issue 35 written by Lee, penciled by Jack Kirby and inked by Dick Ayers. In the story, scientist Henry Pym, who had appeared in an earlier story called "The Man in the Ant Hill" in issue 27 when the book was still a sci-fi fantasy comic title, perfected his formula that allows him to shrink to the size of ant. He then created a special helmet that let him communicate with and control ants, donned a colorful costume and became Marvel Comics' latest superhero. After Lee and Kirby launched the title, the book was handed over to writer Lieber and artist Don Heck. Because of sagging popularity, Ant Man was given a sidekick in the form of Janet Van Dyne, the winsome Wasp, in issue 44, which was written by Lee and drawn by Kirby. Eventually Pym becomes Giant Man in issue 49. Lee explained:

A. You know, it was just—it was not all that successful. And I later realized why it wasn't all that successful. The interesting thing about a character who is that big (indicating), would be to show him against a lot of big things. But somehow no matter which artist drew him, they always made him look life size, They put him in the foreground. So you didn't enjoy the contrast of the little guy next to the big—you know, if they had him near a cigarette in an ashtray, but they always had him somehow where he didn't look like Ant-Man.

Anyway, I hate to give up. So, at some point I changed him to Giant Man. He had the ability to become a giant.
Q. The ant could become a giant?
A. Yeah. And that didn't become too popular either, although he's still running around somewhere in the books.
Q. Who came up with the idea of making—having Ant Man become Giant Man?
A. I'm embarrassed to say it was me.

* * *

Q. Who was it who came up with the idea for Ant-Man?
A. I did.

The next hero on the scene was Iron Man. Stan Lee explained:

Q. Let's talk a little—let's talk about Iron Man. Tell us about how Iron Man came about, how he was created, the back story with regard to Iron Man.
A. I will try to make it shorter. It was the same type of thing. I was looking for somebody new. And I thought—I don't know why I thought it, somebody in a suit of armor. And what if it was iron armor. He would be so powerful. So for some reason I have always been fascinated by Howard Hughes. I thought I would get a hero like Howard Hughes.

He's an inventor. He's a multimillionaire. He's good looking. He likes the women. And but I got to make something tragic about him. And then it occurred to me if he—somehow when he got his iron armor—it's a long story—but he gets into a fight, and he gets injured in his chest. And his heart is injured, and he has to wear this little thing that runs the iron armor. He has to wear that on his chest because it also keeps his heart beating. And that would make him a tragic figure as well as the most powerful guy. So I thought the readers would like him even more with that little bit added to it.

And that was it. Then again—oh, but wait a minute. This one wasn't Jack. I called Don Heck, and I asked Don Heck because I think Jack was busy with something else. That must have been what it was.
Q. Don Heck is another artist?
A. He's another artist that we had who was pretty good. And he drew the first Iron Man. I

think I might have given the cover to Jack to do. I don't remember who did the cover. I think it might have been Jack.

Q. And in coming up with the back story, did you include a love interest?

A. Oh, yeah. I forgot. I made up a name called—a girl who worked for the millionaire. I figured he has—I wanted him to be a playboy, so he has this gorgeous assistant secretary named Pepper Pots. And he's in love with her, and she's in love with him, but he won't admit he's in love with her because he figures he could die any minute with his bad heart. And he loves her too much to make her a widow, and so he never admits to her how he feels about her, which again is a little touch of pathos for the series.

He also has a friend named Happy Hogan, and it goes on and on.

Q. Now, in addition to Don Heck, did your brother Larry Lieber have a role in Iron Man?

A. Oh, yeah. I came up with the idea, but when the script was—when the strip was drawn, I didn't have time to put in the copy. So I asked my brother Larry to write it.

Q. And this happened on other occasions where—

A. Yeah. There were times when I would ask Larry to write something. Mm-hmm.

Iron Man first appeared in *Tales of Suspense* issue 39, released on March 1, 1963. Once again, drawing and writing duties were turned over to Lieber and Heck. Kirby did the pencils for the cover and Heck did the inks. The cover shows someone putting on a suit of armor, and the captions ask "Who?," "Who?," "Who? "Who? Or what, is the newest, most breathtaking super-hero of all?" Readers did not have to wait long to know as the answer appeared below. "Iron Man! He lives! He walks! He Conquers!" Of course, at this point, Marvel Comics already knew of its popularity since *Tales of Suspense* announced that it was "From the talented bull-pen where the Fantastic Four, Spider-Man, Thor and your other favorite super-heroes were born."

Finally, in September 1963, Lee was able to deliver on Martin Goodman's request for a team like the Justice League of America when he and Kirby created *The Avengers*, gathering together Thor, Iron Man, Ant Man, the Wasp, and the Hulk in one title as they faced off against Thor's evil half-brother Loki. *Avengers* issue 1 promised "Super Heroes! Super Villains! Super Thrills! Presented in the fabulous Marvel manner." Once again, Stan Lee wrote the story, while Kirby did the pencils and Paul Reinman inked the book. Lee testified:

Q. Let's focus on The Avengers. How did The Avengers come about? First, tell us who The Avengers are.

A. Well, they're anybody that we wanted to put in the group of our own heroes. I don't even remember who they were in the first issue. It might have been Iron Man, Captain America, Thor, Daredevil. I don't even remember because we kept changing the roster each month, whoever we felt like.

But the idea was that they were organized by—I don't remember which of our heroes organized. Oh, they got together and decided to become a fighting team. Again we wanted something like The Justice League that DC had.

Q. Had you discussed the idea for The Avengers with Martin Goodman?

A. Oh, sure. Oh, sure. I couldn't do any book unless Martin approved of it. And I remember Iron Man who was the rich one. I had them use Iron Man's mansion on Fifth Avenue as The Avengers' headquarters, and Captain America was definitely an Avenger. Iron Man. And Spider-Man never joined them; he was a loaner [*sic*].

But then I would have them—the toughest thing about The Avengers, they were also powerful that we had to find very powerful villains for them to fight. And again, you know, Jack drew it, and it turned out to be popular. They're going to make a movie of that, too.

Q. You needed to have very powerful villains to make it a fair fight.

A. Oh, sure. In fact, it's always best if the villain—if it isn't a fair fight; if the villains seem even more powerful, because then you wonder how will the hero ever get out of this one.

Q. And who came up with the back story for The Avengers?

A. There really wasn't much back story. I did, but just the idea that they all get together and form a group. Because I didn't have to create new characters. We had them. I just needed an excuse for them to get together. And honestly I forget what the excuse was now.

Another Lee and Kirby super team debuted at the same time as *The Avengers*. They were the X-Men, teenage mutants with fantastic powers. Lee described the concept as follows:

Q. Keeping with our discussion, could you tell us about the creation of X-Men? How did that come about?

A. Again, Martin asked me for another team because the Fantastic Four had been doing well. And again I wanted to try something different. And I thought what—I could think of superpowers for them, but how do they get their powers? I have already had cosmic rays and gamma rays and bitten by a radioactive spider. What was left?

So I took the cowardly way out. I said I'm going to just say they were born that way. They're mutants. Now I don't have to figure out gamma rays or anything. So I decided to have a group of young mutants. And I really, the more I thought about it, the more I liked it. I said, they'll go to a school. They have to keep their mutant powers secret, so it will just say a School for Gifted Youngsters. Nobody will know it means mutants.

And we'll get a professor who gets them together. And this guy should also have mutant powers, but I will make him have mental powers. He's got a brain. He can send thought waves all around, and he can send his thought waves around to detect where there's a kid with mutant powers, and then he'll ask that kid to enroll in his school. And again, so that he isn't too powerful, I thought I would make him in a wheelchair. He's the professor.

Q. And what was his name?

A. Professor Xavier. And then I thought of the characters. There would be a girl who can do—called Marvel Girl, who could do crazy things, and a fella called The Beast, who looks a little bit apelike. So to go against type, I made him the smartest and the most articulate of all of them. And a guy named The Angel with wings, and so forth.

And when I went to tell the idea to Martin Goodman, I said—he loved it, but I said, "I want to call it The Mutants."

He said, "That's a terrible name. Nobody knows what the word 'mutants' means." So I went back, and I thought about it. And I thought Professor X, Xavier. And the mutants have extra powers. For some reason I thought I could call them the X-Men. So I went back to Martin. He said, "Oh, that's a good name." And as I walked out, I thought, if nobody knows what a mutant is, how were they going to know what an X-Man is? But I had my name, so I wasn't about to make waves.

Q. And you gave the—this—

A. Oh, yeah, luckily—

Q. —idea to Kirby?

A. Luckily, Jack was free at the time. And again, he did a wonderful job.

Q. Did you, again, with X-Men follow the same pattern you testified before, using the Marvel method?

A. Yeah. I spoke to him. I don't even think I wrote anything. I think we talked about it. And he was on absolutely the same wave length. He saw it the way I did. So I said, "Go on and draw it." And he did, and it came out great. And I wrote the copy, and it became one of our best-selling strips.

Stan Lee also testified about the creation of Nick Fury with Kirby.

Q. Next Nick Fury. Tell us about Nick Fury.

A. Nick Fury, Agent of S.H.I.E.L.D. There was a television series called The Man from U.N.C.L.E. that I used to watch and I liked it. And I thought it would be fun to get something like that as a comic book.

So I remembered we had done a war series called Sgt. Fury and his Howling Commandos, Stories of World War II. And it was quite popular. I don't really like war stories, so after a few years of doing it I asked Martin if we could drop the book so we could concentrate on superheroes. And he said okay. But we got a lot of fan mail. The kids loved the characters. And we kept reprinting those books, and they sold as well as the originals.

So when I wanted to do the thing like The Man from U.N.C.L.E., I thought why don't I take that popular Sgt. fury that was years ago in World War II, why don't I say he's older now and he's a colonel, and he's in charge of this new outfit that I made up, S.H.I.E.L.D, which stood for the Supreme Headquarters International Law Enforcement Division. So I took Sgt. Fury, who now has a patch over one eye, and made him in charge of this group.

And again, there was Jack Kirby. I said, "How would you like to draw Nick Fury, Agent of S.H.I.E.L.D. And it was right up Jack's alley. He loves that kind of stuff. And he came up with all kind of weapons and things.

Q. And again, you had the same process of overseeing and editing it?

A. Yeah. It was always the same process.

Captain America, a previously released golden age character, also made his resurgence during the Marvel Age of Comics. There was no dispute that Kirby and Simon created the character. Lee's writing modernized the character for the Marvel Age. On this, Lee testified:

Q. To your recollection, were there any characters that Kirby had created before he was working with you or anyone at Marvel that he brought to Marvel and then were then [sic] published by Marvel?

A. No, I don't believe so. I don't recall any. Oh, wait a minute. Wait a minute. Captain America, for God's sake. He and Joe Simon had created Captain America.

Q. Right.

A. Now, by the time in the 60s, Jack came to work for us, we weren't—there was no more Captain America We weren't publishing it because Martin Goodman thought it was just a World War II character and people wouldn't be interested in it anymore.

I always loved the character, so I decided to bring it back. And I tried to write a story where he had been frozen in a glacier for years, and they found him and he came back to life, and so forth. And I tried to give him some personality where he always felt—he was an anachronism. He was living in our day, but yet he had the values of 20 or 30 years ago. And I tried to make him a little bit interesting.

And Jack would draw him. And Jack just drew him so beautifully, and the stories worked out so well that he became part of the Marvel superhero characters, the one that I did not create. Yeah. And he's a great character, and they'll be making movies of him soon.

Q. Other than Captain America, you can't remember any—

A. No, I don't remember any others.

Of course, Captain America was the subject of an earlier litigation, as discussed in chapter 5. During that litigation, Kirby wrote, in a July 12, 1966, declaration:

I felt that whatever I did for [Marvel Comics] belonged to [Marvel Comics] as was the practice in those days. When I left [Marvel Comics], all of my work was left with them.

Kirby also signed a copyright registration application for Captain America in which he acknowledged that Marvel Comics was the "proprietor of a copyright in a work made for hire."

Kirby continued to work at Marvel Comics for almost a decade, creating and shepherding what would be known as Marvel House style. At Lee's request, he often provided new-to-Marvel Comics-artists breakdown layouts, over which they would pencil in order to become acquainted with the Marvel Comics house look. As artist Gil Kane described:

> Jack was the single most influential figure in the turnaround in Marvel's fortunes from the time he rejoined the company.... It wasn't merely that Jack conceived most of the characters that are being done, but ... Jack's point of view and philosophy of drawing became the governing philosophy of the entire publishing company and, beyond the publishing company, of the entire field ... [Marvel Comics took] Jack and use[d] him as a primer. They would get artists ... and they taught them the ABCs, which amounted to learning Jack Kirby.... Jack was like the Holy Scripture and they simply had to follow him without deviation. That's what was told to me.... It was how they taught everyone to reconcile all those opposing attitudes to one single master point of view.

The Marvel Method

For the most part, Lee continued to write all the Marvel books during the sixties and early seventies, but as more titles were added, it became more and more difficult for him to keep up. Concerned for the freelance artists, who were paid by the page, and not by a salary, Lee came up with what would come to be known as the Marvel Method. As he described:

Q. Okay. Why don't you describe the Marvel method.

A. There was a time when I was writing so many stories that I couldn't keep up with the artists. I couldn't feed them enough work. And, you see, the artists were freelancers. Now, for example, if Jack was working on a story, and Steve was waiting for me to give him a story because he had had finished what he had been doing—

Q. Jack being Jack Kirby?

A. Jack Kirby.

A. And Steve Ditko?

A. Right. Or it could have been any of the artists. But just using them as an example, if one of them was waiting for a story while I was still finishing writing the story for the other one, I couldn't keep him waiting because he wasn't making money. He was a freelancer. He wasn't on salary.

So I would say: Look, Steve, I don't have time to write your script for you, but this is the idea for the story. I'd like this fill in, and I'd like this to happen, and in the end the hero ends by doing this. You go ahead and draw it any way you want to, as long as you keep to that main theme. And I will keep finishing Jack's story. And when you finish drawing this one, I will put in all the dialogue and the captions.

So in that way I could keep one artist working while I was finishing something for another artist. That worked out so well that I began doing that with just about all the artists. I would just give them an idea for a story, let them draw it any way they wanted to. Because no matter how they drew it, even if they didn't do it as well as I might have wanted, I was conceited enough to think I could fix it up by the way I put the dialogue and the captions in. And I'd make sense out of it even if they may have made—have done something wrong.

And I was able to keep a lot of artists busy at the same time by using that system. And I have never given that long an explanation before.

In addition, Roy Thomas testified that Lee "would come up with the idea for the plots" and Lee would then give the plots to the artists to draw. Similarly, John Romita, Sr., also testified that he and Lee would "get together in a room" to discuss the plot, and then he "would have to do the nuts and bolts" in the pencil drawing. Finally, this was also confirmed by Lieber, who testified:

Q. And where would—how would you get the idea for the story? How would you know what to write about?
A. Well, my brother made up the plot and gave me a synopsis.
Q. And your brother is?
A. Stan Lee. I'm sorry.
Q. And did all of the ideas for stories come from Stan Lee or was there any other way you would get ideas?
A. No, they all came from Stan Lee.

* * *

Q. Who came up with the ideas for the characters that would be in the story?
A. Stan. Well, wait a minute. You say the characters?
Q. Yes.
A. Stan. Yes. Yes. Stan, yes. Yes, sure.
Q. Who was responsible for giving you the assignment to write a particular script or a particular—
A. Stan.

* * *

Q. You mentioned that Stan would give you the synopsis or the plot. How? How would he give that to you? Would he—
A. As far as I remember, it was—you mean written. He would give it written to me.

Under this method, artists would draw out the plots. Sometimes, these artists would make notes on the side of the page. With regard to the margin notes of Kirby, Lee described how Kirby made his notes.

Q. Now, typically, what was the work product after you had given Kirby an assignment? What was the work product that you would receive back from Kirby?
A. I would receive back usually, if the book was 20 pages long, I'd receive back 20 beautifully drawn pages in pencil which told a story.
Q. And did Mr. Kirby ever suggest dialogue?
A. Not orally, but what he would do, when I would give Jack a rough idea for what the story should be, and he went home and he drew it in his own way, laying it out the way he thought it would be best, he would put in the borders, the margins of the pages, he would put little notes letting—so I would understand what he was getting at with each drawing, and he would sometimes put dialogue suggestions also.

[Lee was then given an exhibit that contained a *Fantastic Four* page with margin notes.]

Q. Do you recognize the notes around the pages?
A. Well, that's Jack's handwriting. That's the way he wrote them. Yes.
Q. And could you tell us, for example, in this instance I see that there's a dialogue that's actually in the different blocks. Tell us who did that dialogue. How was the process done?

A. Well, I wrote the dialogue and the captions, but Jack would give me notes. For example, in panel 4 of that page, the next to the last panel—

Q. Right.

A. Jack wrote what he suggested the dialogue might be. "I will rule. My years underground will end." That was to let me know what he felt the fellow should be doing or saying.

So I wrote, "My conquest will be complete. I, the Mole Man, banished from my fellow men half a life time ago, will return at last as Master of the Earth."

Very often I would write dialogue to fill up spaces. In other words, I also indicated where the dialogue balloons and the captions should go on the artwork. And I might not have written so much if he had made the face bigger, but inasmuch as there was that space on the upper right-hand part of the page, I put in more dialogue to sort of dress up the—balance the panel with picture and dialogue. That was something else I had mentioned but I concentrated very much on.

For example, in the panel above it, that panel was an interesting panel, and I didn't want to—I only used three lines of caption. I didn't want to crowd that with copy.

And the same with the first panel. There's so much going on, that I only had a two-line caption that only went part way across, because I wanted the reader to enjoy looking at Jack's artwork with no interference.

Q. And who was it who decided where those—where the dialogue would go?

A. I did. I always made the indications for the letter—before giving my strips to a letterer, I always indicated in pencil after I typed out the dialogue where the dialogue should go in the panel. And the sound effects, also.

Romita also testified that Lee often times ignored any margin notes submitted by the artist with suggestions as to the plot or dialogue in the story.

Q. We talked about this a little bit, but who would write the dialogue?

A. The person who wrote the script, Stan Lee in his cases, Roy Thomas in his cases. They wrote all the dialogue.

Q. Did artists ever write dialogue?

A. The only thing we used to do, because we worked from a plot, we used to write notes above and below the artwork and sometimes in the margins to—we would make notes and say—to remind him what we had talked about in the plot and this is my response to it and this is how I'm building up to it....

Q. So what would Stan do with notes or the dialogue in the margins?

A. I used to write notes that I thought were clever.... He invariably would not use them....

Q. Do you know whether it was just your dialogue he wouldn't use? Would he use anybody else's dialogue in the margins?

* * *

A. I don't think so. I don't think he ever—I think he—more than once I've heard him saying he avoided anybody else's expressions in the scripts.

With regard to payment, it was also clear that Kirby worked for a fixed per page rate for all the work Marvel Comics published. And while neither side was able to produce checks that were given to Kirby during his work at Marvel Comics in the sixties and early seventies (nor did Marvel Comics retain any checks written during that period), both sides agreed that the checks had legends on the back that assigned rights to the freelance work created to Marvel Comics. And while there were no contemporaneous checks, checks were produced from later periods to show that the earlier checks had a similar legend. Kirby's heirs also produced a check issued by Marvel Comics to Stephen Gerber, a freelance artist, in 1973. The back of the check read:

By endorsement of this check: I, the payee, acknowledge full payment for my employment by Magazine Management, Co., and for my assignment to it of any copyright, trademark, and any other rights in or related to the material, and, including my assignment of any rights to renewal copyright.

A second check from 1974 to freelance artist Dick Ayers was found that had the identical statement.

By contrast, the evidence produced showed that Marvel Comics did not explicitly mention that the work being performed was done as work for hire until after the passage of the 1976 copyright act. For example, a 1986 check payable to Kirby bore a legend that stated:

By acceptance and endorsement of this check, payee acknowledges, (a) full payment for payee's employment by Marvel Entertainment Group, Inc., (b) that all payee's work has been within the scope of that employment, and (c) that all payee's works are and shall be considered as works made for hire, the property of Marvel Comics Group, Inc.

Moreover, neither side could produce any contemporaneous documents that showed any kind of a written agreement between Marvel Comics and Kirby relating to any of the early work done. Lee described the relationship:

Q. And were different artists and different writers paid different rates?
A. Oh, yes, according to how valuable we thought they were.
Q. And did it matter—let's take a particular artist, oh, say Jack Kirby. Did it matter whether he—was Mr. Kirby one who got a higher page rate?
A. He got the highest because I considered him our best artist.

* * *

Q. And what was—what were his job responsibilities as an artist?
A. Well, to draw the strip as well and as excited—excitingly and grippingly as possible, and draw it in such a way that the readers would want to see more, more, more.
Q. And who had the right to direct and supervise Mr. Kirby's work?
A. That was me.
Q. And who had the ability to edit and control Kirby's work?
A. That was my job.
Q. And who decided which comic books and characters Kirby would draw?
A. I did.
Q. And who gave him those assignments?
A. I did.
Q. As best you can recall, did Mr. Kirby ever submit work to you or to Marvel that he had done on spec?
A. Not that I remember.
Q. And you mentioned the situation with taking him off the Spider-Man book. In addition to that, were there other instances where you did edit Kirby's work?
A. Well, I edited everybody's work. I don't remember taking him off anything else.
Q. Do you remember Mr. Kirby ever refusing to make any of the edits or changes that you made?
A. As a matter of fact, no. Jack was really great to work with.
Q. To your knowledge, during this period in the 60s, was Kirby working only for Marvel or was he doing work for other comic books?
A. I thought he was working just for us.
Q. Now, typically, what was the work product after you had given Kirby an assignment? What was the work product that you would receive back from Kirby?

A. I would receive back usually, if the book was 20 pages long, I'd receive back 20 beautifully drawn pages in pencil which told a story.

* * *

Q. And looking at paragraph 13 of [Stan Lee's] affidavit, it states, I will read it into the record, "For years I," being you, "received checks from Timely and its successor that bore a legend acknowledging that the payment was for works for hire." Do you recall—that's a true statement; right?

A. Yes, it is.

Q. And do you recall that that was the practice at the time?

A. Yes, it was.

Q. And was that the practice not only with respect to you but with all the writers and artists?

A. Oh, yes.

Q. And that would include Mr. Kirby?

A. Yes. Everybody.

Kirby left Marvel Comics in 1972.

On May 30, 1972, Marvel Comics and Kirby executed a written agreement that assigned to Marvel "any and all right, title and interest [Kirby] may have or control" in all the work that Kirby created for Marvel Comics. The agreement specifically provided assignment of:

(1) Any and all MATERIALS, including any and all ideas, names, characters, symbols, designs, likenesses, visual representations, stories, episodes, literary property, etc., which have been in whole or in part acquired, published, merchandised, advertised and/or licensed in any form, field, or media by [Marvel Comics], their affiliates, and/or their predecessors or successors in interest....

(2) Any and all RIGHTS, including any all copyrights, trademarks, statutory rights, common law rights, goodwill, and any other rights whatsoever relating to the Materials in any and all media and/or fields including any and all rights to renewal or extension of copyright, to recover for past infringement and to make application or institute suit therefor, and including by way of example and without limitation Kirby's claim to renewal copyright in Volume 2, Nos. 1–10 of the work entitled "Captain America Comics," these being evidenced by Registration Nos. R429502, R446534, R446535, R446536, R446537, R446538, R446539, R446540, R446541, and R448324 in the United States Copyright Office.

Kirby briefly returned to work at Marvel Comics in the seventies and signed a three year contract on March 24, 1975. This was the first written employment agreement between Kirby and Marvel Comics. The agreement provided:

Writer/Artist grants to Marvel the sole and exclusive right to all Material delivered to Marvel hereunder including, but not limited to, (a) the exclusive right to secure copyright(s) in the Material in the United States, Canada, and throughout the world, (b) the magazine rights therein of every kind, (c) all film and dramatic rights of every kind, (d) all anthology, advertising and promotion rights therein, and (e) all reprint rights.

During his three year return to Marvel Comics, Kirby worked on characters he had co-created, like Captain America and the Black Panther, as well as new creations like the Eternals, Devil Dinosaur, and Machine Man (which was based on the movie *2001: A Space Odyssey*). Perhaps learning from the past, Kirby did not work with any collaborators on these titles and did them himself. Kirby decided not to renew his contract, which expired on May 1, 1978.

In 1986, Kirby arranged to get some of his original artwork back from Marvel Comics.

As part of the agreement reached, Jack Kirby signed another agreement that stated an "Acknowledgement of Copyright Ownership" dated June 16, 1986. The agreement stated:

> I have no copyright rights and no claim to copyright, or to the renewal or extension of copyright, or any other rights (except only for my ownership of the original physical artwork being returned to me by Marvel) in any artwork, characters, publications or other material ... created or prepared by me for or on behalf of, or which was published by or under the authority of, Marvel Comics Group or any predecessor company.

Since then, Marvel Comics characters have appeared in movies, television and video games. In fact many of the top grossing films of all time are based on Marvel Comics properties that Kirby helped create.

Kirby died on August 6, 2009.

In August 2009, the Walt Disney Company acquired Marvel Comics.

Notice of Termination and the Lawsuit

On September 16, 2009, Kirby's heirs served Marvel Comics with termination notices for 45 Kirby comics published by Marvel Comics between 1958 and 1963, including characters from the *Fantastic Four*, *The Incredible Hulk*, *Journey into Mystery*, *Thor*, *Spider-Man*, *X-Men*, *Avengers*, *Nick Fury* and *The Rawhide Kid*.[3] *Captain America* was not included in these termination agreements.

On January 8, 2011, Marvel Comics made a preemptive strike against Kirby's heirs and filed suit in in the United States District Court for the Southern District of New York seeking declaratory relief that it owned the copyrights. As grounds for the relief, Marvel Comics argued that when Kirby made the comics he did so as works for hire under the 1909 copyright act. This would make the termination notices invalid. Under copyright law, the general rule is that protection initially vests with the author or creator of the work, who can then sell or transfer the protection to a purchaser. However, there is an exception to this rule when the work is a work made for hire. In that case, the employer or entity commissioning the work is considered the author under the law vested with transfer rights.

Kirby's heirs counterclaimed and argued that the work belonged to Kirby and was not made as work for hire.

During discovery, the parties took several depositions that shed light on what it was like to work at Marvel Comics in the Silver Age. For example, John Romita testified about the Marvel Bullpen and what it was like to correct Kirby:

> Q. Did you ever make any changes to any of Jack Kirby's work?
> A. Yes. And it was hard for me, because I idolized the man's stuff. I used to change occasionally girl's faces. Now, Jack used to do girls that I loved. I loved his girls. But Stan used to find sometimes something that he didn't like, an expression, two [*sic*] wide a face, too narrow a face, mostly too wide, and he would ask me to adjust it. He liked the way I did one of the female characters in Captain America better than the way Jack did it, so I would occasionally change the faces. Much to my chagrin, people accused me of being an egomaniac, again, because they thought I was the one changing it. Since I was a de facto art director, they said, "look this Romita, he is changing everybody's work." Barry

Smith almost put a contract out on me because I changed somebody—a girl's face on a Conan cover. To this day I still don't know why he is talking to me. We are friends, but I know he wanted to kill me then.

Q. Whose idea were those changes? Were they ever yours?

A. Uh-uh, never. I would never change anybody—I had to change Jack Kirby's work, Gene Colan's work, John Buscema's work. I idolized all of these guys. I would—it violated me to have to do it. I cringed. And I will tell you, the worst thing is initially we didn't have the equipment or the technology to do it less obtrusively, because originally we didn't have photostats and xeroxes to work with. I erased things. To this minute I —the hair on the back of my neck stands up when I am thinking I am erasing a Jack Kirby face and putting my face in there. That, to me, is a criminal act. I did it because I had no choice. Stan asked me to change it.... I used to actually deface artwork that I idolized. And it was not fun, but I did my duty as I was instructed.

Because Kirby was no longer around to give a deposition, the heirs attempted to show their side of the argument through documentary evidence and the use of two expert witnesses: John Morrow and Mark Evanier. The court described them as follows:

John Morrow is a writer, archivist, and publisher in the comic book industry. Morrow states that Kirby's death in 1994 prompted him to produce a newsletter about Kirby's life and achievements. He still publishes that newsletter today.... Mark Evanier is a comic book writer, columnist, and historian. In 1969, Kirby hired Evanier as an assistant, to conduct research, co-author "letter pages" in Kirby comic books, and to assist Kirby with creating storylines. Evanier helped Kirby with new comic book projects that Kirby was producing for DC Comics in 1969—six years after the relevant period....

On February 25, 2011, both sides moved for summary judgment arguing that based on the undisputed material facts, they were entitled to the relief requested. Marvel Comics argued that the undisputed material facts established that the work done for Marvel Comics by Kirby were all made as work for hire under the Copyright Act of 1909, which means that Marvel Comics owned all aspects of the copyright. In response, Kirby's heirs argued that there were disputed issues of material fact that precluded summary judgment in Marvel Comics' favor. Instead, the undisputed material facts would permit the court to rule in Kirby's favor as a matter of law, i.e., a finding that the work done by Kirby while at Marvel Comics was not work for hire.

The Lower Court Decision

On July 28, 2011, the Southern District Court of New York decided the case in Marvel Comics' favor and found that the Kirby comics were made as work for hire under the Copyright Act of 1909.

The court began its opinion by acknowledging Kirby's contribution: "Jack Kirby is a legend in the comic book industry. During his long association with Marvel Comics, Kirby, working as a freelance artist, played a key role in the creation of a number of iconic characters, including 'The Fantastic Four,' 'The Incredible Hulk,' and 'The X–Men.'"

The court then explained its decision. Initially, the court was careful to point out that the case was covered by the Copyright Act of 1909. This is because the works were created from 1958 to 1963 and works made before January 1, 1978, are governed by the Copyright Act of 1909; works made after are governed by the Copyright Act of 1976. This is very important because each copyright act has a different standard and test for whether something was made as a work for hire. Simply put, it would be much easier to establish work for hire under the 1909 Act, which only mentions the doctrine once: "[I]n the interpretation and construction of this title ... the word 'author' shall include an employer in the case of works made for hire." Because the 1909 Act doesn't define "employer" or "works made for hire," it has been left to the courts to fill in the gap. And while it was clear that the work for hire doctrine would apply in cases where the parties have an employer/employee relationship, courts have also held that there are circumstances when commissioned works can be considered work for hire, such as when the creator is an independent contractor. Consequently, courts needed to establish a bright line. In 1965, judges developed what would be known as the instance and expense test for works made for hire. Under the test, a court will examine who asked for the work to be done, and who was in charge of supervising. It is important to note that there doesn't actually need to be supervision, just the right to direct and supervise the manner in which the writer performs his work.

Whether Kirby's work for Marvel Comics is considered a work made for hire is an important question because it determines whether he had termination rights. This is because the termination provisions in the 1909 and 1976 Copyright Acts do not apply to works made for hire. The logic behind this is that the owner of a work for hire is the employer or company that commissions the work. In this case, if the court were to find that Kirby created the Marvel properties as work for hire, then Marvel Comics would own the copyright and the renewal period. In other words, Kirby would not prevail in terminating his transfer of copyright to Marvel Comics, because he never owned it in the first place because it was made as a work for hire. However, if the court found that the works were not made as works for hire, then Kirby's heirs had the right to terminate the transfer of rights to Marvel Comics and regain ownership of all of Marvel Comics' main characters.

After establishing that it was looking at the work for hire standard established in the 1909 Act, the court had no trouble finding that Jack Kirby's Marvel Comics work was made at Marvel's direction. The court held

> [T]hat there are no genuine issues of material fact, and that the Kirby Works were indeed works for hire within the meaning of the Copyright Act of 1909. Therefore, the ... Termination Notices did not operate to convey any federally-protected copyrights in the Kirby Works to the Kirby Heirs. Marvel's motion for summary judgment is granted; the Kirby Heirs' cross motion is denied.

So the question must be, how did the court reach this decision when there was so much contradiction between how Marvel Comics and Kirby remembered the creation of these characters? To answer this question, it is important to look at how a court evaluates and admits evidence in a case. There are three kinds of witnesses at trial, fact witnesses, expert witnesses, and mixed fact and expert witnesses. Under the rules of court, a fact witness is defined as someone who has a personal knowledge of whether a relevant fact occurred or did not occur. For the most part, fact witnesses are not allowed to give their opinion on what the facts mean; they just tell the court what happened. In other words, they were there and witnessed the events that gave rise to the case but can't say how those facts fit into the argument. An expert witness, by contrast, has no personal knowledge but has a skill set or area of expertise that is helpful to the court in looking at the facts that are presented. These people render an opinion on the facts and can rely on anything, even inadmissible evidence, so long as they would regularly rely on it in their job. The final category is exactly what it sounds like, a person with specialized knowledge that was present at the event and knows the facts firsthand. These mixed fact/expert witnesses can testify about what happened and what it means. The textbook example of this type of witness is the testifying physician that treated the plaintiff after an accident. The doctor personally knows what happened in the accident, but also can help the court understand the medical jargon that describes what damage the victim suffered.

In the *Kirby* case, Marvel Comics presented evidence from several witnesses who were present at the time of the events. Primarily, Marvel Comics relied on the testimony of Lee and then supplemented it with that of several other Marvel Comics writers and artists. As the court explains,

> Marvel's side of the story is told by the most percipient of witnesses: Stan Lee Marvel's editor during the period 1958–1963—when the Kirby Works were created—and a legendary figure in his own right.... Marvel's motion stands or falls on his testimony, although Marvel supplemented Lee's testimony with testimony from Roy Thomas, Lawrence Lieber, and John Romita.

Basically, Lee was the best witness because he was there for all of the conversations with Kirby. He was there for the closed door planning sessions that resulted in the creation of the characters and the comics. The only other witness with as much personal knowledge would have been Kirby, who was no longer alive to give testimony. So the heirs had to tell Kirby's side of the story without relying on Kirby's testimony. The court explained their approach:

> To counter Lee's first-hand testimony, the Kirby Heirs offer the testimony from three comic book artists who also worked as freelancers for Marvel between the 1950s and 1970s. James F. Steranko is a comic book artist and historian who worked for Marvel as a freelance artist between 1966 and 1973. Joe Sinnott is a comic book artist who worked for Marvel as a freelance artist in the 1950s and 1960s. Sinnott also worked as a "freelance inker" and inked many issues of Kirby's "The Mighty Thor" and "The Avengers." Richard Ayers is a comic book artist who worked on a freelance basis for Marvel from 1959 until 1975. Richard Ayers also inked various newspaper comic strips drawn by Kirby (but not for Marvel) between 1959 and 1961.
>
> The Kirby Heirs also offer their own reminiscences about their father and his work, but as they were children during the relevant time period, they do not claim to have first-hand knowledge about their father's business dealings with Marvel.

Marvel Comics moved to strike (i.e., asked the court to ignore) all of these witnesses, and most of their documents. First, Marvel Comics raised a procedural argument that Kirby's heirs did not timely disclose the three comic artists or produce several documents and that their surprise appearance in the case created undue prejudice. The court quickly rejected this argument because all of the witnesses and documents were identified or known to Marvel Comics as they were discussed during depositions or mentioned in documents produced in discovery. In addition, the court determined that these witnesses had relevant information and personal knowledge of that information. As a result, the declarations and testimony of these witnesses were considered by the court.

Marvel Comics also moved to strike Kirby's two expert witnesses on the grounds that they were merely conduits utilized to get facts into the record and offered no real expertise for the court to utilize. The court agreed with Marvel Comics and struck the reports and testimony of Mark Evanier and Tom Morrow.

In reaching this conclusion, the court looked to the substance of the reports. First, Tom Morrow's report looked at: (1) Marvel Comics' history before, during, and after the 1958–1963 time period; (2) the business relationship between Kirby and Marvel Comics during that period; and (3) Kirby's creation or co-creation of certain comic book characters. Like the Morrow report, the Evanier report looked at: (1) the manner in which Kirby created or co-created comic book characters published by Marvel Comics from 1958 to 1963; (2) Kirby's relationship with Marvel Comics during that time period; and (3) the background of the comic book industry, including Marvel Comics' origin, and Marvel Comics' relationship with Kirby.

The court first looked to the fact that neither expert had first-hand personal knowledge of the facts upon which they opined.

> The reason for Evanier and Morrow evidence is clear: to try to rebut Lee's testimony and create issues of fact about the creation of the Kirby Works between 1958 and 1963. Unfortunately for Defendants, Evanier and Morrow lack Lee's "I was there" experience. Evanier admits that he was only six years old in 1958, when the relevant time period began; he did not meet Kirby until over a decade later, when Evanier was 17. Evanier also concedes that, "There's a limit to how much [he] can know about what two men [i.e., Lee and Kirby] did behind closed doors years ago." Similarly, Morrow has no firsthand knowledge about Marvel's practices during the relevant time period, or about the actual creation of the Kirby Works. Morrow testified that his accounts of Marvel's history, its working relationship with Kirby, and the creation of certain characters were based on "what [he has] read throughout the years" and what others have told him. Morrow admits that he learned everything he put in his report from interviews and other secondary sources, in other words, hearsay. Morrow also admits that his only "connection" to the comic book industry prior to 1994 was as a "comics fan."

Finding no personal knowledge, the court then turned on to the witnesses' qualifications to serve as experts and therefore have their declarations and reports admitted as expert opinion. The court found the reports lacking for several independent reasons, each of which could be relied upon to strike the witnesses. The court wrote:

> First, Evanier's and Morrow's purported "expert" reports are merely factual narratives based on their review of secondary sources and interviews that attempt to reconstruct events about which neither has first-hand knowledge.... Second, Evanier's and Morrow's reports address "lay matters which [the trier of fact] is capable of understanding and deciding without the expert's help." Third, Morrow and Evanier also offer their "opinions" about the intent or motivations of Marvel and individuals that worked at Marvel.... Inferences about the intent or motive of parties or others lie outside the bounds of expert testimony. Finally, by purporting to opine on the credibility of Lee's testimony, Evanier has improperly usurped the role of the jury.

Exclusion of the Morrow and Evanier reports was devastating to Kirby's heirs as it allowed Lee's testimony to go essentially unchallenged. This combined with the lower burden necessary under the two-pronged instance and expense test under the 1909 Copyright Act led to the court ruling in Marvel Comics' favor.

Turning to the first prong of the instance and expense test, the court looked at the degree to which Marvel Comics had the right to control or supervise Kirby's work. Put another way, the court was looking at whether Marvel Comics had the power to accept, reject, modify, or otherwise control Kirby's work. If it did, then the work was created at the instance of Marvel Comics.

Applying this test, the court reasoned as follows: "The record on the cross motions admits of but one conclusion: Kirby did not create the artwork that is the subject of the Termination Notices until Lee assigned him to do so."

As a result, the court focused on whether Lee had the right to direct and supervise the manner in which Kirby performed his work. The court stated:

> It is undisputed that at all times between 1958 and 1963 Lee had complete editorial and stylistic control over all work that Marvel published.
>
> In the 1950s and 1960s, Lee supervised the creation of Marvel's comic books from conception to publication. Lee assigned writers and artist [*sic*] to work on comic books and reviewed all work before it was published. Lee also had the authority to ask artists to revise or edit their work before publication and frequently exercised that authority.... If, for instance, Lee wanted a character's frown changed to a smile to suit the story's dialogue, the artist made the change. Lee did not always consult with the artist before making a change to their work.
>
> If Lee did not approve of the artist's work, it was not published. Kirby was no exception. Lee edited Kirby's work and reviewed and approved all of his work prior to publication.... Additionally, it was Lee who generated the plot or synopsis from which an artist created the pencil drawing for each assignment. Lee testified that he assigned an artist to draw a comic book after he had either described the premise in a plot outline or plotting conference, or provided the artist with a detailed script. Lee, who created the plot and dialogue for the characters after the pencil drawing was completed, often times ignored any "margin notes" submitted by the artist with suggestions as to the plot or dialogue in the story.
>
> Lee's testimony is corroborated by both documentary evidence and testimony from other artists.

Consequently, the court determined: "[t]here is no disputed issue of material fact: the undisputed evidence illustrates that the Kirby Works were created at Marvel's 'instance.'"

The court rejected arguments by Kirby's heirs that the absence of a written agreement between Kirby and Marvel Comics meant Marvel Comics lacked the legal right to control his work. This is because contracts can be oral and the ability to supervise and edit an artist's work does not need to be memorialized to prove it existed. The record was clear that Lee gave artists, like Kirby, assignments, reviewed his work, and made changes when necessary. This supervision proved that Marvel Comics did control and supervise all work that it published between 1958 and 1963 regardless of whether there was a written contract.

The court also found that the statements by James Steranko, Richard Ayers, and Joe Sinnott did not create an issue of fact on the question of instance because all three stated that payment for their work was contingent on approval of the work by Marvel Comics' editor.

Turning to the expense prong, which it also found in Marvel Comics' favor, the court determined that Kirby bore no financial risk if a book failed because he was paid a page rate for the work done. Kirby's heirs argued that this prong was not met because Kirby provided his own tools, worked his own hours, paid his own taxes and benefits, and used his own art supplies. The court dismissed these factors and stated: "[T]hese factors 'have no bearing on whether the work was made at the hiring party's expense'; they are relevant only to the issue of whether an artist worked as an employee and not an independent contractor."

Instead, all that was necessary was to show that Marvel Comics paid Kirby a certain sum for his work, and the court held that the flat page rate made by Marvel Comics for Jack Kirby's work alone would be sufficient to meet the expense prong of the test. The court contrasted a situation where the creator of a work receives royalties as payment, which would weigh against finding a work for hire relationship. The court summed up, "[T]he focus is on who bore the risk of the work's profitability."

Kirby's heirs also argued that the fact that Marvel Comics was not contractually or legally obligated to buy his pages, and even rejected some of the pages or asked for major revisions, meant that Kirby ultimately bore the risk of loss and profitability. In support of this, the heirs presented evidence of what is known as turn down fees, which are paid regardless of whether the work is accepted. The court rejected this argument relying on well established precedent that holds that profitability must be considered over the entire project. In this case, the risk was on Marvel Comics that the book would not sell because it paid the cost for producing the book, including printers, the writers, pencilers, inkers, letterers, and colorists. The court also determined that:

> In this case, the evidence that the works were created at Marvel's instance is so overwhelming that its failure to pay Kirby a turn-down fee is effectively irrelevant.
>
> * * *
>
> Kirby took on none of the risks of the success of the many comic books he helped produce. His contribution to the enterprise was plainly critical, but Marvel, not he, bore the risk of its failure. Therefore, the expense factor favors Marvel's work-for-hire claim as well.

The court concluded:

> It is undisputed that Kirby was paid a fixed per-page fee for all work that Marvel published—including the Kirby Works. Therefore, there is no genuine issue of material fact: the works were created at Marvel's expense.

As a result, the court determined that because Marvel Comics faced all the financial risk on the books, Marvel Comics was presumed to be author/owner of all the work done by Kirby for Marvel Comics.

Of course, the instance and expense test only creates a presumption in Marvel Comics' favor that the work was done as a work for hire. This means that Kirby's heirs could have offered evidence to rebut that presumption and show that Kirby was the true author/owner of the work through the use of evidence of a contrary agreement, either written or oral. In order to rebut the presumption, Kirby's heirs claimed that three documents supported their position: the 1972 assignment agreement between Kirby and Marvel Comics; the 1975 employment agreement between Kirby and Marvel Comics; and checks issued between 1973 and 1974 by Marvel Comics to freelance artists other than Kirby. Each of these documents reference a transfer of copyright. Kirby's heirs argued that these documents prove that Marvel Comics could not have owned the original copyright because then there would be no reason to transfer it.

The court rejected the argument of Kirby's heirs. Looking at the first document, the

1972 agreement, the court concluded that it only assigned to Marvel Comics whatever right, title and interest Kirby had at that time in the copyrights and neither proved nor disproved that Kirby's works were created as works for hire within the meaning of the 1909 Act. To the contrary, the court determined that the 1972 assignment actually supported the argument that the material created by Kirby was made as work for hire. The court stated:

> The agreement only purports to assign whatever right, title and interest Kirby "may have" in the Kirby Works; it does not contain language acknowledging that Kirby actually had retained any federally protected copyright in those works at the time he created them.
> What the 1972 agreement does contain is Kirby's admission that he created the works as an employee for hire of Marvel's owners—definitive language that completely eviscerates the Kirby Heirs' claim that the agreement constitutes evidence of an understanding that the Kirby Works were not works for hire.

Moreover, the court found the plain language of the 1972 assignment clearly stated that all of Kirby's work done for Marvel Comics was owned by [Marvel Comics] as it was prepared as a work for hire. This was consistent with other statements made by Kirby, including statements that Captain America belonged to the company for which he created it. Kirby wrote that he "felt that whatever [he] did for [Marvel Comics] belonged to [Marvel Comics] as was the practice in those days." In addition, Kirby signed a 1986 affidavit in which Kirby admitted that the practice at the time he was at Marvel Comics gave ownership of those works to Marvel Comics.

The court determined that the later agreements corroborated the plain language of the 1972 assignment: "None of these statements suggests that the 1972 agreement conveyed any federal copyright from Kirby to Marvel; all of them support Marvel's contention that no agreement exists that contradicts the work-for-hire presumption."

Next, the court turned to the 1975 employment agreement. Once again, the court rejected Kirby's heirs' argument since the agreement covered future works. Finally the court turned to the 1973 and 1974 checks. Kirby's heirs argued that the legend on the check proved that copyright vested with Kirby before it was transferred to Marvel Comics. The court found that the checks did not relate to the time period as neither side was able to produce checks from the relevant time period, and it wouldn't matter if they did:

> Of course, there is absolutely no evidence that checks issued to Jack Kirby between 1958 and 1963 bore a legend identical or similar to the one that appears on the checks from a decade later; one cannot infer what might have been written on a check issued in 1958 from what was written on an analogous check fifteen years later. For that reason alone, the 1973 and 1974 checks do not raise any genuine issue of fact that tends to contradict the work-for-hire presumption.... Further, the language in the legend, which assigns to Marvel the copyright in the work, is not dispositive of whether a work-for-hire relationship exists under the 1909 Act.

After reviewing all the evidence, the court determined that

> [N]one of the evidence submitted none of the evidence submitted by Defendants makes so much as a dent in the "almost irrebutable" presumption that the Kirby Works were works for hire. The Kirby Heirs are not entitled to summary judgment in their favor, and they have not raised any genuine issue of fact necessitating a trial. The Termination Notices were of no force and effect, because Marvel acquired the federal statutory copyright in the Kirby Works by virtue of its status as their "author" under the work-for-hire doctrine. Plaintiffs are entitled to a declaration to that effect.

To sum up, the court found that the facts and evidence presented showed that the work done by Kirby for Marvel Comics constituted works made for hire as a matter of law. As a result, Marvel Comics was the author under the 1909 Act, making the termination notices filed by Kirby's heirs invalid.

Kirby's heirs appealed the decision to the Second Circuit Court of Appeals.

After acknowledging, "That Marvel owes many of its triumphs to Kirby is beyond question," the Second Circuit Court of Appeals affirmed the ruling.[4]

The court determined that:

> Despite the absence of a formal employment agreement, however, the record suggests that Kirby and Marvel were closely affiliated during the relevant time period. Lee assigned Kirby, whom he considered his best artist, a steady stream of work during that period.... And Kirby seems to have done most of his work with Marvel projects in mind.

The Second Circuit agreed with the District Court and concluded that the works were created at Marvel Comics' instance and expense and held:

> Although Jack Kirby was a freelancer, his working relationship with Marvel between the years of 1958 and 1963 was close and continuous.... Understood as products of this overarching relationship, Kirby's works during this period were hardly self-directed projects in which he hoped Marvel, as one of several potential publishers, might have an interest; rather, he created the relevant works pursuant to Marvel's assignment or with Marvel specifically in mind. Kirby's ongoing partnership with Marvel, however unbalanced and under-remunerative to the artist, is therefore what induced Kirby's creation of the works.

On the issue of whether the books were made a Marvel's expense, the Second Circuit determined, "Marvel's payment of a flat rate [to Kirby] and its contribution of both creative and production value, in light of the parties' relationship as a whole, is enough..."

Consequently, the circuit court ruled:

> The evidence suggests ... that Marvel and Kirby had a standing engagement whereby Kirby would produce drawings designed to fit within specific Marvel universes that his previously purchased pages had helped to define ... the district court made no error, in our view, in determining as a matter of law that the works were made at Marvel's instance and expense.

As a result, the court held that Kirby could not terminate the rights as Marvel Comics owned them as work made for hire. The case was over. Or was it?

On March 21, 2014, the Kirby heirs petitioned the United States Supreme Court for *certiorari*, basically requesting the Court to hear the case. The Supreme Court's review, for the most part, is discretionary and the Court hears less than one percent of the estimated 10,000 petitions it receives each year. In order to determine what cases are heard, the justices select cases they believe have merit to be heard in conference. In 2014, the Court decided to debate whether the *Kirby* case should be heard in conference. While this was no guarantee that *certiorari* would be granted, the Court's decision was enough to motive several prominent litigants, including the Screen Actors Guild of America, the Directors Guild of America, the Writers Guild of America and others, to file *amicus curiae* (friend of the court) briefs in support of the Kirby heirs. On September 26, 2014, it was announced that the case was settled.

Kirby and Lee's creations still appear in pages of Marvel Comics and will star in several upcoming feature films. Jack Kirby's name has since been added to the credits.

CHAPTER 15

The Never Ending Battle Begins
Jerry Siegel and Joe Shuster v. DC Comics

The story behind the creation of Superman is a tale of perseverance. It begins in 1932 on the east side of Cleveland, when two students at Glenville High School named Jerry Siegel and Joe Shuster met while working on *The Torch*, the school's newspaper.[1] They quickly realized that they had a common interest in their love of science fiction. Siegel wanted to be a writer; Shuster, an artist. They formed a legendary partnership and created an iconic character that would transform an industry. But the road was not easy for this creative pair.

The Birth of Superman

At the beginning of their partnership, they created *Science Fiction: The Advance Guard of Future Civilization*, a mail-order fanzine. In January 1933, the fanzine featured a short story entitled "The Reign of the Superman." This story introduced a villainous Superman that looked and acted much more like Lex Luthor than the costumed hero he would later become. In the story, Professor Ernest Smalley recruits a transient named Bill Dunn from a bread line to test an experimental potion. The potion gives Dunn psychic abilities that are used to commit crimes in his attempt to take over the world. However, after Dunn murders the mad scientist, he discovers the effects of the potion are only temporary. With the death of its creator, the potion cannot be duplicated and Dunn must return to his prior life on the breadline.

And while the story was interesting, Siegel realized that by simply changing the Superman character from a villain to a hero, it could be so much more. So he began work on creating Superman as a comic book character. Siegel said that he sought to create a character to give hope to the masses, most of whom were suffering, as he did, from the Great Depression.

So, while Siegel began to write the adventures for his new character, Shuster began to sketch the panels of the comic. This effort resulted in a book called *The Superman*. Once again, the character bore little resemblance to the superhero that would follow. Inspired by the pulp characters of Flash Gordon and Tarzan, and the comic book character Detective Dan, this version of Superman possessed no superpowers, but was an athletic strongman.[2] His crime fighting costume consisted of jeans and a t-shirt.[3]

Once they had completed the work, Siegel and Shuster began a quest to find a publisher.

They turned to Consolidated Book Publishing, the publisher of one of Siegel's inspirations, *Detective Dan, Secret Operative*. Consolidated initially accepted the book for publication, but changed their mind and stopped making comics. A devastated Shuster threw all the art for the story into a fireplace. Siegel was only able to pull the cover out of the fire, which is all that remains of the story.

Depressed, but determined, Siegel continued to modify the Superman character. And while Siegel initially attempted to work with other artists on the story, he eventually returned to his partner, Shuster, to draw the story. This time, jaded by their experience in the comic book industry and motivated by the popularity of comic strips, the pair decided that this version of Superman would be released as a daily black and white newspaper strip.[4]

Then, one night in the summer of 1934, inspiration struck Siegel, who was unable to sleep in the summer heat. He began to come up with the concept for a new Superman character. In his own words, "I was up late counting sheep and more and more ideas kept coming to me, and I wrote out several weeks of syndicate script for the proposed newspaper strip. When morning came, I dashed over to Joe [Shuster]'s place and showed it to him."

This time the character was less a pulp action hero and more of a mythic hero in the vein of Hercules, but in a modern setting. Once again, Siegel borrowed heavily from the plots of the pulps, which often featured earthborn heroes transplanted to a foreign galaxy or planet, where they are imbued with amazing powers. However, Siegel turned this setting on its head by making Earth the foreign planet visited by the hero. So, using the same formula that enabled Edgar Rice Burroughs to allow John Carter to soar over the skies of Barsoom, Superman would leap through the skies of Metropolis.

Perhaps inspired equally by the stories of Tarzan and Moses, Siegel envisioned his savior as the sole survivor of a distant planet who was sent to Earth as a baby. The differences between his planet and Earth imbue the hero with powers well beyond those of mortal men. These powers included superhuman strength, speed, invulnerability and the ability to leap one-eighth of a mile (as well as tall buildings) in a single bound. But, unlike the villain who wreaked havoc in the short story, this Superman was here to save the people of Earth.

Another major change in this version of the Superman character was the creation of the hero's mild mannered alter ego. When not saving the world, Superman hid his face behind thick glasses and worked as a meek reporter named Clark Kent. The Clark Kent identity not only humanized the character but, along with the introduction of fellow reporter Lois Lane, also helped create romantic tension in the form of a most unique love triangle. Clark was in love with Lois, who only had eyes for Superman.[5]

Once Siegel had handed his scripts over to Shuster, the young artist began to draw the story and design the look for the new Superman, including his now famous spit curl. Specifically, it was Shuster who came up with the idea for Superman's costume, complete with a tight-fitting blue leotard with red briefs, boots, and matching red cape. Shuster also came up with one of the most recognized symbols in pop culture as he decided to draw a red "S" logo on Superman's chest in an inverted triangle. He also designed the uniform for Clark Kent, which consisted of a plain blue suit with matching fedora, combed back hair and thick black-rimmed glasses. If it weren't for the fact that Clark and Superman were the same person, then the two would have nothing in common.

Siegel's script and Shuster's designs were combined into four weeks' worth of comic strips.[6] They worked together to put these together with Shuster providing the pictures and Siegel providing the final dialogue. Siegel also had drafted some prose material for their submission, including a one paragraph preview of future Superman adventures as well as a nine page summary for the next three weeks of material.

The two then set off again on a search for a new publisher for their new creation. They pitched the book to numerous companies over the next several years. They faced rejection after rejection. Siegel and Shuster had created the first superhero, but no one cared.[7] One of the companies to reject Superman was the McClure Newspaper Syndicate.

With their hopes of a Superman newspaper strip dashed, Siegel and Shuster found work in the comic industry with other projects. Together they created Slam Bradley, a hard-nosed detective that closely resembled the second incarnation of Superman, and The Spy for publisher Major Malcolm Wheeler Nicholson. In 1937, DC Comics acquired the rights to these titles, among others, when the Major went out of business.

Siegel and Shuster had a new boss. On December 4, 1937, the pair signed an employment agreement which stated, in part, that the duo would create these comics exclusively for DC Comics for a period of two years and gave DC Comics a right of first refusal for any new comics created. DC Comics had sixty days to publish the new material. The agreement provided:

> AGREEMENT OF EMPLOYMENT entered into in the Fourth day of December, 1937, by and between [DC COMICS]..., hereinafter referred to as the Employer, and Jerome Siegel and Joe Shuster..., referred to as the Employees.
>
> 1. The Employer hereby agrees to employ, and does hereby employ the Employees as Artists, for a period of two years, commencing with December 4, 1937 and terminating December 3, 1939, and pay them for such services and for all of the matters hereinafter set forth, the sum of Ten Dollars ($10) per page.
>
> 2. The Employees agree to give their exclusive services as artists in producing features known as "Slam Bradley" and "The Spy" during said periods of employment, to the Employer, and agree that all of these products and work done by said Employee for said Employer during said period of employment, shall be and become the sole and exclusive property of the Employer, and the Employer shall be deemed the sole creator thereof, the Employee acting entirely as the Employer's employee.
>
> 3. In the event that the Employee leaves the service of the Employer prior to the termination date set forth in the Agreement or subsequent thereto, and for any reason whatsoever, the Employees agree that they will not, directly or indirectly, and through any means whatsoever, use, duplicate, simulate or bring into being any of the products or work or creations or characters or plots used, made or created by him while in the employ of the Employer.
>
> 4. It is understood that any new and additional features which the Employees produce for use in a comic magazine are to be first submitted to the Employer, who reserves the right to accept or reject same within a period of Sixty days.

Shortly thereafter, DC Comics began seeking new material for a new comic magazine, which would be entitled *Action Comics*. As part of this quest, DC Comics reviewed previously rejected submissions from newspaper publishers, including the McClure Newspaper Syndicate, and discovered the failed pitch for the *Superman* comic strip. This time, DC Comics was very interested in Superman. But, DC Comics did not want to print Superman as a strip. Instead, DC wanted the story told in 13 full color pages in *Action Comics*.

On February 1, 1938, DC Comics contacted Siegel and Shuster and asked them to take the existing *Superman* newspaper comic strip and convert it into a 13-page comic book story. This required the creators to recut and reformat their daily strip into the multi-grid format utilized in comics by pasting the original panels on new boards.[8]

On this, Shuster stated:

> The only thing I had to do to prepare Superman for comic book publication was to ink the last three weeks of daily strips which I had previously completely penciled in detail. In addition, I inked the lettering and the dialogue and story continuity and inked in the balloon containing the dialogue.
>
> Certain panels I trimmed to conform to [DC Comics'] page size. I drew several additional pictures to illustrate the story continuity and these appear on page 1 of the first Superman release. This was done so that we would be certain of having a sufficient number of panels to make a thirteen page release. Finally, I drew the last panel appearing on the thirteenth page. [DC Comics'] only concern was that there would be panels sufficient for thirteen complete pages. Jerry told me that [DC Comics] preferred having eight panels per page but in our judgment this would hurt the property. I specifically refer to the very large panel appearing on what would be page 9 of the thirteen page release. We did not want to alter this because of its dramatic effect. Accordingly, on this page but six panels appeared.

In addition, Siegel recalled:

> Upon receiving word from [DC Comics] that we could proceed, Joe Shuster, under my supervision, inked the illustrations, lettering and dialogue balloons in the three weeks of daily strips that had been previously penciled. In addition, he trimmed certain pictures to meet [DC Comics'] panel specifications and extended others. To assure ourselves of having the proper number of panels we added several pictures to illustrate the story continuity, I had already written. Added as well for this reason was the scientific explanation on page 1 of the release and the last panel at the foot of page 13.

On or around February 16, 1938, Siegel and Shuster finished their work and delivered the Superman story to DC Comics. DC Comics took the pages and, at Siegel's suggestion, took a panel from the book to use as a cover template for *Action Comics* issue 1. The panel chosen, page nine, panel three, featured the now iconic image of Superman lifting a car over his head as several thugs run away in terror.

On March 1, 1938, DC Comics paid Siegel $130 for the 13-page Superman story.[9] DC Comics also enclosed a new written agreement along with the payment, which Siegel and Shuster soon signed.

This agreement provided:

> I, [Jerry Siegel and Joe Shuster], am an artist or author and have performed work for strip entitled "SUPERMAN"
>
> In consideration of $130 agreed to be paid by [DC Comics], I hereby sell and transfer such work and strip, all good will attached thereto and exclusive right to use of the characters and story, continuity and title of strip contained therein, to [DC Comics] and [its] assigns to have and hold forever and be [DC Comics'] exclusive property and I agree not to employ said characters or said story in any other strips or sell any like strip or story containing the same characters by their names contained therein or under any other names at any time hereafter to any other person, firm or corporation, or permit the use thereof by said other parties without obtaining [DC Comics'] written consent therefor. The intent hereof is to give [DC Comics] exclusive right to use and acknowledge that you own said characters or story and the use thereof, exclusively. I have received the above sum of money.

This assignment of ownership rights was later confirmed in a September 22, 1938, employment agreement in which Siegel and Shuster acknowledged that DC Comics was not only "the exclusive owners" of the other comic strips created for Major Nicholson but *Superman* as well. This agreement stated that the pair would continue to supply create these comics for the next five years and that DC Comics had the "right to reasonably supervise the editorial matter" of those existing comic strips; that Siegel and Shuster would not furnish "any art or copy ... containing the ... characters or continuity thereof or in any wise similar" to said comic strips to a third party. The agreement also reaffirmed DC Comics' right of first refusal on new material:

> In the event [Siegel and Shuster] shall do or make any other art work or continuity suitable for use as comics or comic strips, [Siegel and Shuster] shall first give [DC Comics] the right to first refusal thereof by submitting said copy and continuity ideas to [DC Comics]. [DC Comics] shall have the right to exercise that option for six weeks after submission to us at a price no greater than offered to [Siegel or Shuster] by any other party.

DC Comics heavily promoted the first issue of *Action Comics* in many of its comics with a cover date of May 1938, including *More Fun Comics* issue 31 and *Detective Comics* issue 15. Each of these books contained a full page black and white advertisement that reproduced, on a reduced scale, the cover to *Action Comics*.

On April 18, 1938, Superman was introduced to the world when *Action Comics* issue 1 premiered on the newsstands with a cover date of June 1938. The story began with a one-page origin that included "a Scientific Explanation of Clark Kent's Amazing Strength."[10] In the story, Superman stops a wrongful execution, saves a battered wife, rescues Lois Lane from grabby thugs, and uncovers a corrupt senator.

Of course, the Superman that appeared in 1938 was very different from the character that regularly appears in the pages of DC Comics today. In three-quarters of a century, the qualities, powers, and look of the character have changed and been refined and developed over thousands of appearances. For example, the Superman in *Action Comics* did not possess the power of flight or his super senses (superhearing, telescopic vision, X-ray vision, and heat vision). He also did not develop a weakness to kryptonite until that element was introduced on the radio program in 1943.[11] Superman's origin would also be refined by Siegel himself in a later-produced McClure newspaper strip. *Action Comics* issue 1 did not mention the name of the planet (Krypton), his father (Jor-El), or an explanation as to why he was the only person to survive the destruction of the planet. And while Lois Lane has been present from the beginning, much of Superman's supporting cast, like Perry White and Jimmy Olson, would come later—once again as elements of the radio program. In fact, Clark Kent did not even work at the *Daily Planet* until nearly two years later in *Action Comics* issue 23. Prior to that he was a reporter at the *Daily Star*, mistakenly referred to as the real life *Cleveland Evening News* in *Action Comics* issue 2, under editor George Taylor. Over the years, the Superman Universe has been expanded to include a rogues' gallery of villains, a Fortress of Solitude, Superboys, Supergirls, Superwomen, and a variety of super pets, including a super dog, a super cat, a super horse and even a super monkey. None of these elements were even hinted at in the first issue. Even the character's trademark chest symbol has changed over time, originally appearing only as a small, yellow, inverted triangle with a red letter "S" in the middle, but evolving over time to its current version, a large red rounded five-sided shield, filled in with yellow and containing a red letter "S" in the middle.

The Superman comic in *Action Comics* issue 1 became a huge success for DC Comics.[12] On September 12, 1938, Siegel and Shuster executed another employment agreement with DC Comics that provided:

> [DC Comics] was "the exclusive owner[]" of not only the other comic strips they had penned for Nicholson (and continued to pen for [DC Comics]), but Superman as well; that they would continue to supply the artwork and storyline (or in the parlance of the trade, the "continuity") for these comics at varying per-page rates depending upon the comic in question for the next five years; that [DC Comics] had the "right to reasonably supervise the editorial matter" of those existing comic strips; that Siegel and Shuster would not furnish "any art copy ... containing the ... characters or continuity thereof or in any wise similar" to these comics to a third party; and that [DC Comics] would have the right of first refusal (to be exercised within a six-week period after the comic's submission) with respect to any future comic creations by Siegel or Shuster.

As a result of the success of *Superman*, DC Comics had Siegel and Shuster stop working on their other comic book projects to focus solely on the Man of Steel. DC Comics and the creators of Superman entered a supplemental employment agreement on December 19, 1939. This agreement increased the payments made to Siegel and Shuster and also reiterated that DC Comics was the "sole and exclusive owner" of Superman including "all rights of reproduction" and "all copyright and all rights to secure copyright registration in respect of all such forms of reproduction...."

Superman Becomes a Superboy

The popularity of Superman spawned many imitators. As explained in chapter 4, DC Comics sued several publishers that they claimed had created Superman-like characters. DC Comics sued Wonder Comics because they published comics featuring Wonder Man, a Superman clone created by Will Eisner. DC Comics also sued to prevent the publication of *Master Man* and *Captain Marvel* from Fawcett Comics and *Steel Sterling* from Zip Comics. It was only a matter of time before DC Comics would seek to imitate itself. Once again, Siegel's imagination paved the way. Siegel's idea was to show the adventures of Superman when he was a boy.

Siegel called this character Superboy.

Siegel described the concept as:

> Superboy ... would relate the adventures of Superman as a youth.... I'd like the strip to have a large number of pages, such as 13 so that I could develop it as well as Superman.... The strip would feature super-strength, it would be very much different from the *Superman* strip inasmuch as Superboy would be a child and the type of adventures very much different. There'd be lots of humor, action, and the characters would be mainly children of about 12-years rather than adults. Also, inasmuch as this strip will probably be used as a newspaper feature, I should think that you would want to own all rights to it by having it first appear in your magazine.

Siegel officially pitched his idea for *Superboy* on November 30, 1938, in writing and by mail. The pitch was made under the terms of the contract dated September 12, 1938, which meant DC Comics had the right to accept or reject the pitch within six weeks. With a letter dated December 2, 1938, DC Comics said that it was deferring consideration of the *Superboy* comic strip until some future time. This means that, under the terms of the employment agreement, DC Comics, in effect, had rejected the comic by declining to publish in the six week period.

Meanwhile, Superman's popularity increased. In 1939, McClure Syndicate began publishing a *Superman* newspaper strip. In the summer of that same year, Superman received his own self-titled series. On February 12, 1940, the *Adventures of Superman* appeared on the radio. In 1941, the Fleischer Brothers brought *Superman* cartoons to the movie theaters. The animated Superman was soon joined by a live action version, played by Kirk Alyn, in 1948. Superman was rapidly becoming a multi-media sensation. The character was used to endorse everything from cereal to toys to bread to gas. And while Siegel and Shuster were certainly proud of the success of their creation, they did not receive any royalties. Of course, Siegel and Shuster were not doing badly either. By the 1940s, they had made enough money to afford a stable of comic creators to supply material to DC Comics. In 1940, the pair's gross earnings were $75,000, which would equate to over a million dollars today.

Siegel repitched the concept for *Superboy* in December 1940. This time, Siegel submitted a more complete pitch, including a completed script and outline for the continuity, supporting cast, and dialogue for the *Superboy* comic. In addition, Siegel included a synopsis for future issues. Once again, DC Comics did not respond within six weeks, effectively rejecting Siegel's new pitch for *Superboy*.

The 1942 cover of *Superman* issue 18 features Superman facing the unified threat of the Japanese and Nazi Germany. In July 1943, Siegel, like his greatest creation, faced these enemies when he enlisted in the army and fought in World War II. Little did Siegel realize that his greatest struggle would not be fought on the battlefields of Europe, but rather in the courtrooms of America.

In December 1944, while Siegel was still in the army and stationed abroad, DC Comics released *More Fun Comics* issue 101.[13] The comic, written by Don Cameron and drawn by Shuster, contained a five-page story entitled "Superboy," the first appearance of the character. The story included many of the elements and characters present in Siegel's two earlier pitches but was published without notice to Siegel and, more importantly, without his consent. The character was an immediate success. Superboy would go on to star in *Adventure Comics* before getting his own self-titled series in 1949.

When Siegel found out about the Boy of Steel he was livid. Upon his return to the United States after the war in January 1946, Siegel and DC Comics negotiated over *Superboy*. During these negotiations, DC Comics offered to pay Siegel for *Superboy* at the same rate he was paid for *Superman*, which would have been $200 for the thirteen pages.

There had already been disagreement between the creators and DC Comics over whether DC Comics had adequately compensated them for the success of *Superman*. The publication and negotiation over *Superboy* only served to further disgruntle the already-displeased Siegel. And while Siegel and Shuster were doing well, they knew that DC Comics was doing better. Under the 1939 agreement, Siegel and Shuster eventually received $1,000 per release plus royalties from newspaper syndication and other forms of commercial exploitation. By 1947, the creators had earned over $400,000 in total compensation from all sources for the strip, which would equal $5 million today when adjusted for inflation. In 1948, Siegel and Shuster were receiving $35 a page for their work on the comics.

In contrast, DC Comics was making millions on comics, media, and merchandise related to Superman and Superboy. Siegel was incensed. In his mind, not only had DC Comics stolen his creations, but they were giving him and Shuster less work. Eventually, Siegel and Shuster and DC Comics parted ways.

The New York State Litigation

In 1947, Siegel and Shuster sued DC Comics in an effort to obtain what they believed was their fair share of the money earned by DC Comics from the exploitation of their Superman creation, as well as the profits generated from characters like Superboy, which had his roots in the original Superman character. Specifically, the creators argued that the contract should be annulled (i.e., made as if it had it never existed) and rescinded because there was no agreement, the two sides having never mutually agreed as to what was being sold or paid (referred to as "a lack of mutuality and consideration"). The suit also specifically alleged on behalf of Siegel that DC Comics did not own *Superboy* and violated his rights by unlawfully publishing it. Siegel and Shuster did not make a claim that DC Comics violated his copyright in the character, which is why the case was brought in state court.

As part of the suit, Siegel argued that DC Comics had no right to publish his *Superboy* creation.[14] Siegel argued that the two *Superboy* submissions became his property when DC Comics failed to exercise its right of first refusal under the parties' September 1938 contract and thus DC Comics unlawfully took his ideas and concepts when it published *More Fun Comics* issue 101. In short, according to Siegel, DC Comics stole Superboy from him and claimed him as their own. In the alternative, Siegel argued that plot, concept, and incidents in *Superboy* were substantially similar to and based upon and the plot, conception and incidents of the Superman character created by Siegel and Shuster. Consequently, Siegel argued that DC Comics tricked the public into thinking that Siegel was the author of *Superboy* by failing to seek his consent and publishing the story and therefore hurt Siegel's reputation. As a result, Siegel asked the court to stop DC Comics from publishing *Superboy* and for an accounting of the profits generated from *Superboy*'s publication.

On November 21, 1947, after a trial, Judge Addison Young concluded that the *Superman* contract was valid. Consequently, the court concluded that "plaintiffs transferred to [DC Comics], all of their rights in and to the comic strip Superman, including the title, names, characters and conception.... [DC Comics] became the absolute owner of the comic strip Superman." The court wrote:

> 1. By virtue of the instrument of March 1, 1938, plaintiffs transferred to [DC Comics] all of their rights in and to the comic strip SUPERMAN including the title, names, characters and concept as same were set forth in the first release of said comic strip published in the June 1938 issue of the magazine "Action Comics" and by virtue of said instrument [DC Comics] became

the absolute owner of the comic strip SUPERMAN, including the title, names, characters and concept as the same were set forth in the said first release.

The court also concluded that *Superboy* was a work solely created by Siegel that was separate and distinct from *Superman*. When DC Comics did not purchase the character under its right of first refusal in the September 1938 contract, Siegel retained the rights to the character. As a result, the referee concluded:

It is quite clear to me, however, that in publishing Superboy the [DC Comics] acted illegally. I cannot accept [DC Comics'] view that Superboy was in reality Superman. I think Superboy was a separate and distinct entity. In having published Superboy without right, [Siegel and Shuster] are entitled to an injunction preventing such publication and under the circumstances I believe [DC Comics] should account as to the income received from such publication and that [Siegel and Shuster] should be given an opportunity to prove any damages they have sustained on account thereof.

On April 12, 1948, Judge Addison Young issued a thirty-six page findings of fact and conclusions of law that expanded upon his earlier ruling. With regard to *Superman*, he wrote:

7. [DC Comics] is the sole and exclusive owner of and has the sole and exclusive right to the use of the title SUPERMAN and to the conception, idea, continuity, pictorial representation and formula of the cartoon feature SUPERMAN as heretofore portrayed and published ... and such sole and exclusive ownership includes, but is not limited to the fields of book and magazine publications, newspaper syndication, radio broadcasts, dramatic presentations, television, motion picture reproduction and all other forms of reproduction and presentation, whether now in existence or that may hereafter be created, together with the absolute right to license, sell, transfer or otherwise dispose of said rights.

With regard to *Superboy*, he wrote:

Siegel is the originator and the sole owner of the comic strip feature SUPERBOY, and ... that [DC Comics] ... are perpetually enjoined and restrained from creating, publishing, selling or distributing any comic strip material of the nature now and heretofore sold under the title SUPERBOY.... Plaintiff Siegel, as the originator and owner of the comic strip feature SUPERBOY has the sole and exclusive right to create, sell and distribute comic strip material under the title SUPERBOY.

Both sides appealed. However, before the appeal could be resolved, Siegel and Shuster settled the case for $94,000. The settlement agreement asked the court to vacate the earlier decision and required Siegel and Shuster to agree that DC Comics owned all the rights to Superman and was "the sole and exclusive owner" of Superboy. Specifically, the agreement read:

[DC Comics] is the sole and exclusive owner of and has the sole and exclusive right to the use of the title SUPERBOY and to create, publish, sell and distribute and to cause to be created, published, sold and distributed cartoon or other comic strip material containing the character SUPERBOY....

On May 21, 1948, the referee entered a final consent judgment that vacated the findings of fact and conclusions of law entered on April 12, 1948. The court wrote:

ORDERED AND ADJUDGED that plaintiffs, their agents, servants and employees, be and they hereby are enjoined and restrained from creating, publishing, selling or distributing or permitting or causing to be created, published, sold or distributed any material of the nature heretofore created, produced or published under the title SUPERMAN, or any material created, produced or published in imitation thereof, or from using, permitting or causing to be used in connection with any comic strip or other material created by them the title SUPERMAN or any title imitative of the title SUPERMAN or which shall contain as part thereof the word "SUPER."

The court also expressly acknowledged that DC Comics was the "sole and exclusive owner of and has the sole and exclusive right to the use of the title SUPERBOY."

Shortly afterwards, Siegel and Shuster were both fired and their names were removed from the credits in the comic books.

Things turned bad for the duo after the decision. Siegel tried without success to create new characters, such as Funny Man. Later, Siegel would claim that DC Comics had blackballed him in the comics industry. In fact, Siegel was so desperate that he actually returned to DC Comics and worked on *Superman* in the early 1960s as an uncredited writer before becoming a mail clerk. Things were worse for Shuster, who was growing blind in one eye. He could no longer draw and lived in a trailer park. What is not clear, however, is what happened to the money received from DC Comics. According to papers filed during various litigations, by the time Siegel and Shuster filed their 1947 lawsuit, DC Comics had paid Siegel and Shuster over $400,000 for their work on *Superman*. Somehow, Siegel and Shuster went from high income to destitution in a very short time. By 1969, both creators had fallen upon hard times.

New York Federal Litigation

The expiration of the initial copyright term for Superman in the mid–1960s allowed Siegel and Shuster to challenge DC Comics for ownership of their characters again in 1969.[15] This time, the creators filed suit in the United States District Court for the Southern District of New York and asked the court to declare that they were the owners of the copyright renewal rights in *Superman*. Instead, the court found, based on the 1947 decision and settlement, that Siegel and Shuster transferred "all their rights" in *Superman* to DC Comics in the final consent judgment. This meant that the creators had assigned not only *Superman's* initial copyright term but the renewal term as well, even though those renewal rights did not exist yet. Also of interest was the court's conclusion that Siegel and Shuster were employees of DC Comics when they created *Superman* and therefore the character was a work for hire that belonged to the company. The court found this despite the fact that Siegel and Shuster created the character five years before coming to work for DC Comics.

Siegel and Shuster appealed to the United States Court of Appeals for the Second Circuit in 1974. Because the Second Circuit determined "Superman and his miraculous powers were completely developed long before the employment relationship was instituted," it disagreed with the lower court and determined that *Superman* was not a work made for hire. Despite this distinction, the Second Circuit ultimately agreed with the lower court and held that Siegel and Shuster had, through the consent order, signed away all their rights and "all rights in Superman, including the renewal copyright, have passed forever to [DC Comics]."[16] Both cases relied on the same Supreme Court case (*Fred Fisher Music v. M. Witmark*) to determine the renewal rights were assignable during the initial copyright term.

The second battle for *Superman* and *Superboy* was over. Siegel and Shuster had lost again.

Pensions for Life

By the end of the lawsuit, Superman had appeared in radio shows, movie serials, live action movies, several animated serials, a live-action TV series and a Broadway musical called "*It's a Bird It's a Plane It's Superman.*" Neither Siegel nor Shuster had profited from any of it and had fallen on hard times. In 1973, a new big budget Superman movie was announced. The movie, written by Mario Puzo and directed by Richard Donner, would star Gene Hackman, Marlon Brando, and an unknown actor named Christopher Reeve in the title role. With so much on the line, DC Comics could hardly afford any bad press. So, after battles in both state and federal court, Siegel tried his next case in the court of public opinion.

In October of 1975, Siegel wrote a press release attacking DC Comics. In the same flowery prose that made him a comic legend, Siegel wrote that DC Comics "killed my days, murdered my nights, choked my happiness, strangled my career." He also guaranteed national coverage by adding, "I, Jerry Siegel, the co-originator of SUPERMAN, put a curse on the SUPERMAN movie! I hope it super-bombs. I hope loyal SUPERMAN fans stay away from it in droves. I hope the whole world, becoming aware of the stench that surrounds SUPER-MAN, will avoid the movie like a plague." After chronicling his courtroom defeats, Siegel concluded, "But I can write this press release and ask my fellow Americans to please help us by refusing to buy Superman comic books, refusing to patronize the new Superman movie, or watch Superman on TV until this great injustice against Joe and me is remedied by the callous men who pocket the profits from OUR creation." The press release was picked up by both comics-industry and mainstream press.

Siegel's plan was successful and allies soon appeared. Comic book professionals, including artists Neal Adams and Jerry Robinson, helped wage a public relations campaign for fair treatment for the creators. Jerry Robinson garnered the support of both the Screen Cartoonist's Guild and the Writers Guild of America, while Neal Adams rallied the comic book community. Ultimately, DC Comics reached an agreement with Siegel and Shuster on December 24, 1975. Under the terms of the agreement, both Siegel and Shuster would receive a modest annual pension (somewhere between $10,000 and $35,000 a year) and medical benefits, which, upon their deaths, would pass on to their respective heirs. More important to the creators, however, was the agreement that the words "Superman created by Jerry Siegel and Joe Shuster" would appear on all printed matter and media.

In fact, when *Superman: The Movie* premiered in 1978, Siegel and Shuster were given a full screen credit as the creators of Superman as they have been in all subsequent movies, TV shows, comics, and cartoons. Over the years, the amount of Siegel and Shuster's pension was raised. In 1992, Shuster was reportedly receiving $85,000 a year. Four years later, Siegel's stipend was in the six figures. In exchange, Siegel and Shuster once again acknowledged that DC Comics was the exclusive owner of all rights and title to *Superman*.

Joe Shuster died on July 30, 1992, at the age of 78. Jerry Siegel followed his collaborator on January 28, 1996. Upon Siegel's death, annual payments and media coverage were transferred to his widow, Joanne Siegel, who, ironically, was also the original model for Lois Lane, for the remainder of her life. Shuster did not leave a wife or any children.

But, the story does not end there.

CHAPTER 16

The Never Ending Battle Continues
Joanne Siegel v. DC Comics

After Siegel and Shuster signed their deal with DC Comics, the copyright law changed. In 1976, a provision was added that allowed creators another opportunity to reclaim their rights in their works provided certain steps were followed. The termination of the grant may be effected at any time during a five year window that begins at the end of 56 years from the date copyright was originally secured (i.e., when the book was published). Notices for termination must be served not less than two or more than 10 years before their effective date. *Superman* was eligible for termination beginning on April 18, 1994, and ending on April 18, 1999 (as measured from the original *Action Comics* issue 1 publication date of April 18, 1938) and any termination notices would need to have been served between April 18, 1984, and April 18, 1997. Shuster died before the termination date without heirs. Perhaps because he did not want to endanger his settlement, Siegel never terminated the agreement during his lifetime. As a result, DC Comics continued to own both *Superman* and *Superboy*. However, after the death of Siegel, something changed. These changes resulted in Siegel's heirs filing two lawsuits in federal court in California to challenge DC Comics' ownership of both Superman and Superboy.

Termination Notices

On April 3, 1997, Laura Siegel Larson, Jerry Siegel's daughter, and Joanne Siegel served DC Comics with a termination notice for *Superman* effective April 16, 1999.[1] The notice stated that it "applie[d] to each and every work (in any medium whatsoever, whenever created) that include[d] or embodie[d] any character, story element, or indicia reasonably associated with SUPERMAN or the SUPERMAN stories, such as, without limitation, Superman ... Superboy, ... [or] Smallville."[2] If valid, this revocation would have meant that the Siegel heirs have owned 50 percent of the Superman character since mid–April 1999.[3] On April 15, 1999, DC Comics denied the letter of termination and stated "[Y]ou are hereby put on notice that DC Comics rejects both the validity and scope of the notices and will vigorously oppose any attempt by your clients to exploit or authorize the exploitation of any copyrights, or indeed, any rights at all, in Superman."

There were extensive negotiations between the Siegel heirs and DC Comics regarding the *Superman* notice of termination. At one point, DC Comics paid the Siegel heirs a $250,000 advance for *Superman* royalties. After four years, these negotiations culminated in an October 19, 2001, letter that stated the Siegel heirs have "accepted D.C. Comics offer of October 16, 2001." The letter also included "five pages of terms outlining substantial compensation for the heirs in exchange for DC Comics' continued right to produce Superman works...." This agreement covered "all Superman, Superboy and related properties (including, for example, *Supergirl, Steel, Lois & Clark*, and *Smallville*), and the Spectre property,[4] and included all pre- and post-termination works (including the so-called *Superman* library, characters, names and trademarks relating to the property." The Siegels' attorney thanked DC Comics' attorney for his "help and patience in reaching this monumental accord."

However, before the agreement could be finalized and placed in contract form, the Siegel heirs changed lawyers and withdrew their acceptance of the agreement. On September 30, 2002, the Siegel heirs sent a letter stating that the negotiations were over.

On November 8, 2002, the Siegel heirs filed notices of termination of transfer of copyright in the Superboy character. If effective, the termination would have meant that DC Comics would have ceased to own Superboy on November 17, 2004. On August 27, 2004, DC Comics denied the notices of termination related to Superboy.

The California Federal Lawsuit

On October 8, 2004, the Siegel heirs filed suit in the United States District Court for the Central District of California to assert their claim that they owned 50 percent of the interest in *Superman*. On November 11, 2004, DC Comics filed an answer and counterclaim that disputed the Siegel heirs' charges. The case was eventually assigned to Judge Ronald S.W. Lew and the parties asked the court to rule before the trial.

On October 22, 2004, the Siegel heirs sued to assert their claim to co-ownership of *Superboy* in the United States District Court for the Central District of California. On November 11, 2004, DC Comics filed an answer and counterclaim that disputed the Siegel heirs' charges. Both parties asked the court to rule before the trial, which led to interesting results.

Initially, United States District Court Judge Ronald S.W. Lew, in a March 23, 2006, decision, ruled that the Siegel heirs had recaptured the copyright to *Superboy*. Moreover, Judge Lew stated, "Enough facts are presented that this Court, contrary to [DC Comics'] request, could find that the main character in Smallville, is, in fact, Superboy" and ordered a trial to determine the amount of damages. This was a very strong ruling for the Siegel heirs.[5] However, on October 30, 2006, the case was reassigned to the Honorable Stephen G. Larson.

With the presence of a new judge, DC Comics immediately moved for reconsideration of the March 23, 2007, decision. On July 27, 2007, Judge Larson granted DC Comics' motion and determined that *Superboy* was a joint work between Siegel and Shuster and that DC Comics had received permission from Shuster's heirs (see chapter 17) to publish the character. Moreover, since Shuster's heirs did not seek to terminate, this meant that DC Comics could not be held liable for any infringement of the Superboy character. At the time, this was considered a major victory for DC Comics. However, this victory was short lived.

On March 26, 2008, Judge Larson issued a 72 page opinion, complete with color illustrations and a copy of *Action Comics* issue 1. The court summarized its ruling by saying:

> After seventy years, Jerome Siegel's heirs regain what he granted so long ago—the copyright in the Superman material that was published in Action Comics Vol. 1. What remains is an apportionment of profits, guided in some measure by the rulings contained in this Order, and a trial on whether to include the profits generated by DC Comics' corporate sibling's exploitation of the Superman copyright.

In short, the court held that the Siegel heirs have owned 50 percent of the domestic copyright to *Action Comics* issue 1 since 1999. Despite this, the ruling also makes clear that certain items are not included. For example, the court did not award the use of Superman trademarks that are independent of the comic (S shield t-shirts, necklaces and hats) or any derivative works created from 1937 through 1999 created by DC Comics. The other thing the court did not determine was how much money DC Comics owed to the Siegel heirs. Instead, the court set the damages issue for a trial, including whether proceeds from movies and television earned by Time Warner, DC Comics' parent, should be paid. Needless to say, this figure would have been substantial.

The parties moved for reconsideration. The court summed up these motions:

> In sum, defendants complain that the Court's March 26, 2008, Order went too far, while plaintiffs complain that the Court's Order did not go far enough. As set forth below, the Court affirms its conviction that its Order went as far as, and no further than, required by the issues properly before it and, accordingly, denies both motions.

Specifically, the court found that the terminations did not specifically list the ads that ran in *More Fun Comics* and *Detective Comics*. As a result, the court awarded:

> [DC Comics] may continue to exploit the image of a person with extraordinary strength who wears a black and white leotard and cape. What remains of the Siegel and Shuster's Superman copyright that is still subject to termination (and, of course, what defendants truly seek) is the entire storyline from *Action Comics*, Vol. 1, Superman's distinctive blue leotard (complete with its inverted triangular crest across the chest with a red "S" on a yellow background), a red cape and boots, and his superhuman ability to leap tall buildings, repel bullets, and run faster than a locomotive, none of which is apparent from the announcement.

DC Comics appealed the decision to the Ninth Circuit. And the saga continued.

The Ninth Circuit Appeal

The case was heard by Circuit Judges Reinhardt and Thomas and District Judge Sedwick, who was sitting by designation from the United States District Court for the District of Alaska. Arguments were held on November 5, 2012.

On January 10, 2013, the Ninth Circuit reversed the District Court's March 2008 grant of summary judgment, finding that the October 19, 2001, letter from the Siegel heirs' then-attorney constituted acceptance of an oral settlement offer made on October 16, 2001, and created a binding settlement under California law. "The October 19, 2001, letter itself plainly states that the heirs have 'accepted DC Comics' offer of October 16, 2001, in respect of the 'Superman' and 'Spectre' properties." Noting that the objective, not subjective, understandings of the parties determine whether they reached an agreement, and that by looking at the parties' actions they could determine whether the offer referred to in the letter had, in fact, been made, the Ninth Circuit concluded:

> Statements from the attorneys for both parties establish that the parties had undertaken years of negotiations, that they had resolved the last outstanding point in the deal during a conversation on October 16, 2001, and that the letter accurately reflected the material terms they had orally agreed to on that day.

In reaching its conclusion, the Ninth Circuit held that the contract was valid despite the fact that further negotiation was necessary to finalize the contract, even if those negotiations are material, "as long as the terms of any contract that may have been formed are sufficiently definite that a court could enforce them (as is undoubtedly the case here)." As a result, the court determined that parties may bind themselves to a contract even if they anticipate that some material aspects of the deal will be set in writing in the future, or even absent an express reference to a future agreement. This is exactly what the October 19, 2001, letter did, so the Ninth Circuit concluded that a settlement agreement was formed.

Joanne Siegel died on February 12, 2011. After her death, her daughter, Laura Siegel Larson, took over the case in her own name and as executor of the estate of Joanne Siegel.[6]

The court remanded the case back to Judge Larson with instructions to reconsider the counterclaims in light of the 2001 settlement agreement. The Ninth Circuit added that if the court ruled in favor of DC Comics, it would "appear to render moot all of the other questions in this lawsuit."

On remand, Judge Larson granted summary judgment to DC Comics on the grounds that the October 19, 2001, agreement continued to be effective. This was because the Siegel heirs did not rescind the contract and DC Comics continued to assert their rights under that contract through more than eight years of litigation.

So, the parties ended up where they began. DC Comics owned Superman and continues to publish his monthly adventures. The Siegel heirs have vowed to continue their fight. Despite this, Superman's ownership will stay with DC Comics.[7]

At least until the character enters the public domain in 2033.

CHAPTER 17

The Never Ending Battle Ends?
DC Comics v. Pacific Pictures Corporation

The previous chapter explored what happened to Jerry Siegel's half of Superman. But, what happened to the part owned by Joe Shuster?

As previously discussed, Jerry Siegel and Shuster created a pitch for a Superman comic strip. After shopping the idea around without success, the pair eventually sold the idea to DC Comics on March 1, 1938, for $130. The book premiered in 1938 and was a huge success. Believing they were not being adequately compensated, the creators brought several unsuccessful lawsuits against DC Comics to reclaim their character.

And although Siegel and Shuster were never awarded a dime in court, they eventually obtained relief from DC Comics in the form of a December 24, 1975, agreement under which DC Comics promised the creators an annual pension, medical benefits and that the words "Superman created by Jerry Siegel and Joe Shuster" would appear on all printed matter and media. In exchange, Siegel and Shuster agreed that DC Comics owned all Superman-related copyrights. Over the years, DC Comics has continued to make voluntary increases to the annual payments and make periodic cost-of-living adjustments. In addition, DC Comics has provided special bonuses and paid to have Siegel, Shuster, and their families travel to Superman-related events. It has been estimated that Siegel and Shuster have received in excess of $4 million under the 1975 agreement without considering medical benefits or bonuses.

The Shuster Heirs

Shuster died on July 30, 1992, at the age of 78. At the time of his death, he was unmarried and childless. As a result, his sister Jean Peavy was named in his will as sole beneficiary and executrix of his estate. On August 22, Jean Peavy wrote to DC Comics asking for help with Shuster's bills. She wrote, "[a]ny help that Time Warner could give to the family of Joe Shuster to pay his final debts and expenses would be warmly appreciated." In response, DC Comics offered to cover Joe's debts and increase survivor payments to his brother, Frank Shuster, from $5,000 to $25,000 per year.

On September 10, 1992, Frank Shuster wrote to DC Comics expressing his pleasure at the increase and directed, "after discuss[ing] this good news with [Jean Peavy]," that payments be made directly to Jean, who would "send [Frank Shuster] whatever money [he] wanted as a gift which would not be taxable to [him]." In response, Paul Levitz, vice president of DC Comics, stated, as he did to all the authors and heirs he dealt with, that while DC Comics agreed to make payments, "this agreement would represent the author/heir's last and final deal with DC Comics, and would fully resolve any past, present, or future claims against DC Comics." Frank Shuster and Jean Peavy confirmed their agreement in 1992.

On October 2, 1992, the parties signed a new agreement that provided that DC Comics would pay for Shuster's debts and also pay Jean $25,000 a year for the rest of her life in exchange for Jean Peavy's and Frank Shuster's agreement to regrant all of Joe Shuster's rights back to DC Comics and their vow never to assert a claim to such rights. That agreement provides:

> [DC comics] ask you to confirm by your signatures below that this agreement fully settles all claims to any payments or other rights or remedies which you may have under any other agreement or otherwise, whether now or hereafter existing regarding any copyrights, trademarks, or other property right in any and all work created in whole or in part by your brother, Joseph Shuster, or any works based thereon. In any event, you now grant to us any such rights and release us, our licensees and all others acting with our permission, and covenant not to assert any claim of right, by suit or otherwise, with respect to the above, now and forever.

Levitz regularly corresponded in nearly 60 letters back and forth between himself and Jean Peavy and Frank Shuster over the next decade. In these correspondences, Jean Peavy thanked DC Comics and reaffirmed the 1992 agreement. Occasionally, Jean Peavy would request bonus payments over the amount of the contract. For example, in a 1993 letter she wrote that she was displeased with the deal but assured DC Comics that, at that time, she and Frank Shuster were "not planning to reclaim the Superman copyright. [And that they] believe [they] have a right to expect that [DC Comics would] be fair with [them] as well and will grant [their] request for increased payment."[1] They added that they intended to "stick to [their] bargain which [they] signed, dated as of October 1, 1992."

On April 3, 1997, the wife and daughter of Jerry Siegel served DC Comics with a termination notice for *Superman*. However, because Joe Shuster died before the termination period without a proper heir, his estate was unable to do the same. In 1999, Congress amended the copyright statute as part of the Sonny Bono Copyright Term Extension Act so that it would permit the Shuster estate to terminate the grant of *Superman* rights. Once Jean Peavy learned about what the Siegels had done, she wrote to Levitz and stated: "I have learned from the Internet that Joanne Siegel has filed a copyright claim for Superman. I want you to know that I intend to continue to honor our pension agreement. I would, however, appreciate a generous bonus for this year as you had done many times in the past."

DC Comics paid several bonuses that ranged from a low of $10,000 to a high of $25,000 to Jean Peavy in the years 1993, 1994, 1995, 1996, 1998, 1999, 2000, and 2001.[2]

Termination Notices and Lawsuit

In May of 2009, Jean Peavy had a stroke that left her incapacitated. As a result, Jean Peavy's 50-year-old son, Mark Warren Peary, took over as the substitute executor of the Shuster Estate.

On November 7, 2003, Mark Warren Peary retained Marc Toberoff, the Siegels' lawyer, and served DC Comics with a notice of termination for *Superman*. Shortly thereafter, Mark Warren Peary assigned the rights to the Pacific Pictures Joint Venture with his lawyer, Marc Toberoff. Later in the case, DC Comics filed suit against Pacific Pictures, the estate, and Toberoff.[3]

The case was assigned to Judge Otis D. Wright, II.

DC Comics moved for summary judgment on several grounds. First, DC Comics argued that the 1992 agreement barred Shuster's heirs from pursuing termination. Second, DC Comics argued that the Shuster heirs lacked the majority interest necessary to terminate because they assigned their rights to Pacific Pictures. Third, there was no statutory basis for the termination because Shuster died without a proper heir before the law changed to permit termination. In response, the heirs argued that an author or his estate may exercise termination rights "notwithstanding any agreement to the contrary."

The court issued its opinion on October 17, 2012, granting DC Comics' motion. In reaching its decision in favor of DC Comics, Judge Wright first considered whether the 1992 agreement barred the Shuster heirs from pursuing termination. First, the court concluded that the 1992 agreement settled and released all claims, rights, and remedies that the heirs had concerning the Shuster copyrights, and regranted such rights to DC Comics. As a result, this agreement revoked and superseded any earlier grants by Shuster and gave the heirs one shot to renegotiate the terms of Shuster's pre–1978 grants of his copyrights. In reaching this conclusion, the court rejected the heirs' argument and held that an author or his estate may exercise termination rights notwithstanding any agreement to the contrary." The court disagreed that the 1992 agreement constituted an impermissible agreement to the contrary.[4] No one could have known that Congress would have changed the law to create a second termination right when Shuster died and his heirs entered into the 1992 agreement. As a result, the heirs had signed away their termination rights. This ruling had the effect of nullifying the termination notices Joe Shuster's heirs had filed and served on DC Comics.

The court next rejected DC Comics' second argument related to the transfer of interest to Pacific Pictures. The court held that, under the Copyright Act, the right to serve a termination notice cannot be transferred to a third party. This means that, under law, the heirs could not have transferred the termination rights even if they thought they could. Accordingly, the heirs retained the requisite majority share.[5]

The court did not address DC Comics' third argument, that Shuster lacked a statutory heir.

The court also addressed the transfer between the Shuster heirs and Pacific Pictures and held that the transfer violated copyright law, which provides:

> A further grant, or agreement to make a further grant, of any right covered by a terminated grant is valid only if it is made after the effective date of the termination. As an exception, however, an agreement for such a further grant may be made between the author or [his heirs] and the original grantee or [its successor], after the notice of termination has been served....

This meant that between the date of service of the termination notice and the effective date of the termination, DC Comics was the only party that could have entered into an agreement with the Shuster heirs regarding the Superman copyrights.

The heirs appealed and the case went up to the Ninth Circuit where it was heard on November 5, 2012, by Circuit Judges Reinhardt and Thomas, and District Judge Sedwick, the same judges who decided the *Siegel* case. On January 10, 2013, the Ninth Circuit affirmed the case holding, "The district judge correctly held that the 1992 Agreement, as a matter of New York law, superseded the 1938 assignment of copyrights to DC, and therefore operated to revoke that assignment and re-grant the Superman copyrights to DC." The Supreme Court declined to hear the case on appeal on October 6, 2014.

In short, DC Comics still owns Shuster's half of Superman.

With their appeals exhausted, it appears that, for the Shuster heirs, the never ending battle has ended.

Or has it?

CHAPTER 18

Public Domain in Brief

While the discussion of the public domain is merely a subset of the copyright law, given the importance of the subject matter, it needs to be addressed as a separate topic. The public domain can provide a source of inspiration to reinvigorate and reinvent older properties.[1]

What Is Public Domain?

A public domain work is a creative work that may be freely used by anyone without permission. There are three ways for a work to enter the public domain: (1) the material is produced by the United States government; (2) at the request of the author; or (3) at the expiration of the original copyright.

The first method is the simplest. Works created by any agency of the United States government are public domain as soon as they are created. While there are laws that limit the public's access (such as privacy laws), these documents are generally free to use. Perhaps the best example of this concept would be the 9/11 Report, which was circulated by numerous publishers after it was released by Congress. Other examples of governmental public domain documents include federal court opinions, legislative history and census information.

The second method for works to enter public domain is also straightforward. Although it is very rare, sometimes creators do not wish to protect their work. In this instance, a creator can voluntarily move his or her creation into the public domain by expressly authorizing that the work is public domain.

The final method of entering the public domain, lapsed copyright, is what most people visualize when they think of public domain. Most non-governmental works enter public domain because the work was either created prior to 1923 or the original copyright has lapsed. A detailed explanation of this process is explained in chapter 3. This chart serves a summary of those principles.

Date	Term
Published before 1923.	Already public domain.
Published 1923–63.	28 year initial term plus an additional renewal term of 67 years. Works not renewed are already public domain.
Published 1964–77.	95 years after the publication date.

Date	Term
Created before 1-1-78 but not published.	The greater of the creator's life plus 70 years (if work of corporate authorship, 95 years from publication) or 12-31-2002.
Created before 1-1-78 but published between then and 12-31-2002.	The greater of the creator's life plus 70 years (if work of corporate authorship, 95 years from publication) or 12-31-2047.
Created after 12-31-2002.	The creator's life plus 70 years or, if work of corporate authorship, 95 years from publication.

Once a work enters the public domain, it can be freely used. This means that the original material can be reproduced verbatim or the characters can be utilized in a derivative work. It should be noted that when public domain material is used to create original work, the new work would be protected by the intellectual property laws. For example, while Mina Murray, Allan Quatermain, and Captain Nemo are public domain characters, Alan Moore's *League of Extraordinary Gentlemen* is a copyrighted and trademarked work.[2] The same would apply to the retconned history and successor characters of the Quality Comics characters, which belong to DC Comics. This is true despite the fact that, with the exception of the casts of *Plastic Man*, *Blackhawk*, and *The Spirit*, all Quality Comics characters have lapsed into the public domain.

Several prominent literary and comic characters are public domain. In addition to the aforementioned *Project Superpowers* characters, Quality Comics characters, fairy tale characters, and the ensemble cast of the various *League of Extraordinary Gentlemen* series, several other characters are public domain and free to be used. For example, characters from Arthurian legends; Norse, Greek, and Roman myths; and Shakespearean literature are all public domain. Similarly, several other comic book characters have become public domain, including those originally published by Barsoom, Centaur Publications, and Fawcett Comics.

If copyright law does not change, existing public domain characters may get some famous neighbors. Mickey Mouse[3] and friends will enter the public domain in 2023. Superman enters in 2033 and will be quickly followed by the rest of DC Comics' golden age characters.[4]

Public domain allows an outlet for reinvigoration and provides a new generation of readers with access to classic characters rewritten with a modern spin.

CHAPTER 19

Business Structure in Brief

As can be seen throughout the cases described in this book, comic creators can use a variety of corporate structures from which to run their comic businesses. As a result, it may be helpful to provide a general overview of the different kinds of entities that are available to today's comic creator. At the risk of repetition, it is important to point out that the following discussion is not meant to be an all-encompassing detailed description or survey of the law of business structures, and many states may have different rules and requirements. Anyone seeking to incorporate or form a limited liability entity should work with a qualified attorney.

The primary options for comic creators to conduct their business include a sole proprietorship, a partnership, a corporation, a limited partnership, or a Limited Liability Company. There are key advantages and disadvantages to each form of business, and specific business and personal circumstances may impact the choice. The determination of what organization works best should be made after considering such factors as tax status, the desire for limited liability, the need to raise capital, and other business decisions. In fact, over the life of a creator, he or she may see a need to use more than one form of organization to accomplish their goals.

What follows is a brief description of each structure.

Sole Proprietorship

The sole proprietorship is the simplest business form under which a comic creator can operate. In fact, a sole proprietorship is not a separate legal entity at all. Instead, the term refers to an organization where the owner assumes all obligations of the business. Basically, the owner is the business. The sole proprietorship can operate under the name of its owner or it can do business under a fictitious name. Use of a trade name doesn't change the analysis of whether a business is a sole proprietorship. For example, Han can call his smuggling operation by his name or Millennium Falcon Trading and it will still be considered a sole proprietorship.

A major benefit for the use of sole proprietorship is its simplicity. A creator need not create any paperwork or pay a fee to form the entity.

On the other hand, there is a major disadvantage to the use of a sole proprietorship. Because there is no separate organization, the owner is personally liable for all the business's debts. So, if the business has financial trouble, then creditors can personally sue the owner for the unpaid debts. More importantly, if the business runs out of money these creditors can reach the personal assets of the owner. Lawsuits can be filed against the business owner to pay the business's debt. This also applies to liability for injuries. People who are hurt or otherwise seek to sue the business will sue the owner, and there is no limit on the amount of liability that the owner could be personally obligated to pay. On the other hand, unlike corporations, sole proprietorships can bring lawsuits using the name of the sole proprietor owner.

In fact, the sole proprietorship has no separate identity under the law. From a practical point, a sole proprietor typically will sign contracts in his or her own name. In most instances, customers will make payments directly to the owner, as opposed to the business. A benefit of this is that sole proprietor owners can, and often do, commingle personal and business property in a way that is impossible under the other forms. Frequently, sole proprietors have their bank accounts for the business in the name of the owner.

Similarly, there are no formal management requirements. For example, there is no need to hold meetings or elections for the company as the owner controls it. Of course, this also means that proprietors cannot raise capital by selling an interest in the business. As a result, sole proprietorships do not survive the death or incapacity of their owners and so do not retain value. Many businesses begin as sole proprietorships and graduate to more complex business forms as the business develops.

Finally, because a sole proprietorship is not separate from its owner, the income earned by a sole proprietorship is considered earned by its owner. As a result, the company does not have to file a separate tax return. Instead, a sole proprietor reports the sole proprietorship income on his or her own tax return.[1]

General Partnership

Much like a sole proprietorship, a general partnership is a default organization when two or more people work together in a business to make a profit. Absent agreement among the partners, the partners in a general partnership are equally responsible for running the partnership and share all profits and losses equally. Partners can enter into partnership agreements to alter the profit sharing or control default rules. A general partnership is very flexible and does not require any formal filings to exist.

A general partnership is what is referred to as a pass through entity for tax purposes. This means that partnership does not pay separate taxes. Instead, the partnership files a tax return and the gains and losses are distributed to each of the individual partners, who are taxed on their personal income tax returns. Each partner can also deduct losses from the business on his or her own individual tax return. This pass-through tax treatment is one of the most beneficial advantages of forming a partnership as there is no double taxation that is present with corporations. With pass-through tax treatment, filing is relatively easy. There is no taxation to the business itself; all income, deductions, and credits "pass through" to the individual partners and are reported on their individual tax returns.

Another benefit of general partnerships is their simplicity and flexibility. Like a sole proprietorship, the partnership is the default form and thus much less expensive and requires less paperwork to form than corporations, limited partnerships, or limited liability partnerships. There is also flexibility in management as the general partners can choose either a centralized management structure, like a corporation, or a completely decentralized structure, where every partner is actively involved in the management of the business. Similarly, the general partners can agree how to combine resources and share the financial commitment.

Despite the advantages outlined above for general partnerships, there are hefty disadvantages to conducting business through general partnerships. First, and foremost, like a sole proprietorship, a partner is personally liable for the obligations of the partnership. Even worse, because any partner is able to bind the partnership, a partner may be liable for debts and obligations taken on by his partners. Sometimes this personal liability makes it hard for a general partnership to raise money.

Limited Partnership

The next type of organization is a limited liability partnership, which is a hybrid entity that contains at least one general partner and one or more limited partners. The general partners participate in management and have 100 percent of the liability for partnership obligations and are treated exactly like a partner in a general partnership. Limited partners cannot participate in the management and have no liability for partnership obligations beyond their capital contributions, protecting them against personal liability for the partnership's debts and other obligations. They do, however, receive a share of the profits for their involvement as limited partners.

Many partnerships are formed as limited partnerships because the limited liability is attractive to passive investors. Business persons find it easier to market limited partner interests as an investment, and general partners can raise money without involving outside investors in the management of business. Assets are also protected in a limited partnership. Unlike corporate law, which allows a shareholder's stock to be confiscated in a personal lawsuit, there are provisions that protect a partner's interest in a limited partnership from being taken away when that partner is sued personally. A limited partnership also enjoys the advantages of pass-through tax treatment, as it is taxed like a general partnership in that the profits and losses pass through to the partners who then include their allocated income on their personal tax returns.

Besides the obvious advantages of limited liability for limited partners, a limited partnership can also allow the general partners to use their expertise to make important decisions in managing the business. However, having general partners can also be a disadvantage, in that they still assume 100 percent personal liability. Limited partnerships also have more filing formalities than a typical general partnership. In addition, limited partners lose all of their limited liability if they participate in any management functions within the company.

Corporations

When people think of corporations, they picture large multinational entities like Pepsi, Apple, Microsoft and LexCorp. In reality, a number of corporations are simply small operations or even home-based businesses. The main difference between a corporation and the entities discussed thus far is that a corporation is a separate legal entity under law. As such, there are certain advantages and disadvantages to having a corporation. As described above, in a sole proprietorship or partnership, the business and the owners are one and the same. In contrast the corporation has shareholders who do not own the business directly, but instead own stock in the company. There is no limit to the amount of shareholders a corporation can have, but the rules are the same regardless of whether a corporation has one shareholder or a billion shareholders.

Forming a corporation requires quite a bit more work than a partnership or a sole proprietorship and, in most instances, probably should be done with at least the help of an attorney. First, the owners need to draft something called Articles of Incorporation,[2] which contain the purpose and the rules governing the management of a corporation, and the total number of shares issued.[3] This document is then filed with the Secretary of State to create the corporate entity.[4] Once established, the corporation has to apply to the Internal Revenue Service for an Employer Identification Number (called an EIN). Next, the corporation will need to draft bylaws, which are the specific rules that govern things like establishing officers, creating a board of directors, and the procedures for electing directors. A lot of thought and planning should go into the formation documents, preferably with the assistance of counsel.

Because a corporation is a separate entity, its existence is not tied to anyone. For example, unlike a partnership or a sole proprietorship, either of which lasts only as long as the life of its owners, a corporation can go on indefinitely with its shares being owned by many different people over time.

Another major difference distinguishing corporations from partnerships and proprietorships is that the shareholder owners do not run the company. Instead, the shareholders elect a board of directors.[5] These directors make general business decisions for the corporation, which are implemented by the corporation's officers, who are appointed by the directors in accordance with the bylaws.

The main advantage of using a corporate form to conduct business is limited liability. A corporation is responsible for its debts and liabilities. It can sue and be sued in its own name.[6] Because of this, the shareholders,[7] directors, and officers are not personally liable unless they take some action that makes them liable. For example, a comic book writer that works through a corporation where he is the sole shareholder will still be personally liable for injuries that arise from his writing (e.g., copyright violation or libel) because he personally performed the task. However, if the same corporation contracts with a printer and then goes out of business while still owing money for printing costs, the printer, for the most part, should not be able to personally collect against the writer/owner.[8]

There is a disadvantage in using a corporation to conduct business and that is how it is treated for tax purposes. Corporations are taxed as separate entities. Corporations file different returns, calculate income differently, and have their own corporate tax rates. At the discretion of the directors, the earnings of the corporation can also be distributed in the form of dividends, which are taxed to the shareholder.[9] Although these dividends are traditionally taxed at a special lower tax rate, dividends are, in reality, taxed twice, once at the corporate level and then at the shareholder level.[10] Let's take a simple example:

Assume Thanos has a funeral home business and he forms a corporation called I Love Death, Inc., and he makes $1,000,000 and is taxed at 35 percent at the corporate level. That means he pays $350,000 in taxes and has $650,000 to distribute to himself as the sole shareholder. If he reinvests it, there are no tax effects, but if he distributes the whole $650,000 to himself (and is at a tax bracket of 40 percent), he will have to pay an additional $260,000 in taxes. This means that I Love Death, Inc., and Thanos pay a total of $610,000 in taxes.

But, if Thanos operates his business as a sole proprietorship, profit will all flow directly through to him and the $1,000,000 will only be taxed once, at Thanos's 40 percent bracket. Thus, Thanos will only have to pay $400,000, which results in a tax savings of $210,000.

In short, double taxation is something that should be considered with the advice of a tax specialist.[11]

Limited Liability Company (LLC)

The desire for pass through taxation, simplified organization, and limited liability resulted in the creation of a new type of business organization—the limited liability company, affectionately referred to as LLCs.

The LLC is a flexible form of enterprise that blends elements of partnership and corporate structures. Like a corporation, the LLC is treated as a separate legal entity and conducts business in its own name. This provides limited liability to the owners of an LLC, called members. These members are given the same protection as shareholders, directors and officers in a corporation so that, generally, members are not personally liable for the debts and liabilities of the LLC.[12]

For tax purposes, an LLC can elect to be treated as a pass-through entity, like a sole proprietorship or partnership, or as a regular corporation.[13] This means that the members of an LLC are not subject to double taxation.

The requirements for forming an LLC vary from state to state. Generally, an LLC requires the following: (1) filing formal paperwork, usually called articles of organization, and paying a filing fee; (2) creating an LLC operating agreement, which sets out the rights and responsibilities of the LLC members; (3) publishing a notice of your intent to form an LLC; and (4) obtaining an EIN for the entity. Of course, forming an LLC is a complex matter and usually requires the assistance of a lawyer.

Conclusion

As can be seen, there are a lot of choices available. However, with some planning and forethought the modern creator can choose an entity that best suits their needs.

CHAPTER 20

Censorship and the
Comics Code in Brief

For as long as there has been the written word, there has been censorship. And for as long as there has been censorship, there have been dedicated defenders of free speech. For example, Benjamin Franklin stated, "If all printers were determined not to print anything till they were sure it would offend nobody, there would be very little printed."

Any discussion of censorship begins with the First Amendment: "Congress shall make no law respecting an establishment of religion, or prohibiting the free exercise thereof; or abridging the freedom of speech, or of the press; or the right of the people peaceably to assemble, and to petition the Government for a redress of grievances."

The First Amendment clearly protects all free speech, not only that which people are comfortable with or agree with. Obscenity, on the other hand, is not protected. Throughout history, it has been very difficult to establish the line between the two. This is especially true in the comics medium, which tends to attract children as readers. Parents have a right to protect their children. That is a noble goal, but sometimes people overcompensate. When things are taken too far, the result is censorship.

Sadly, censorship arising from moral panic is a constant presence in the history of comics. From the 1930s to the modern day, moral crusaders have attacked the medium as corrupting and warping young minds. This outcry led to a rash of public criticism in popular magazines and newspapers. In fact, it got so bad that people actually were led to comic book burning.

In response, the Association of Comics Magazine Publishers was created in 1948 to regulate the industry and create rules which were modeled loosely after the 1930 Hollywood Production Code. Essentially, this code banned graphic depictions of violence and gore in crime and horror comics, as well as the sexual innuendo of what aficionados refer to as good girl art. But the organization never took off.

Dr. Fredric Wertham

Dr. Wertham was a child psychologist who worked with juvenile delinquents. Juvenile delinquency was on the rise in America in the 1950s and he tried to figure out why. He discovered that many of his patients read comics. As a result, he concluded that comics were a corruptive influence on children. Apparently, he was also a media hound who was always looking for way to be in the spotlight, and he used his anti-comics soapbox as a tool to gain celebrity.

The apex of his anti-comics work was the 1954 book *Seduction of the Innocent*, which vilified horror, crime, and superhero comics. This book led to severe censorship of comics in the 1950s. As a result of Wertham's crusade, the Senate Subcommittee on Juvenile Delinquency held hearings in 1954. Wertham was asked to testify to a room of sympathetic senators. He made a convincing case. He stated: "...I think Hitler was a beginner compared to the comic-book industry. They get the children much younger. They teach them race hatred at the age of 4 before they can read."

On the same day, Congress also heard from William Gaines, the publisher of EC Comics. EC Comics printed crime and horror comics, including titles such as *Tales from the Crypt*, *The Vault of Horror*, *Shock SuspenStories*, *Weird Science*, and *Two-Fisted Tales*, which featured stories with content above the level of the typical comic. Gaines volunteered to appear at the hearing. He was defiant in his testimony and met with disdain from the senators. In short, his testimony was a public disaster and led to further public backlash against comics.

Gaines made the following opening remarks to Congress:

Entertaining reading has never harmed anyone. Men of good will, free men should be very grateful for one sentence in the statement made by Federal Judge John M. Woolsey when he lifted the ban on Ulysses. Judge Woolsey said, "It is only with the normal person that the law is concerned." May I repeat, he said, "It is only with the normal person that the law is concerned." Our American children are for the most part normal children. They are bright children, but those who want to prohibit comic magazines seem to see dirty, sneaky, perverted monsters who use the comics as a blueprint for action. Perverted little monsters are few and far between. They don't read comics. The chances are most of them are in schools for retarded children. What are we afraid of? Are we afraid of our own children? Do we forget that they are citizens, too, and entitled to select what to read or do? Do we think our children are so evil, so simple minded, that it takes a story of murder to set them to murder, a story of robbery to set them to robbery? Jimmy Walker once remarked that he never knew a girl to be ruined by a book. Nobody has ever been ruined by a comic.

During the hearing Gaines was showed a cover of *Crime Suspense Stories*, which featured a killer carrying the severed head of a woman and an axe, and was asked whether he thought it was in good taste. The transcript reveals the following testimony:

CHIEF COUNSEL HERBERT BEASER: Let me get the limits as far as what you put into your magazine. Is the sole test of what you would put into your magazine whether it sells? Is there any limit you can think of that you would not put in a magazine because you thought a child should not see or read about it?

BILL GAINES: No, I wouldn't say that there is any limit for the reason you outlined. My only limits are the bounds of good taste, what I consider good taste.

BEASER: Then you think a child cannot in any way, in any way, shape, or manner, be hurt by anything that a child reads or sees?

GAINES: I don't believe so.

BEASER: There would be no limit actually to what you put in the magazines?

GAINES: Only within the bounds of good taste.

BEASER: Your own good taste and saleability?

GAINES: Yes.

SENATOR ESTES KEFAUVER: Here is your May 22 issue. [Kefauver is mistakenly referring to *Crime Suspenstories* #22, cover date May.] This seems to be a man with a bloody axe holding a woman's head up which has been severed from her body. Do you think that is in good taste?

GAINES: Yes sir, I do, for the cover of a horror comic. A cover in bad taste, for example, might be defined as holding the head a little higher so that the neck could be seen dripping blood from it, and moving the body over a little further so that the neck of the body could be seen to be bloody.

KEFAUVER: You have blood coming out of her mouth.

GAINES: A little.

KEFAUVER: Here is blood on the axe. I think most adults are shocked by that.

The Comic Book Code Authority

After the devastating Senate hearings, the comics industry was faced with an angry public and the fear of congressional interference through adverse regulations. In response, the industry, under the leadership of New York Magistrate Charles F. Murphy, created the Comics Code Authority, a self-policing code of ethics and standards for the comic book industry. The Comics Code Authority responded to the public outcry by creating the 1954 Comics Code, which banned graphic depictions of violence and gore in crime and horror comics, as well as the sexual innuendo of what aficionados refer to as good girl art.

The 1954 Comics Code was very similar to the 1930 Hollywood Production Code, which was created by the Motion Pictures Producers and Distributors of America after state governments created censorship boards in the wake of a 1915 Supreme Court decision, *Mutual Film Corporation v. Industrial Commission of Ohio*, which held that free speech did not extend to motion pictures. The Hollywood Production Code contained a series of "Don'ts" and "Be Carefuls" for filmmakers that ranged from child pornography to heavy kissing.

The Comics Code was more strict than the Hollywood Production Code. For example, the 1954 Code barred the following: sympathetic criminals; details or methods of crime; disrespectful portrayal of law enforcement officers, judges or government officials; glamorized crime or criminals; evil winnings; violence, torture, unnecessary knife and gun play; concealed weapons; murder of law enforcement officers; kidnapping; the words "Horror" or "Terror" (or emphasis of the word "Crime") in a title; lurid, unsavory, gruesome illustrations; walking dead, torture, vampires and vampirism, ghouls, cannibalism and werewolfism; profanity, obscenity, smut, vulgarity; references to physical afflictions or deformities; excessive slang and colloquialisms; attacks on any religious or racial group; nudity and indecent or undue exposure; suggestive and salacious illustrations or suggestive posture; inappropriate dress; exaggeration of the female form; humorous treatment or desirable portrayal of divorce; illicit sexual relations; violent love scenes as well as sexual abnormalities; disrespect for parents, the moral code, or anything that would not encourage honorable behavior; anything that would deemphasize the value of the home and the sanctity of marriage; anything that would stimulate the lower and baser emotions; the suggestion of seduction and rape; sexual perversion or any inference to same; and all elements or techniques not specifically mentioned, which are contrary to the spirit and intent of the Code that were considered violations of good taste or decency.

This self-regulatory body appeared to calm the growing hysteria against comics, but there was a large price to pay—free speech. The Code was de facto censorship. After its enactment, the number of comics on the stands dropped from 650 to around 250 and several companies (like EC Comics, Star Press, Sterling, Toby Press, Eastern Color, and the comic book division of United Features Syndicate) were forced out of business. Essentially, comics for older teens and adults disappeared for nearly fifteen years.

The Underground Comix Movement

From 1966 through 1973, a movement called underground comix emerged as an uncensored art form that challenged attitudes toward class, sexuality, equality, politics, and drugs. Underground comix thrived for less than ten years because of changes in the law stemming from a criminal case involving *Zap Comix*. Although *Zap Comix* was the gold standard for underground comix, it was also the first to be found legally obscene.

As more fully described in chapter 21, there was a story in *Zap Comix* issue 4 that was the subject of a sting operation and retailers who offered it were prosecuted for (and found guilty of) selling obscenity in New York. The book was also prohibited from being sold over the counter in New York.

Shortly after the *Zap Comix* decision in 1973, the United States Supreme Court laid down the standard for what constitutes unprotected obscenity for First Amendment purposes in *Miller v. California*. "Obscenity" is not protected by the First Amendment. The *Miller* test for determining what constituted obscene material has three parts:

1. Whether "the average person, applying contemporary community standards," would find that the work, taken as a whole, appeals to the prurient interest,

2. Whether the work depicts/describes, in a patently offensive way, sexual conduct specifically defined by applicable state law,

3. Whether the work, taken as a whole, lacks serious literary, artistic, political or scientific value.

The work is considered obscene only if all three conditions are satisfied. The first two prongs of the *Miller* test are held to the standards of the community, and the last prong is held to what is reasonable to a person of the United States as a whole. After the *Miller* decision, content businesses braced for combat and many shops simply removed questionable material from their shelves. Basically, it was a fatal blow for underground comix.

Progressive Changes

An interesting thing happened in the late sixties and early seventies: while the underground was dying, mainstream comics were thriving. In 1971, Stan Lee, at the request of the government, wrote a Spider-Man comic dealing with drug abuse.[1]

This comic violated the Comics Code and did not receive approval, but Marvel Comics still released the book. The success of the book and the importance of the issue led to the amendment of the code to allow drug use so long as it was depicted as a vicious habit.

In the 1980s, organized fandom revitalized comics through the use of conventions and specialty stores. These led to the creation of what has become known as the direct market and for the bringing of Japanese manga into America. As a result, the eighties saw a huge surge of comics published for adults. For example both independent books, like *Fantographics*, *Cerebus*, and *Elfquest*, and the experimentation done by Marvel Comics and DC Comics, with titles like *Epic Illustrated* and Alan Moore's run on *Swamp Thing*, were produced during this time. However, the new comics revolution really started with the release of the *Dark Knight Returns* and *Watchman*, which put comics on the forefront as a means to offer commentary on society. Also at this time, Viz Media began to bring manga to American audiences with more adult themes and simple line art. In short, comics (along with pop culture, in general) were being viewed as having artistic merit.

Of course, with the increased exposure and recognition of artistic merit came added exposure and, at times, overzealousness on the part of law enforcement authorities. As described in chapter 22, Michael Correa was arrested in 1986 on charges of displaying obscene material. In response, Denis Kitchen raised money for Correa's defense, which led to the creation of the Comic Book Legal Defense Fund. As described later, this organization has been instrumental in defending the rights of comic creators.

The Death of the Comics Code Authority

While the Comics Code Authority seal appeared on comics books for nearly fifty years, eventually comics outgrew the system. Advertisers no longer cared who had the seal and who didn't. Comic readers were growing up and the market needed to respond. New publishers didn't join the Comics Code Authority, while member companies became lax in their use of the seal. Some member companies made a conscious decision not to include the seals on their books for mature readers. Other member companies, like Archie Comics, were placing the seal on books that were not submitted for approval. Milestone Comics put the seal on approved books, but still released unapproved books without the seal.

In 2001, Marvel Comics was the first publisher to completely abandon the code, when it created its own age group ratings system. In 2010, Bongo Comics stopped using the code. In January 2011, DC Comics stopped participating in the Comics Code Authority review process and would follow Marvel Comics with a rating system approach. A day later, Archie Comics, the only publisher still using the seal, announced it too was withdrawing.

The Comics Code was dead.

On September 29, 2011, in a bit of free speech justice, the Comic Book Legal Defense Fund acquired the intellectual property rights to the Comics Code Seal. The organization uses it on their fundraising merchandising and as a reminder of the censorship that occurred.

CHAPTER 21

Pulled from the Underground
People of New York v. Kirkpatrick

In 1954, the Comics Code Authority instituted a series of industry-wide prohibitions governing what could appear in comic books. In short, the Comics Code stifled artistic creativity in the mainstream comic book industry. In response, several creators, inspired by the horror comics produced by EC that had borne the brunt of the public backlash, started what would be known as the underground comix movement. Underground comix presented a stark, uncensored commentary on society. The books focused on 1960s counterculture subjects like recreational drug use, politics, rock music, and free love. To avoid confusion with the mainstream all-ages books sold in convenience stores and newsstands, the publications were known as "comix." Of course the "X" also emphasized the frequently X-rated nature of the books. Comix were usually only available in headshops (i.e., places that sold drug paraphernalia).

Zap Comix

Zap Comix issue 1 premiered in 1968, coming from the creative mind of Robert Crumb, an underground comix visionary from San Francisco. The book had a false start when the original publisher reportedly left the country with Crumb's artwork. (Crumb would later use photocopies of the art and release them as *Zap Comix* issue 0.) With only 3,500 printed copies (printed by Charles Plymell), *Zap Comix* issue 1 was released by publisher Don Donahue under the Apex Novelties imprint. In true underground fashion, the first issue was sold in San Francisco's counterculture headquarters, Haight-Ashbury, out of a baby stroller pushed by Crumb's wife, Dana.

Zap Comix issue 1, labeled "Fair Warning: For Adult Intellectuals Only," was a big success. And while there were others before it (such as Jack Jackson's *God Nose, Das Kampf*, Robert Ronnie Branaman's *Bacchanal, The Adventures of Jesus, and Lenny of Laredo*), *Zap Comix* is frequently considered to be the true beginning of the popular underground comix movement. *Zap Comix* was eventually expanded to include several other artists, including S. Clay Wilson, Robert Williams, "Spain" Rodriguez, Gilbert Shelton, and two artists with reputations as psychedelic poster designers, Victor Moscoso and Rick Griffin.

Despite the growing popularity of *Zap Comix* and limited distribution, there was an ongoing attack against underground comix. There were arrests across the country. A Berkeley bookstore named Moe's and the Phoenix Gallery were raided. An employee of Third Eye bookstore was arrested for selling *Zap Comix* issue 2. These charges never resulted in any convictions.

Despite the attempts to shutdown underground comix, the success of *Zap Comix* continued. But with issue 4, released in August 1969, the book would become infamous. That was because of a story by Crumb called "Joe Blow" that attacked social conventions. "Joe Blow" was drawn in a simple, Walt Disney style and featured a white-collar executive who, after a hard day at the office, enjoyed spending quality time with his nuclear family. Of course, this quality time consisted of an incestuous orgy (with the motto "the family that lays together, stays together"), thus providing a unique commentary on the hypocrisy of America. Almost immediately, *Zap Comix* issue 4 was targeted by law enforcement in an effort to remove it from circulation.

The Arrest

On the East Coast, *Zap Comix* issue 4 was the subject of a sting operation by the Morals Squad in New York. On August 25, 1969, Patrolman Megna, an undercover policeman from the Morals Squad, walked by the East Side Bookstore and saw a showcase in front of the sales counter with copies of *Zap Comix* issue 4. In trial, Megna testified that he bought a copy from Terrence McCoy for 50 cents. On August 25 and again on September 17, 1969, Officer Megna made similar purchases from Peter Kirkpatrick, a 23-year-old bookshop manager who was behind the counter at the New Yorker Bookstore. Also on September 17, Megna purchased a copy of *Zap Comix* issue 4 from Peter Dargis at the East Side Bookstore and "observed numerous copies" of that magazine in a glass case.

Megna personally arrested McCoy. Kirkpatrick was arrested for "promoting obscenity." Across town, Peter Dargis, manager of East Side Bookstore, was also arrested for selling *Zap Comix* issue 4. The police also arrested the owner of the New Yorker Book Store, Pete Martin, and the owner of the East Side Bookstore, James Rose, but the charges against Martin and Rose were dropped.

The case was assigned to Judge Joel Tyler, former commissioner of licenses who previously issued the ruling that labelled the movie *Deep Throat* obscene (thus making it famous). The people of New York were represented by Manhattan Assistant District Attorney Richard Beckler, who had a unique trial strategy. As the court stated, "The People introduced no evidence, whatsoever, as to the character or contents of *Zap No.* 4, but merely urged the court that its examination would reveal that the material contained therein is obscene 'as a matter of law.'" Basically, Beckler simply provided the court with a copy of *Zap Comix* issue 4 and asked for it to be found obscene. Under New York law at the time, "A person who promotes obscene material, or possesses the same with intent to promote it in the course of his business, is presumed to do so with knowledge of its content and character." Thus, any ruling that *Zap Comix* issue 4 was obscene as a matter of law would have the effect of shifting the burden of proof back to the accused to prove that they did not know the book was obscene when it was sold it to the undercover police officer.

At trial, Kirkpatrick and Dargis were represented by Robert Levine and Stephen Rohde, who argued that *Zap Comics* issue 4 had redeeming social value and thus could not be declared obscene under the law. To prove its case, the defense relied on the testimony of four expert witnesses. First, Gil Kane, a mainstream DC Comics artist, expressed his admiration of Crumb and compared his work to that of an expressionist painter. Second, Robert M. Doty, curator of New York's Whitney Museum of American Art, testified that he displayed Crumb's art at the Whitney Museum's exhibit, "Human Concern and Personal Torment: The Grotesque in American Art." Third, Steven Marks, a teacher and writer, stated that he regularly used Crumb's strips in his humanities course at Columbia University. Fourth, Sidney Jacobson, an editor at children's publisher Harvey Publications, argued that underground comix should be respected as a medium to express adult stories and adult situations.[1]

During examination of Jacobson, Judge Tyler revealed his views on the case when the subject of Archie Comics came up:

A. I certainly think that Archie is certainly a little sexy comic book.
Q. Archie is supposed to be a child's comic?
A. Yes.
Q. You think that it is sexual?
A. I know.
JUDGE TYLER: You know? Is there more than one Archie?
A. Archie Comics, which would be Archie and who—the teenage character.
JUDGE TYLER: But there is just one Archie that you mentioned is that so?
A. I'm sorry–
JUDGE TYLER: You mean a magazine? Is there any other comic book called Archie?
A. No, there is the famous one that's about twenty years old that has been successfully going.
JUDGE TYLER: You are talking about that, Mr. Jacobson, only one?
A. As far as I know.
JUDGE TYLER: You say that deals in sexuality
A. Absolutely.
JUDGE TYLER: Tell me in what way.
A. What way?
JUDGE TYLER: Yes.
A. Purposely written and drawn to arouse sexualities in teenagers. I think this is done without question.
Q. What do you mean by "sexuality" in Archie?
A. I mean by that the publishers, the editors and writers are putting in—the people involved in drawing and creating Archie are trying within it to appeal to the sexual desires of their public, which is a little different.
Q. Would you say arousing the prurient interest?
A. No, I wouldn't say that. I would say arousing the sexual interest.
Q. Would you say that Zap No.4 arouses sexual interest?
A. No, not really.
Q. So, it would seem to me, on the sliding scale of yours, that Archie would arouse more interest of the sex appeal than Zap No.4, is that correct?
A. Yes, to its reader.
JUDGE TYLER: How about Archie? Is that obscene?
A. No, I don't think it's obscene, I think it's sexual.
JUDGE TYLER: Do they intend in Archie to appeal to the sexuality of the teenager?

A. Yes, they do.

JUDGE TYLER: Do you deem that an obscene purpose?

A. No, I don't.

The court also heard from several fact witnesses. First, Patrolman Megna testified about the purchases and the arrests.

McCoy took the stand and denied that he was in the bookstore on August 25, 1969, or that he sold the copy to Patrolman Megna. The court also took notice that McCoy had long straight hair and was 5 feet 8½ inches tall, in contradiction to the arrest warrant, which describes the person who sold *Zap Comix* issue 4 to Officer Megna as having curly hair and being 6 feet 1 inch tall. McCoy testified that the warrant described Bob Gillespie, another employee. A "day sheet" was put into evidence, showing those employees working each day and indicating that McCoy did not work that day.

Dargis testified that while he ordered 200 copies of *Zap Comix* issue 4, he had never read or discussed the comic. He remembered unpacking the book and looking at the cover, which was clearly labeled "Adults Only." He also testified that underground comix represented less than 1 percent of the gross sales of the East Side Bookstore. Finally, he confirmed that McCoy did not work on August 25.

Kirkpatrick testified that he performed such office work as billing invoices, accounting, and reorders, and that he sold in the store and had personally sold 25 to 30 copies of *Zap Comix* issue 4. Kirkpatrick also said that had never read *Zap Comix* issue 4, and he confirmed that, like the East Side Bookstore, the sales from underground comix represented less than 1 percent of total sales.

The court issued its opinion on October 28, 1970. First, the court acquitted McCoy based on the testimony that the arrest warrant described the seller as one having physical characteristics substantially different from those of McCoy; that the records of the bookshop indicated, and its manager testified, that McCoy was not working on the day of the sale; and McCoy's own denial of his presence and of the sale, all of which created reasonable doubt.

However, the court found Kirkpatrick and Dargis guilty as charged beyond a reasonable doubt. The court found *Zap Comix* issue 4 was obscene as a matter of law and concluded:

It is material utterly unredeemed and unredeemable, save, perhaps, only by the quality of the paper upon which it is printed. It is patently offensive. It has gone substantially beyond "the present critical point in the compromise between candor and shame at which the community may have arrived here and now." It is a part of the underworld press—the growing world of deceit in sex and it is not reality or honesty, as they often claim it to be. It represents an emotional incapacity to view sex as a basis for establishing genuine human relationships, or as a normal part of human condition. It is what Dr. Benjamin Spock characterizes as "shock-obscenity," representing a brutalizing trend in our society. The development of understanding of, or making proper comment about, sex is vitiated by its graphic and venal exploitation of sexuality. And such exploitation is an unfortunate concomitant of our times. Zap No. 4 is an exploiter; its effect is to purvey "filth for filth's sake." It is hard-core pornography. Perhaps that type of obscenity contains its own antidote and eventually becomes a repetitious bore—but, unfortunately by that time it has rendered its victims shock-proof, jaded and permissive to the point of indifference toward moral values and tolerable behavior. The material must fail by any legal test yet announced, including [the New York obscenity law], and stands condemned as a violator of that law. The magazine is legally obscene.

The court also ruled that that the presumption that the defendants "knew" the material they were selling was obscene was valid. The court stated:

I disagree that the defendants cannot be presumed, to know, in general, the contents and character of the material they offer to sell and sell.... It is "based on life and life's experience" to expect merchants to know something about the items they sell in their business, without expecting them to have examined each carefully. Is it farfetched, as defendants maintain, to presume that a bookseller or magazine vendor who sells obscene material in the course of his business knows something of its contents and character? I believe not, and to maintain such a position is to divorce oneself from the realities of "life's experience." "No corner hardware merchant would long prosper," remarks Richard H. Kuh in his interesting book (Foolish Fig Leaves? Pornography In-And-Out-of-Court, 1967, p. 264) "lacking general familiarity with the items he had for sale. No Wall Street broker could succeed, ignorant of fluctuations in the securities he marketed. Similarly, honest book and magazine dealers have some general knowledge of the character of the wares they order, put on their shelves, sometimes display, and ultimately hope to sell." ... It is not unreasonable for the law to presume that the bookseller knows his merchandise, since to expect less would, as Mr. Justice FELIX FRANKFURTER noted, permit the bookseller to insulate "himself against knowledge about an offending book" and "thereby free to maintain an emporium for smut."

Nor, does this presumption create an unreasonable hardship upon defendants. The presumption is not conclusive; "it gives him every opportunity to rebut the presumption * * * merely calling upon him to explain * * *. And even if he offers no explanation, the jury may still refuse to convict. The burden of proof upon the entire case, the duty of establishing guilt beyond a reasonable doubt, remains as ever with the prosecution. Defendants' right to a fair trial continues undiminished; no hardship is imposed, no constitutional right or safeguard impaired." ...

[The New York Statute] raises no presumption of knowledge, by mere possession of obscene material. The presumption is operable only if the material is actually sold (lent, delivered, etc.) in "the course of his business," or if possessed with intent to sell (lend, deliver, etc.) "in the course of his business."... Accordingly, our presumption cannot operate against a private individual who sells or lends or delivers, etc. an obscene book to another, unless he does so "in the course of his business," nor can it operate against a retailer who does not sell or intend to sell an obscene item in the course of his business. [The New York Statute] was intended to raise presumptions against those in the business of regularly dealing in obscene material, either in large or small quantity, and as to them, there is a rationality and logic to the expectation that those who sell or intend to sell such material in the course of their business, know something of the character of the contents thereof.

In reaching the conclusion that the book was obscene, the court rejected the opinions of the experts:

I find that all of these witnesses failed to particularize in understandable lay terms their generalizations that the cartoonists were "original," or how they were "influencing a new generation of cartoonists" or how they showed "enormous vitality" or where was the satire or parody of the sexual experiences depicted; or why was the explicit sexuality, as demonstrated, necessary to the theme (i.e., a commentary on conventional relationships in middle-class society); or how do these cartoons, dealing as they do in the main with perverted sexual experiences, attempt to "humorously outrage" the reader and place in perspective human values.

Instead, the court substituted its own view:

In the final analysis, the Court must be the expert in assessing what is the dominant theme, prurient interest, community standards, any redeeming social value, and the like.... Merely because the magazine in question does not appeal to the prurient interest of the sophisticated or other small group of intellectuals does not remove it from the prohibition [against obscenity]. To do so would permit the substitution of defendants' sophisticated and intellectual experts for those of the average person in the contemporary community.

Kirkpatrick and Dargis were fined $500, and if the fine was not paid, ordered to serve 90 days in jail.[2]

The Appeal

After paying the fine, Kirkpatrick and Dargis appealed. The Appellate Term affirmed the lower court's decision, so they again appealed by leave of an associate judge of the New York Court of Appeals, the highest state court level in New York. The Court of Appeals affirmed with a 4–3 decision. The majority concluded:

> The fact of obscenity need not be dwelt upon at this time. Most of this court agrees with the courts below that the material sold was obscene, and its nature was discussed by the trial court in its elaborate opinion determining the case. What remains at issue, with disagreement in this court, is whether the record contained sufficient evidence to establish that the booksellers knew of the obscene contents and by way of alternative ratio decided whether the statutory presumption that a seller of obscene materials knows the contents of what he sells is valid.

The majority relied on the trial courts findings to determine that:

> The trial court both found actual knowledge and applied the statutory presumption.... It is evident then that the trial court found scienter [knowledge of wrongdoing] both by reason of the statutory presumption not having been rebutted and by its own inference of the fact of knowledge from the evidence. Since the attack on the validity of the presumption rests in part on the probabilities of knowledge by the booksellers of what kind of material they were selling, it necessarily follows that the probabilities supporting the validity of the presumption, the failure to rebut it successfully, and the inference of knowledge overlap. The conviction should be affirmed on either view of the case.

The majority then addressed First Amendment concerns raised by the presumption that the defendants knew what they were selling was obscene:

> Notably, the [Supreme Court] recognized that any obscenity statute applicable to a bookseller will induce some tendency to self-censorship, but also indicated that the decision did not require meeting the problem. The importance of the expressed restraint is of course that otherwise any effective control of obscenity would become impossible. The "hardcore" obscenity to which modern efforts are directed is largely of the kind where the authors and publishers are or would be largely anonymous or disguised. It is at some point of distribution that the offense may be uncovered and only sometimes worked backward to the makers of the contraband. In any event, so long as the Supreme Court has not viewed obscenity as beyond legislative control, it behooves the courts to sustain rational efforts at control and not, indirectly on attenuated constitutional speculations, to overthrow serially every restrained effort at control. So long as obscenity measures are restricted to the type of material now involved, the social redeeming value qualification retained, and only rebuttable presumptions based on rational connection or probabilities are utilized, the risk to constitutionally protected speech or press is invisible.

In short, the majority upheld the constitutionality of a statutory presumption that the seller of obscene materials knows the contents of that material and also held that there was sufficient independent evidence of scienter (i.e., knowledge of wrongdoing) to support the conviction.

The dissenters did not agree that the trial court found actual knowledge of the contents of the magazine. Chief Judge Fuld, writing for the dissent, stated:

> Despite the indisputable fact that there was not a word of testimony or evidence presented during the People's case that either defendant knew the content or nature of Zap No. 4, the trial judge, after the prosecution rested, reserved decision on the defense motion to dismiss on the ground that evidence of scienter was lacking. This ruling demonstrates that the judge necessarily relied on the statutory presumption of knowledge; had he not done so, he would, of course, have granted the motion. In any event, after decision on their motion had been reserved, the defendants took the stand quite obviously to attempt to rebut that presumption....
>
> In short, implicit both in the court's conduct of the trial and in its treatment of the case is a determination that, absent reliance upon the presumption, the proof offered did not establish that the defendants knew the allegedly obscene nature of the material. This being so, our court may not make a new finding of fact even though we were to assume that the trial judge could have made such a finding.

Turning to the presumption, the dissent stated:

> A statutory presumption violates due process, the Supreme Court has held, if there is "no rational connection between the fact proved and the ultimate fact presumed, if the inference of the one from proof of the other is arbitrary because of lack of connection between the two in common experience. * * * [W]here the inference is so strained as not to have a reasonable relation to the circumstances of life as we know them, it is not competent for the legislature to create it." ... It is most unlikely that a bookseller—especially in a store such as those in which the defendants were employed—would have knowledge of the content of the publications being offered for sale.... Reason and experience tell us that it would be impossible for a bookseller in either store to acquaint himself with the content and character of so large a number of titles. In any event, it may not be said with "substantial assurance"—as required by the cases—that such booksellers may be "presumed" to know the content and character of a publication merely upon proof that they sold it.
>
> However, even if the statutory presumption were able to withstand an attack based on due process grounds, I would be impelled to stamp it unconstitutional as an infringement on the freedom of expression guaranteed by the First Amendment. The presumption violates that amendment because it creates and occasions a system of "self-censorship" on the part of booksellers which affects the sale and distribution of all books—those that are constitutionally protected as well as those that are obscene... "By dispensing with any requirement of knowledge of the contents of the book on the part of the seller, the ordinance tends to impose a severe limitation on the public's access to constitutionally protected matter. For if the bookseller is criminally liable without knowledge of the contents, and the ordinance fulfills its purpose, he will tend to restrict the books he sells to those he has inspected; and thus the State will have imposed a restriction upon the distribution of constitutionally protected as well as obscene literature. * * * And the bookseller's burden would become the public's burden, for by restricting him the public's access to reading matter would be restricted. If the contents of bookshops and periodical stands were restricted to material of which their proprietors had made an inspection, they might be depleted indeed. The bookseller's limitation in the amount of reading material with which he could familiarize himself, and his timidity in the face of his absolute criminal liability, thus would tend to restrict the public's access to forms of the printed word which the State could not constitutionally suppress directly. The bookseller's self-censorship, compelled by the State, would be a censorship affecting the whole public, hardly less virulent for being privately administered. Through it, the distribution of all books, both obscene and not obscene, would be impeded." ...

Although the State may generally regulate the allocation of the burden of proof through legislation, it is clear that a statute may not, where the First Amendment is involved, declare a person presumptively guilty of a crime or presume that he has committed one of its material elements. Freedom of speech is too important a right to allow it to be seriously impeded or impaired by a presumption.

The Supreme Court

After yet another loss, Kirkpatrick and Dargis applied to the Supreme Court for a writ of certiorari. The Supreme Court dismissed the petition for want of substantial federal question without opinion. More interesting, however, were the dissents.

Justice Douglas wrote that he was "of the view that state obscenity regulation is prohibited by the Fourteenth and First Amendments" and noted that he would rule there was "probable jurisdiction in this case and reverse judgment of conviction." Justice Brennan (joined by Justices Stewart and Marshall) wrote that:

> It is my view that "at least in the absence of distribution to juveniles or obtrusive exposure to unconsenting adults, the First and Fourteenth Amendments prohibit the State and Federal Governments from attempting wholly to suppress sexually oriented materials on the basis of their allegedly 'obscene' contents." Since it is clear that, when tested by that constitutional standard, the word "obscene" in [the New York Law], renders [the statute] unconstitutionally overbroad and therefore facially invalid, I disagree with the holding that the appeal does not present a substantial federal question, and therefore dissent from the Court's dismissal of the appeal.

Of course, the effect of the Supreme Court's action in Kirkpatrick has been hotly debated. This dismissal, in its procedural context, was equivalent to an adjudication of the federal issue on its merits. However, many courts have found the dismissal of the appeal in Kirkpatrick ambiguous or inconclusive on the issue of the constitutionality of the presumption challenged.

Conclusion

The *Kirkpatrick* decision stands as stark reminder as to why comic creators and dealers must remain vigilant. Interestingly, reprints of *Zap Comix*, as well as many other underground comix, are available in mainstream bookstores. Robert Crumb has been featured in museums. If this case were decided today, things would hopefully be different.

CHAPTER 22

And There Came a Day
Illinois v. Correa (The Friendly Frank's Case)

Police Officer Anthony Van Gorp had a very important job. He was responsible for protecting the youth of Lansing, Illinois. Specifically, youth officer investigator Van Gorp was charged by the Lansing police department with the task of monitoring and observing areas where youths congregate. That is what brought him to the Friendly Frank's comic book store on the afternoon of November 28, 1986. The record isn't clear as to what made Officer Van Gorp and his partner enter the Friendly Frank's store on the day after Thanksgiving. But, this Black Friday would prove to be the darkest in the history of the shop.

Officer Van Gorp wandered through the store and perused the books on the shelves of the comic shop. Some of the books depicted scenes of sexual conduct and nudity. More troubling to the policemen was the fact that the offensive books were intermixed with the other comics and not segregated behind the counter. Van Gorp and his partner returned to the station and reported the store to their supervisor.

On December 3, 1986, the following Wednesday, officer Van Gorp returned to the Friendly Frank's shop and picked out fifteen comics that he determined depicted scenes of sexual conduct and nudity. The books selected were *Omaha the Cat Dancer*; *The Bodyssey*; *Bizarre Sex*; *Weirdo*; *Heavy Metal*; *Elektra: Assassin*; *Love & Rockets*; *Ms. Tree*; *Murder*; *Swords of the Swashbucklers*; *The Chronicles of Corum*; *Ex-Mutants*; and *Elfquest*. Officer Van Gorp took his purchases to the register where Michael Correa, the manager of Friendly Frank's, rang them up. The books totaled $41.10 and Officer Van Gorp paid using police department funds. At the end of the sale, Correa gave Van Gorp a receipt and his change, and probably wished him a good day.

One week later, on December 10, 1986, Officer Van Gorp returned to the Friendly Frank's store, this time with Sergeant Jack Hoestra. Buying comics was not on either officer's agenda. Earlier in the day, Officer Van Gorp swore out a criminal complaint charging Correa with obscenity because he possessed obscene magazines with intent to distribute them. Specifically, Officer Van Gorp found seven of the fifteen magazines to be obscene. The offenders were *Omaha the Cat Dancer* numbers 1 through 3; *the Bodyssey*; *Bizarre Sex* number 5; and *Weirdo* 17 and 18.

Officer Van Gorp and Sergeant Hoestra entered the shop on December 10 and arrested Correa for obscenity. Under Illinois law:

233

[A] person commits the offense of obscenity when he or she, inter alia, creates, buys, procures, or possesses obscene material with the intent to disseminate it, with knowledge of the nature or content of the material, or recklessly failing to exercise a reasonable inspection that would have disclosed the nature or content of the material.

Correa was placed into handcuffs and taken to jail. The police confiscated the seven so-called obscene books and closed down Friendly Frank's for five days. Correa waived his right to a jury and his case was heard by the court. On January 1, 1988, New Year's Day, The Honorable Paul T. Foxgrover of the Circuit Court of Cook County found Correa guilty as charged. After the conviction, the court sentenced Correa to court supervision for one year and ordered Correa to pay $750 in fines and costs.

Perhaps the most interesting and lasting part of this story was occurring outside of the courtroom. After the arrest of his employee, Frank Mangiaracina, the owner of Friendly Frank's, sent requests for aid to publishers and fellow retailers. Denis Kitchen, the publisher of Kitchen Sink Press who published *Omaha the Cat Dancer*, one of the offensive books, responded to the request. Kitchen soon met with a retailer named Greg Ketter at a convention in Minnesota and, together, they sought to raise funds for Correa's defense. In 1987, Neil Gaiman, then an up-and-coming writer, did a signing that raised nearly $10,000 for Correa. Kitchen also created an art book called *Benefit Portfolio in Defense of the First Amendment—The Comic Book Legal Defense Fund* that would help raise money to pay for the defense. *Benefit Portfolio in Defense of the First Amendment—The Comic Book Legal Defense Fund* featured art from fourteen artists, including Sergio Aragones, Hilary Barta, Reed Waller, Steve Bissette, Bob Burden, Richard Corben, Robert Crumb, Howard Cruse, Will Eisner, Frank Miller, Mitch O'Connell and Don Simpson, and Eric Vincent. Kitchen also found a printer who produced the portfolio at cost and Mangiaracina convinced the International Association of Direct Distribution to carry the benefit portfolio at a lower-than-normal discount. The book had a limited run of only 1,500 and the first 250 were numbered and signed. The proceeds from the project were placed into a bank account Kitchen dubbed The Comic Book Legal Defense Fund.

With the fundraising proceeds, Correa was able to hire a renowned First Amendment lawyer named Burton Joseph to represent him in his appeal. On appeal, Joseph argued: (1) the magazines on which the State based its prosecution are not obscene; (2) the trial court erred in completely disregarding evidence relating to the literary and artistic value of the magazines; (3) the State failed to prove beyond a reasonable doubt the essential elements of the offense; and (4) the criminal complaint was duplicitous and, therefore, void. The appeal was heard by Justices Linn, Jiganti, and McMorrow, who were sitting on the Appellate Court of Illinois, First District, Fourth Division.

On November 16, 1989, with an opinion written by Justice Linn, the Appellate Court reversed the lower courts. In reaching its conclusion, the court first pointed out that comic books are indeed subject to the protections of free speech afforded by the United States and Illinois constitutions regardless of the fact that they are sold for profit and are primarily for entertainment. The court next stated that sexuality is not synonymous with obscenity and, more importantly, expression that is sexually oriented but not obscene would still be considered protected speech. The appellate court then reviewed each of the seven comic books at issue. With regard to *Omaha the Cat Dancer* issues 1, 2, and 3 and *the Bodyssey*, the court found that the depicted nudity and sexual conduct contained in the books were an incidental part of the plot. As a result, the court determined that the books, taken as a whole, did not lack serious literary or artistic value. The court was not as kind to *Bizarre Sex* Number 5 or *Weirdo* Numbers 17 and 18 as it concluded that they were in poor taste, made no sense, and had no serious literary or artistic value. Despite this, the court still determined the content of the books did not equate to hard-core obscenity. As a result, the court concluded:

> We are not impressed with the literary or artistic merit of the cartoon comic books before us. However, that is not the standard which we must apply. We hold that none of the cartoon comic books on which the State based its prosecution constitutes patently offensive hard-core obscenity as stated in the statute. Consequently, defendant's conviction and sentence must be reversed.

But the story does not end there.

After celebrating their victory in the case and paying all the bills, Kitchen found that the fundraising was so successful that several thousand dollars remained in the Comic Book Legal Defense Fund bank fund. Fearing that the prosecution of Correa was a sign of things to come, Kitchen used the bank account to help create a permanent organization to protect comic retailers and creators. He decided to use the same name as the bank account, and the Comic Book Legal Defense Fund (otherwise known as the "CBLDF") was born.

The CBLDF was granted non-profit status under section 501(c)(3) of the Internal Revenue Code in 1990. The organization is dedicated to the protection of the First Amendment rights of the comic art form and its community of retailers, creators, publishers, librarians, and readers. The CBLDF provides legal referrals, representation, advice, assistance, and education in furtherance of its goals. Funds for CBLDF are raised primarily through membership programs for individuals, retailers, and corporations and through the sale of autographed books and comics. In addition, as the CBLDF is always looking for volunteers to assist its education, administrative and fundraising work. More information can be found at CBLDF.ORG.

If a creator believes that they have a First Amendment problem, the first call they make should be to the CBLDF at 800-99-CBLDF or 212-679-7151.

Conclusion

I hope that you have enjoyed reading this book as much as I have enjoyed writing it. As you can guess, it only touches the rich history of comics. And while I have attempted to include all major topics and cover the most influential cases, I obviously cannot have included them all. As technology adapts new issues may arise. For example, I would have liked to include chapters on social networking and social fundraising, but those areas are too new and haven't fully developed. Likewise, international topics, as well as film and television licensing, were just too voluminous to include. Similarly, there are comic book cases that were only touched upon, like those involving Air Pirates, Tony Twist, and Blade to name a few, that would have been more fleshed out if space permitted. Sadly, there just wasn't room.

I should add a word about sources. The stories in this book come entirely from the public records in the cases. All quotes are from the judicial opinions, the deposition or trial testimony, or, in a few minor cases, the exhibits used in the case. Care was taken to eliminate personal information, such as home addresses, as well as other personal identifiers unless relevant to the outcome of the case. In addition, negative comments either by or about the litigants or their lawyers have been omitted unless directly relevant to the outcome of the case.

In closing, it may be helpful to summarize some of the lessons that these stories teach. First, always remember to be clear in any business arrangement, as this can avoid lawsuits later. Second, get it in writing. Make sure that all the terms are clear and in the contract. And while this may not always avoid the lawsuit, it will certainly make it easier to win if there is one. Third, remember to keep all the records. Without the documents, it may come down to one person's word against another's. Finally, if necessary, you should hire professional help. Whether it be a lawyer to help with contracts, an accountant to help with taxes, or the CBLDF to help with a First Amendment issue, the comic creator should not try to navigate these difficult subject matters without a trained professional.

Good luck to you on all of your comic related ventures.

Chapter Notes

Introduction

1. In some of the stories, there are no winners and no losers because the cases settled.

Chapter 1

1. In a jury trial, a group of private citizens are selected to determine the facts of a case; the judge will then determine the applicable law to apply to those facts. In a bench trial, the judge serves as both the fact finder and the legal authority.

2. For example, a court can eliminate opening or closing arguments. In some cases, the court may order the direct testimony by written questions.

3. Interestingly, a large number of the cases in this book were reversed on appeal. This may indicate the complexity of intellectual property law or a general lack of understanding by the courts as to what comic books are.

Chapter 2

1. A patent is a form of intellectual property that provides protection to an inventor, or their assignee, for any new, useful, and non-obvious process, machine, article of manufacture, or composition of matter. More information on patents is available on the website for the United States Patent and trademark Office at http://www.uspto.gov/.

2. For example, when Marvel Comics was creating the *Ultimates*, a re-imagining of the Avengers, for their Marvel Ultimate line of comics, the company obtained permission from actor Samuel L. Jackson and redesigned the character of Nick Fury to look like him. Jackson would later portray Nick Fury in several Marvel movies and on television. David Hasselhoff has also portrayed Nick Fury in an unrelated television movie, but the character has never been portrayed as him in a comic.

3. There is a split as to whether the celebrity must be alive to have the right of publicity. While the predominant view is that the right survives the celebrity's death, some courts have held that the right of publicity dies with the celebrity, while others have only permitted the celebrity's heirs to assert the right. Some states have enacted statutes determining how long the right lasts.

4. During the trial, evidence was produced that Mc-Farlane also produced and licensed Spawn logo hockey pucks, hockey jerseys and toy Zambonis, and conducted a Spawn-themed promotional event at a minor league hockey game. Twist also put on evidence that he had lost a major endorsement deal as a result of the connection with the character.

5. The Supreme Court did not address claims related to whether advertising for the comic books, which may have implied that the Winter brothers endorsed the product, violated the musicians' publicity rights. On remand, the Court of Appeals determined that the Winter brothers would not be able to prevail on any advertising claims.

Chapter 3

1. Most recently, this can be seen in the Digital Millennium Copyright Act, which relates to the downloading of music off the internet.

2. Many creators may take issue with this argument, feeling that they draw because they love comics. Sadly, the founding fathers did not share their passion for sequential art.

3. Censorship and the First Amendment are discussed in more detail in chapter 20.

4. Before enacting the Constitution, the fledgling United States was governed by the Articles of Confederation. Under the Articles, each individual state was encouraged to adopt its own copyright rules. Madison served on the committee that created this provision in the Articles.

5. Although the first work was registered within two weeks, most writings were never registered.

6. It should be noted that the Copyright Act of 1976 took effect beginning January 1, 1978 (two years later). As will be seen, this Act was updated many times, but not substantially changed.

7. The same concept applies to plot outlines. At its basic level, a plot outline is a mere idea and there is no copyright protection unless there is sufficient detail to be considered expression.

8. A closely related concept involved the merger doctrine, which provides that if there is only one way to express an idea, then the idea and expression merge and the expression cannot be protected. On this, courts have held that boilerplate rules and language in sweepstakes forms could not be protected as they were the only way to express the idea and protecting the expression would prevent others from using the idea. In the world of comics, a disclaimer that "Any similarity to persons living or dead is purely coincidental" would probably fall under this exception.

9. Comics actually fit under two categories of the Copyright Act and can be registered as visual art works or literary works. Generally, comics are considered works of the visual arts; however, if textual elements are preponderant, they should be registered as literary works.

10. As discussed elsewhere, these items may sometimes be protected under state law doctrines or state and federal trademark laws. In fact, as discussed in chapter 3, in some circumstances, courts have held ideas to be protected in cases where there is a pre-existing relationship between the parties.

11. It should also be noted that toys are generally not considered useful articles, and are thus copyrightable. However, at least one court found that Halloween costumes are useful objects, like clothing, and thus not protected by copyright.

12. The originality requirement is met because the compiler chose the selection and organization of the work.

13. The case involving Sam Spade related to the film version of *The Maltese Falcon*.

14. There was a case involving James Bond homage in a Honda commercial that explains the "story being told" test and summarized cases involving Sam Spade, Rocky Balboa, Mickey Mouse and Tarzan. Of course the court did not look at whether James Bond was actually copyrighted but whether there was a likelihood that the court could find James Bond to be copyrightable (MGM sued Honda and asked the court to stop the commercial [an injunction] pending the release of the real decision and needed to prove that "they were likely to succeed on the merits"). The court stated, "Indeed, audiences do not watch Tarzan, Superman, Sherlock Holmes, or James Bond for the story, they watch these films to see their heroes at work. A James Bond film without James Bond is not a James Bond film." As a result, the court held that "Plaintiffs will probably succeed on their claim that James Bond is a copyrightable character under either the 'story being told' or the 'character delineation' test."

15. The general rule is that the person who conceives of the copyright expression is the owner rather than the person who causes it to be fixed or provided. This allows for editorial work and administrative work to be done without creating joint copyright. It is unclear whether a letterer and a colorist are entitled to joint work status. For example, the *Spawn* case, which discusses the process and implies joint ownership, did not give the letterer or colorist to *Spawn* issue 9 any of the copyright. Of course, the letterer and colorist could have been employees or working under a work for hire contract, but if that were relevant, it should have been discussed in the opinion. Moreover, the *Spawn* decision applies the minority view. The majority view is that a joint author's contribution must be more than de minimis and independently copyrightable. This book will not comment on the debate as to whether comic book lettering or coloring is independently copyrightable. It should be noted that typesetting is not covered by copyright; typefaces are exempt from copyright; yet scalable fonts are covered by copyright (as part of a computer program) while other bitmapped fonts are not. In short, it would probably come down to a facts and circumstances test and the courts could go either way, depending on the court's level of comic book sophistication.

16. As described more fully in chapter 3, courts have occasionally found the right to recover for the unauthorized use of an idea.

17. Stan Lee's career and employment contracts are discussed in more detail in chapter 9.

18. The entire list contained in the statute includes: collective works; part of a motion picture; translation; supplementary work; compilation (e.g., an index or table of contents); instructional text; test; answer material for a test; or an atlas.

19. In fact, not every work has all five rights. For example, it is not possible for an artist to perform a sculpture.

20. While this law applies to books published at any time, the copy must have been made after September 16, 1996, the effective date of the Copyright Law Amendment, 1996, PL 104–197. The policy reasons for this change was made clear in the legislative history. For example, Dr. Tuck Tinsley, head of the American Printing House for the Blind, testified:

"The [new proposed statute] proposed by the National Federation of the Blind, the Association of American Publishers, and the Library of Congress will greatly assist with the provision of educational materials to blind students at the same time the materials are available to their sighted peers. This amendment will provide long-overdue enrichment to the lives of blind students. It is time to put an end to the unintended effect that copyright has of censoring blind students' access to current ideas, information, and educational resources. On behalf of all of the legally blind student population of our country, the American Printing House for the Blind salutes the Association of American Publishers for going to the National Federation of the Blind and working toward [a statue] which is beneficial to all."

President Clinton signed the bill into law on September 16, 1996.

21. In the comics industry, some licensors separately license the rights to make comics and the right to make manga (Japanese comics) to two different companies.

22. There is also a limitation for works purchased in another country. For example, assume that a United States comic company tries to sell a copy of their hit World War II series entitled *This "A" Doesn't Stand for France* in Europe. They send 10,000 units for sale in Paris. Not getting the joke, the Parisian market bottoms out requiring French comic shops to deeply discount the book even while it continues to sell out in the United States. A clever American named Joe Comicbookfan, on vacation in France, sees the book and quickly buys all 10,000 copies with the hopes of reselling them in the United States for a huge profit. This will violate the right to distribution, the first sale doctrine will not apply, and Joe, as an infringer, will most likely be prevented from exporting the books into the United States.

23. The Rome Act of 1928 was the first legal international treaty to recognize the concept of moral rights.

24. The statute provides for waiver of moral rights, but only by a signed, written agreement specifying the work and the precise uses to which a waiver applies.

25. The 1976 Copyright Act originally only provided for a protection period of the life of the creator plus 50 years. This period was increased as part of the Sonny Bono Copyright Term Extension Act of 1998, which was signed into law on October 27, 1998. The change was made, in part, to help align the copyright law in Europe and the law in the United States. Apparently, this change was quite controversial and even unsuccessfully challenged in court when publishers and librarians filed a suit arguing the Act was unconstitu-

tional. On January 15, 2003, the U.S. Supreme Court held that the Copyright Term Extension Act was constitutional by a 7–2 decision.

26. Unpublished works were still covered by copyright, but that protection arose under state common law copyright, which lasted until publication. Common law basically means that the law was created by courts in cases instead of through laws made by legislature. In short, under the old state judge-made law, copyright never expired on unpublished works.

27. Under the 1909 Act, only the original author could apply for the renewal. If the author died before the 28th year, the surviving spouse or children of the author could apply for renewal. If there were no children or spouse, then the executor of the author's will could apply. If the author had no will, then the author's statutory next of kin had the right to apply for renewal.

28. As discussed in the *Josie and the Pussycats* case in Chapter 10, the 1976 Copyright Act was meant to replace all existing state common law copyright laws. This is called federal preemption, which refers to the fact that, with some exceptions, a federal law will always invalidate a state law when the two are in conflict.

29. Someone good at math will figure out that all works published before 1923 are not covered by copyright and are in the public domain. Similarly, under this rule, no new works will enter the public domain until 2018. The public domain is explored in chapter 18.

30. This question is further complicated by the 1998 Sonny Bono Copyright Term Extension Act. Prior to the Sonny Bono Act, the works in the second renewal period were only given protection for 75 years from the date of first publication. So, if *Sidekick* was published in 1920, with a proper renewal in 1948, under the pre–Sonny Bono provisions of the 1909 Copyright Act, *Sidekick* would have lost its copyright protection in 1995 (1920+75). Because this work lost its copyright protection prior to the enactment of the Sonny Bono Act in 1998, it will remain unprotected.

31. This means that for works published after 1964, the work is automatically renewed. There is still optional voluntary renewal, however, with various statutory incentives, including a presumption of validity in litigation of copyright.

32. At one time, there was a question as to whether an author could assign the future renewal right since that defeated the purpose of the 1909 Copyright Act to protect the future bargaining position of the author. The Supreme Court rejected this position in *Fred Fisher Music Co. v. M. Witmark & Sons* and held that the transfer of a future renewal interest is permissible. However, the sale of the renewal must be specifically mentioned and if it is not included in the contract then the renewal will not be considered transferred. This was at issue in the *Superman* case, discussed in chapter 15, and the *Captain America* case discussed in chapter 5.

33. At this risk of repetition, this issue would not arise under the current copyright law as there is no renewal period for works created after January 1, 1978.

34. The creation date of the work is irrelevant.

35. In 1998, Congress amended the copyright statute as part of the Sonny Bono Copyright Term Extension Act so that it would permit estates to terminate the grant of rights.

36. This is a different result from the 1909 Act where the author in the residual period could prevent exploitation of the derivative right if he or she chose to keep the work during the renewal period after it is transferred for the first period.

37. The date of death and the date of creation are irrelevant to this determination.

38. There are exceptions under copyright law for when the work isn't published. An owner of a transferred copyright has a five year period in which to send a notice of termination. If publication of the property is not involved, this five year period begins thirty-five years from the date of the execution of the grant. Alternatively, if the grant covers publication of a work (as most comics contracts do), the five year period begins at the earlier of 35 years from publication or 40 years from the signing of the grant. Section 203(a)(3) provides:

> Termination of the grant may be effected [1] at any time during a period of five years beginning at the end of thirty-five years from the date of execution of the grant; or [2], if the grant covers the right of publication of the work, the period begins at the end of thirty-five years from the date of publication of the work under the grant or [3] at the end of forty years from the date of execution of the grant, whichever term ends earlier.

The reason for the two different periods when publication is involved is simple and explained in House Report No. 94–1476, "the alternative method of computation is intended to cover cases where years elapse between the signing of a publication contract and the eventual publication of the work." In fact, book publishers lobbied for this provision because publishing contracts are frequently signed before the book is written. This could result in several years passing between the signing of a contract and publication of a book. Thus, applying a single thirty-five years from execution of the grant would be unfair to these publishers as it provides a much shorter time to exploit the covered work before termination.

39. There is a concept known as limited publication. This is basically when an author distributes copies to a limited audience for a limited purpose. For example, a limited publication of this book was created when it was printed and sent to close friends for their editing and comments. A general publication, i.e. an unrestricted distribution of copies to the public, occurred when McFarland printed and distributed it to public.

40. Although beyond the scope of this book, it should be noted that the copyright symbol ("©") is not used for sound recordings. Instead, the symbol for phonorecording is "℗."

41. In 1988, the United States agreed to join the Berne Convention for the Protection of Literary and Artistic Works, an international treaty that was created to create uniform copyright laws around the world.

42. The cure could take many forms. First, if only a few copies lacked notice, then the failure to include notice on these copies was ignored. Second, if the publisher had agreed to include a notice and accidentally left it off the publication, then the lack of notice was ignored. Third, if a work was simply published without notice, the failure could be cured if the author (1) registered the work with the copyright office within five years of publication and (2) took reasonable effort to add notice to all copies that were distributed domestically.

43. There is a common misconception that copyright can be established by having a creator mail themselves the work in a sealed envelope and then keep the postmarked envelope. This practice is referred to as the

Poor Man's Copyright and has no legal effect in the United States. After extensive research, no cases have relied on it and the copyright statutes don't provide for it. In short, the Poor Man's Copyright is an urban legend.

44. Registration is a prerequisite to filing suit for domestic works. Foreign works that are covered by the Berne convention don't need to be registered before their creators can sue for infringement.

45. In the interest of completeness, there is a three month grace period for registration of copyright, if infringement occurs within this period and then the owner registers the work within the first three months, but after infringement, then the statutory liquidation damages and attorney's fees remedies are still available. For example, assume Barry publishes a book in January and Bart infringes the book in February. If Barry is fast enough to register the copyright by March, he could still sue Bart for statutory liquidated damages and obtain attorney's fees if he prevails.

46. This circular can be found at http://www.copy right.gov/circs/circ44.pdf.

47. Because the court is only looking for evidence of copying, the similarities of the two works could be in any element of the work, including things like common ideas or factual material, which are not protected.

48. A very famous non-comic example is the *A&M Records, Inc. v. Napster, Inc.* case, which involved peer to peer music sharing. The Ninth Circuit held that Napster was vicariously liable because it derived a financial benefit from the infringing activities and had the right and ability to prevent infringement. The Ninth Circuit also held that Napster was liable for contributory infringement because its peer to peer file sharing network had violated the exclusive rights of distribution and reproduction.

49. As described above, this defense is not available if proper notice is placed on the book.

50. For example, some parodies would be included in the fair use exception. The key factor courts have looked at to determine fair use is whether the parody is transformative. In other words, does the parody add something new? For comics, the best example of this is the *Mad* case, discussed in chapter 8, in which *Mad* was allowed to parody 23 popular copyrighted songs.

51. FL-102 is available at http://www.copyright. gov/fls/fl102.html.

52. There are exceptions for law enforcement and other education purposes beyond the scope of this book.

53. For example, a copy machine can be viewed as a device that can be used to circumvent copyright. However, the primary use of a copy machine is not to make infringing copies, but to make legitimate copies.

54. This is not a strict liability offense (i.e. it takes intent to violate the statute). As a result, liability is only imposed if the violator knows or has reasonable grounds to know that tinkering with the information will facilitate infringement.

Chapter 4

1. For purposes of this book, predecessor entities will be referred to by their current incarnation unless the distinction is relevant. For example, DC Comics will be used to refer to National Comics and Marvel Comics will be used to refer to Timely Comics and Atlas Comics.

2. Comic fans will no doubt recognize Zatara as the father of Justice League member Zatanna.

3. In a strange bit of metafiction, if a character had, or was given, his own comic book series he could only be an honorary member in the Justice Society of America.

4. In later years, Eisner would remember these events and this testimony differently.

5. There is some truth to this argument given the similarities of *Superman* to other works of art. For example, in addition to the myths and pulps listed by Bruns, the Man of Steel had much in common with Doc Sampson, the Man of Bronze, including an unwavering moral code and the name Clark (Sampson's first; Superman's last—both apparently based on actor Clark Gable). Similarly, the names Kent and Lane were featured in *The Shadow*. Even the explanation of Superman's great strength was nearly identical to those offered in *Gladiator* by Philip Wylie and Edgar Rice Burroughs's *Princess of Mars*. Wylie had actually considered suing over *Superman*.

6. Of course, Bruns Publishing did not learn their lesson and were back in the United States District Court for the Southern District of New York in 1942 for copying DC Comics. In awarding $2,000 in damages and $500 in attorneys' fees Judge Bright held:

> The defendant Fox Publications, Inc. (formerly known as Bruns Publications, Inc.), does not seem to have profited by its experience in the [Bruns case].
>
> A comparison of the cartoons of "The Lynx" with "Blackie the Mystery Boy" published by the defendant Fox Publications, Inc., in its magazine "*Mystery Men Comics*" ... with the cartoons of "The Batman" with "Robin the Boy Wonder," published by the plaintiff in its magazines "*Detective Comics*" and "The Batman," convinces me there has been a deliberate copying by the defendant of drawings and cartoons of the Batman and his companion Robin as contained in the issues of "*Detective Comics*." ... These publications were all duly copyrighted by the plaintiff.

7. Elvis Presley was a big fan of Captain Marvel, Jr. Presley modeled his haircut and his stage outfits to mimic the character and painted a Marvel lightning bolt on the logo for his band, Taking Care of Business. Presley's collection of *Captain Marvel, Jr.* comics is currently on display at Graceland.

8. Unlike Captain Marvel, Mary Marvel got her power from saying an acronym of various "goddesses": Selena for grace; Hippolyta for strength; Ariadne for skill; Zephyrus for fleetness and flight; Aurora, for beauty; and Minerva for wisdom. Later, Ariadne would be exchanged for Artemis and Aurora would be exchanged for Aphrodite.

9. Interestingly, in the seven years since it filed suit, it was DC Comics that had apparently taken from Fawcett as it introduced a bald Sivana-like mad scientist in the form of Lex Luthor as well as a Captain Marvel, Jr.–like character with Superboy. (Although Supergirl is very similar to Mary Marvel, she would not be created until 1959.)

10. Under the 1909 Copyright Act, publication without a proper notice affixed meant that the owner of the copyright waived protection under the Copyright Act.

11. This is not the first time that a court reached this type of conclusion as the principle is common in trademark law called the generic trademark. A general trademark refers to a brand name that is used so frequently that it becomes synonymous with the general class of

product or service. For example, aspirin was originally a brand name. Because the company did not adequately protect its brand name, a court allowed the use of aspirin as a generic term for the drug.

12. Marvel Comics has been very careful to keep *Captain Marvel* comics in print. To date, there have been several versions of the character. First there was the Kree warrior named Mar-Vell in the sixties through the early eighties. When that character died, Monica Rambeau, an Avenger that transformed into energy, took on the identity in the eighties and nineties. Next, Marr-Vell's son, Genis Vell, took up the mantle in the nineties. After Genis sacrificed himself, his younger sister, Phyla-Vell, became Captain Marvel in the 2000s; she also ended up sacrificing herself to save the Guardians of the Galaxy. Next, the original Captain Marvel apparently returned; however, he was soon discovered to be a shape-shifting alien Skrull. More recently, a character named Noh-Varr took the name Captain Marvel when he joined the villains turned heroes in *Dark Avengers*. Most recently, Carol Danvers, the previous Ms. Marvel, took on the mantle of Captain Marvel in honor of the original character. Perhaps the reason for all of these comics is so that Marvel Comics can ensure that the trademark in the name Captain Marvel isn't abandoned and claimed by DC Comics.

Chapter 5

1. Text stories were regularly included in comics in an attempt to get preferential postage rates.

2. The word *amicus curiae* is Latin for "friend of the court" and is used to describe a person or entity that is not a party to a case who offers information that bears on the case but that has not been solicited by any of the parties to assist a court.

Chapter 6

1. This particular Batmobile only lasted three pages before the Joker sent it over a cliff in "The Riddle of the Missing Card." However, an identical version of the car was back by "Book of Enchantment," the second story in the book.

2. ABC, in turn, contracted with Greenway Productions, Inc. and Twentieth Century–Fox Television, Inc. to work on and create the television series. Greenway Productions, Inc. and Twentieth Century–Fox Television, Inc. own the copyright registrations for all of the episodes of the 1960s *Batman* television series.

3. This agreement also provided that DC Comics would pay ABC a share of the income derived from the exploitation of this exclusive merchandising right. As a result, DC Comics possessed an exclusive right to sell, distribute, and manufacture products derived from the elements that appeared in the *Batman* television show, including the Batmobile.

4. Apparently, Barris used the Lincoln Futura because there was insufficient time to create an original car as filming was set to begin three weeks after ABC approached Barris for a Batmobile. Instead, Barris utilized a concept car from his personal collection, which was then modified by custom builder Gene Cushenberry for the show. Barris Kustom City retained ownership of the Batmobile until 2013, when he sold it at auction for $4,620,000.

5. A separate agreement, signed on August 15, 1966, acknowledged that:

Notwithstanding anything to the contrary herein contained, [DC Comics] acknowledges [Barris Kustom City] is the owner of the vehicle known as Batmobile I as used in the BATMAN television series and feature motion picture and that [20th Century–Fox Television Inc. and Greenway Productions Inc. and Barris Kustom City.] are the joint owners of the design of said Batmobile I as provided for in Article 7 of that certain agreement between [20th Century–Fox Television Inc. and Greenway Productions Inc. and Barris Kustom City.], dated September 1, 1965.

6. The term "Additional elements" was defined as "any device or thing newly created by [Batman Productions] and which, but for the operation of this agreement, would constitute an infringement of DC Comics' copyright or trademark in or to any device or thing contained in the Property."

7. Furst created this Batmobile pursuant to a work for hire agreement with Warner Bros. Productions.

8. DC Comics explicitly reserved the rights to copyright and trademark any additional characters or elements featured in future Batman motion pictures.

9. On March 26, 1990, Anton Furst won an Academy Award for Art Direction for his work on the *Batman* film.

10. Towle also manufactured and distributed various automobile parts and accessories featuring the Batman trademark and did business through a variety of websites that display DC Comics' trademarks to promote Towle's business.

11. On October 1, 2010, DC Comics filed for an intent to use trademark for the mark "Batmobile" in the field of "Automobiles" or for "Custom Manufacturing in the Field of Automobiles."

12. DC Comics filed an amended Complaint on November 22, 2011, which added more copyright registrations.

13. Towle also argued that DC Comics did not have any rights in these designs.

14. Related to this, Towle described how DC Comics was aware that he was making Batmobiles, yet took no steps to stop him for at least eight years prior to filing suit.

15. The court also determined that, even if DC Comics did not have direct standing to sue, they could have brought suit since they owned the literary rights and the Batmobile replicas were derivative works based on those literary works.

16. The fact that the Batmobile is not a person does not diminish its standing as a character. For example, Freddy Krueger's glove (from the *Nightmare on Elm Street* film series) has been held to meet this standard in *New Line Cinema Corp. v. Bertelsmann Music Group, Inc.*

17. The court was ruling on motions for summary judgment, which requires the court rule as a matter of law relying only on the undisputed material facts.

Chapter 7

1. The studios was named for the fact that it was located on Gower Street in London.

2. Years later, Spider-Man would also work for the *Daily Bugle*. There is no evidence of any connection between the two.

3. In 1977, Mick Anglo produced *Nostalgia: Spotlight on the Fifties*. This book contains a reprint of Young Marvelman art. The copyright on the art has a copyright notice that says it is owned by Mick Anglo Ltd.

4. Issue 8 was a fill-in issue containing mostly reprints of the pre–Moore stories.

5. A hand written notation amends the contract to provide "or as agreed from time to time."

6. Gaiman also received a four percent royalty on reprints.

7. According to this agreement, Eclipse Comics agreed that it owned two-thirds of the rights to *Miracleman*, with Gaiman and Buckingham sharing one-third.

8. Originally, it was announced that *X-men* artist Whilce Portacio and longtime *X-Men* writer Chris Claremont would also be founders, but neither one opted into to becoming a partner and neither creator formed an Image imprint.

9. This number and duration would change over time; for example *Spawn* issue 9 reduces this number to 100 years.

10. Gaiman testified that he took the *Spawn* work because he had a 12-year-old son and he was mostly writing adult comics at the time. With *Spawn*, he could write something his son could read.

11. The same amount was paid to Sim, Moore, and Miller. McFarlane testified that the same amount was paid to each writer because he expected the writers to talk to each other and he didn't want anyone upset that one writer was paid more than another.

12. Medieval Spawn receives his name later as the character is only referred to as Spawn in the script.

13. At the time Gaiman was writing his script, there were no previous Spawns featured in the series.

14. Specifically, there was concern that readers would not realize that the *Angela* mini-series was related to the *Spawn* series.

15. Issue 25 was apparently completed but not colored at the time Eclipse Comics ceased publication. In fact, the company had also announced a new series entitled *Miracleman Triumphant*, which was to be released concurrently with issue 25.

16. McFarlane also paid Gaiman for royalties on a statuette made by McFarlane's toy company at this time.

17. On February 14, 1999, Gaiman's lawyer sent McFarlane's negotiator a letter that stated that he was withdrawing all previous offers. The letter stated that Gaiman had created the characters of Medieval Spawn, Angela, and Cogliostro not as work for hire but "pursuant to the terms of an oral agreement under which Mr. McFarlane agreed that Mr. Gaiman would be compensated on the same terms as set forth in Mr. Gaiman's DC Comics Agreements dated August 1, 1993." The letter requested that McFarlane "immediately forward all monies which are currently owed to Mr. Gaiman in accordance with the terms of the DC Agreement."

18. In 1997 and 1998, McFarlane also sent Gaiman royalty checks totaling around $16,000 that referred to Gaiman as "Co-Creator of Medieval Spawn, Angela and Cogliostro."

19. In 2005, Image Comics released a hardcover tenth anniversary book. McFarlane's section included Miracleman. This is later explained, in *Spawn* issue 150, to be the Man of Miracles, a shape changer who appears as what people want to see. McFarlane also released a statue and an action figure of Miracleman at the San Diego ComicCon.

20. This project would be released as *Marvel 1602*.

21. As McFarlane is co-owner of the works under the copyright law, he cannot be sued for infringement by unilaterally publishing a jointly owned work. Instead, it is more correct to say that Gaiman was requesting relief from McFarlane's conversion or misappropriation of his share of the profits as joint owner.

22. An interesting moment occurred at the end of the trial when McFarlane asked Gaiman to sign one of the comics that was used as an exhibit during the trial for a young boy who was in the courtroom. Gaiman signed and the two creators put aside their differences to pose for a picture with the boy. McFarlane even joked that he saved Gaiman the sweet spot on the cover.

23. Perhaps Gaiman, or his attorneys, realized that the transfer agreement between Skinn and Leach to Eclipse required the company to stay in business to avoid reversion. If this was true, the only thing that was transferred to McFarlane as a result of the bankruptcy purchase was United States Patent and Trademark Office registration number 1,447,456, which related to the name *Miracleman*. Given that Marvel Comics agreed to allow the book to be released as *Marvelman* once again, this trademark would have had very little value.

24. Under the terms of the Big Entertainment agreement, Gaiman provided one paragraph descriptions for five characters and created the world they inhabited in exchange for $45,000 and 8 percent in royalties on sales and 33 percent royalties on derivative rights. In 1995, the books were released under the Tekno Comix imprint. Gaiman's books were: *Neil Gaiman's Lady Justice*; *Neil Gaiman's Mr. Hero the Newmatic Man*; *Neil Gaiman's Phage: Shadow Death* (a six-issue limited series); *Neil Gaiman's Teknophage*; and *Neil Gaiman's Wheel of Worlds* (released as two one-shots). Tekno Comix stopped publishing by 1997.

25. The court did award $33,639.40 to Gaiman to reimburse attorney fees based on the right of privacy claim because that was required under the statute.

26. McFarlane conceded that Angela was a joint creation and therefore not included in this argument.

27. This argument is based on a doctrine called *Scène à faire*, which is French for "scene to be made" or "scene that must be done." Under the doctrine, certain elements of a creative work cannot be copyright protected because they are generic or required by certain genres. For example, science fiction movies need aliens, and mysteries need detectives. As Judge Learned Hand stated in *Nichols v. Universal Pictures Corp*, which involved two separate comedies about interfaith marriage, "The less developed the characters, the less they can be copyrighted; that is the penalty an author must bear for marking them too indistinctly." The logic behind the doctrine is twofold. First, it avoids confusion as to whether an alleged violator was taking from copyrighted material or from the public domain. Second it avoid situations whereby authors would have to obtain numerous releases anytime they wanted to create new works.

28. As more fully described in chapter 2, this amount was later reduced and the case ultimately settled.

29. As pointed out by the Judge Crabb, "Angela's wings are on her headpiece; Tiffany's are on her back; and Domina's are on her shoulders."

30. McFarlane also drew a variant cover.

31. McFarlane asked for a jury trial on the issue, but the court denied the request.

32. This testimony is consistent with the fact that there is a World War II Spawn, a Gunslinger Spawn, and both a Medieval and Dark Ages Spawn. This time period was expressed as 50 years in *Spawn* issue 9.

33. The court also held that the fact that Brian Holguin testified that he made no effort to base his Dark Ages Spawn on Medieval Spawn was irrelevant. Instead, the court relied on the fact that he had access to Medieval Spawn before he created Dark Ages Spawn. This is because there is no intent requirement for copyright violation and subconscious copying is still copying.

34. Presumably, a resolution to the Miracleman/Marvelman issue was also reached since Marvel Comics announced, in October 2013, that it was the owner of Marvelman and Miracleman and would be releasing the Warrior and Eclipse reprints and announced a new Marvelman series. The series has since been released with Alan Moore credited as "the Original Writer." Interestingly, Marvel Comics also introduced Angela to the Marvel Universe in the *Ultron Unleashed* mini-series. The character regularly appears in *Guardians of the Galaxy* and recoined her own solo series in 2014.

35. While the settlement details are confidential, some limited public financial information was available from McFarlane's bankruptcy. For example, on February 24, 2012, the $382,000 (plus interest) was released to Gaiman in part payment for the suit. Then, on May 1, 2012, McFarlane filed a Post Confirmation Summary of Disbursements for the quarter ended March 31, 2012. The report states that McFarlane paid $1,100,000 for a Gaiman Settlement. This number is not broken down further and may include McFarlane's attorney's fees. McFarlane's bankruptcy was closed on April 12, 2012.

Chapter 8

1. Several states have enacted their own trademark protection laws modeled after the Lanham Act.

2. The act was named after Fritz G. Lanham, a Representative of Texas, who served from 1919 until 1947 and was a proponent of strong trademark protection.

3. The certification mark was owned by the Comics Magazine Association of America. In 2011, the Comic Book Legal Defense Fund acquired the intellectual property rights to the Comics Code seal from the Comics Magazine Association of America.

4. Similarly, the shape of a product or even its color can be trademarked. However, that is beyond the scope of this chapter.

5. The complaint identified ten defendants by name and referred to 100 additional John and Jane Doe defendants. Each defendant sold knockoff Power Ranger toys in New York City, including helmets and action figures.

6. To determine whether a trade dress is nonfunctional, a court will apply a two-step test. First, is the trade dress essential to the use or purpose of the article, or does it affect the cost or quality of the article? If it is essential to the use, then the product is functional and cannot be protected. Second, if the answer to question one is that it affects the quality or cost, then the court must examine whether the exclusive use of the trade dress put other competitors in the same business at a significant non-reputation related disadvantage. If the answer is no, then the trade dress will be considered a nonfunctional aesthetic. Note that if the answer to these questions is yes, then the trade dress could still qualify for a patent, which is beyond the scope of this chapter and book.

7. Vertigo is a trade name as well as a trademark. A trade name is a commercial designation used by a person to identify their business. Trade names include the names of companies, partnerships and proprietorships. A trade name cannot be registered under the Lanham act as such; however, the trade name also could be registered as a trade name or a service mark—for example, if, like the Vertigo imprint, the name identifies the source of the goods from others and distinguishes them. In addition, business owners that have unprotected trade names that could not also be considered trademarks have a remedy at law if someone else tries to use their name. As described above, the original trade name owner could sue under the doctrine of unfair competition.

8. Also included in the category are pictures of the product. For example, a picture of an apple on apple juice.

9. For this purpose the definition of secondary meaning is used to describe the situation where the mark has become so popular that the average consumer recognizes it not only for its primary meaning, but also as an indication of the source of the product or service. This is typically proved by consumer surveys or testimonials that the product name has become associated with the product. Other companies have also shown advertising budgets and sales figures to prove secondary meaning. An example of secondary meaning is the trademark on the word superhero.

10. This is referred to as genericization.

11. It is also important to mention that a term that may be generic in one industry may be arbitrary in another. A fine gem store called "Diamond" would not be permitted, but a comic book distributor with the same name would be okay. Similarly, "Apple" could not be used a trademark used to describe a fruit seller, but can be used to name a computer company.

12. To determine whether a mark is confusingly similar, courts will look at the likelihood of consumer confusion between the two marks using the same standard as determining where there is infringement. This is discussed later in this chapter.

13. A state by state comparison is beyond the scope of this book. Instead, it will focus on state common law and the federal statute. For more information on state statutes go to: www.uspto.gov/trademarks/process/State_Trademark_Links.jsp.

14. At one time, this travel with the goods factor strictly required affixation of the mark to the product. In recent years, affixation has become less important. More important is the requirement that the mark is made known to customers in the ordinary course of business in a manner that associates the mark with the goods or services of the merchant.

15. As described more fully below, dilution claims arise when the power of the mark is weakened through its identification of dissimilar goods or when the mark is cast in an unflattering light.

16. Under either application process, current trademark law provides that once the mark is registered, the registration creates what is known as constructive use during the period between the filing of the application and the ultimate approval. This will allow the applicant to have priority over anyone who has used the mark after the application has been filed but before registration is finalized. Under state common law, the first to actually use the mark has priority.

17. Of course, the legislative history makes clear that use in the ordinary course will vary by industry. Factors that can be considered when determining whether a use

is ordinary include (1) how much use; (2) what kind of transaction the use is being performed in; and (3) industry standards.

18. This test is fairly easy to meet as sales in a test market or infrequent sales of large ticket items would qualify as bona fide for purposes of this test.

19. More information can be obtained from the Patent and Trademark Office at http://www.uspto.gov/trademarks/basics/index.jsp.

20. While it is generally recommended that a creator hire a lawyer to do a trademark search, an applicant may conduct a search free of charge on the USPTO Web site using the Trademark Electronic Search System (TESS). Applicants may also conduct a trademark search by visiting the Trademark Public Search Library, between 8:00 a.m. and 8:00 p.m. at the Public Search Facility, Madison East, 1st Floor, 600 Dulany Street, Alexandria, VA 22313. Use of the Public Search Library is free to the public. Applicants may check on the status of an application or registration through the Trademark Applications and Registrations Retrieval (TARR) database or by calling the Trademark Assistance Center at 1-800-786-9199 or 1-571-272-9250 to check the status.

21. This is true even if the mark is just an unstyled word

22. A complete listing of current fees can be found at http://www.uspto.gov/web/offices/ac/qs/ope/fee010114.htm.

23. The TEAS Plus system has strict filing requirements. Under TEAS Plus, the applicant must: (1) file a "complete" application (including optional parts); (2) select the description of goods/services from the Manual of Acceptable Identifications of Goods and Services; (3) pay for all classes to be covered by the application at the time of filing; (4) agree to file future correspondence, such as Responses to Office Actions, though TEAS; and (5) agree to receive communications from the Examining Attorney by email. In short, the TEAS Plus system can be used to trademark easily described goods and services by a technologically sophisticated merchant.

24. Renewal currently costs $400 per class. As described below, even after a mark receives a registration certificate, the current law still allows anyone damaged by the registration to petition to have it cancelled.

25. A bona fide attempt to use is not defined in the statute. According to the legislative history, a bona fide attempt to use means a fair objective determination of the applicant's intent based on all circumstances and must reflect good faith circumstance around the intended use.

26. A listing of current fees can be found at http://www.uspto.gov/web/offices/ac/qs/ope/fee010114.htm.

27. This period can be extended for an additional six months for a $150 fee per class. The applicant can request further extensions upon a showing of good cause (and by paying more fees) for up to 24 months.

28. A trademark owner may also establish enforceable common-law rights based on its natural zone of expansion. Under this doctrine, a prior user who can prove neither use nor current association with the mark in the disputed area can still prevail over a subsequent good-faith user by establishing that the area is within the zone of the prior user's probable or natural expansion. Of course, this doctrine is rarely used by courts and is usually limited to a small geographic area.

29. In addition, federal law provides something called the incontestability provision. If a registered mark is used for five continuous years it will be considered in-

contestable if the trademark holder files certain paperwork. The effect of this is that the valid filing is conclusive evidence of the validity of the mark unless: (1) the registration was fraudulent; (2) the mark has been abandoned; (3) the registered mark misrepresents the good; (4) fair use is being made of the mark; (5) good faith use was made in a remote geographical area before the mark was registered; (6) there was prior registration and use of the same mark; (7) the mark violates anti-competition or antitrust laws; or (8) equitable defenses apply. This status is highly sought because, if it is achieved, no one can challenge the mark on the grounds that it is not distinctive. The mark is considered conclusively distinctive if it is incontestable.

30. The concept of nationwide notice and use is a very important right under the federal law as it expands the registrant's geographical rights beyond the common law. As a result, anyone who uses the mark after the application cannot claim to have used it in good faith before the applicant. In short, a registrant can enjoin anyone from using the mark so long as that person wasn't using the mark at the time the application was being filed. For example, assume that two people, Hal and Kyle, each use the symbol of a green ring in the shape of a lantern inside a green circle as their symbol in connection with their security businesses. Hal begins using the symbol in 1959 in Coast City, California; Kyle begins using the symbol, in good faith without knowledge or notice of Hal's business, in 1994 in New York City (a geographically remote location from Coast City). In 1996, Hal registers the mark under the federal law. In 1998, Hal opens a jewelry store in Metropolis, Illinois, using the trademark symbol. If Kyle attempts to block Hal from using the mark, he would be unable to do so because Hal has constructive notice and use after 1996 in all areas that Kyle did not have a business. If Hal attempted to use the mark in New York City, then Kyle could block him because he was already doing business there.

31. This is the same standard used to determine whether to deny trademark registering of a trademark based on prior use by others.

32. Of course, different cases describe these terms differently, and no court has claimed that this list is exhaustive, so there may be more factors that are relevant in each individual case. Application of these factors can be found in the Batmobile case discussed in Chapter 6.

33. Batgirl is a comic book character regularly appearing in DC Comics and has been featured in a number of television shows, movies and videos. Sky Girl is a character in a young adult series of books available from Martin Sisters Publishing by the author of this book.

34. This case was further complicated by the fact that DC Comics and Ingersoll-Rand reached an agreement in 1983 to allow the word Kryptonite to be used on the locks so long as they were not associated with Superman and both sides claimed that agreement was breached. That part of the decision is beyond the scope of this example.

35. Dilution is discussed below. Unfair competition is addressed in chapter 2.

36. This factor has been become less important in recent years.

37. The same concept applies in copyright; see chapter 3. However, the concept of fair use in the trademark law is not as broad as the application of fair use in copyright.

38. There are also issues involving freedom of speech under the First Amendment that will be discussed in Chapter 20 where the court compares the importance of the freedom of expression to the potential for confusion.

39. Indeed, this was exactly what was at issue in a case between *Playboy* and a former Playmate of the Year. The bunny was allowed to use various *Playboy* marks on her website in the masthead, the banner ads, and the metatags because these marks truthfully identified her as a former Playmate and did not imply current sponsorship by *Playboy*. However, the court cautioned that she could have been found to infringe if she used the trademark so frequently that search engines would rank her site above *Playboy*'s. Similarly, the court found that the use of the trademarks on downloadable wallpaper was not a nominative use of the mark as it was not necessary in order to describe herself.

40. Token use of the mark will not save it from abandonment.

41. Perhaps this is the reason why Marvel Comics continuously puts out different version of its *Captain Marvel* books and continues to use the name.

42. In recognition of the difficulty in determining actual damages, the federal law permits courts to increase damages up to three times (referred to as treble damages) to adequately compensate the trademark owner.

43. Once again, the court has the ability to increase or decrease the award of profits based on the facts of the case.

44. An award of treble damages is highly unlikely absent a showing of bad faith on the part of the infringer.

45. The federal trademark law contains provisions allowing for the marking of trademarked goods and for the display of one of three designations in the vicinity of the trademark: (1) "Registered in the United States Patent and Trademark Office." (2) an abbreviation of (1), or (3) the letter R inside a circle ("®"). The law also prohibits the use of counterfeit marks, defined as a spurious designation that is identical with or substantially similar to a registered mark. The use of the counterfeit mark can result in the imposition of a higher level of damages, including treble damages, attorney's fees, prejudgment interest, and seizure order.

46. The dilution cause of action first arose under state common law, which was eventually adopted into state trademark laws. In 1995, Congress passed the Federal Trademark Dilution Act of 1995, which protects famous trademarks from unauthorized commercial use if such a trademark begins after the trademark had become famous and lessons the power of the famous trademark to identify the original goods or services or the distinctive quality of the trademark. The Trademark Dilution Revision Act of 2006, which was passed on October 6, 2006, revised several of the provisions of the Act.

47. This is even true in cases where there can be no confusion that the original mark owner sanctioned the trademark's use.

48. In 1917, a superhero was an accomplished public figure. In 1934, Doc Savage was called a superhero on his radio program.

49. See U.S. Trademark Serial Nos. 72243225, 732220 79, 1140452, 1179067, for example. The copyrights were renewed in 2006.

50. The one case, *Burgh man, Pittsburgh's Super Hero*, involved a technical problem with the opposition as they missed the deadline.

Chapter 9

1. Up until the 1960s, comic books were required to contain at least one one-page text story to satisfy U.S. Postal Service requirements for preferential magazine rates.

2. It is believed that Lee has a contractual clause that requires Marvel Comics to include him in these movies. If this is so, then there is an agreement separate and apart from the 1998 agreement reprinted below, which does not provide for guaranteed cameos (although it does provide for an Executive Producer credit).

3. *Marvel Superheroes* was a half-hour animated cartoon series produced by the Grant-Ray-Lawrence Company. The show first aired in syndication from September 1, 1966, through December 1, 1966. As an interesting bit of trivia, one of the syndicated stations, WNAC-TV in Boston, also included live action segments, which were scripted by Superman co-creator Jerry Siegel.

4. Marvel Comics had some modest success on live action television with a *Dr. Strange* television pilot, two *Captain America* movies, and a *Spider-Man* television series. Marvel's biggest success came on November 4, 1977, with the premiere of *The Incredible Hulk on* CBS starring Bill Bixby as David Banner (TV executives thought Bruce sounded too feminine), Lou Ferrigno as the Hulk, and Jack Colvin as Jack McGee. The series lasted until 1982, and also continued in several made for television movies: *The Incredible Hulk Returns* (featuring Thor); *The Trial of the Incredible Hulk* (with Daredevil); and *The Death of the Incredible Hulk* (with the Black Widow sort of). Plans for a fourth television movie, *The Revenge of the Incredible Hulk*, were cancelled when Bill Bixby's health declined as a result of cancer.

5. There was also a direct to video *Captain America* movie starring Matt Salinger, the son of J.D. Salinger, released in 1990 and an unreleased version of the *Fantastic Four* produced by Roger Corman in 1994.

6. Marvel Comics' bankruptcy proceeding lasted from December 1996 through October 1998. During this period, several executives vied for control of Marvel. While the events surrounding Marvel's bankruptcy are fascinating, a discussion of this topic is beyond of the scope of this book. Luckily, it has been the subject of several books

7. Under paragraph 4(c) of the Agreement, Stan Lee was given 150,000 valuable stock options which Lee exercised for a net gain of approximately $1.4 million.

8. Paul also lost his license to practice law. In 1983, Paul was sent back to prison when he pled guilty to making false statements to customs inspectors after he was caught traveling to Canada using the identity of a deceased person.

9. Lee also provided his voice for the character of Izayus, the mentor that gathers the heroes together and guides them in their adventures.

10. Only the first twenty episodes aired online. After the bankruptcy of Stan Lee Media, the final two episodes were only available on television.

11. The stock price eventually dropped below the agreed upon sale limit, which resulted in a lawsuit. The rights were eventually sold in the bankruptcy, which was challenged in another lawsuit by Stan Lee Media, who alleged the company had been misled into relinquishing the rights during its 2002 bankruptcy proceedings. On October 22, 2013, the Ninth Circuit affirmed the District Court's ruling that dismissed the case and validated the sale.

12. The US Attorney in New York charged that Paul violated SEC Rule 10b-5, a securities laws felony. Specifically, prosecutors alleged that Paul, along with a co-conspirator, manipulated the market price of the stock of Stan Lee Media and artificially inflated the stock to a peak value of $350 million through the use of transactions through and between accounts that Paul controlled but maintained in the names of others. It was also alleged that Paul and his co-conspirators misused the brokerage account to borrow more than $4 million from Merrill Lynch to buy real estate, travel and make political contributions. Stan Lee was never implicated in the scheme

13. Wolfman sued Marvel Comics over the Blade character, and others, in the bankruptcy proceeding arguing he did not create the character under a work for hire contract. In 2000, the bankruptcy ruled in Marvel Comics' favor. The court wrote:

> Wolfman has likewise not provided the court with sufficient evidence to show that he developed Blade and Deacon Frost prior to the publication of "*The Tomb of Dracula*" issue number ten
>
> * * *
>
> Here, Wolfman merely had a nascent idea for a character and story. Even assuming that Wolfman produced a half-page write up of the character's background and look, Wolfman had not completely developed the characters of Blade and Deacon Frost as the plaintiffs had in Siegel. Wolfman's Siegel argument does not account for the transition from a story idea to a story ready for publication. Wolfman spent time and energy while employed at Marvel developing a script with proposed panel art and text for "The Tomb of Dracula." Wolfman performed this work at the instance and expense of Marvel. Thus, even if this court assumes that Wolfman had produced a half-page origin story of Blade and Deacon Frost, that story and those characters [were not completely developed].
>
> * * *
>
> The court further holds that the characters Wolfman created while employed by Marvel were made at Marvel's instance and expense and are, therefore, works made for hire. Because Wolfman could not show an agreement to the contrary, the court finds that Marvel is the author of all of the characters in dispute....

14. Marvel's toy division also reported over $100 million in sales of *Spider-Man: The Movie* toys in 2002, alone.

15. There also a dispute in the later lawsuit as to whether the deals were correctly described as term gross participation or whether they were actually gross profit contracts.

16. There has also been an unrelated defamation lawsuit between Lee and Paul, but that is beyond the scope of this book.

Chapter 10

1. As *Fantastic Four* readers are aware, Willie Lumpkin would go on to become the regular mailman for the Baxter Building.

2. Several of Archie Comics' books at this time promoted President Kennedy's call for the youth of America to get more physically fit. This was also the subject of DC Comics' "Superman's Mission for President Kennedy," which was delayed because of President Kennedy's assassination in 1963. The story was eventually released in *Superman* issue 170 in 1964, at the request of the White House and President Johnson.

3. Pepper did have a brief cameo in *Tales from Riverdale* issue 24.

4. The show had an impressive voice cast. Janet Waldo voiced Josie; Barbara Pariat played Valerie Brown; Jackie Joseph was Melody and Casey Kasem voiced Alexander Cabot III. The singing voices for the Pussycats were portrayed by different actresses: Cathy Dougher was Josie McCoy; Patrice Holloway, sister of Motown star Brenda Holloway, sang for Valerie; and future *Charlie's Angels* star Cheryl Ladd, working under her real name, Cheryl Jean Stoppelmoor, portrayed the singing voice of Melody. These voices were featured as Josie and the Pussycats on a soundtrack for the cartoon series.

5. During this period, Josie and the Pussycats released their second album, a soundtrack for the film.

6. DeCarlo also moved to disqualify Archie Comics' lawyers. But that is beyond the scope of this book.

7. This is different than the 1976 Copyright Act, which does not require formal publication. Instead, federal copyright protection attaches upon the fixation of a work in tangible form.

Chapter 11

1. Both Betty and Veronica have since married Archie Andrews in two alternate timelines.

2. This was the court's reasoning for ruling against DeCarlo in the earlier case.

3. He also incorporated by reference the counter-claims previously dismissed by the court in order to preserve his issue for appeal.

4. Archie Comics also moved to strike (i.e., dismiss) the parts of the answer that reasserted the dismissed counterclaims dismissed. The court denied this motion stating, "The motion to strike is of a stripe properly characterized as dilatory." Because the claims were dismissed and only included to preserve the record, there was no practical reason to re-litigate the issue in front of the court.

5. DeCarlo also took issue with some of the alternative arguments raised by Archie Comics to support its request for a declaration, but the court did not reach that argument.

6. A jury trial is where a group of private citizens are selected to determine the facts of a case; the judge will then determine the applicable law to apply to those facts. In a bench trial, the judge serves as both the fact finder and the legal authority. As one can guess, there were several reasons why DeCarlo would want to present his case to a potentially more sympathetic jury, especially in light of Judge Kaplan's comments on his arguments. However, a jury trial is not available in all types of cases. For example, it is not permitted in cases that seek declaratory judgment as opposed to monetary relief. Presumably, Archie Comics made a strategic decision to withdraw its contract claim in order to avoid the jury.

7. The court first issued its opinion on March 31, 2003. However, it granted a motion for reconsideration. A revised opinion was issued on April 23, 2003.

8. The court also admonished DeCarlo's lawyers for not properly following local rules related to summary judgment motions, but that is beyond the scope of this book.

Chapter 12

1. Some contracts need to be in writing. For example, if a task cannot be performed in a year, it must be

in writing. Similarly, as seen in earlier chapters, certain contracts transferring intellectual property rights must be in writing.

2. The perfect example of how relationships can break down is the recent lawsuit between Robert Kirkman and Tony Moore over *The Walking Dead*. Moore and Kirkman grew up together. Still, Moore filed suit in the Superior Court of the State of California on February 9, 2012, alleging that he had been tricked into assigning his interest in the material over to Kirkman in a later agreement and wasn't sufficiently compensated. In response, Kirkman counterclaimed alleging that he had overcompensated Moore and that Moore had breached a confidentiality provision of their agreement. The lawsuit was eventually removed to federal court when a copyright ownership claim was added by Moore. The parties eventually settled on September 24, 2012. The terms of the settlement were sealed.

3. The artist could say, "no, I will not draw pencils for a three issue limited series for a hundred dollars a page, but I would do it for two hundred." This is not acceptance, it's a counter offer. The writer then has the option to accept or reject the new counter offer.

4. "Exposure" can also be a consideration. So, if someone writes or draws a book for free with the understanding that they will be listed in the book, there is valuable consideration under the law.

5. Examples of several types of contracts are included in this book.

Chapter 13

1. Marvel Comics has a history of recycling character names. For example, the Human Torch was the moniker of a golden age android before becoming associated with the young hothead Johnny Storm in the *Fantastic Four*. Similarly, a character named the Avenging Angel appeared years before Warren Worthington joined the *X-Men* as the winged mutant called Angel.

2. Magazine Enterprises was also the publisher of Jerry Siegel's *Funnyman*, a slapstick-comedian hero. Although Siegel was hopeful to create another character with the popularity of Superman, Funnyman simply could not find an audience.

3. The Magazine Enterprises library of characters, including its version of Ghost Rider, was reprinted by AC Comics in the 1980s. While the copyrights have lapsed due to non-renewal, AC renamed the Ghost Rider as the Haunted Horseman, due to Marvel's ownership of the Ghost Rider trademark.

4. After the success of the Johnny Blaze *Ghost Rider* series in the 1970s, the Western stories (along with new original backup stories) soon reappeared in *The Original Ghost Rider Rides Again*. Eventually, Marvel Comics decided to rename its western-version Ghost Rider to avoid confusion with the modern supernatural version of the character. Initially, in 1974 and 1975, Marvel Comics used the name Night Rider. However, because that name was also used to describe members of the Ku Klux Klan (who also dressed all in white), the character's name was again changed to Phantom Rider in 1975.

5. The colorist is not credited.

6. A second movie entitled *Ghost Rider: Spirits of Vengeance* was released in 2011.

7. As discussed in Chapter 3, the 1976 Copyright Act was meant to replace all existing state common law copyright laws. This is called federal preemption, which

refers to the fact that, with the some exceptions, a federal law will always invalidate a state law when the two are in conflict.

Chapter 14

1. There is debate as to whether an earlier released *Detective Comics* issue 225, which is the first appearance of the Silver Age Martian Manhunter, actually signifies the start of the Silver Age.

2. Like many other Silver Age characters, the Human Torch has nothing to do with his Golden Age predecessor.

3. Kirby's heirs also made a claim for the Rawhide Kid, who was created by Lee, Kirby, and Dick Ayers in 1960. The court summarized:

> Lee developed "*The Rawhide Kid*" because Goodman loved westerns and liked titles that included the word "kid." Lee also wrote the comic book's first issue. Kirby drew the pencil artwork. Eventually, the writing and artwork for "*The Rawhide Kid*" was reassigned to Lieber. The first issue of the comic book was published in August 1960.

4. The Second Circuit also ruled that a New York court only had jurisdiction over Kirby's two (of four) children. That part of the ruling is beyond the scope of this book.

Chapter 15

1. The fictional high school newspaper on the television show *Smallville* is named in honor of this paper.

2. This version of Superman was more Slam Bradley, a later creation of Siegel and Shuster.

3. Grant Morrison would return Superman to jeans and a t-shirt when DC Comics would revamp their entire line with the New 52.

4. At this time, most comic books were simply newspaper strips collected in comic book format. In fact, Mark Evanier, a comic book historian and expert witness in the Superman case, testified that one of the main reasons that comic books began including original material was because the companies were unable to procure reprint rights to existing newspaper strips and instead hired young comic strip artists "to simulate the same kind of newspaper strip material."

5. In many ways, the character of Clark Kent represented the real persona of the reader, whereas Superman represented the ideal the reader wanted to be.

6. According to the witnesses, only the first week's worth of strips was completely finished and ready for publication. The remainder of the strips had completed pencils and lettering, but still needed to be inked.

7. Siegel later stated that one publisher was interested in Superman but only if the project could be expanded into a full color comic book. However, after being burnt by their Consolidated Book Publishing experience, Siegel was not interested.

8. DC Comics required eight panels per page. Unfortunately, Siegel and Shuster did not have enough material to fit this requirement. Instead, some pages were produced with less than the required eight panels such as page one (seven panels), page five (seven panels), page nine (six panels), page twelve (five panels) and thirteen (seven panels). Shuster was able to meet the requirement on the remaining pages by splitting existing panels or drawing additional panels using the existing dialogue.

9. The check was actually issued in the amount of $412. According to the line items, the additional amounts related to payments for other line items including "D.C," "Adv," and "Fun." These notations most likely relate to the duo's work on *Detective Comics, New Adventure Comics*, and *More Fun Comics*, which included several of their creations including Doctor Occult, Federal Men, and Slam Bradley.

10. In the example, Superman is compared to both an ant and a grasshopper to explain how he can perform his great feats. This explanation was very similar to the one provided to explain the strength and prowess of Hugo Danner, the main character in the novel *Gladiator*, a pulp novel by Philip Wylie that was reviewed by Siegel in his early fanzines. However, Siegel does not list the book among his influences and has specifically stated that he was not influenced by *Gladiator* when he developed the concept.

11. Apparently, the star of the program, Bud Colyer, needed a vacation. So, the writers created kryptonite to permit Superman to be out of action for a few episodes. Interestingly, Siegel had already come up with the concept, but it was rejected by DC Comics. The court explained that "K-Metal from Krypton" featured "the first appearance of the kryptonite concept (referred to in the material as K-Metal derived from meteorite debris from the planet Krypton) and its debilitating effects on Superman's powers."

12. There is some perception that DC Comics immediately knew it had a hit with Superman even before the comic hit the stands. The evidence doesn't necessarily bear this out. For example, while Superman did indeed appear on the cover of the first issue of *Action Comics*, he was not featured or even mentioned on the cover again until issue 7, cover date December, 1938. In fact, he would not regularly appear on the cover until issue 16, cover date September, 1939.

13. DC Comics also filed for copyright protection for all the contents of *More Fun Comics* issue 101 and obtained Copyright Registration No. B653651.

14. Shuster could not be included in this cause of action because he drew the pages under an employment agreement with DC Comics.

15. As explained in chapter 3, the Copyright Law of 1909 provided works were protected for a period of 28 years from the date of publication. After that period the work could be renewed by the owner and, absent agreement, would revert back to the original owner.

16. Both the trial court and the Second Circuit made use of April 1948 vacated findings as well as the parties' May 1948 final consent judgment in their final opinions. Despite this, there was disagreement as to whether these court documents had a binding effect with the district court relying on both and the Second Circuit only relying on the final consent judgment.

Chapter 16

1. The notice package consisted of 546 pages and weighed nearly six pounds.

2. In a strange coincidence, the plaintiff and Jerry Siegel's widow, Joanne Siegel, also served as the original model for Lois Lane.

3. The termination only applied to the original version of the character and not any derivative versions created by DC Comics. Interestingly, for a time in 1998 prior to the termination date, DC Comics changed Superman in an electric blue version with different powers

and abilities. Eventually, this character would become Superman Red and Superman Blue when he was split in two. Eventually, the original version of the character reappeared after a major crossover event without explanation in 1999.

4. Although the focus of the Siegel lawsuits has been Superman and Superboy, there was another Siegel character at issue in the case. In addition to terminating the copyright on the man and teen of steel, Siegel's heirs also issued a termination notice for the Spectre, which would have become effective November 27, 2000. The Spectre was created by Jerry Siegel and Bernard Baily in 1939 and first appeared in *More Fun Comics* issue 52. The story featured a murdered policeman named Jim Corrigan, who was condemned by an omnipotent entity referred to only as "The Voice" and tasked with eliminating all evil from the world. The Spectre was a charter member of the Justice Society of America in 1940 and played major roles in all of DC Comics' major crossover events from *Crisis on Infinite Earths* through *Kingdom Come*. Perhaps in response to the Siegel heirs' termination, Jim Corrigan found redemption and no longer served as the Spectre. In the late 1990s, the former Green Lantern known as Hal Jordan became the Spectre. In 2006, the *Day of Vengeance* miniseries featured a hostless Spectre that wreaked havoc among DC Comics' mystical community. As a result of that storyline, a murdered Gotham City detective named Crispus Allen became the latest mortal to adopt the guise of the Spectre. Not much is known about the current Spectre that appears after DC Comics reimagined its entire line of books as part of its New 52.

5. On April 24, 2006, the Kids WB announced the concept for a new show entitled *Superboy and the Legion of Superheroes*. However, when the show debuted on September 23, 2006, the title was changed to *The Legion of Superheroes* and the show starred a young Superman instead of Superboy.

6. The court also held that the Copyright Act "expressly permits an agreement transferring ownership of a copyright to be signed by a 'duly authorized agent' of the copyright owner, and [the Siegel heirs do] not contest that the heirs' attorney was such an agent."

7. It is important to realize that the court's decision does not mean that the Siegel heirs are not receiving compensation for Superman. Instead, the court determined that the Siegel heirs are entitled to the amounts agreed to in the settlement, which are presumably substantial.

Chapter 17

1. Peavy and Frank Shuster not only requested an increase in payments, but also "a yearly increment to account for inflation."

2. DC Comics, in response to one of Jean Peavy's bonus requests, reiterated that Jean Peavy had no legal right to make such requests, but that it would pay her a bonus anyway. Jean Peavy thanked DC Comics for the bonus.

3. There were some side issues in the case related to Toberoff's representation in the *Superman* cases, but those are beyond the scope of this book and will not be discussed.

4. As discussed in chapter 5, the Second Circuit reached a different conclusion related to the *Captain America* terminations.

5. The court also found that the agreements prevent-

ing the heirs from making any deal with DC Comics without Toberoff's and the Siegel heirs' consent violated the Copyright Act.

Chapter 18

1. For example, Alan Moore used several literary characters to form his various *League of Extraordinary Gentlemen* books. Bill Willingham features several famous fairy tale characters in *Fables*. Dynamite Comics publishes many stories featuring classic pulp heroes. Alex Ross created *Project Superpowers*, which stars heroes originally published by Fox Comics, Crestwood Publications and Nedor Comics.

2. One of the only original characters in the series, Campion Bond, was excluded from the movie adaptation probably because of similarities to the copyrighted character of James Bond.

3. A few Mickey Mouse comics accidentally entered public domain and were published by Eternity Comics as issue 1 and 2 of the *Uncensored Mouse*. Eternity Comics included a notice that "Mickey Mouse is a registered trademark of Walt Disney Productions" so as to avoid trademark claims. Disney filed a lawsuit and the series was cancelled.

4. The trademark on each of these characters would remain in effect unless they are abandoned by their owners.

Chapter 19

1. More information can be found at IRS.gov. It is strongly suggested that a creator consult a tax professional if they have any question.

2. These are also referred to as the Certificate of Incorporation or the Corporate Charter.

3. The total number of shares a corporation may issue is arbitrary. However, the corporation must issue at least one share of stock for each shareholder.

4. A corporation can be formed in any state. Most form, or at least register, in the state where they are located. However, a lot of corporations choose Delaware or Nevada because of a preferential corporate-friendly law. The choice for state of incorporation is a complicated one and beyond the scope of this book.

5. Once again, corporations must have at least one director, but there is no upper limit. Procedures for electing directors should be in either the articles or the bylaws or both.

6. A corporation must be represented by a lawyer in court, which can add expense.

7. A shareholder's loss will be limited to their investment, the price paid for the stock.

8. There are ways for creditors to collect directly from shareholders. These topics, which would include piercing the corporate veil and nominee/alter ego, are beyond the scope of this book.

9. Shareholders who perform services through the corporation are considered employees, and will be required to pay taxes on their salary.

10. Corporations may have other costs, like licensing fees and franchise taxes as well as minimum insurance requirements. These topics are beyond the subject matter of this book

11. There is a type of corporation called an S Corporation that allows for limited liability and pass through taxation. There are a lot of restrictions on these types of entities, including who can be a member and what type of income can be earned.

12. Because of the newness of the LLC structure, many potential creditors (such as banks and service providers) still require the members to co-sign for the LLC; thus they would still be liable.

13. If no election is made, the entity will be treated as a pass-through entity.

Chapter 20

1. The book was requested by the United States Department of Health, Education and Welfare. The three issue story ran in issues 96 through 98 (cover date of May–July 1971). Interestingly, the Comics Code at the time did not specifically forbid depictions of drugs. Instead, Marvel Comics ran afoul of a clause prohibiting "All elements or techniques not specifically mentioned herein, but which are contrary to the spirit and intent of the code, and are considered violations of good taste or decency." At the time, acting administrator John L. Goldwater, publisher of Archie Comics, refused to grant Code approval based on the depiction of narcotics being used, regardless of the context. Even more interestingly, the CCA had previously approved a story involving drugs, in *Strange Adventures* issue 205 (Oct. 1967), in which Deadman fought opium smugglers.

Chapter 21

1. Judge Tyler admitted to regularly reading Harvey Comics and took issue with the fact that Jacobson said they were intended for the lowest age group.

2. When Judge Tyler retired, he said, referring to the Deep Throat decision, "If I were to write that appendix today, I would be deemed a fool, given the substantial change in our outlook." Given the recognition of Crumb, Pekar, and many other underground creators, I think he would agree that the statement would equally apply to the *Zap Comix* decision. Judge Tyler died in January 2012 at the age of 90.

References

The text of this book is based upon a review of the publicly available records and information related to the following cases, statutes, and government websites.

A&M Records, Inc. v. Napster, Inc., Case Nos. No. 00-16401, No. 00-16403 (9th Cir. 2001)

Abadin et al. v. Marvel Entertainment et al., Case No. 09-0715 (USDC SDNY 2009)

Archie Comic Publications, Inc. v. Josette Dumont DeCarlo, Executrix of the Estate of Daniel S. DeCarlo, Case Nos. 00 Civ. 5686 and 02 Civ. 8466 (SDNY 2000)

Community for Creative Non-Violence v. Reid, No. 88-293 (US SCT 1988)

Copyright Act of 1909 (Pub. Law 60-349)

Copyright Act of 1976 (Pub. L. 94-553)

Copyright Law Amendment (Pub. Law 104-97)

Copyright Term Extension Act (Pub. L. 105-298)

Dan DeCarlo v. Archie Comics Publications et al., Case No. 00 Civ. 2344 (SDNY 2000)

DC Comics v. G5 Barbers LLC et al., Case No. 6:11-1600 (USDC MDFL 2011)

DC Comics v. Kryptonite Corp., 1:00-cv-05562 (SDNY 2000)

DC Comics v. Mark Towle d/b/a Gotham Garage et al., Case No. CV 11-3934 (USDC CDCA 2011)

DC Comics v. Pacific Pictures et al., Case No. 2:10-cv-03633 (USDC CD CA 2010)

Delaware Limited Liability Company Act

Detective Comics, Inc. v. Bruns Publications, Case No. 203 (USDC SDNY 1939)

Detective Comics, Inc. v. Fox Publications (USDC SDNY 1939)

Digital Millennium Copyright Act (Pub. L. 105-304)

Donald Molony et al. v. Boy Comics Publishers et al. No Case No. in Original (SDNY 1950)

Edgar Winter et al. v. DC Comics et al., Case No. BC145670 (California 1996)

Federal Rules of Appellate Procedure

Federal Rules of Civil Procedure

Federal Rules of Criminal Procedure

Federal Rules of Evidence

Federal Trademark Dilution Act, H.R. 1295

Folsom v. Marsh, Case No. 4,901 (C.C.D. Mass. 1841)

Fred Fisher Music Co. v. M. Witmark & Sons, Case No 327 (US SCt 1943)

Gary Friedrich v. Marvel Characters, Incorporated, Case No. O8:CV:01533 (USDC SDNY 2008)

Harry C. Fisher v. Star Company (NY 1919)

In re: Marvel Entertainment Group, Case No. 97-638 (D. Del. 2000)

In re: Todd McFarlane Productions et al., Case No. 06-08 (USBC DDEL 2006)

International News Service v. The Associated Press, Case No. 221 (US SCT 1918)

IRS.gov

Irving Berlin et al. v. E.C. Publications, Inc., Case No. No. 255 (2d Cir. 1964)

Jazan Wild d/b/a Carnival Comics v. NBC Universal, Case No. 2:10-cv-03615 (USDC CDCA 2010)

Jerome Siegel and Joe Shuster v. National Comics Publications et al., No Case No. in Original (New York 1947)

Jerome Siegel and Joe Shuster v. National Periodical Publications, Inc., Case No. 69-civ-1429 (USDC SDNY 1969)

Joseph Simon v. Martin Goodman, No Case No. in Original (NY 1966)

Joseph Simon v. Martin Goodman et al., No Case No. in Original (USDC NY 1967)

John Doe (AKA Tony Twist) v. Todd McFarlane, Case Nos. ED78785 and ED85283 (Mo. 2004)

The Lanham (Trademark) Act (Pub. L. 79-489)

Laura Siegel Larson et al. v. Warner Bros. Entertainment, Inc. et al., Case Nos. CV 04-8400; 04-8776 (USDC CDCA 2004)

Marvel Comics v. Joseph Simon, Case No. 1:00cv1393 (USDC SDNY 2000)

Marvel Worldwide et al. v. Lisa Kirby et al., Case No. 10-141 (USDC SDNY 2010)

MGM v. Honda, Case No. CV 94-8732 (USDC CDCA 1994)

Michael Anthony Moore v. Robert Kirkman et al., Case No. 2:12cv6811 (CDCA 2012)

Michael Anthony Moore v. Robert Kirkman et al., Case No. BC478780 (CA. 2012)

Miller v. California, Case No. No. 70-73 (US SCT. 1973)

Mutual Film Corporation v. Industrial Commission of Ohio, Case No. No. 456 (US SCT 1915)

National Comics v. Fawcett Publications, et al. No Case No. in Original (SDNY 1941)

Neil Gaiman v. Todd McFarlane, Case No. 02-cv-48 (USDC WDWA 2002)

New Line Cinema Corp. v. Bertlesman Music Group, Inc., Case No. 88 Civ. 5181 (S.D.N.Y. 1988)

New Kids on the Block v. News America Publishing, Inc., Case Nos. 90-56219, and 90-56258 (9th Cir. 1992)

Nichols v. Universal Pictures, Case No. 04 (2d Cir. 1930)

The People of the State of Illinois v. Michael Correa, Case No. 1-88-1558 (Illinois 1988)

The People of the State of New York v. Charles Kirkpatrick et al., No Case No. in Original (NY 1970)

Playboy Enterprises v. Welles, Case No. 98-CV-0413 (S.D. Cal. 1998)

Revised Uniform Limited Liability Company Act

Saban Entertainment et al. v. 222 World Corp. et al., Case No. 94 Civ. 6043 (S.D.N.Y. 1994)

Stan Lee v. Marvel Characters et al., Case No. 02-8945 (USDC SDNY 2002)

Stan Lee Media v. Conan Sales et al., Case No. 2:11-cv-06861 (USDC CDCA 2011)

Stan Lee Media v. Marvel Comics, Case No. 1:2007 cv02238 (USDC SDNY 2007)

Stan Lee Media v. Stan Lee et al., Case No. 2:2007 cv04438 (USDC CDCA 2007)

Stan Lee Media v. The Walt Disney Company, Case No. 1:12-cv-02663 (USDC CO. 2012)

Stan Lee Media et al. v. Stan Lee, Case No. 2:07-cv-00225 (USDC CDCA 2007)

Stewart vs. Abend, Case No. 88-2102 (US S Ct 1990)

Trademark Dilution Revision Act of 2006, H.R. 683

Uniform Limited Liability Act (1996)

Uniform Limited Partnership Act (1985)

Uniform Limited Partnership Act (2001)

Uniform Partnership Act (1914)

Uniform Partnership Act (1997)

The United States Constitution

United States Senate Subcommittee on Juvenile Delinquency, Eighty-Third Congress, Second Session, Hearings (April 21–22 and June 4, 1954)

USPTO.gov

The Visual Artists Rights Act of 1990 (Pub. L. 101-650)

Walt Disney Productions v. Air Pirates, Case No. C-71-2021 (USDC NDCA 1971)

Warner Brothers v. Columbia Broadcasting Systems, Case No. 13457 (9th Cir. 1954)

Warner Brothers et al. v. American Broadcast Companies, Inc. et al., Case Number 81-1551 (USDC SDNY 1981)

Index

253